After the Holocaust

For the last decade scholars have been questioning the idea that the Holocaust was not significantly talked about in any significant way until well into the 1970s. *After the Holocaust: Challenging the Myth of Silence* is the first collection of authoritative, original scholarship to expose a serious misreading of the past on which, controversially, the later claims for a 'Holocaust industry' rest.

Taking an international approach this bold new book exposes the myth and opens the way for a sweeping reassessment of Jewish life in the postwar era, a life lived in the pervasive, shared awareness that Jews had narrowly survived a catastrophe that had engulfed humanity as a whole but claimed two-thirds of their number. The chapters include evaluations of the work of survivor-historians and memoir writers, studies of David Boder, theatrical productions made by survivors and films, and a discussion of the different types, and meanings, of 'silence'

A breakthrough volume in the debate about the 'Myth of Silence', this is a must for all students of Holocaust and genocide.

David Cesarani is Research Professor in History at Royal Holloway, University of London, UK. He has written and edited over a dozen books, including *Eichmann: His Life and Crimes* (2004), and *Major Farran's Hat: Murder, Scandal, and Britain's War Against Jewish Terrorism, 1945–1948* (2009). For his work in establishing a Holocaust Memorial Day in Great Britain he was awarded an OBE in 2005.

Eric J. Sundquist is Andrew W. Mellon Professor of Humanities at John Hopkins University, USA. His publications include *Kings Dream* (2009), *Strangers in the Land: Blacks, Jews, Post-Holocaust America* (2005) and *To Wake the Nations: Race in the Making of American Literature* (1993).

After the Holocaust

Challenging the Myth of Silence

Edited by
David Cesarani and Eric J. Sundquist

Routledge
Taylor & Francis Group

LONDON AND NEW YORK

First published 2012
by Routledge
2 Park Square, Milton Park, Abingdon, Oxon OX14 4RN

Simultaneously published in the USA and Canada
by Routledge
711 Third Avenue, New York, NY 10017

Routledge is an imprint of the Taylor & Francis Group, an informa business

British Library Cataloguing in Publication Data
A catalogue record for this book is available from the British Library

Library of Congress Cataloging in Publication Data
After the Holocaust : challenging the myth of silence / edited by David Cesarani
and Eric J. Sundquist.
p. cm.
Includes index.
Holocaust, Jewish (1939-1945)--Influence. 2. Holocaust, Jewish (1939-1945)--
Historiography. 3. Holocaust, Jewish (1939-1945)--Moral and ethical aspects.
4. Memory--Social aspects. I. Cesarani, David. II. Sundquist, Eric J.
D804.348.A38 2012
940.53'1814--dc22
2011015444

ISBN: 978-0-415-61675-1 (hbk)
ISBN: 978-0-415-61676-8 (pbk)
ISBN: 978-0-203-80314-1 (ebk)

Typeset in Bembo
by Taylor & Francis Books

Printed and bound in Great Britain by
CPI Antony Rowe, Chippenham, Wiltshire

Contents

List of figures

Notes on contributors

Lawrence Baron has held the Nasatir Chair of Modern Jewish History at San Diego State University since 1988. He is the author or editor of four books, including *Projecting the Holocaust into the Present: The Changing Focus of Contemporary Holocaust Cinema* (2005) and *The Modern Jewish Experience in World Cinema* (2011).

David Cesarani is Research Professor in History at Royal Holloway, University of London, UK. He has written and edited over a dozen books, including *Arthur Koestler: The Homeless Mind* (1998), *Justice Delayed: How Britain Became a Refuge for Nazi War Criminals* (2001), *Eichmann: His Life and Crimes* (2004), and *Major Farran's Hat: Murder, Scandal and Britain's War Against Jewish Terrorism, 1945–1948* (2009). For his work in establishing a Holocaust Memorial Day in Great Britain he was awarded an OBE in 2005.

Beth B. Cohen is Gold/Weinstein Visiting Professor of Holocaust History at Chapman University, California, USA. Her research interests include survivors in the early postwar years, the topic of her book, *Case Closed: Holocaust Survivors in Postwar America* (2007), and numerous articles. She is currently studying the experiences of child survivors and how various Jewish organizations interpreted the charge to rescue and rehabilitate those children.

Rachel Deblinger, a doctoral candidate in the Department of History at UCLA, USA, is currently completing a dissertation, "Constructions of Survival: Framing Holocaust Narratives in Postwar America," that explores early accounts of the Holocaust in the United States and the factors that shaped first expressions of Holocaust memory. Her research has been supported in part by the Andrew W. Mellon Foundation, and in 2011–12 she will be a Samuel and Flora Weiss Research Fellow at YIVO.

Hasia R. Diner, the Paul S. and Sylvia Steinberg Professor of American Jewish History at New York University, USA, won the 2010 National Jewish Book Award for *We Remember with Reverence and Love: American Jews and the Myth of Silence After the Holocaust 1945–62* (2009). She has also published several books in the field of American Jewish history, American women's history, and the history of immigration and ethnicity.

Margarete Myers Feinstein is Research Scholar at the UCLA Center for the Study of Women, USA. She has written extensively about the legacies of Nazism, Jewish displaced persons, and postwar German national identity. Her recent book, *Holocaust Survivors in Postwar Germany, 1945–1957* (2009), tells the story of a community of survivors rebuilding their lives in the aftermath of the Shoah.

Kirsten Fermaglich is Associate Professor of History and Jewish Studies at Michigan State University, USA. The author of *American Dreams and Nazi Nightmares: Early Holocaust Consciousness and Liberal America, 1957–1965* (2006) and co-editor of the Norton Critical Edition of Betty Friedan's *The Feminine Mystique* (forthcoming in 2013), she is currently working on a book tentatively entitled "A Rosenberg By Any Other Name," which will deal with the history of Jews and name-changing in the twentieth century.

Laura Jockusch is the author of *Collect and Record! Jewish Holocaust Documentation in Postwar Europe, 1943–1953* (forthcoming from Oxford University Press). She is currently Feodor Lynen Minerva Postdoctoral Fellow at the Avraham Harman Institute of Contemporary Jewry at the Hebrew University of Jerusalem and at the Department of Jewish History at Ben-Gurion University of the Negev. Her current research includes a critical edition of early postwar Jewish Holocaust texts and a study of Jewish conceptions of retributive justice in postwar Germany.

Alan Rosen is the author, most recently, of *The Wonder of Their Voices: The 1946 Holocaust Interviews of David Boder* (2010) and *Sounds of Defiance: The Holocaust, Multilingualism, and the Problem of English* (2008), and the editor of *Approaches to Teaching Wiesel's Night* (2007). He has taught at universities and colleges in Israel and the United States, and lectures regularly on Holocaust Literature at Yad Vashem's International School for Holocaust Studies. His current book project is entitled *Killing Time, Saving Time: Calendars and the Holocaust*.

David G. Roskies is the Sol and Evelyn Henkind Professor of Yiddish Literature and Culture at the Jewish Theological Seminary and Visiting Professor of Jewish Literatures at Ben-Gurion University of the Negev. He has published extensively on Jewish responses to catastrophe. With Naomi Diamant, he is the co-author of *Holocaust Literature: A History and Guide* (forthcoming from the University Press of New England), from which his contribution to this volume is excerpted.

John K. Roth is the Edward J. Sexton Professor Emeritus of Philosophy and the Founding Director of the Center for the Study of the Holocaust, Genocide, and

Human Rights (now the Center for Human Rights Leadership) at Claremont McKenna College, USA. His most recent books include *Ethics During and After the Holocaust: In the Shadow of Birkenau* (2007); *Anguished Hope: Holocaust Scholars Confront the Palestinian-Israeli Conflict* (2008); and *The Oxford Handbook of Holocaust Studies* (2011).

Mark L. Smith is a doctoral candidate in Jewish History at UCLA, where his work has been supported in part by the Andrew W. Mellon Foundation. His dissertation, "The Yiddish Historians and the Struggle for a Jewish History of the Holocaust," argues for recognition of a specifically Yiddish orientation in Jewish historiography, focusing on the early postwar period. Related work includes entries in the Encyclopedia Judaica (Isaiah Trunk) and the Encyclopedia of American Women's History (Lucy Dawidowicz), as well as papers at the Berkeley Yiddish Conference and the Association for Jewish Studies.

Michael E. Staub teaches English and American Studies at Baruch College, City University of New York, USA. His books include *Voices of Persuasion: Politics of Representation in 1930s America* (1994), *Torn at the Roots: The Crisis of Jewish Liberalism in Postwar America* (2002), and *Madness Is Civilization: When the Diagnosis Was Social, 1948–1980* (2011), a history of the influence of psychiatric and anti-psychiatric perspectives on American culture and politics from the 1940s to the 1980s.

Eric J. Sundquist is Andrew W. Mellon Professor of the Humanities at Johns Hopkins University, USA, where he teaches in the Department of English. His books include *King's Dream* (2009); *Strangers in the Land: Blacks, Jews, Post-Holocaust America* (2005), which received the Weinberg Judaic Studies Institute Book Award; and *To Wake the Nations: Race in the Making of American Literature* (1992), which received the Christian Gauss Award from Phi Beta Kappa and the James Russell Lowell Award from the Modern Language Association.

Acknowledgments

The editors wish to acknowledge the support of the Andrew W. Mellon Foundation, whose Distinguished Achievement Award to Eric J. Sundquist (then a faculty member at UCLA) in 2007 made possible a three-year program of teaching and research activities on the Holocaust in American and modern culture, including a conference on the topic of "the myth of silence" that led to this volume. We are indebted to UCLA and especially to the UCLA Center for Jewish Studies for its gracious support of this program. We wish also to acknowledge the kind and discerning assistance of Eve Setch, Laura Mothersole, Emma Hudson and Jacqueline Dias at Routledge. The Publisher would like to thank Yad Vashem and Photofest, Inc.

INTRODUCTION

David Cesarani

In the mid-1990s, a comfortable consensus existed amongst historians concerning post-1945 responses to the wartime persecution and mass murder of Europe's Jews. They agreed, more or less, that the liberation of the concentration camps and the trials of Nazi leaders had attracted a flurry of attention in 1945–46, but with the focus on Western Europe and within the narrative of the war. The identity of the Jewish victims was often blurred or ignored. Partly thanks to the skewed focus of the International Military Tribunal at Nuremberg, the massacre of the Jews in Eastern Europe and the death camps remained shrouded in mystery. In any case, soon afterwards the world lost interest in what had happened to them. By the late 1940s, even the Jewish communities of Israel and the Diaspora seemed reluctant to engage with the recent past. Due to the onset of the Cold War, efforts to resolve the economic and political issues stemming from the implementation of genocide were quietly discontinued. The Jewish survivors were shunned and neglected. Little historical research was undertaken.[1]

Historians broadly concurred that this trend was reversed by the trial of Adolf Eichmann in Jerusalem in 1961–62. Then came the 1967 Israel–Arab war, which revived in Jews the memories of threatened extermination and made Jewish youth, in particular, more sympathetic towards what their elders had endured. The public at large was similarly jolted by the television mini-series 'Holocaust', shown around the world in 1978–79. For all its faults, 'Holocaust' marked a watershed in public awareness of the events it portrayed. Survivors of Nazi persecution who had been empowered by the Eichmann trial now found willing audiences for their testimony. Politicians, creative figures and cultural entrepreneurs were all alerted to the potential of what became known universally as 'the Holocaust'.[2] Finally, the end of the Cold War enabled the completion of unfinished business in Eastern Europe and created a political and intellectual framework in which the past could be confronted more honestly.[3]

However, in an article in *New Left Review*, in July 1997, Norman Finkelstein argued that the steadily increasing salience of 'the Holocaust' was actually due to a deliberate campaign by Jewish organizations and that it was instrumentalized for the benefit of Jews in the USA and Israel. Two years later, in *The Holocaust in American Life*, Peter Novick proposed a similar explanation although with a different emphasis. Finkelstein published a book length version of his polemic, *The Holocaust Industry*, in 2000. It became an international best seller. With remarkable speed this revisionism became the new orthodoxy. It was soon *de rigueur* to maintain that the public prominence of 'the Holocaust' was mainly due to the efforts of Jewish organizations to make people aware of this history with the intention of building sympathy for the Jews at large and Israel in particular.[4]

More recently, in *The Holocaust and Memory in the Global Age*, Daniel Levy and Natan Sznaider have argued that by the end of the twentieth century, the Nazi crime against the Jews had become a universal symbol of evil. This development was in part a response to the undermining of moral certainty due to postmodernism and the search for some agreed benchmarks of good and bad; but it was also a result of the 'Americanization' of 'the Holocaust', a process of globalization that accentuated its universal features and utility as a yardstick of evil.[5] This thesis (regardless of its merits) and the case made by Finkelstein and Novick (notwithstanding the variations between them), hinge on the notion that after the war there was a 'silence' about the attempted annihilation of the Jews until it was in the interests of the organized Jewish community in America to break it by 'constructing' what we know today as the historical event and cultural subject called 'the Holocaust'. But was there really a 'silence' after the war? Is the 'globalization' of knowledge and awareness of the genocide against Europe's Jews really something new?

The purpose of this essay collection is to present evidence that in the wake of the Second World War the Jewish survivors of Nazi persecution and mass murder were not 'silent' and that, over the ensuing fifteen years, the world was gifted a plenitude of information about the horrors that had so recently occurred in Europe. In so doing, several contributors pose the question of why, if this material existed, historians got it so wrong? One reason is that many Jewish survivors who lived through that period, and whose personal experiences informed the work of later researchers, tended to maintain that there had been a 'silence'. Yet, as we can now understand, their memory of those years was affected by the extraordinary salience that the horrendous events they had lived through assumed later on (and perhaps somewhat belatedly), and by their own enhanced status as 'survivors'. In comparison with the recognition heaped upon them in the 1990s and the ubiquity of 'the Holocaust' in historiography and public discourse, the 1950s did look in retrospect like an unknowing and uncaring decade.[6]

This is why it is apposite to use the term 'myth' to describe the phenomena being scrutinised here. Because what started out as a historical construction, an interpretation of the past based on evidence, turned into a set of beliefs almost immune to contrary data. A few concrete examples may illustrate this curious development. It is helpful to begin with Judith Miller's pioneering work of reportage *One, by One, By*

One: Facing the Holocaust, published in New York in 1990. Miller captured not only the work of historians up to that point, but also the aggrieved voice of survivors in several countries. It was a potent combination. 'Immediately after the war,' she wrote, 'the survivors who came to America wanted to forget their experiences and build new lives. The communities in which they lived encouraged little else.' She interviewed Abe Foxman and cited his experiences in support of her argument. Foxman recalled that after arriving in the USA his parents had tried to explain what they had been through, but gave up in the face of incomprehension. In a gloss on his comments, which were rather more nuanced than her own observations, she added: 'People like Foxman's father wrote, but mostly for themselves, in diaries and memoirs, few of which were published.' She concluded that:

> Outside their homes, there was little organised support for the victims. Their pain was not recognised by organised American Jewry. Survivors were not exactly excluded as a group; but they were not included either. Neither the Jewish community – nor gentiles – were interested in their harrowing tales.[7]

As we will see, however, some survivors in the United States were vocal and did find audiences. Several published memoirs and much about the Nazi persecution of the Jews was told in a variety of genres, if not in the historical narrative form that we would recognise today. Nevertheless, the assumed 'invisibility of the Holocaust' seemed to relieve researchers of the need to probe more deeply. Hence a succession of books appeared that seemed to confirm what was fast becoming orthodoxy.[8] Thus Aaron Hass could assert bluntly on the first page of *The Aftermath: Living with the Holocaust* that 'For several decades after its conclusion, little was written about the Holocaust.' Conversely, he claimed, 'No one wanted to know what the survivors had seen and endured.'[9] At the end of the decade, the British Jewish academic Victor Jeleniewski Seidler interwove the threads of his own experiences growing up as the child of survivors in postwar London with this burgeoning literature to make a similar set of assertions. 'Anglo-Jewry in the 1950s,' he wrote, 'was in many ways a frozen, traumatized community that had not really begun to come to terms with the Shoah.' To buttress this claim he quoted the bitter reflections in *Return to Auschwitz*, Kitty Hart's memoir of her time in Auschwitz and her arrival after the war in England. He added that:

> She kept her silence till the 1970s and her own family were grown up before she started to share some of her experiences. Post-war England wanted to turn its back on the suffering of the war and did not want to be reminded of what happened to European Jewry.[10]

Yet Kitty Hart had published her first memoir, *I Am Alive* in 1961. It appeared a year later in a mass-market paperback edition under the Corgi imprint. The book carried a dedication to 'my darling David and Peter to explain why their Mummy appears a little preoccupied at times'.[11] Now there may be many reasons why Seidler seems to have overlooked this fact, but there is no doubting the convenience of its omission for his overall argument. By the turn of the century, the majority of commentators, historians, and survivors simply assumed that with the exception of a brief and partial outburst of publicity immediately after the liberation of the camps, the years 1945 to 1970 were a desert as far as testimony, memoirs, historiography, films and other forms of representation were concerned. If there was nothing there, it was not even worth exploring. As Alan Rosen writes in this volume, 'The myth of silence organizes the facts to suit its purposes.' The 'silence' assumed mythic proportions; it had gone beyond the realm of verifiability and become a self-generating, self-justifying, and self-reflecting story that fulfilled various social or political functions.

Its functionality was its undoing. As long as the 'myth of silence' served to justify museum building and memorial enterprises, research grants and university courses, and to bestow heroic status on those who 'broke' it, Jewish communities and the wider world could accept it without question. But once the myth was put to what many considered malign purposes, the consensus on which it rested was shattered. When Peter Novick suggested that the organised Jewish community in the United States had colluded in the 'silence' in the 1950s and then purposefully ruptured it from the late 1960s in order to blunt assimilation and out-marriage, contest anti-semitism, and bolster support for Israel, it ceased to be a useful or desirable part of the American Jewish historical narrative. When Norman Finkelstein took the 'silence' as a fact and used it to claim that there was now a 'Holocaust industry' hell bent on extorting money from the Germans and anyone else who could be labelled a perpetrator or Nazi collaborator, it became not just an embarrassment but a liability.[12]

This is not to suggest that the essays in this collection or the conference from which they emerged reflect a deliberate pushback mounted for communal or political reasons. Much of the research on which they draw was underway before the most egregious manipulation of the 'myth of silence' and several trail-blazing publications that undermined the accepted version had already appeared.[13] On the other hand, the backlash triggered by Novick's book and Finkelstein's polemic created the space for a re-examination. It became easier to present evidence that apparently ran against the grain of memory and lived experience. Even so, as Hasia Diner observes in her essay in this volume, presentations on this theme are still likely to encounter incomprehension, disbelief, and flat out denial. If this book has just one purpose, it is to set out in accessible form a body of evidence that will enable a discussion of facts rather than a fruitless stand-off between hard-won data and deeply entrenched dogma.

In the first chapter David Cesarani sets the scene with an overview of efforts by Jewish survivors to record and publish accounts of their grim odysseys through ghettos and camps. Cesarani stresses the global nature of this enterprise, which commenced even before the war was over. He identifies Warsaw and Paris as nodal points for the generation of written accounts, but follows the movement of survivor-writers and translations across the Atlantic and into various languages. This was a vast collaborative effort that has not been fully appreciated, which in terms of historical research anticipated the major historical commissions of the 1990s. Cesarani also argues that the amount of testimony and historical inquiry is increased markedly if we include texts by non-Jews that did not foreground the fate of Jews and by Jews in which the Jewish identity of the author was 'effaced'. Furthermore, if the established, and restrictive, definitions of 'Holocaust literature' and 'Holocaust historiography' are put to one side, the volume of published information swells still further. This leads to his conclusion in which he seeks, in part, to understand how the 'myth of silence' was born. He argues that, if anything, by the end of the 1940s too much had been published on the suffering of the Jews and it had been held in the spotlight for too long. The public suffered a sort of 'compassion fatigue' that made it harder for subsequent waves of writers and memoirists to break through. But they were thwarted less by indifference and ignorance, than by the exhaustion of the market.

While it remains puzzling why historical researchers and literary historians failed to engage with the significant amount of published writing that appeared in the late 1940s and early 1950s, it is perhaps easier to understand why they overlooked the more ephemeral creations of the immediate postwar period. The Displaced Persons [DP] camps for Jews were the location of an intense cultural life and a hothouse of early research. But it was conducted in Yiddish, a language that was then pre-eminent in Jewish life but suffered rapid attrition thereafter. The products of this intense environment were treated carelessly because the camps were always intended to be transitory, although they lasted far longer than anticipated. When they eventually broke up, and the DPs moved on, their literary remains were scattered. Few archives existed to take DP journals or play bills, fewer had any interest in doing so, and fewer still had the resources to make them publicly accessible. However, the wrong language and inconvenience are not sufficient to explain the condescension of posterity towards the survivor-writers, memoirists and early historians. As Margarete Feinstein explains, the 'myth of silence' inhibited scholarship and this, in turn, reinforced the impression that there was no subject to investigate. The truth could not be more sharply different.

By examining the writing and performance of plays in the DP camps in allied-occupied Germany Feinstein exposes the myth that survivors were all traumatized and unable to articulate their experiences. In the camps they 'talked and talked' about what they had endured. Jews with pre-war experience of the Yiddish theatre wrote plays and organised companies to perform them. They were astonishingly bold and candid, confronting terrifying and distressing moments that would have been uncomfortably familiar to their audiences. They critiqued the Jewish leadership of the ghettos, held kapos under the spotlight, and probed the awful, heartrending decisions Jews had to make in order to survive. In the process, they helped Jews come to terms with their losses and the compromises they had made. The plays were, quite literally, an 'acting out' in a psycho-therapeutic sense. Feinstein also shows how writers, actors and audiences located themselves in terms of the ideological currents that swirled through the DP camps. They were anything but helpless, passive victims. Rather they were 'waging a battle to reclaim the Jewish heritage, to revive the Jewish soul, and to imagine the Jewish future'. Feinstein concedes that while the Jewish survivors may have been voluble, not everyone was ready to hear them. But today there can be no excuse for ignoring what they said and wrote. Recognising the importance of Yiddish and tracking down the creative works of the DP era transforms our perceptions.

'Rediscovering the survivors' words', Feinstein concludes, 'is a crucial step in correcting the historical record.'

Indeed, once we gain access to the 'Yiddish public sphere' we are overwhelmed by the extent of activity and its richness. Mark Smith looks at the role of the survivor historians who created the first historiography of the catastrophe and, at the same time, conducted a reflective, sometimes agonised, conversation with Yiddish-reading Jews around the world. Philip Friedman, Josef Kermish, Natan Blumental, Isaiah Trunk, Mark Dworzecki, Jonas Turkow and others were responsible for hundreds of publications. Few of these have been translated or republished. Although Friedman is perhaps the best known of this cohort and many of his pioneering essays have been collected and published, the bulk of his Yiddish oeuvre awaits translation. The result of this absence is a partial appreciation of his achievement as a researcher and his historiographical project. Although Friedman and his colleagues argued vigorously among themselves, they agreed that they were not simply outside observers but part of the history they were narrating. They understood its emotional charge, but sought ways to embrace sentiment rather than adopt a pose of Olympian detachment. This stance and their extensive use of testimony long anticipated Saul Freidländer's aspiration for an 'integrated history'.[14]

Several of the historians discussed by Smith participated in an extraordinary conference held in Paris at the end of November 1947. It was convened by Isaac Schneersohn, the founder and guiding spirit of the Centre de Documentation Juive Contemporaine [CDJC]. Schneersohn and his immediate co-workers, including Leon Poliakov, were of East European Jewish origin, but they were able to embrace French-born Jews and even interest French government officials in the task of documenting the plight of Jews in France under the Vichy administration and German occupation. Laura Jockusch explains that the politically astute Schneersohn depicted his Centre's mission as an adjunct to efforts by France to come to terms with the war years. Its publications typically attributed anti-semitism in France to external influences and reduced the despoliation and deportation of Jews to the work of a collaborationist clique that betrayed the true principles of the Republic. Under this guise, however, the Centre was able to publish twenty substantial collections of documents and historical works, many with the endorsement of prominent French figures. Schneersohn was less successful in his aspiration to make Paris the hub for research, documentation and memorial activity. The international conference that assembled with high hopes degenerated into a series of disputes: should the historians look at resistance or all Jewish responses to persecution; should they focus on the victims or also chronicle the actions of the perpetrators; should they collect and publish testimony or present documentary sources; should they privilege Yiddish? Behind these disagreements were political and ideological divisions that reflected both deep currents in modern Jewish history and also the immediate response to the catastrophe. Within a short time this international network broke up and decades would pass before such a collaborative enterprise was undertaken again. But the work of the CDJC went on and it achieved a huge amount, culminating in the dedication of a prominent memorial to the murdered Jews of Europe.

This memorial was abstract, unlike the one by Nathan Rapoport erected in 1947 on the site of the Warsaw Ghetto and duplicated later at Yad Vashem in Jerusalem. To David Roskies, the two sides of the memorial represent the two distinct narratives that emerged in Yiddish writing during the postwar decade. One strand celebrated resistance and heroism; the other the martyrdom of helpless innocents. Both were grounded in ideology and understandings of Jewish history. In his sweeping survey, Roskies examines how a panoply of Yiddish and Hebrew writers including Leyb Rochman, Zvi Kolitz, Abraham Sutzkever, Mordechai Strigler, and Ka-Tzetnik (Yehiel Dinur) wrestled with the catastrophe both in terms of representation and interpretation. In diaries, memoirs, poetry, novels, anthologies, and memorial books they organised once inchoate events according to some principle that would give them meaning and lend dignity to those who had perished. 'To sanctify the memory of the dead,' he writes, 'the Holocaust was read backwards in time. Everyone who perished was deemed holy and everything they had created was rendered holy, too.' This was a collective enterprise, like the writing of history, and it was conducted mainly in Yiddish, 'for Yiddish was still the universal Jewish language and the Yiddish press was to remain for decades the main purveyor of Holocaust memory'. By the close of the 1950s, Jewish readers could pick one of two distinct narrative responses: a naturalistic and a liturgical version. Above all, 'the Holocaust became part of the metanarrative of destruction and rebirth'.

Without that architecture, and before the historical narrative gelled, it was very hard indeed to make sense of what survivors were saying. In their analysis of the early audio recordings made by David Boder, Alan Rosen and Rachel Deblinger shed light on the context in which he worked and the impact he had. Rosen stresses that although Boder travelled alone in Europe in 1946, his expedition resulted from institutional and financial support that made it a collective effort. And he continued to get grant money for the analysis and dissemination of his research for nearly a decade afterwards. Boder had his own peculiar scientific agenda, but he also under-stood that he had a duty to educate Americans about what had befallen the Jews. Consequently, he pressed his interviewees to explain everything. Even though he had difficulty getting all his interviews published, his mission was hardly forlorn. Rosen shows how a range of social scientists utilised his findings: 'On multiple levels, Boder's interviews found an engaged lay and scholarly American audience.'

Boder's achievement was all the more remarkable because he was operating at the frontiers of both technology and knowledge of the immediate past. He did not have histories of Nazi policy or settled accounts of the ghettos and camps to help him frame his questions. As Deblinger shows, he frequently interrupted his interviewees to seek clarification about what they were telling him: it was initially incomprehensible because it was unprecedented. Many of these things were being said for the first time and he was the first hearer. As a result, people told him things and he asked questions that would later be deemed impolitic or indelicate. His interviews captured details of sexual abuse, prisoner-on-prisoner violence in the camps, and violent revenge taken by liberated Jews. Because Boder's interviews were overlooked by later authorities on 'Holocaust historiography' and 'Holocaust literature' many of these topics failed to enter the 'canonical narrative'. The 'rediscovery' of his amazing work reveals material that 'seems both to anticipate later themes and to complicate the historical narrative by recalling themes that have since been filtered out'.

Ironically, Boder's published interviews seem to have had more impact on the social sciences in general and on history writing that was not concerned with the Nazi period. Erving Goffman, for example, found inspiration in them for his work on prisons. Then again, as Michael Staub shows, a range of political scientists and social scientists in the USA registered the impact of the Jewish catastrophe in their work. This influence was apparent in the debates over *The Authoritarian Personality* by Theodor Adorno, Else Frenkel-Brunswick, Daniel Levinson and Nevitt Sandford, which was part of a project funded by the American Jewish Committee to lay bare the roots of prejudice and identify why societies fall prey to dictators. Staub insists that the entire project made no sense without reference to the Nazi takeover in Germany and the subsequent fate of the Jews. However, few Americans were ready to swallow the bitter pill served up to them by the researchers – even though several of them had had personal encounters with Nazism. The research faced an avalanche of criticism and was ultimately buried. When the insight of Adorno and his team came back into fashion in the 1960s it was adopted without any sense of its original historical mooring, as if this early response to Nazism had never happened as such.

The same process of 'forgetting' seems to have afflicted the realm of theology. Between 1945 and 1952, Karl Jaspers, Abraham Joshua Heschel and Martin Buber all penned searching reflections on the catastrophe, although it took time for their ideas to permeate wider theological circles. This was richly ironic because one subject that preoccupied them was: silence. This was, of course, the silence of God in the face of horrific acts perpetrated by his creation, man, upon other men. There was, however, no blanket 'silence' about this silence either. As early as the 1950s, Franklin Littell was starting out on what would become a trail-blazing career examining the troubled relationship between Christianity and Nazism.

Needless to say, such deep investigation and sophisticated reflection took time to complete and to see the light of day, let alone to register an impact in academic circles, the clergy or laity. The same was not true of certain areas of the creative industries that were able to respond flexibly and with alacrity to current affairs. Consequently, as Lawrence Baron shows, a number of films dealing with the Third Reich and Nazi criminality appeared from the early 1940s onwards. Filmmakers depicted Nazi atrocities during the war, sometimes blurring the identity of the victims, but at other times, as in *None Shall Escape* (1943), referring explicitly to Jews. After the war, when Nazis faced justice, Baron argues that the figure of the Nazi criminal fugitive was a popular screen trope. Major figures in Hollywood including Orson Welles and Sam Fuller tackled the subject. Indeed, the studios brought to a mass audience films of the liberated concentration camps that had previously only been seen fleetingly in newsreels or at the Nuremberg Tribunal. Baron thus challenges the chronology structuring conventional histories of 'film and the Holocaust' which only acknowledge the importance of *The Young Lions* (1958) and *Judgment at Nuremberg* (1959), implying that before these productions there was 'silence'.[15]

Two of the best known films that can be seen as a response to the war and the persecution of the Jews were *Gentleman's Agreement* and *Crossfire*, both released in 1947. They do not address 'the Holocaust' as an historical event, even as it was understood in the late 1940s, but they do explore anti-semitism in America. To this extent it is myopic not to see them as responses to the recent Jewish tragedy. Indeed, both feature Jewish GIs, recently returned from the war. Yet *Gentleman's Agreement*, like Arthur Miller's 1945 novel *Focus*, is equally interested in the varied behaviour patterns of Jews confronting prejudice. Their reactions cannot be dissociated from their knowledge of the catastrophe recently enacted in Europe or the plight of survivors, whose stories repeatedly erupted onto the front pages of US newspapers, long after the war ended, when they clamoured for permission to emigrate from Europe to British-administered Palestine.

This is the context for the epidemic of name changing examined by Kirsten Fermaglich. Through a close reading of petitions to alter surnames that sounded 'Jewish' or 'foreign' and the debates which this practice attracted, Fermaglich is able to chart one of the most personal, intimate and, as yet, unnoticed impacts of the Nazi onslaught against the Jews. Some explained that they wanted to circumvent the handicap that a 'Jewish' name posed or to avoid drawing the unwanted attention of those who disliked Jews. Fermaglich argues that refugees and survivors who reached America sought to distance themselves from the horrors perpetrated by Germans and other Europeans. Commentators in the Jewish press and Jewish writers, including Laura Zametkin Hobson, author of *Gentleman's Agreement*, and Bernard Malamud, discussed this practice in the light of the war years. Fermaglich concludes that: 'Far from repressing the knowledge of the Holocaust, American Jews in the late 1940s and 1950s used European genocide as a lens through which to interpret their most fundamental public identities in the United States.'

It was, after all, hard to avoid hearing about the fate of Jews on the radio, seeing DPs in newsreels, or reading about them in the newspapers. Jewish Americans in many cities were also likely to encounter pre-1939 refugees and post-1945 survivors, living embodiments of the catastrophe. Beth Cohen investigates how they reacted and, in particular, the conduct of social workers tasked with assisting them. She cites many transplanted Jews who complained that 'nobody wanted to listen' or that 'nobody ever asked' about what they had suffered. Consequently, the refugees and survivors tended to talk about their experiences between themselves, in their families, and in old-country immigrant associations called *landsmanshaftn*. They were not 'silent', she concedes, but it took time for them to find an audience outside these circles. Social workers, however, were obligated to engage with the remnant that made it to America; so how did they treat them? Cohen finds that for a variety of reasons social work professionals preferred not to delve too deeply into the bad times. Some may have wanted to avoid causing needless pain or feared arousing guilt in those who had somehow survived. Others were simply incredulous, while in certain cases they were believing but had already heard all they wanted to hear. It was a complex situation, full of shades, and not reducible to sweeping generalizations about a postwar 'silence'.

For, the harder the historian looks, the more there is to find. In the last chapter, Hasia Diner asks why, if there was no hush, the 'myth' developed in the first place. Her monumental study *We Remember With Reverence and Love: American Jews and the Myth of Silence After the Holocaust* was one source of inspiration for this volume, which in its title pays tribute to her industry and achievement.[16] Diner does not seek to summarise the vast quantity of data she excavated from historical writing, communal archives, synagogue magazines, publishers' lists, journals of opinion, liturgies, Sunday school curricula, youth movement programmes, all of which chronicled the destruction of European Jewry, referred to it as a subject for urgent debate, lamented and commemorated it. Instead, she drives the analysis forwards in time and seeks to understand how or why all this was ignored. She notes that Jewish communal activists in the 1960s, so-called 'New Jews', exploited the progressively benign environment in America to adopt a more extrovert and expansive Jewish identity and, concurrently, belittled the comparatively restrained expressions that typified their parents' generation. They claimed that they 'discovered' the history of wartime Jewish suffering and defied the sensibility of the public at large by confronting them with it. Their behaviour and the story they told of their genesis correlated with sociological descriptions of the 'ethnic revival'. It seemed, therefore, to make sense that previously there had been little of either Jewish ethnicity or the knowledge of 'the Holocaust' that increasingly underpinned it. The purveyors of the 'myth of silence' in turn seized on the self-aggrandising comments of 1960s and 1970s Jewish activists and the apparently dispassionate findings of social scientists to prove what they suspected or wanted to find. Yet the entire edifice rested on the hyperbole and false heroics of young Jewish baby-boomers: 'Inherent in the constant iteration and perpetration of the myth of silence is a valorization of what a later generation of American Jews did vis-à-vis the Holocaust and the kind of memorial practices which it constructed.' Of such things are myths made.

The focus of Diner's work seems a long way away from the DP camps in postwar Europe, but as well as taking issue with the 'myth of silence' all the chapters are linked by a number of common and overlapping themes. They all demonstrate, perforce, the sheer volume of talking, recording, writing, representation in various media, and publishing that went on from 1945 well into the 1950s. If anything, they show a continuity rather than a tapering off followed by a new wave of activity at the time of the Eichmann trial. But they also reveal a series of tensions and paradoxes that rendered this thread hard to discern from the perspective of the 1990s.

Language played a curious, Janus-faced role. As Cesarani, Feinstein, Smith, Jockusch, Roskies, Rosen and Deblinger explain, Yiddish was essential to the conversation conducted amongst Jews. Contrary to the glib argument that much of the early testimony, memoir literature, and historiography was in the wrong language, and was looked down upon by scholars, their contributions demonstrate that language was no barrier to expression and that Yiddish actually helped to disseminate information. Millions of Jews around the world spoke Yiddish as their first language. The existence of the Yiddish-speaking Jewish diaspora facilitated the rapid translation and distribution of key texts. Scholarship in Yiddish flourished. However, the precipitous decline of Yiddish and the contraction of language competency closed off much of this source material, finally creating the illusion that it had never even existed. Sheer ignorance and linguistic ineptitude, from the 1970s to the 1990s, was more important than prejudice in the 1940s and 1950s.

The use of Yiddish and its decline are related to one of the tensions that ran through the Jewish world after 1945: whether the Jewish diaspora could once again prosper in safety or whether a Jewish state represented the only secure future for the Jewish people. The break up of the DP camps and the dispersion of their inhabitants gave one answer. Had 250,000 Yiddish speaking Jews remained in central Europe on the free side of the Iron Curtain, the course of scholarship and commemoration might have taken a very different path. But, after 1948, most went to Israel or the USA, which were increasingly uncongenial environments for the Yiddish language and scholarship in Yiddish. This rupture concretized the ideological divide, but its outcome was not fore-ordained.

Another, and not unconnected, tension was the struggle to agree on a narrative of the catastrophe. This, in turn, hinged on whether the Jewish fate was defined and understood in particular or universal terms. Feinstein, Smith and Roskies show Jewish intellectuals wrestling to come up with explanations for what had happened (especially for Jewish behaviour). Was it an end or a beginning? Zionists, at least, could draw the lesson that Jewish life could only flourish in a Jewish homeland and depicted the liberation of the survivors as a potential rebirth. Of course, the Zionist interpretation was predicated on a certain, particularistic reading of Jewish history. But was the destruction of Jewish communities really a result of the exceptional Jewish situation or were Jews simply one victim group amongst many? Even if they were acknowledged as the victims of Nazi racism, it was possible to point out many other targets for murderous racial-biological policies. This interpretative tension helps to account for the curious silence and non-silence that characterised many countries after liberation from German occupation. On the one hand everyone knew what had happened to the Jews and knew equally well that there had been extensive collaboration and profiteering. For obvious reasons, few people wanted to talk about this openly and Jews, who were hardly in a strong position to do so, felt inhibited about broaching the subject themselves. But this did not mean that they were silent. Instead, non-Zionist Jews sought to craft narratives that would articulate the Jewish disaster in broadly acceptable terms.

Jockusch and Staub both illustrate the contortions of Jewish thinkers who sought to represent the specific Jewish tragedy in a universal framework. Over time, it became easy to miss the nuances of what they were trying to achieve and to forget what was, in the immediate aftermath of the war, blazingly obvious. Instead, later generations came to read patriotic accounts or universal explanations as 'self-effacement' and a form of 'silencing'. We can now see that in the absence of an agreed narrative and the contest over definitions there was a vigorous debate that was the opposite of a hush, but it has been necessary to go back to the sources, Yiddish in particular, in order to recover it.

Jewish populations in Europe in the wake of the war were demographically weakened, where they still existed at all, economically shattered, and ideologically fractured. Even where they were intact, in the USA, or relatively undamaged, in the UK and pre-1939 USSR, they operated in uncongenial political environments. There is no comparison with the formidable Jewish communal organisations of the late twentieth century and the scholarly institutions that provide narrative continuity and guarantee the reproduction of research. So it is even more astonishing that the early research and creative endeavours had such extensive and long lasting impacts. Yet Roskies, Rosen, Staub and Baron illustrate the many ways in which these early explorations and representations permeated 'high' and 'low' culture from the late 1940s onwards. While not recognisable as 'the Holocaust', the fate of the Jews was the starting point for academic studies of prejudice and authoritarianism, and inscribed in poetry, novels, and films. Roth explains how German barbarity conducted by Christians and occasionally in the name of Christ caused Christian theologians to reflect on their faith, just as it challenged Jewish thinkers to wrestle with questions of theodicy in Judaism. If the choice of names is considered a manifestation of popular culture, it was, as Fermaglich shows, registered here, too. In their different ways, both Cohen and Diner reveal how the tragedy impinged on the everyday life of Jews in America. Whether they responded in ways that we would now consider inappropriate or with sensitivity and sympathy, communal leaders and social workers could not avoid the aftershocks of the disaster.

Ironically, the very success with which Jews overcame the trauma of genocide and the razing of their communities in much of Europe may have fostered the 'myth of silence'. The liquidation of the DP camps, the creation of Israel, and the integration or reintegration of survivors obscured the intensity of the years 1945–48. These processes also broke the threads of continuity, allowing the illusion of silence and inaction to develop amongst later generations. As Diner shows, their 'rediscovery' of the war years and its bitter after-effects, combined with the vainglorious characterisation of their efforts as 'heroic' in contradistinction to the conduct of their parents, gave birth to the myth that before them little had been said and less done. That myth has now been exposed; the way is open to a root and branch reassessment of Jewish life in the postwar era, a life lived in the pervasive, shared awareness that Jews had narrowly survived a catastrophe which was one facet of an apocalyptic conflict that had engulfed humanity as a whole but claimed two-thirds of their number.

Acknowledgments

Much of the research for this article was conducted at the Library of the United States Holocaust Memorial Museum, Washington, DC. I would like to acknowledge the generosity of the J B and Maurice C Shapiro Charitable Trust for making it possible for me to spend the academic year 2008–9 at the USHMM Centre for Advanced Holocaust Studies where an early version of this study was presented.

Notes

1 For a paradigmatic text that summarises the state of research on a range of countries in the mid-1990s, see David S Wyman ed., *The World Reacts to the Holocaust* (Baltimore: Johns Hopkins University Press, 1996).

2 See contributions in Wyman ed., *The World Reacts to the Holocaust*, on France by David Weinberg, pp. 3–44; on Italy by Meir Michaelis, pp. 514–53; on the Netherlands by Deborah Dwork and Robert-Jan van Pelt, pp. 45–77; on Britain by David Cesarani, pp. 599–641; the United States, by David S Wyman, pp. 693–748; on Israel by Dalia Ofer, pp. 836–923.

3 The significance of the end of Communism for the history and memory of the war years was identified by Tony Judt in his essay, 'The Past Is Another Country: Myth and Memory in Postwar Europe' that first appeared in István Deák, Jan T Gross and Tony Judt eds, *The Politics of Retribution in Europe: World War II and Its Aftermath* (Princeton, NJ: Princeton University Press, 2000), 293–323. Judt gave greater salience to memory of the Jews' fate in the 'Epilogue' to his monumental work *Postwar: A History of Modern Europe Since 1945* (London: Heinemann, 2005), entitled 'From the House of the Dead. An Essay on Modern European Memory', 803–31. For variations on this theme and its working out in specific national contexts, see Jan-Werner Müller, *Memory and Power in Post-War Europe* (Cambridge: Cambridge University Press, 2002); Klas-Göran Karlson and Ulf Zander eds, *The Holocaust on Post-War Battlefields: Genocide as Historical Culture* (Malmo: Sekel, 2006); Richard Ned Lebow, Wulf Kansteiner, Claudio Fogu eds, *The Politics of Memory in Postwar Europe* (Durham, NC: Duke University Press, 2006).

4 Norman Finkelstein, 'Daniel Jonah Goldhagen's "Crazy" Thesis', *New Left Review*, 224 (July/August 1997), 39–87. Peter Novick, *The Holocaust in American Life* (New York: Houghton Mifflin, 1999); Norman Finkelstein, *The Holocaust Industry: Reflections on the Exploitation of Jewish Suffering* (London: Verso, 2000).

5 Daniel Levy and Natan Sznaider, *The Holocaust and Memory in the Global Age* (Philadelphia: Temple University Press, 2006)

6 See Henry Greenspan, *The Awakening of Memory: Survivor Testimony in the First Years after the Holocaust* (Washington, DC: United States Holocaust Memorial Museum, 2000).

7 Judith Miller, *One, By One, By One: Facing the Holocaust* (New York: Simon and Schuster, 1991), 220–21.

8 Edward T Linenthal, *Preserving Memory: The Struggle to Create America's Holocaust Museum* (New York: Viking, 1995), 7–8. Cf. the more nuanced overview in Rochelle Saidel, *Never Too Late to Remember: The Politics Behind New York City's Holocaust Museum* (New York: Holmes and Meier, 1996), 16–26 and 28 where the author speaks of a 'latent awareness'. It is pertinent to note that both these books celebrate the creation of institutions dedicated to rescuing and preserving memory, so the authors had an incentive to stress, even to exaggerate, the earlier failure to do so.

9 Aaron Hass, *The Aftermath: Living with the Holocaust* (Cambridge: Cambridge University Press, 1995), 1.

10 Victor Jeleniewski Seidler, *Shadows of the Shoah: Jewish Identity and Belonging* (Oxford: Berg, 2000), 11–12, referring to Kitty Hart, *Return to Auschwitz* (London: Sidgwick and Jackson, 1981).

11 Kitty Hart, *I Am Alive* (London: Abelard-Schuman, 1961, reissued by Corgi, 1962).

12 It is interesting to note that in 1990 Judith Miller had already used the phrase 'Holocaust industry' and cited many voices suggesting that the tragic history of the Jews was being over-used, not least to mute criticism of Jewish behaviour and to generate sympathy for Israel: *One, by One, By One*, 230–31.

13 See, for example: Stuart Svonkin, *Jews Against Prejudice: American Jews and the Fight for Civil Liberties* (New York: Columbia University Press, 1997); Jeffrey Shandler, *While America Watches: Televising the Holocaust* (New York: Oxford University Press, 1999).

14 Saul Friedländer, *Nazi Germany and the Jews: The Years of Persecution 1933–39* (London: Weidenfeld and Nicolson, 2005) and idem *Nazi Germany and the Jews 1939–1945: The Years of Extermination* (London: Weidenfeld and Nicolson, 2007). For a full discussion of Friedländer's approach and its precursors, see the essays in Paul Betts and Christian Wiese

eds, *Years of Persecution, Years of Extermination: Saul Friedländer and the Future of Holocaust Studies* (London: continuum, 2010).

15 Compare, for example, Annette Insdorf, *Indelible Shadows: Film and the Holocaust* (New York: Cambridge University Press, 1989 2nd edition).

16 Hasia Diner, *We Remember With Reverence and Love: American Jews and the Myth of Silence After the Holocaust* (New York: New York University Press, 2009).

1

CHALLENGING THE 'MYTH OF SILENCE'

Postwar responses to the destruction of European Jewry

David Cesarani

Jews began documenting Nazi policies of racial persecution and the destruction of their communities in Europe even while these horrors were occurring. This was not simply a passive reaction, chronicling their fate as it was played out. Acting individually and collectively they also made Herculean efforts to disseminate the information or at least to preserve it for a time when it could be used. The work of the Oyneg Shabes group in Warsaw is the most famous example. Tragically, as Samuel Kassow observes, Oyneg Shabes 'had more luck in saving documents than in saving people'.[1]

The Centre de Documentation Juive in France was more fortunate. It was the brainchild of Isaac Schneersohn, an Orthodox Jew of distinguished rabbinic lineage who had fled from German-occupied Paris to Grenoble. In April 1943 he called a meeting of Jewish organizations and convinced them that it was essential to chronicle the depredations of the Vichy Regime and the Germans so as to provide a basis for restitution proceedings and retribution after the war. However, little could be achieved under wartime conditions. In December 1944, Schneersohn resumed operations in liberated Paris. He was assisted by a small team of gifted young men, some with academic (though not necessarily historical) training, including Leon Poliakov and Joseph Billig. Within a short time the centre, renamed the Centre de Documentation Juive Contemporaine (CDJC) published several groundbreaking collections documenting Vichy and German anti-Jewish measures.[2]

Schneersohn was a shrewd political operator. He realized the importance of forging links with the French state and put the Centre's resources at the disposal of the French delegation to the Nuremberg Tribunal. This co-operation paid dividends. One of the French prosecutors, Henri Monneray, ensured that the Centre received the documentation assembled to support the charges of war crimes and crimes against humanity. By 1949 the CDJC had amassed several tons of this material.[3]

The same sense of history animated the survivors of Polish Jewry. As early as August 1944 Philip Friedman, a historian of pre-war eminence, and several others with historical training set up a Jewish Historical Commission in Lublin. Its immediate aim was to collect eye-witness testimony from Jewish survivors to supply evidence for postwar trials and to ensure that the Polish authorities were fully appraised of Jewish suffering and losses under the German occupation. Like Schneersohn, the Commission realized the importance of cooperating with state authorities in war crimes investigations, both to further the achievement of justice and to legitimate its own activity.[4]

In February 1945, the Commission became a branch of the officially recognized Central Committee of Polish Jews. Friedman was appointed director. The founders were now able to network a number of other committees that had sprung up in newly liberated cities. At its height, the central historical commission presided over 25 branches and employed around 100 staff. Amongst the professionally trained historians working alongside Philip Friedman were Rachel Auerbach and Hersz Wasser, the sole survivors of Oyneg Shabes; Josef Kermisz; Natan Blumental; Artur Eisenbach; Michel Borwicz; Isaiah Trunk; Nella Rost; and Josef Wulf. All would go on to make major contributions to historical research. Between 1944 and 1949, the commission distributed numerous questionnaires and conducted about 5,000 interviews. Given that the number of survivors of the camps and ghettos in Poland was 40,000–50,000, this demonstrates a significant willingness to record and talk, but certainly not 'silence'.[5]

Under Friedman's direction, the central commission made a great effort to recover hidden Jewish archives. With the assistance of the official Main Commission for the Investigation of German Crimes in Poland it also amassed captured German records. Commission members participated in the state investigations at Auschwitz, Chelmno and Treblinka. They supplied material to the Polish delegation at Nuremberg and were essential to the subsequent prosecution of Hans Biebow and Rudolf Hoess. At the same time, they churned out publications at a staggering rate. A visitor from America, Jacob Pat, recalled that 'They all work in a kind of fever, as if they feared that every day, every hour's delay, might make them late.' If to some in the West the death camps remained shrouded in mystery, it was not for lack of effort by Polish Jewish historians.[6]

A parallel movement developed amongst Jewish survivors in the Displaced Persons (DP) camps in allied-occupied western Germany. The first historical commission there was initiated in October 1945 at Hohne-Belsen, in the British Zone. A month later a commission was established in Munich in the American Zone. They soon spread. At their greatest extent there were 47 historical commissions in both zones, employing well over 60 people. About 40 were based in Munich which became the coordinating centre. As in Poland, the commission activists (who were mainly untrained), prioritized the collection of eye-witness accounts. Over a four-year period the Central Historical Commission collected 2,250 testimonies. It also drew up and distributed statistical surveys and questionnaires. Around 8,000 completed forms were returned to individual branches and collated centrally.[7] The Munich office even published a journal, *Fun Letsten Hurbn*, dedicated to disseminating testimony and encouraging further submissions. Inaugurated in February 1946, it ran to ten issues, each of many pages, with a print-run of about 1,800. Copies were circulated throughout the Yiddish-speaking world, reaching the USSR, France, Palestine, North and South America.[8]

The survivors of the Jewish partisan groups formed their own association, with the acronym PAHAH (from *Partizanim, Hayalim, Halutzim* – Hebrew for partisans, soldiers, pioneers), and used the Jewish DP journal *Fam Folk* as a vehicle for publishing testimony and accounts of armed Jewish resistance. The story of Tuvia Bielski appeared there as early as 1946. PAHAH accumulated no fewer than 700 biographies of individual resisters and 100 depositions. These reports in Yiddish were quickly picked up and translated into English by the first historians of Jewish resistance. Several appeared in the pioneering anthology, *The Root and the Bough*, edited by Leo Schwarz and they supplied much of the material for Marie Syrkin's history of Jewish resistance, *Blessed is the Match*, which appeared in 1948.[9]

For other survivors, like Tuvia Friedman in Vienna, and Simon Wiesenthal in Linz, the impulse to collect documents and to amass depositions came from the hope of achieving retribution. Their work may have been eccentric and unprofessional but it resulted in the capture of significant information that later historians would utilize.[10] In Italy the drive towards historical research began with inquiries into the fate of the Jews deported from Italian territory. A few months after Rome was liberated Colonel Massimo Adolfo Vitale established the Comitato Ricerche Deportati Ebrei (CRDE) under the auspices of the Union of Italian Jewish Communities. His methods were rather erratic but gradually the CRDE accumulated an impressive archive. With the assistance of the Italian Ministry of Justice, in March 1947 Vitale traveled to Cracow to attend the trial of Rudolf Hoess. While there he obtained an interview with Hoess and collected important documents from the Polish prosecution team. On this basis he was able to compile the first account of Auschwitz to be made available in Italian. Vitale also arranged for over 190 testimonies to be taken from Italian Jewish survivors (nearly a third of the total).[11]

Efforts at documentation and the collection of testimony were almost ubiquitous, spanning areas under Soviet influence, countries of the Atlantic alliance, and former neutrals. In Budapest, the National Relief Committee for deportees in Hungary (DEGOB) established an office which eventually employed around 30 interviewers who took depositions from over 3,600 Jewish survivors of forced labour, ghettoisation and deportation.[12] In London, staff at the Central Jewish Information Office (later known as the Wiener Library) sporadically collected eye-witness statements, some to assist war crimes investigations. They also published half a dozen testimonies during 1945–46.[13] There was even a centre in Sweden where Nella Rost set up a small unit to document the rescue efforts of Norwegians, Danes and Swedes, and collected testimony from Jews evacuated to Sweden from camps in Germany in 1945.[14]

The transnational character of the catastrophe, the migration of survivor-historians, and the knowledge in each centre that similar efforts were underway elsewhere was a spur to international cooperation. Within a short time the work of historiography was globalized. Philip Friedman was possibly the first to realize the potential and importance of establishing cross-border networks. In July 1947, the Yad Vashem Foundation convened a conference in Jerusalem to discuss the progress of research and to establish Jerusalem's claim as the eventual repository for all relevant document collections. Due to the troubled state of Palestine few Europeans or Americans could attend. Nevertheless, Friedman was able to represent the historical commissions in Germany (where he now resided), Natan Blumental attended on behalf of the Polish historians, and the CDJC was represented.[15]

The early efforts of Yad Vashem to monopolize research did not deter Isaac Schneersohn from pursuing his own vision of making Paris the centre for scholarship and commemoration. At the invitation of the CDJC, between 30 November and 9 December 1947, 32 delegates representing Jewish historical commissions and research centres in 13 countries assembled in Paris for a conference. This gathering represents a crucial moment in the postwar research effort and the formation of an early historiography. For a short while it focused a transnational enterprise of remarkable dimensions. However, apart from unanimity that the record of Jewish resistance should be at the forefront of any joint efforts, the delegates could not find common ground. There was not even agreement on which language to use for their own discussions. Although the conference concluded with a resolution to set up a European coordinating committee, its members never met. Schneersohn was running short of funds and, in any case, the Jewish historical commissions proved to be transitory. Following the establishment of Israel, many of the historians emigrated and arranged for the archives to be sent to Yad Vashem. Others moved to America. Those who stayed in eastern Europe found their work suffocated by forced conformity to the Soviet version of the war.[16]

In hindsight the Paris conference marked the high point of early efforts to document the wartime catastrophe using the most modern methods of collective historical research, including the mobilization of grass roots activists and the writing of history on an industrial scale by teams of historians. It would be 40 years before a similar undertaking would be attempted. Yet the failure of the 1947 initiative and the disintegration of the historical commissions was not inevitable. Circumstances rather than an imposed or voluntary silence conspired to derail a promising bid to embark on a global historiography.[17]

Even under the best of conditions, time would have been needed to process the mass of raw material obtained by the commissions and documentation centres. Much of what they collected went into archives in New York, London, Paris, Warsaw and Jerusalem, where it was subject to the whims of archivists, fluctuating budgets, and fashions for historical research. It would necessarily take time before the stories locked away in these files would impinge further on public awareness. For this reason it is important to look at early memoirs, reports, and testimony that were published in Europe and to investigate their wider dissemination.

Despite the disruption of communications and disputed borders, authors, witnesses as well as manuscripts criss-crossed war-shattered Europe. With extraordinary speed, accounts by survivors from one country appeared in another, frequently translated into a third language. The westward migration of survivors itself aided the dissemination of information about events in Eastern Europe. Consequently, the focus of many of these accounts was overwhelmingly on Eastern Europe – ghettos, mass shootings, death camps, and Jewish resistance.

Twelve months after his liberation Philip Friedman had written in Polish and Yiddish on the destruction of the Jews of Lwow and a general account of the extermination of Polish Jewry. His history of Auschwitz, *This Was Oswiecim. The Story of a Murder Camp*, was transmitted to England, translated from the Yiddish by the poet and critic Joseph Leftwich, and published as a booklet in 1946 with a foreword by the Polish Ambassador.[18] The remnant of the Bund that reconstituted in Warsaw in 1945 was responsible for publishing Marek Edelman's narrative of the Warsaw Ghetto uprising. Within a year it had been translated into English by Zofia Nalkowska, a well-known Polish author who chaired one of the state commissions investigating German crimes in Poland, and published in New York by the American section of the Bund.[19] Bernard Goldstein's account of the Warsaw ghetto revolt made its way from Poland to the USA in under two years and from Yiddish to English in the next two years. Goldstein was a veteran Bundist and a leader of the uprising. After the war he emigrated to America where he published his memoir in Yiddish, *Finf Yor in Varshever geto*. It was printed in just 2000 copies, but elicited such a response that Viking Press commissioned a translation by Leonard Shatzkin. The English edition appeared under the (rather unhelpful) title *The Stars Bear Witness* and it was widely and well reviewed.[20] These combined efforts illustrate both the extent of the global effort at diffusion and the absence of an immediate postwar 'silence'.

After Poland, Paris was the most active centre for publishing memoirs and histories.[21] In 1945, Calmann Levy published Ber Baskind's memoir of the Warsaw Ghetto, *La Grande Épouvante: Souvenirs d'un rescapé du ghetto de Varsovie*. Baskind had been captured during the uprising and sent to the Poniatowa labor camp. He later escaped and went underground, but when he heard that the Germans were offering sanctuary to Jews with the citizenship of certain neutral countries he obtained the necessary papers and was sent to the internment camp at Vittel, in southern France, where he was finally liberated. His memoir is a good example of how the movement of survivors brought detailed information from East to West. It is not often remarked, but Vittel became a living archive of events in Eastern Europe. The fact that his report was quickly translated and printed by a notable publishing house also indicates that there was a yearning for narratives that were explicitly and unequivocally centred on the tragedy of the Jews.[22]

In Italy, the first account of the terrible round up in Rome on 16 October 1943 appeared in print just months after the war ended. It was written by a pre-war litterateur Giacomo Debenedetti. He was in hiding at the time of the *razzia* but the record he assembled from subsequent newspaper reports and eye-witnesses was sufficient to depict that day in detail. Nor did Debenedetti fail to mention the 1938 racial laws and the discrimination against Jews under Fascism. The slim volume appeared with a preface by the novelist Alberto Moravia, much of which was dedicated to recalling his own troubles under Fascism and the racial laws.[23]

Many anthologies of 'Holocaust literature' and literary studies exclude or ignore a swathe of early survivor narratives because the authors were not Jewish, allegedly 'marginalized' the treatment of Jews in the camps or 'effaced' them altogether. There is no doubt that some memoirs by non-Jewish returnees from the camps did ignore the Jews. One of the earliest and most widely read accounts which rendered the Jewish presence invisible was by Pelagia Lewinska, a member of the Polish underground. Although her narrative begins with her in a prison cell in Cracow with seven Jewish prisoners, she hardly mentions Jews once her narrative reaches Auschwitz. Lewinska's memoir was published in Paris in 1945 and eventually sold over 40,000 copies.[24]

However, such examples are less common than reports that acknowledged a Jewish presence but framed it within the perspective of the moment, at a time when the genocide against the Jews was not seen as the central event of the Nazi era or the war. To modern sensibilities this may resemble myopia, but if non-Jewish authors did not devote extensive passages to Jewish suffering this does not mean that they were colluding in its displacement or distorting its singularity. On the contrary, it may have been so obvious to them that it did not have to be underlined or highlighted. Often a brief reference in these texts says more about the plight of the Jews than volumes written subsequently. The brevity of such allusions may indicate the opposite of indifference or ignorance. So much was known, or thought to be known, that more was simply not required.

The most famous camp memoir published in France at this time was *L'univers concentrationnaire* by David Rousset, who had been imprisoned in Buchenwald. It was a bestseller and was quickly translated into English, appearing in New York in 1947. Annette Wieviorka, who wrote the landmark history of early camp literature in France, chides Rousset for suggesting that the difference between Auschwitz-Birkenau and other camps was one of 'degree not kind', thus blurring its genocidal function which was specific to the Jews. However, Rousset was hardly consistent. While he dubbed the prisoner population a 'race' he nevertheless marked the distinctions between groups and differentiated the functions of the camps: 'The camps for Jews and Poles', he wrote, entailed 'extermination and torture on a large scale.' In other books he acknowledged that the Jews faced a different destiny. Indeed, it would otherwise be hard to explain why Isaac Schneersohn and the CDJC were happy to cooperate with him in the production of a book about Nazi repression.[25]

The impact made in France by Rousset's memoir was paralleled in Germany by Eugen Kogan's report on Buchenwald. Kogon was arrested in Austria for anti-Nazi activities in March 1938 and incarcerated in Buchenwald from September 1939 until the liberation. He was subsequently invited by the US Army to write a report on the camp. The resulting document was so comprehensive and powerful that the US occupation authorities arranged for it to be published as a book. Appearing as *Der SS-Staat,* it quickly sold 135,000 copies and was soon translated into English. For years it was the standard work on the Nazi concentration camps.[26] Kogon's book was not about the 'Final Solution'. He admitted that he knew little about Auschwitz or the death camps. But he was acutely aware from his own experience, and what he learned from Jewish prisoners, that they had been subject to the harshest regimen everywhere and that the aim of German policy towards the Jews was extermination. His book devotes a chapter to their uniquely tragic situation. Importantly, he included unmediated testimony by survivors who recalled experiences in Treblinka, Auschwitz, the Warsaw Ghetto uprising, the Riga ghetto and other camps. With good reason, Philip Friedman praised the work for setting 'the framework in which the Jewish fate was the most horrible and tragic manifestation' and writing about the Jews with 'profound understanding'.[27]

We Were in Auschwitz, the collective memoir by three Polish inmates of Auschwitz, Janus Nel Siedlecki, Krystyn Olszewski and Tadeusz Borowski, begins in a patriotic, universalistic spirit. The three authors maintain that the experience of one prisoner was the same as that of all the others. However, before long, the Jewish presence in the camp is admitted and a distinction drawn between the treatment of Jews and that of non-Jews. The three authors state that during 1942 Auschwitz mutated from being a 'Polish camp' into 'an enormous international extermination camp for many millions of European Jews'. They observe that 'A separate element of camp life was the transports of Jews from the whole of Europe to the gas.'[28] In 1948 Borowski's contribution was published separately, to great acclaim, and twenty years later reached audiences in English, but wrenched from its original context. The result has been a significant misreading of his famous 'story' 'This Way to the Gas Ladies and Gentlemen. ...' Borowski was writing testimony, not fiction. Furthermore, his focus on Jews tells strongly against the notion that the fate of the Jews was routinely effaced in postwar Poland.[29]

In almost every country in Europe from which Jews were deported, published accounts by survivors appeared within just a few years or even months after liberation or the end of the war. Until recently, histories of 'Holocaust literature' and historiographical surveys have ignored most of these, either because they did not appear in English or because they did not address the fatal peculiarity of the Jewish situation.[30] And, indeed, there is a curious lack of self-referentiality and evasiveness in these early testimonies. After they returned from camps many Jewish survivor writers hid their identity or stressed their patriotism. Others wrote from a left-wing standpoint and transmuted their experiences into a universal lesson for mankind, demonstrating the evils of fascism or capitalism. Yet this should be a cause for understanding rather than censure. As the historian Pieter Lagrou observes,

> anti-fascist discourse offered a formal legal recognition to survivors of the Holocaust, with both symbolic and material benefits; it offered social support and sociability through organizations capable of delivering a powerful sense of mission. Specific recognition of Jewishness, even through the recognition of a tragically distinctive persecution, was not what many survivors, whose survival had depended on the opposite, asked for at the time.[31]

A good example is *Smoke Over Birkenau* [*Dymy nad Birkenau*] written by Seweryna Szmaglewska in 1946. Szmaglewska, who was Jewish, was chosen to give evidence at the Nuremberg Tribunal, but did not advertise the fact that she was Jewish. She hid her identity in her memoir, too. However, in the foreword she remarked that about 5 million people died in Auschwitz of whom 'more than 3 million were Jews'. Of course these figures were incorrect, but the magnitude of the disaster that had occurred to the Jews was evident. Even if she masked her own Jewishness, Jews are present throughout her account. Szmaglewska was one of the first memoirists to record the story of Mala Zimmetbaum (here called Zimmerman). Her recollections were quickly translated into English and published in America as *Smoke Over Birkenau*.[32]

Krystyna Zywulska, like Szmaglewska, concealed her Jewish origins. She was born Sonia Landau in Lodz and following the German occupation of western Poland fled to the Soviet zone. She returned to Warsaw in 1941 and entered the ghetto, but subsequently escaped and lived underground on the 'aryan side'. She was caught in mid-1943 and held in the Pawiak prison before she was sent to Auschwitz-Birkenau. Although she retained her assumed persona in her memoir she frequently referred to Jews in Birkenau and never concealed their dreadful situation. When Polish survivors of the Warsaw uprising entered the camp in Summer 1944, she reassured them, 'They only burn Jews. Don't worry.' Zywulska's memoir was translated into English and went through several editions.[33]

By contrast, in the first version of his camp memoir *Ein Psycholog Erlebt das Konzentrationslager*, published in Vienna in 1946, but now famous as *Man's Search For Meaning*, Victor Frankl hid his Jewish identity. He concealed the fact that he spent two years in Theresienstadt with his wife and parents because he was a Jew. After being transported to Auschwitz he was quickly assigned to Kaufering and then Turkheim labour camps. He claims that it was in the lesser camps like these 'where most of the real extermination took place'. For Jews, of course, that was hardly the case.[34] But Frankl was an extreme case of 'effacement' and his motives seem to be personal. Other Jews certainly did universalize their experiences, but only because they were writing within the convention of resistance narratives or anti-fascist ideology which had no place for racial persecution or the specifics of Jewish suffering.

Giacomo Debenedetti expressed this viewpoint powerfully in *Eight Jews*, his 1945 essay about the trial of perpetrators responsible for the massacres at the Ardeatine Caves in March 1944. 'Proper redress', he wrote, 'would be to set Jews once again amid other peoples' lives, in the circle of all human fate, and not to segregate them, even for benevolent reasons.'[35] Even so, most memoir writers chose to signal their Jewish identity to the attentive reader. Instead of condemning the dejudaisation of such texts, it may be more appropriate to respect the reluctance of their authors to be identified solely as Jews and to see their writing as lightly coded.

The testimony by Suzanne Birnbaum, who was arrested in January 1944 and deported via Drancy to Auschwitz, offers another example. Birnbaum was denounced as a Jew and arrested by the French *milice*. While she does not address the mass murder of the Jews, as such, she entitled her memoir *Une Française Juive Est Revenue*. In it she describes the transports that arrived from different countries carrying Jews to the gas chambers. Birnbaum's testimony was amongst the first to recall the story of

Mala Zimmetbaum, the young Polish Jewish woman who escaped from Birkenau and, when recaptured, committed suicide at the gallows rather than allow the SS guards to hang her. Her patriotism, indicated in the title of her recollections and present throughout the text, and the fact that she does not write as a Jew does nothing to mask their fate.[36]

Italian Jewish victims also tended to write within the framework of anti-fascist ideology rather than leading with their Jewish identity and usually published with small local presses that restricted their audience.[37] But does this matter? Guiliana Tedeschi's narrative, *There Is a Place on Earth: A Woman in Birkenau*, published in Milan in 1946, did not centre on her Jewishness but did include a chapter describing the celebration of the Jewish New Year in Birkenau.[38] In a similar fashion Liana Millu recalled Hannukah in Birkenau, a festival, she wrote, 'symbolizing resistance and victory'.[39] Alba Valech barely mentions why she was doomed as a Jew to be deported to Auschwitz in the Autumn of 1943, but she dedicated her book, *A24029*, to the members of her family who were seized by fascist militia and to 'all the Jews who suffered martyrdom' dreaming of 'the Promised Land'.[40]

Yet Jewish memoirs have been ignored not only because they were written in a patriotic or anti-fascist spirit or in the wrong language, such as Yiddish or Polish, or published in the wrong place. It is striking just how many memoirs published by mainstream publishers *in English* between 1945 and 1950 have not entered the 'canon'. These narratives deal overwhelmingly with Auschwitz and events in Eastern Europe. Their exclusion has created a false impression of silence in the Anglo-Saxon world and ignorance about what happened in Eastern Europe. A few examples may suffice to indicate the scale of this neglect.

Olga Lengyel was a Jewish doctor deported from Hungary in 1944. After she was liberated she made her way to France where she had a cousin. Her memoir was written between March and December 1945 and translated into French under the title *Souvenirs de l'au-delà*. It appeared in 1946 and was an immediate success. The English version, *Five Chimneys*, was published a year later, by which time she had emigrated to New York where it was widely reviewed. This is a striking instance of the migration and translation of survivor narratives.[41] Yet it is not mentioned in any early anthologies of 'Holocaust literature' or any of the early studies of the genre.[42]

Nor is *Beyond the Last Path*, the memoir of Eugene Weinstock, a Hungarian-born Jewish cabinet-maker from Antwerp who was sent to Buchenwald thanks to his involvement in the Belgian resistance. His memoir appeared in English in New York in 1947. After only a few pages he recalled how he obeyed the call for Jews to report to the authorities. 'Then we made our first tragic error,' he wrote. 'We were aiding them in exterminating us.' In Buchenwald Weinstock encountered Jews who had passed through Auschwitz and he recounts some of what he heard from them. His narrative reads very well, thanks to the involvement of Ira Wallach, the playwright, novelist and screenwriter. Wallach's contribution indicates the widespread interest in such projects and, again, illustrates the global enterprise of bringing the experiences of survivors to diverse audiences soon after the war ended.[43]

The omission from the 'canon' of Renya Kulkielko's account of Jewish resistance in Poland, *Escape from the Pit*, may be explicable on account of its poor structure and rough style. Kulkielko was born near Kielce into a prosperous family with a Zionist outlook. Her account, which takes the form of a diary, extends from the outbreak of war, through her involvement in the Jewish resistance, to her arrival in Palestine in March 1944. It was written on Kibbutz Dafna in the summer of 1946, then sent to America where it was published in New York in 1947 by a small Zionist publishing house. Even so, it carried a foreword by the well-known author Ludwig Lewisohn.[44]

Studies of 'Holocaust literature' and historiography have also ignored reports on the plight of the survivors authored by allied medical personnel, relief workers and the emissaries of Jewish organizations. This is a curious, hybrid genre but it contradicts many of the assumptions about the effacement of the Jews and the preoccupation with Western concentration camps. It may seem bizarre that what we think of as 'the Holocaust' was initially viewed as a public health catastrophe but that was how dozens of British doctors and nurses – including 97 medical students from all over Britain who were flown in to assist – confronted it during the relief of Belsen. The operation was such an extraordinary challenge that the medical and health professionals who were part of the effort wanted to share their experience with others of their calling.[45]

This impulse led to a stream of articles in specialist publications that extended awareness of the disaster. Between May 1945 and June 1953, ten items touching on Belsen and other concentration camps appeared in *The Lancet*, the leading journal of the medical profession in Britain. In 1946 the *British Medical Journal*, the 'trade paper' of British doctors, carried six items, including four substantial reports.[46] Articles appeared in a dozen other medical publications in the UK between 1945 and 1947, usually written by medical students. These items merit close attention because they reveal how medical and relief workers identified the victims of Nazism. For example, an extensive report by Lt Col F M Lipscombe that appeared in *The Lancet* on 8 September 1945, stated that 'Russians and Poles predominated. Czechs, Belgians, French, Italians and Yugoslavs were also present. The great majority were Jews.'[47] In March 1946, the journal carried a special article by Dr Lucie Adelsberger that gave a concise account of her experiences in Auschwitz. Adelsberger commenced by introducing herself:

> I was arrested in May 1943, and was sent to Birkenau concentration camp. This was the climax to a series of restrictions that began in March, 1933, with my removal from a post at the Robert Koch Institute, Berlin, because I was a Jewess.

Adelsberger thereby put the span of Nazi anti-Jewish policy in a nutshell. She then described what she had witnessed in the course of her employment as an 'internee woman doctor', including selections from Jewish transports.[48]

Articles appeared in other publications serving health professionals. The *British Dental Journal* carried an exhaustive (and gruesome) study of facial gangrene amongst inmates of Belsen. The research by Maj J Dawson was based on ten case studies, each of which opened with a brief biographical comment. Dawson identified eight as Jews, of whom six were Hungarian.[49] A study of psychological breakdown amongst inmates of Belsen, published in the *Journal of Mental Science* in January 1946, was based on 20 brief case histories – 11 of which were identified as Jewish.[50] Although much of the early psychological literature to come out of the war concerned perpetrators or undifferentiated victims of the camps, Jewish psychologists and social workers in the United States were responsible for several that contained historical data and testimony. Kopel Pinson, later to make his mark on historiography, published one of the earliest accounts of life in a DP camp in *Jewish Social Studies* in 1947. Paul Friedman's study of 'concentration camp psychology' was based on interviews with over 170 inmates of the British-run detention camp on Cyprus. Both researchers set survivor behavior against the background of torment by the Nazis.[51]

Less technical and far more emotional were the accounts by emissaries of Jewish organizations sent to Poland to investigate the condition of the surviving remnant. Jacob Pat was a Polish-born activist in the Jewish Labour Committee in New York. In 1946 he made a fact-finding trip to Poland and on his return wrote up his experiences in Yiddish as *Ash un Faye. Iyber di Churbos fun Polin*. The volume was quickly translated into English by Leo Steinberg (later to achieve fame as an art historian and critic) appearing as *Ashes and Fire* in 1947. Although the book moves erratically between wartime events and scenes that Pat witnessed himself, it is stuffed with historical material, narratives and testimony. It is, in effect, an early oral history of the disaster that overwhelmed Polish Jews and the first stage of their recovery.[52] In April 1946 Joseph Tenenbaum, a Polish-born official of the World Jewish Congress, followed in Pat's footsteps. His subsequent account was published as *In Search of a Lost People – The Old and the New Poland* in New York later that year. His narrative, like Pat's, moves awkwardly between the history of the Jews in Poland, the German occupation, and the current situation. Yet it is possible to find accounts of the death camps and numerous testimonies. It was pioneering and crude, but it was full of crucial historical information and insights into the dire situation of Jews in post-bellum Poland.[53]

When Polish Jews fled west after the Kielce pogrom they swelled the population of the Jewish DP camps and added to the clamour for emigration. The campaign waged by the Jewish DPs and the Zionist movement for migration to the Jewish national home in Palestine ensured that the linkage between the uprooting of Jewish life in Europe and the demand for a Jewish state was constantly being made. Remarkably, 'Holocaust historiography' has scarcely noted the debates about Zionism even though every international commission that investigated the plight of the Jewish DPs or the question of Palestine ended up linking the two and brought the recent past into the mainstream of public discourse.[54]

The first of these investigations was mounted by Earl G Harrison at the behest of President Truman following allegations of abuses against Jewish DPs committed by US troops. Harrison's report made it absolutely plain that the Jews had suffered singularly under Nazi rule: they had survived 'extermination'. As a result, few wanted to return to their homes and most expressed a preference for migration to Palestine. That linkage became the curse of Britain's Palestine policy and ensured that as long as Palestine was in the headlines so was an awareness of what the Jews had suffered during the war.[55]

The well-known journalist I F Stone covered the Harrison mission for the New York paper *P.M.* In 1946 he was invited to accompany a group of American sailors who had volunteered to crew one of the illegal immigration ships running the British naval blockade of Palestine. His report of this adventure, *Underground to Palestine*, was the first of its kind and attracted enormous attention.[56] Through the story of one boatload of refugees, Stone transmitted the horrors of the war. He recalled meetings with survivors of the ghettos in Sosnowicz, Lodz, Lwow, Kovno, Vilna, and Bialystok. He retold what he heard about Majdanek and Auschwitz. He recorded how a group of young survivors on a train journey through central Europe sang songs of the ghettos and camps. Stone even recorded the story of a Jewish officer in the Red Army who boasted of killing 2,500 surrendered Germans in revenge for the Jews.[57]

In London, while en route to Palestine, Stone met with Richard Crossman, a recently elected Labour Party MP. Crossman served as a British member on the Anglo-American Committee of Inquiry into the Problems of European Jewry and Palestine set up in response to President Truman's recommendation that 100,000 Jewish DPs be allowed to emigrate to Palestine.[58] His book about his role on the Committee, *Palestine Mission*, published in 1947, was widely read, not least because he created a huge controversy by coming out against his party's position. Again, it is not 'Holocaust literature' but it is laced with reflections on anti-semitism, the war, and offers glimpses into the experiences of Jewish survivors. Following sessions of the committee in Washington and London, Crossman traveled to Vienna where he met DPs face to face. At a camp in Villach, Austria, he interviewed survivors of Auschwitz and heard graphic stories about their experiences. He heard more from survivors during sessions in Palestine.[59] Bartley Crum, celebrity lawyer, newspaper proprietor, and champion of liberal causes, was one of the American members of the Committee. His account of its work, *Behind the Silken Curtain*, performed a similar function for Americans. Like Crossman, Crum included several passages based on testimony by Jewish survivors and remarked tellingly that 'We found very few Jewish children left alive in Europe.'[60]

The UN Special Committee on Palestine (UNSCOP) in 1947 was the third international commission in as many years tasked with investigating the situation of Jewish survivors of Nazi persecution and the role of Palestine in alleviating their condition. One of the members was Jorge Garcia-Granados, a Guatemalan diplomat. He subsequently wrote a book about his experiences, *The Birth of Israel: The Drama As I Saw It*, published in New York by Knopf. It is routinely cited by historians of Israel and the Middle East but few have noted that it also sheds light on the Jewish tragedy in Europe.[61] Even before UNSCOP visited Europe it was exposed to the experiences of survivors. At Kiryat Anavim, a Jewish settlement in Palestine, they met a 17 year old girl who told them she was born in Poland but came 'from Bergen-Belsen'. To Garcia-Granados:

That told everything. I asked no more questions. ... I knew the story of those children. Of hundreds and thousands of other children. I knew the story of the gas chambers, of the crematoria, of the parents, of the brother and sisters of those children.

Later Garcia-Granados visited Belsen and went with his colleagues to several DP camps in Germany where he heard witnesses recite their experiences in Auschwitz.[62]

Meyer Levin, a writer and journalist who made his name in the 1930s, first encountered survivors of Nazi persecution when he was in Europe in Autumn 1944 as a military correspondent. In a Paris synagogue he met a Jew whose

tales were interspersed with place-names which I had not yet heard, and the world had not yet heard, but assumed they were familiar to me, for what Jews had not lived with them in the forefront of their consciousness? Drancy, Treblinka, Ravensbrück, Auschwitz.[63]

Subsequently he reported on the liberation of Ohrdruff, Buchenwald, and Belsen. The experience was so shattering that he threw himself into the effort to get Jews out of Europe and made a film about Jewish immigration to Palestine that was intended to raise support and money for the Zionist movement. While that may have been its goal, *The Illegals* (which premiered in mid-1947), was one of the first cinematic attempts to confront the destruction of Europe's Jews. Levin's 1950 autobiography *In Search* morphs into an account of the camps, including snatches of testimony.[64]

While it has long been acknowledged that there was a connection between awareness of Jewish suffering during the war and sympathy for Zionism, a dyad made flesh by the Jewish DPs, too often the linkage has been treated as a matter of vague and fleeting sentiment generated by a brief burst of publicity following the liberation of the camps. In fact, the political and diplomatic struggle waged for Palestine between 1945 and 1948 resulted in the sustained dissemination of material about the wartime experience of the Jews. When it is remembered that this process was running alongside various Nazi war crimes trials, it should be evident that rather than a spasm of attention followed by silence there was, in fact, a persistent drum beat about the fate of the Jews.[65]

Much has been written in criticism of the International Military Tribunal at Nuremberg (IMT). It has been lambasted for failing to delineate Nazi crimes against the Jews and give proper weight to the massacres and the death camps in Eastern Europe. The investigators have been chided for barely touching on several murderous agencies of the Third Reich, overlooking even Eichmann's office and failing to probe the complicity of the German Army.[66] There is much force in this criticism, but did the Tribunal blight the writing of history, as Donald Bloxham alleges? Did it obscure the specific fate of the Jews?[67]

Arguably, a closer examination of Jewish involvement in the IMT and its legacy suggests a very different picture.[68] The Polish government's Main Commission for the Investigation of German Crimes published its findings primarily in Polish, but the first two volumes of material used for the Nuremberg tribunal – which included the contributions of Jewish researchers – were translated into English in 1946. There was no attempt to hide or distort the singular treatment of the Polish Jews or the function of the camps on Polish soil.[69] The Central Jewish Historical Commission in Poland enjoyed a mutually beneficial, though not necessarily harmonious, relationship with the Polish war crimes investigators. The Polish government made it possible for several Polish Jewish survivors to give evidence at Nuremberg: Seweryna Szmaglewska on Auchwitz-Birkenau, Samuel Rajzman on Treblinka, and Israel Eisenberg on Majdanek.[70]

Leon Poliakov and Joseph Billig were both seconded by the CDJC to work for the French delegation in Nuremberg. This work was recognized. The French Judge at the IMT, François de Menthon and two of the prosecutors, Edgar Faure and Henri Monnery, later contributed to the Centre's publications. Telford Taylor wrote a preface for the volume on German crimes in the East. There could be no clearer refutation of the idea that the IMT in some way masked the atrocities against Jews in Poland and the USSR.[71] Other forms of cooperation were less formal, but no less important. In the acknowledgments to his pioneering study *The Final Solution*, Gerald Reitlinger thanked Major Elwyn-Jones, one of the British prosecution team, for 'the loan of an almost complete set of documents, relating to the persecution of the Jews and extracted from the enormous files of the Wilhelmstrasse case' which had not yet been published.[72] One of the earliest collections of Nuremberg documents, *Nazi Germany's War Against the Jews*, published by the American Jewish Conference in 1947, was compiled by Seymour Krieger who had been a member of Justice Robert Jackson's staff. His compilation gave prominence to the crimes of the Wehrmacht and the Einsatzgruppen, as well as the operation of the death camps.[73]

The IMT was followed by a spate of books that crystallized the evidence about the genocide against the Jews and made it readily accessible. Peter Calvocoressi, writing in Britain in 1947, and Victor Bernstein, who covered the trial for *P.M.* newspaper, both devoted chapters to the mass murder of the Jews – in which they implicated the German Army. They also drew attention to Eichmann's role.[74] If Nuremberg did not constrain the writing about Nazi crimes against the Jews nor did it necessarily promote a top-down, 'intentionalist' version of the past. Evidence for this can be found in the articles published in *Jewish Social Studies* between 1946 and 1950. These contributions were weighted overwhelmingly towards the experience of the victims and explaining Nazism as a grass roots phenomena.[75]

Yet, towards the end of the decade, conditions for the study of the Nazi era and the persecution of the Jews changed. In late 1947, Isaac Schneersohn complained about 'the forgetfulness, lies, indifference, which endanger more and more the memory of the martyrs'. He also protested against 'The indifference, lassitude, lost respect for written materials, manifest amongst Jews too. The CDJC and the historical commissions don't get enough support from Jewish organizations.'[76] Three years later, Mark Turkow, editor of the important and woefully neglected Yiddish book series 'Dos Poylishe yidntum' published in Buenos Aires, told the Yiddish poet and writer Chaim Grade: 'People want us to stop printing books about the catastrophe.

They don't want to read them anymore; that's the sentiment.'[77] When Leon Poliakov completed his pioneering account of 'the Final Solution' in 1951, he was told by several editors that 'the theme was considered impossible from a commercial point of view'. He only succeeded in finding a publisher thanks to help from Raymond Aron. *Harvest of Hate* went on to be widely reviewed and achieved good sales, but Poliakov was dismayed by the lack of interest in the USA.[78]

So what had happened? There is no doubt that the Cold War inhibited scholarship and publishing about the Nazi years. In 1952, Nehamiah Robinson wrote in the foreword to a series of booklets published by the Institute for Jewish Affairs, tellingly entitled 'Lest We Forget', that the new political approach to the Germans 'of necessity modified also the moral approach to the Germans. It was morally impossible to treat an ally as the incarnation of evil.'[79] But something else was at work, too. Paradoxically, the first wave of memoirists and historians had succeeded too well. At the same time as proclaiming their inability to convey the unimaginable cruelty and suffering in the ghettos and camps, they had proven exactly the opposite, on a grand scale. To grasp this we have to bear in mind that the first publications appeared in 1944, grew in number through 1945, and became a flood in 1946–47. The literature accumulated at such a pace that it was almost impossible to keep up with it. Because so much has been overlooked we have the *illusion* that little was recorded in those early years; but voices from that time tell a different story. Writing in 1952, Samuel Gringausz remarked on 'the innumerable monographs on the Nazi system of ideologically organized inhumanity'.[80] Two years later, Phillip Friedman echoed him: there were so many books on the Warsaw ghetto alone, 'that it is impossible even to enumerate the more important studies'.[81]

Quantity was not the only daunting aspect of this vast library. Much of the memoir literature was raw, angry, graphic and, by its nature, unresolved. Written a few months or years after the events in question, these reports were unmodified by the knowledge of a life lived in the aftermath. The authors had no inkling if their personal losses and horrific experiences would be redeemed in some way or placed in a larger context that gave them a kind of meaning. Finally, they were composed at a time when hatred of the Nazis and Germany was unrestrained and brutal images of the war filled the media. There were few inhibitions about what could be said: sexual abuse, depravity, prisoner-on-prisoner violence, cannibalism, graphic descriptions of filth, squalor and human degradation, as well as explicit accounts of revenge are common. Reading these memoirs and testimonies it is easy to understand why, by the end of the 1940s, the public turned away.

In the introduction to his 1952 study (and part memoir), *Human Behavior in the Concentration Camps*, the Dutch Jewish survivor Elie Cohen remarked that

> Any writer of a book on German concentration camps is under no delusion that nowadays there is a great deal of general interest in the subject. Though it is only a very few years ago, that the survivors left these camps ... and the world learned of the horrors that had occurred, interest in them is very much on the wane.

This syndrome was not due to indifference: it was a reaction to the first wave of camp literature. In the words of a previous memoir writer, the Jewish-born doctor Eddy de Wind, who like Cohen was sent from Westerbork to Auschwitz, 'the reader who has thus had to take the author's burdens upon his shoulders very soon felt he had enough'. The flagging interest and impatience was aggravated wherever it was felt that sectional groups were engaging in special pleading on the basis of their wartime suffering.[82]

Building on these contemporary observation it is my contention that the chief reason for the recession of interest in the story of Jewish suffering and struggle that was so evident by the end of the 1940s is that, quite simply, enough was enough. However, this regression should not be equated with 'silence' or lack of awareness. New studies on the 1950s show that consciousness of the Jewish catastrophe which had been so assiduously fostered in the immediate postwar years had filtered into both popular culture and intellectual life, especially in America. But it did not take the form that we would recognize today as 'Holocaust consciousness'; indeed, it would be foolhardy to expect otherwise.

Best-selling autobiographical novels of the Second World War by ordinary service-men reflected their engagement with the tragedy. Stefan Heym's *Crusaders* (1948) and Irwin Shaw's *The Young Lions* (1949) both dealt with the liberation of the camps and the encounter with Jewish survivors. American Jewish writers who had not served in Europe preferred to write about their own experiences and reflected the Nazi disaster in their combative attitude towards domestic anti-semitism. Hence, Arthur Miller, Laura Zametkin Hobson, and Saul Bellow all wrote books about anti-Jewish dis-crimination. Hobson's was made into a highly successful film, *Gentleman's Agreement* (1947), which along with *Crossfire* (1947) tackled anti-Jewish prejudice in a way and at a time that only makes sense if the horrific outcome of European anti-semitism is seen lurking in the background. These were the creations of 'Holocaust-haunted American Jews' and found their counterpart in historical studies of anti-semitism, social and psychological research into prejudice funded by the American Jewish Committee, and the committee's campaign against discrimination.[83]

Few were as haunted as Meyer Levin, whose obsession with Anne Frank became infamous.[84] Shock and incomprehension pervades the essays of Isaac Rosenfeld.[85] It erupts into the journals of Alfred Kazin, who met survivors in DP camps during a visit to Europe in 1946. In one memorable passage, Kazin recalled an afternoon spent with Hannah Arendt and her husband, Heinrich Blucher in their Upper West Side apartment: 'Hitler may be dead and gone, but here the *shock* of him – for Hannah even more than Heinrich – is in the air they both breathe.'[86] Irving Howe's turn to Yiddish in the mid-1950s is explained partly by his acute sense that the Jewish civilization of Eastern Europe had been destroyed and would only live for future generations in translations of the great storytellers.[87] In fact, the 1950s are framed by two popular-izations of that history, both of which enjoyed massive success. John Hersey's novel about the Warsaw Ghetto, *The Wall*, was on the NY Times bestseller list for 23 weeks. *Exodus*, by Leon Uris, was a bestseller for 80 weeks. In between, was *The Diary of Anne Frank* which was a bestseller for 20 weeks after its publication in 1952.[88]

It is common to dismiss these works as 'middle brow' in the case of the fiction and a de-judaised moral tract in the case of the *Diary*. However, as Alan Mintz notes, despite the artistic compromises necessary to bring these novels to the screen, they vastly enlarged the circle of historical awareness. The same was true of the films spawned at the end of the decade: *The Young Lions* (1958), *The Diary of Anne Frank* (1959) and *Judgement at Nuremberg* (TV version, 1960; feature film, 1961). They may not accord with the paradigm of 'the Holocaust' as it exists today but to expect otherwise is anachronistic and ahistorical. More pertinently, Alan Mintz observes from his own experience growing up in postwar America that Jews watching these films knew exactly what they were about – and welcomed them.[89]

During the late 1950s, intellectuals who feared the effects of mass society and conformism turned to the Third Reich as a paradigmatic case and even constructed analogies between Nazi Germany and the USA. Stanley Elkins drew on psychological studies of inmate behavior by Elie Cohen and Bruno Bettelheim to explain the behavior of slaves in the antebellum American South. Betty Friedan infamously compared the condition of the married suburban housewife in her home to the plight of the inmate in a concentration camp.[90] The role of psychological studies, rooted in wartime experience, as a 'place of memory' is equally pronounced in England. Norman Cohn's *The Pursuit of the Millenium* (1957) ostensibly dealt with millenarianism in the Middle Ages but it was inspired by his wartime service and his belief that Nazism and anti-semitism were mass psychoses. In the Conclusion to the 1970 edition, Cohn advised that 'The story told in this book ended some four centuries ago, but it is not without relevance to our own times.' He observed 'how closely the Nazi phantasy of a world-wide Jewish conspiracy of destruction' was related to the phantasies of millenarians and how the two phenomena shared the same roots in social dislocation. Although Cohn and his collaborators did not tackle the genocide against the Jews head-on, their work was clearly rooted in the tragedy of the Jews and was a response to it.[91]

And what of France? We end where we began: with the survivors in postwar Europe. Within the anti-fascist paradigm and the glorification of resistance, Jewish memory was acknowledged, even if only partially and in ways that today would even seem offensive. In 1949, General de Gaulle unveiled a plaque at the Vel d'Hiv which declared that:

> On 16 July 1942, 30,000 Jewish men, women, and children, victims of racial persecution were confined in this place by order of the Nazi occupier, all separated from each other, they were deported to Germany and the concentration camps. Free men remember.

The audience at this ceremony was being called upon to remember a mythic version of the past rather than the whole truth. But at least it was a form of recognition.[92] A year later, Isaac Schneersohn opened his campaign for a Jewish memorial to the deported Jews. The project touched a popular nerve amongst Jews in France and around the world. Funds flowed in and in May 1953 the foundation stone was laid.

Some 7,000 people, including civic dignitaries, attended the opening ceremony. Although it was predominantly secular and patriotic in tone, Kaddish was sung and at that moment hundreds in the crowd wept. The monument was completed and dedicated in October 1956. It was marked by compromise, but it represented the successful interpolation of Jewish memory into national memory of the war years.[93] Two years later, Andre Schwartz-Bart published *The Last of the Just*. It became an instant bestseller and won the Prix Goncourt. The same year in Italy, Einaudi republished Primo Levi's *If This Is a Man* .... It went on to achieve a world-wide audience and, if anything, served to obscure earlier, more rough hewn memoirs of survival in the camps. Contrary to the notion that individual survivors were silent or too traumatized to act, they had mounted a frenetic, global effort to transmit information about the Jewish catastrophe. If anything, they succeeded too well, too soon. 'The Holocaust' as we know it is not to be found in these postwar accomplishments, but by the 1950s the first layer of historiography and literature had been laid. Everything else rested on this achievement.

Notes

1 Samuel D Kassow, *Who Will Write Our History? Emanuel Ringelblum, the Warsaw Ghetto and the Oyneg Shabes Archive* (Bloomington, IN: Indiana University Press, 2007), passim on Warsaw and 210–12 on other ghettos.

2 The most authoritative account is Laura Jockusch, "'Collect and Record. Help to Write the History of the Latest Destruction". Jewish Historical Commissions in Europe, 1943–1953', D.Phil. New York University, 2007, 56–90. I am grateful to Laura Jockusch for allowing me to read her outstanding dissertation which will soon be published. See also, Georges Bensoussan, 'The Jewish Contemporary Documentation Centre (CDJC) and Holocaust Research in France, 1945–70' in David Bankier and Dan Michman eds, *Holocaust Historiography in Context: Emergence, Challenges, Polemics and Achievements* (Jerusalem: Yad Vashem/Berghahn Books, 2008), 245–54.

3 On the early work of the CDJC see the reports in *Les Juifs en Europe (1939–1945). Rapports Présentés A La Premiere Conference Européenne Des Commissions Historiques Et Des Centres de Documentation Juifs* (Paris: Éditions Du Centre, 1949), 25–31, 34–37, 55–57, 58–62 and Léon Poliakov, *L'auberges des musiciens: mémoires* (Paris: Mazarine, 1983), 69–152, 163–70.

4 Roni Stauber, 'Philip Friedman and the beginning of Holocaust Studies' in Bankier and Michman eds, *Holocaust Historiography in Context*, 83–102; Natalia Aleksiun, 'The Central Jewish Historical Commission in Poland 1944–47', Gabriel N. Finder, Natalia Aleksiun, Antony Polonsky and Jan Schwarz eds, *Polin: Studies in Polish Jewry*, vol. 20, *Making Holocaust Memory* (Oxford: Littman, 2007), 74–97. For pioneering work in this field, see Shmuel Krakowski, 'Memorial Projects and Memorial Institutions Initiated by the She'erit Hapletah, 1944–48' in Yisrael Gutman and Avital Saf eds, *She'erit Hapletah, 1944–1948. Rehabilitation and Political Struggle* (Jerusalem: Yad Vashem, 1990), 388–98.

5 For a contemporary account of the activities of the Central Jewish Historical Commission in Poland between 1944 and 1947 see the report by Jozef Kermisz in *Les Juifs en Europe (1939–1945)*, 140–44. See also, Jockusch, "'Collect and Record!'", 146–212; Aleksiun, 'The Central Jewish Historical Commission in Poland 1944–47', 77–95. For an early published selection of interviews with Jewish child survivors, see Maria Hochberg-Mariaska and Noë Grüss, *The Children Accuse*, trans. Bill Johnston (London: Vallentine Mitchell, 1996).

6 Kassow, *Who Will Write Our History?*, 1–2; Natalia Aleksiun, 'Organising for Justice: Jewish leadership in Poland and the Trial of the Nazi War Criminals at Nuremberg', in

J-D Steinert and Inge Weber-Newth eds, *Beyond Camps and Forced Labour: Current International Research on Survivors of Nazi Persecution. Proceedings of the International Conference, London, 11–13 January 2006* (Osnabrück: Secolo, 2006), 184–94. On the work of the Central Historical Commission, its metamorphosis into the Jewish Historical Institute and decline, see Feliks Tych, 'The Emergence of Holocaust Research in Poland: The Jewish Historical Commission and the Jewish Historical Institute (ZIH), 1944–89' in Bankier and Michman eds, *Holocaust Historiography in Context*, 227–39. Jacob Pat, *Ashes and Fire* (New York: International Universities Press, 1947), 133.

7 For on-the-spot insights into the Central Jewish Historical Commission in Munich, see the report by Moshe Faygenbaum in *Les Juifs en Europe (1939–1945)*, 149–51 and Koppel Pinson, 'Jewish Life in Liberated Germany. A Study of the DPs', *Jewish Social Studies*, 9:2 (1947), 109. Laura Jockusch, 'A Folk Monument to Our Destruction and Heroism: Jewish Historical Commissions in the Displaced Persons Camps of Germany, Austria and Italy', in Avinoam Patt and Michael Berkowitz eds, *"We Are Here": New Approaches to Jewish Displaced Persons in Postwar Germany* (Detroit: Wayne State University Press, 2010), 31–73; Ada Schein, '"Everyone Can Hold a Pen": The Documentation project in the DP Camps in Germany' in Bankier and Michman eds, *Holocaust Historiography in Context*, 103–34; Boaz Cohen, 'Bound to Remember – Bound to Remind. Holocaust Survivors and the Genesis of Holocaust Research', in J-D Steinert and Inge Weber-Newth eds, *Beyond Camps and Forced Labour. Current International Research on Survivors of Nazi Persecution. Proceedings of the International Conference, London, 29–31 January 2003* (Osnabrück: Secolo, 2006), 290–300.

8 Boaz Cohen, 'Representing the Experiences of Children in the Holocaust: Children's Survivor Testimonies Published in *Fun Letsten Hurbn*, Munich, 1946–49', in Patt and Berkowitz eds, *We Are Here*, 74–97.

9 Jockusch, '"Collect and Record"', 247–49, 310–11; Orna Kenan, *Between Memory and History: The Evolution of Israeli Historiography of the Holocaust, 1945–1961* (New York: Peter Lang Publications, 2003), 19–35. Leo Schwarz ed., *The Root and the Bough: The Epic of an Enduring People* (New York: Rinehart, 1949); Marie Syrkin, *Blessed is the Match: The Whole Story of Jewish Resistance in Europe* (London: Gollancz, 1948).

10 See Tuvia Friedman, *The Hunter*, ed. and trans. David C Gross (London: Anthony Gibbs and Phillips, 1961) and Simon Wiesenthal, *Justice Not Vengeance* (London: Weidenfeld and Nicolson, 1989). For a contemporaneous report by Wiesenthal, see *Les Juifs en Europe (1939–1945)*, 37–40.

11 Iael Nidam-Orvieto, 'Fighting Oblivion: The CDEC and its Impact on Italian Historiography', in Bankier and Michman eds, *Holocaust Historiography in Context*, 293–96; Liliana Picciotto Fargion, 'La Liberazione dai campi di concentramento e il rintraccio degli ebrei italiani dispersi' in Michele Sarfatti ed., *Il vitorno alla vita: vicende e diritti degli Ebrei in Italia dopo la seconda guerra mondiale* (Florence, Giuntina, 1998), 13–30; Liliana Picciotto, *Il libro della memoria: gli Ebrei deportati dall'Italia (1943–45)* (Milan: Mursia, 2002 edn), 19–20.

12 Rita Horvath, '"A Jewish Historical Commission in Budapest": The Place of the National Relief Committee for Deportees in Hungary [DEGOB] Among the Other Large-Scale Historical-memorial Projets of She'erit Haplethah After the Holocaust (1945–48)', in Bankier and Michman eds, *Holocaust Historiography in Context*, 475–96.

13 Report on the activity of the Jewish Central Information Office (Wiener Library) by Alfred Wiener, in see *Les Juifs en Europe (1939–1945)*, 125–28. See Ben Barkow, *Alfred Wiener and the Making of the Holocaust Library* (London: Vallentine Mitchell, 1997), 111–21.

14 Report of Nella Rost in *Les Juifs en Europe (1939–1945)*, 57–58. See also Simone Erpel, 'Documented Traumas. Interviews with Polish Survivors of Ravensbrück Women's Concentration Camp, Carried out in Sweden in 1945/46', in J-D Steinert and Inge Weber-Newth eds. *Beyond Camps and Forced Labour. Current International Research on Survivors of Nazi Persecution. Proceedings of the International Conference, London, 29–31 January 2003* (Osnabrück: Secolo, 2003), 301–10.

15 Tych, 'The Emergence of Holocaust Research in Poland', 234; Jockusch, '"Collect and Record"', 355–57; Roni Stauber, *The Holocaust in Israeli Public Debate In the 1950s. Ideology and Memory*, trans. Elizabeth Yuval (London: Vallentine Mitchell, 2007), 21–22.

16 A capacious and frank record of the conference is in *Les Juifs en Europe (1939–1945). Rapports Présentés A La Premiere Conference Européenne Des Commissions Historiques Et Des Centres de Documentation Juifs* (Paris: Éditions Du Centre, 1949). See also the summary and analysis by Jockusch, '"Collect and Record"', (2006) 376–95.

17 Jockusch, '"Collect and Record"', 414–23. Schein, '"Everyone Can Hold a Pen"', 132–35; Tych, 'The Emergence of Holocaust Research in Poland', 236–39.

18 Philip Friedman, *This Was Oswiecim: The Story of a Murder Camp* (London: United Jewish Appeal, 1946).

19 Marek Edelman, *The Ghetto Fights* (New York: American Representation of the General Jewish Workers Union of Poland, 1946). Zofia Nalkowska, the translator, also wrote a short book of semi-factual stories based on her experiences investigating war crimes. *Medaliony* appeared in Warsaw in 1946, and achieved critical acclaim as well as reaching a wide audience with its frank descriptions of Jewish suffering during the occupation: Zofia Nalkowska, *Medallions*, trans. Diana Kupel (Evanston, IL: Northwestern University Press, 2000).

20 Bernard Goldstein, *The Stars Bear Witness*, trans. Leonard Shatzkin (New York: Viking Press, 1949). It is worth noting that many of these early memoirs not only lacked the word 'Holocaust', but went under titles that gave no hint of the content.

21 Annette Wieviorka, *Déportation et génocide: entre la mémoire et l'oubli* (Paris: Pluriel, 1992).

22 Ber Baskind, *La Grande Épouvante: souvenirs d'un rescapé du ghetto de Varsovie*, trans. E Brunet-Beresovski (Paris: Calmann-Levy, 1945). Wieviorka, *Deportation et génocide*, 184, 291, 472.

23 Giacomo Debenedetti, *16 October, 1943. Eight Jews*, trans. Estella Gibson (Notre Dame, IND: University of Notre Dame Press, 2001), 21–62. Giacomo Debenedetti, *16 ottobre 1943* and *Otto Ebrei* were first published in Rome in 1945.

24 Pelagia Lewinska, *Vingt mois à Auschwitz* (Paris: Éditions Nagel, 1945), 67–68, 91, 126–39.

25 David Rousset, *L'univers concentrationnaire* (Paris: Éditions du Pavois, 1946). The quotations are from the English version, *The Other Kingdom*, trans. Ramon Guthrie (New York: Reynal and Hitchcock, 1947), 29, 58–60, 61, 63–66, 109, 114. Wieviorka, *Déportation et génocide*, 85–86. Compare David Rousset, *Le pitre ne rit pas* (Paris: Éditions Du Centre, 1948), 243. This is a curious book. Rousset believed Nazism practiced a form of modern slavery. In his argument, which is stated ironically and in fragments, the specific oppression of the Jews is taken to illuminate the general system of exploitation and enslavement.

26 Eugen Kogon, *Der SS-Staat. Das System Der Deutschen Konzentrationslager* (Berlin: Verlag des Druckhaus Tempelhof, 1947), 5–18. See also, Publishers' Introduction to the 1950 US edition, *The Theory And Practice of Hell,* trans. Heinz Norden (New York: Farrar, Strauss Cuddahy, 1950), 5–12 and Nikolaus Wachsman, Introduction, *The Theory And Practice of Hell* (New York: Farrar, Strauss, Giroux, 2006), xi–xxi.

27 Kogon, *The Theory and Practice of Hell* (1950 edn), pp. 174–97. Philip Friedman and Koppel S Pinson, 'Some Books on the Jewish Catastrophe', *Jewish Social Studies*, 12:1 (1950), 88–89.

28 *Bylismy w Oswiecimiu* (Munich: Oficyna Warszawska na Obczyznie, 1946); quotes from *We Were in Auschwitz*, trans. Alicia Nitecki (New York: Welcome Publishers, 2000), 5–6, 14, 15. To add to the effect, the original edition was bound in cloth taken from the uniforms of Auschwitz prisoners.

29 Tadeusz Borowski, *This Way to the Gas Ladies and Gentlemen* …, trans. Barbara Vedder (New York: Viking, 1967). The translator's note about the original location of the stories is misleading. The edition published by Penguin includes an introduction by Jan Kott but this too fails to mention *We Were In Auschwitz*.

30 Zoë Waxman, *Writing the Holocaust: Identity, Testimony, Representation* (Oxford: Oxford University Press, 2006), 100–112; cf. Wieviorka, *Déportation et génocide*, 264–92.

31 Pieter Lagrou in Jeffrey M Diefendorf ed., *Lessons and Legacies*, vol. 6, *New Currents in Holocaust Research* (Evanston, IL: Northwestern University Press, 2004) 482–83.

32 Seweryna Szmaglewska, *Dymy nad Birkenau* (Warsaw: Czytelnik, 1945). Quotes from *Smoke Over Birkenau*, trans. Jadwiga Rynas (New York: Henry Holt, 1947), vii, 281, 341–42. On her evidence at Nuremberg, see Lawrence Douglas, *The Memory of Judgment: Making Law and History in the Trials of the Holocaust* (New Haven, CT: Yale University Press, 2001), 78, 79.

33 Krystyna Zywulska, *Przezylam Oswięcim* (Warsaw: Spoldzielnia Wydawnicza "Wiedza", 1946). Quotes from Krystyna Zywulska, *I Came Back*, trans. Krystyna Cenkalska (New York: Roy Publishers, 1951), 22, 53 143, 151, 156–57, 158–59.

34 Victor Frankel, *Ein Psycholog Erlebt das Konzentrationslager* (Vienna: Verlag für Jugend und Volk, 1946) published in English as, *From Death Camp to Existentialism. A Psychiatrist's Path to a New Therapy*, trans. Ilse Lasch (Boston: Beacon Press, 1959), 1–5, 7. For an analysis of Frankel's memoirs see Timothy E Pytell, 'Redeeming the Unredeemable: Auschwitz and Man's Search for Meaning', *Holocaust and Genocide Studies*, 17:1 (2003), 89–113.

35 Debenedetti, *16 October, 1943: Eight Jews*, 21–62.

36 Suzanne Birnbaum (Luce), *Une Française juive est revenue* (Paris: Éditions du Livre français, 1945), passim and 145. For bibliographical information see the reprint of *Une Francaise juive est revenue* (Paris: Hérault-Editions 1994), 11.

37 Manuela Consoni, 'The Written Memoir: Italy 1945–47' in David Bankier ed., *The Jews Are Coming Back. The Return of the Jews to their Countries of Origin after World War Two* (Jerusalem: Yad Vashem/ Berghahn Books, 2005) 169–80.

38 Giuliana Tedeschi, *C'e un punto della terra ... Una donna nel lager di Birkenau* (Florence: Giuntina, 1988), 130–32; originally published in Milan, 1946.

39 Liana Millu, *Il fumo di Birkenau* originally published in Milan 1947: see *Smoke Over Birkenau*, trans. Lynne Sharon Schwartz (Philadelphia: Jewish Publication Society of America, 1991), 68–72.

40 Alba Valech Capozzi, *A24029* (Siena: Soc. An. Poligrafica, 1946; rpr Institute for the History of the Resistance 1995).

41 Myrna Goldenberg, 'Olga Lengyel (1908–2001)' in Kramer ed., *Holocaust Literature*, 738–41.

42 See, for example, Albert Friedlander ed., *Out of the Whirlwind: A Reader of Holocaust Literature* (New York: Union of Hebrew Congregations, 1968); Jacob Glatstein, Israel Knox, Samuel Margoshed eds, *Anthology of Holocaust Literature* (Philadelphia: Jewish Publication Society of America, 1969). See, Irving Halpern, *Messengers from the Dead: Literature of the Holocaust* (Philadelphia: Westminster Press, 1970); Lawrence Langer, *The Holocaust and the Literary Imagination* (New Haven, CT: Yale University Press, 1975); Alvin Rosenfeld, *A Double Dying: Reflections on Holocaust Literature* (Bloomington IN: Indiana University Press, 1980).

43 Eugene Weinstock, *Beyond the Last Path*, trans. Clara Ryan (New York: Boni and Gaer, 1947).

44 Renya Kulkielko, *Escape from the Pit* (New York: Sharon Books, 1947). On Renya Kulkielko and other Polish Jews who reached Palestine during the war, see Dina Porat, 'First Testimonies on the Holocaust: The Problematic Nature of Conveying and Absorbing them, and the Reaction in the Yishuv', in Bankier and Michman eds., *Holocaust Historiography in Context*, 437–60, here esp. 440, 445, 455.

45 See Ben Shephard, *After Daybreak. The Liberation of Belsen, 1945* (London: Jonathan Cape, 2005).

46 *The Lancet*: 12 May 1946, 603, 604–5; 9 June 1945, 750; 16 June 1945, letters page; 8 September 1945, 313–15; 20 October 1945, letters page; 2 March 1946, 317–19; 7 August 1946, book review; 13 November 1946, letter; 7 August 1946, 228–29; 6 June 1953, 1138–39. *British Medical Journal*, 9 June 1945, 814–16; 9 June 1945, 813; 23 June 1945, 883–84; 5 January 1946, 4–8; 23 February 1946, 273–75; 21 December 1946, 953–55.

47 'Medical Aspects of Belsen Concentration Camp', *The Lancet*, 8 September 1945, pp. 313–15. See also the earlier report, 'Belsen Concentration Camp', *The Lancet*, 12 May 1945, pp. 603–5.

48 'Medical Observations in Auschwitz Concentration Camp', *The Lancet*, 2 March 1946, pp. 317–19. In 1956 she published an extended memoir that achieved a wide readership in Germany although it was not translated for 40 years: Lucie Adelsberger, *Auschwitz. A Doctor's Story*, trans. Susan Ray (Boston: Northeastern University Press, 1995).

49 'Cancorum Oris', *British Dental Journal*, 79:6 (21 September 1945), 151–57.

50 'Psychological Investigation of A Group of Internees At Belsen Camp', *Journal of Mental Science*, 92:386 (January 1946), 60–74. Compare to Herbert A Bloch, 'The Personality of Inmates of Concentration Camps', *American Journal of Sociology* 52:4 (1947), 335–42, which claims that ethnic or other identity did not matter. See also, J Tas, 'Psychical Disorders Among Unmates of Concentration Camps and Repatriates', *Psychiatric Quarterly* 25:4 (1951), 679–90, based in part on the author's own experiences in Westerbork and the Jewish section of Belsen.

51 Koppel Pinson, 'Jewish Life in Liberated Germany: A Study of the Jewish DPs', *Jewish Social Studies*, 9 (1947), 101–26; Paul Friedman, 'Some Aspects of Concentration Camp Psychology', *American Journal of Psychiatry*, 105:8 (1949), 601–5. Cf. M. Niremberski, 'Psychological Investigation of a Group of Internees At Belsen Camp', *Journal of Mental Science*, 92:386 (1946), 60–74.

52 Jacob Pat, *Ashes and Fire,* trans Leo Steinberg (New York: International Universities Press, 1947), 156–58, 162–223, 224–40.

53 Joseph Tenenbaum, *In Search of a Lost People – The Old and the New Poland* (New York: Beechhurst Press, 1946), vii–vii, 26–43, 91–192,

54 One of the few to make the connection is Lawrence Baron, 'The Holocaust and American Public Memory, 1945–90', *Holocaust and Genocide Studies*, 17:1 (2003), 62–88.

55 Earl G Harrison, *The Plight of the Displaced Jews in Europe: A Report to President Truman*, reprinted in Leonard Dinnerstein, *America and the Survivors of the Holocaust* (New York: Columbia University Press, 1982), 291–305 and available online at: http://www. ushmm.org/museum/exhibit/online/dp/resourc1.htm

56 I F Stone, *Underground to Palestine* (New York: Boni and Gaer, 1946), xiii, 4.

57 Stone, *Underground to Palestine*, 29–31, 46, 66–876, 79–81, 167–68.

58 Amikam Nachmani, *Great Power Discord in Palestine: The Anglo-American Committee of Inquiry into the Problems of European Jewry and Palestine 1945–1946* (London: Frank Cass, 1987), 66–81.

59 R H S Crossman, *Palestine Mission: A Personal Record* (London: Hamish Hamilton, 1947), 16–22, 32, 38–53, 60–65, 82–106.

60 Bartley Crum, *Behind the Silken Curtain* (New York: Simon and Schuster, 1947), 69–102. For a vivid narrative of Crum's activity drawing on unpublished letters and diary entries, see Patricia Bosworth, *Anything Your Little Heart Desires: An American Family Story* (New York: Simon and Schuster, 1997), 167–206.

61 Jorge Garcia-Granados, *The Birth of Israel: The Drama As I Saw It* (New York: Knopf, 1949). Lawrence Baron is one of those who does.

62 Garcia-Granados, *The Birth of Israel*, 27, 99–101, 172–82, 216–25, 229–32.

63 Meyer Levin, *In Search* (New York: Horizon, 1950), 9, 174.

64 Levin, *In Search*, 174–89, 232–72, 298, 359–506. Lawrence Baron, 'From DPs to *Olim*: Depicting Jewish refugees in American Films, 1946–49' in J-D Steinert and Inge Weber-Newth eds, *Beyond Camps and Forced Labour: Current International Research on Survivors of Nazi Persecution. Proceedings of the International Conference, London, 11–13 January 2006* (Osnabrück: Secolo, 2006), 752.

65 This cumulative process is surveyed and analysed in Hasia Diner, *We Remember With Reverence and Love: American Jews and the Myth of Silence after the Holocaust, 1945–1962* (New York: New York University Press, 2009), 180–94.

66 David Cesarani, *Justice Delayed: How Britain Became a Refuge for Nazi War Criminals* (London: Heinemann, 1994), 169–76; idem, 'British War Crimes Policy and National

Memory of the Second World War', in K Lunn and M Evans eds, *War and Memory in the Twentieth Century* (Oxford: Berg, 1997), 27–42; Douglas, *The Memory of Judgment*, 11–94; Donald Bloxham, 'Genocide on Trial: Law and Collective Memory' in H R Reginbogin and C J M Safferling eds, *Die Nürnburger Prozesse. Völkerstrafrecht seit 1945* (Munich: K G Saur, 2006), 73–84. Cf. Michael Marrus, 'The Holocaust at Nuremberg', *Yad Vashem Studies*, 26 (1998), 5–42.

67 Donald Bloxham, *Genocide on Trial: War Crimes Trials and the Formation of Holocaust History and Memory* (Oxford: Oxford University Press, 2001), 63–69, 74–75, 84, 101–10, 124–28, 129–31.

68 See also the counterargument by Michael Marrus, 'A Jewish Lobby at Nuremberg: Jacob Robinson and the Institute of Jewish Affairs, 1945–46', in Reginbogin and Safferling eds, *Die Nürnburger Prozesse*, 63–71, and Mark A Lewis, 'The World Jewish Congress and the Institute of Jewish Affairs at Nuremberg: Ideas, Strategies, and Political Goals, 1942–46', *Yad Vashem Studies*, 36:1 (2008). 181–210.

69 *Biuletyn Glownej Komisji Badania Zbrodni Niemickich w Polsce*, 2 vols (Warsaw, 1946) translated as Central Commission for Investigation of German Crimes in Poland, *German Crimes in Poland*, 2 vols (Warsaw 1946). The references are to the facsimile edition published in 1982: volume 1, on Oswiecim, 27–94; on Treblinka, 95–108; on Chelmno, 109–24; on Polish Jewry, 125–70. For specific quotes, see, 40 and 95. Volume 2, on Belzec, 89–98 esp. 93; on Sobibor, 99–104, esp. 99; on Warsaw Ghetto, 127–29.

70 Aleksiun, 'Organising for Justice', 186–87.

71 *Les Juifs en Europe* (1939–45), 32–33. Henri Monneray ed., *La persécution des Juifs en France et dans les autres pays de l'Ouest: présentée par la France à Nuremberg* (Paris: Éditions Du Centre, 1947); idem ed., *La persécution des Juifs dans les pays de l'Est* (Paris: Éditions Du Centre, 1949).

72 Gerald Reitlinger, *The Final Solution: The Attempt to Exterminate the Jews of Europe 1939–45* (London: Valentine Mitchell, 1953), xi.

73 [Seymour Krieger ed.], *Nazi Germany's War Against the Jews* (New York: American Jewish Conference, 1947), xix, I/1-I/75.

74 Peter Calvocoressi, *Nuremberg: The Facts and the Consequences* (London: Macmillan, 1947), 43–44, 59–60, 89–90, 106–9, 121–23; Victor Bernstein, *Final Judgment: The Story of Nuremberg* (New York: Boni and Gaer, 1947), 181–209, 250.

75 Samuel Gringauz, 'The Ghetto as an Experiment of Jewish Social Organisation. (Three years of the Kovno Ghetto)', *Jewish Social Studies*, 11:1 (1949), 3–20; Hannah Arendt, 'Social Science Techniques and the Study of the Concentration camps', *Jewish Social Studies*, 12:1 (1950), 49–64; Solomon Bloom, Towards the Ghetto Dictator', *Jewish Social Studies*, 12:1 (1950), 73–82.

76 Schneersohn, *Les Juifs en Europe*, p. 9.

77 Schwarz, 'A Library of Hope', 183.

78 Poliakov, *L'auberge des musiciens*, 178–79. See also, Bensoussan, 'The Jewish Contemporary Documentation Centre (CDJC) and Holocaust Research in France, 1945–70', 246–48.

79 Nehamiah Robinson, foreword to Anatole Goldstein, *From Discrimination to Annihilation* (New York: Institute for Jewish Affairs, 1952), 7–8.

80 Samuel Gringauz, review of Friedman, *Oshwiencim*, *Jewish Social Studies*, 14:4 (1952), 376–77.

81 Philip Friedman, 'The Jewish Ghettos of the Nazi Era', *Jewish Social Studies*, 16:1 (1954), 61–88. See Diner, *We Remember With Reverence and Love,* 88–123.

82 Elie A Cohen, *Human Behaviour in the Concentration Camps*, trans. M H Braaksma (London: Jonathan Cape, 1953), xiii, 4. Cohen was citing E De Wind, *Eindstation Auschwitz*, which was published in Amsterdam in 1946. Cf. Bensoussan, 'The Jewish Contemporary Documentation Centre (CDJC) and Holocaust Research in France, 1945–70', in Bankier and Michman eds, *Holocaust Historiography in Context*, p. 252 and more generally, Pieter Lagrou, 'Return to a Vanished World. European Societies and the

Remnants of their Jewish Communities, 1945–47', in David Bankier ed., *The Jews are Coming Back: The Return of the Jews to Their Countries of Origin After WW II* (Jerusalem: Yad Vashem/Berghahn Books, 2005), pp. 1–24.

83 Sidra DaKoven Ezrahi, *By Words Alone. The Holocaust in Literature* (Chicago: Chicago University Press, 1980), 176–97. See also, Emily Miller Budick, 'The Holocaust in the Jewish American literary imagination', in Michael Kramer and Hana Wirth-Nesher eds, *Cambridge Companion to American Jewish Literature* (Cambridge; Cambridge University Press, 2003), 215–16. Edward Shapiro, *A Time for Healing: American Jewry since World War II* (Baltimore: Johns Hopkins University Press, 1992), 9–20, 29, 36–39; Stuart Svonkin, *Jews Against Prejudice: American Jews and the Fight for Civil Liberties* (New York: Columbia University Press, 1997), 11–20, 22–25, 77–89.

84 Meyer Levin, *The Obsession* (New York: Simon and Schuster, 1974). On the tussle over Anne Frank see, Ralph Melnick, *The Stolen Legacy of Anne Frank: Meyer Levin, Lillian Hellman, and the Staging of the* Diary (New Haven, CT: Yale University Press, 1997).

85 Steven Zipperstein, *Rosenfeld's Lives: Fame, Oblivion and the Furies of Writing* (New Haven, CT: Yale University Press, 2009), 122–26.

86 Alfred Kazin, *A Lifetime Burning Every Moment* (New York: HarperCollins, 1996), 45–46, 87–89, 107, 108.

87 Irving Howe and Eliezer Greenberg eds, *A Treasury of Yiddish Stories* (New York: Viking, 1954). See Steve Zipperstein, *Imagining Russian Jewry: Memory, History, Identity* (Seattle: University of Washington Press, 1999), 28–32, for reflections on Howe.

88 Ezrahi, *By Words Alone,* 34–38; Alvin H Rosenfeld, *Anne Frank and the Future of Holocaust Memory* (Washington, DC: United States Holocaust Memorial Museum, 2004), 3–4. See also, Jordan William Paul, 'Overcoming Apathy: Constructing A Holocaust Consciousness in America, 1950–67', unpublished MA Thesis, Michigan State University, 1996, 12–30, 34–40, 76–77.

89 Alan Mintz, *Popular Culture and the Shaping of Holocaust Memory in America* (Seattle: University of Washington Press, 2001), 16–19, 85–100, 102–3 and Lawrence Baron, 'The First Wave of American "Holocaust" Films, 1945–59', *American History Review Forum,* 8–9, 24–35.

90 Kirsten Fermaglich, *American Dreams and Nazi Nightmares: Early Holocaust Consciousness and Liberal America, 1957–1965* (Waltham, MA: Brandeis University Press, 2006). 18.

91 Norman Cohn, *The Pursuit of the Millennium* (Oxford: Oxford University Press, 1970 edn), 285.

92 Caroline Wiedmer, *The Claims of Memory: Representations of the Holocaust in Contemporary Germany and France* (Ithaca, NY: Cornell University Press, 1999), 34–44.

93 Jockusch, '"Collect and Record"', 106–45. Cf. Weinberg, 'France' in Wyman ed., *The World Reacts to the Holocaust,* 20.

2

RE-IMAGINING THE UNIMAGINABLE

Theater, memory, and rehabilitation in the Displaced Persons camps

Margarete Myers Feinstein

> When the children first arrived at Kloster Indersdorf, they talked and talked – about their experiences in the concentration camps and as slave laborers. Horror stories were intermingled with ordinary events, with little show of emotion. It took time for them to relax or play. Nearly all of the first creative plays presented by the children included scenes from the concentration camps, punctuated with wry bits of humour that did not seem funny to the UNRRA [United Nations Relief and Rehabilitation] workers.[1]

Regardless of the sensibilities of Anglo-American social workers who objected to what they considered to be a morbid obsession with the past, child and adult survivors in the Displaced Persons (DP) camps dramatized their wartime experiences. DP plays valorized partisans and resistance fighters, allowing non-combatant survivors to imagine that they had participated in the fight against the Nazis and providing role models for the struggle against the British mandate in Palestine. Creating a narrative of their past, present, and future, the DPs connected their experiences to the need for a Jewish state in the Land of Israel. Far from remaining silent about their experiences, survivors reenacted their most traumatic memories. These performances reveal the need of survivors to understand their past and to shape their own future.

DP theaters

Most DP actors were amateurs, with perhaps some experience in school or youth group productions before the war. Some had performed secretly in ghettoes and concentration camps. Others had spent the war years with no outlet for their creative urges and now hurried to join drama circles and theatrical troupes. The demographics of the survivors meant that many had limited experience with prewar theatrical life. Concentration camp survivors tended to be between 15 and 25 years old, so most were between the ages of 12 and 20 when the war deprived them of the opportunity to attend professional performances or to participate in school plays. In addition, traditional parents had attempted to shelter their children, though not always successfully, from the theater that permitted the mixing of men and women and that tempted young minds to think of frivolous, worldly things. Thus, the initial number of survivors who had the experience, knowledge, and skills to stage productions was small. Later, Polish Jews who had survived the war years in the Soviet Union arrived in the DP camps, bringing older and more culturally knowledgeable individuals who contributed to DP theatrical life.

In 1946 and 1947 reports from Jewish DP committees indicated that those involved in theater were older than the average survivor. The ages of the eight-member Markt-Oberdorf drama circle averaged 28 years. The youngest member was 21 and the oldest 45. At Leipheim, the average age of the thirteen drama circle members was 30, with the youngest 22 and the oldest 52. The 26 performers at Landsberg (20 actors, one choral director, and five orchestra musicians) had an average age of 32 with the youngest at 17 and the oldest at 50. Most were amateurs with

FIGURE 2.1 Sonia Boczkowska reciting the poem "Shoes from Majdanek" at the Belsen DP camp
Source: Yad Vashem, courtesy of Hadassah Rosensaft.

middle school educations. The professionals and older performers, such as those in the Landsberg drama circle, often had some advanced education.[2]

The vast majority of Jewish DPs resided in the American and British zones of occupied Germany. The British zone had a professional troupe soon after liberation. Director Sami Feder gathered together surviving professional Yiddish theater people from around Germany to form the Belsen Katzet-Teater. Trained in Berlin's prewar avant-garde theater scene, Feder's staging had an expressionist, modern sensibility. Despite transportation problems, the troupe performed for thousands of DPs outside Belsen, in Hanover, Brunswick, and Harzburg. In its two-year existence, the Kazet-Teater staged 7 programs, 10 musical revues, 47 theatrical performances, and at the Belsen hospital 22 revues and an evening of classical and Yiddish folk music. The troupe won acclaim in Germany and on a summer 1947 tour in Belgium and France.[3] (see image 2.1)

The American zone received its first professional theater in spring 1946 with the arrival of the Musical Yiddish Cabaret Theater (MIKT). Formed in Poland on March 30, 1946 by a group of Yiddish actors and community leaders to perform revues and concerts, the troupe quickly transformed its mission into reforging the links to Yiddish theater culture with a classical repertoire. The precariousness of life in post-war Poland and the promise of eager Yiddish-speaking audiences in the American zone of Germany brought the troupe to Munich later that spring. DP audiences and press liked their revues and their staging of Sholem Aleichem's comedy *The Jackpot*. On June 12, 1946 a plenary session of the Central Committee for Liberated Jews in the U.S. Zone granted MIKT official status and promised to subsidize the theater. Later, breakaway actors using the same name forced the theater to change its name to the Munich Yiddish Art Theater (MIT). In 1946 the troupe toured DP camps and Jewish communities in Germany, staging 3 premiers and 66 performances, and reaching 50,000 viewers. Frequently over 400 patrons attended a single performance in the larger camps, and in 1948 MIT reported total attendance figures of 180,000 during its first two years of existence.[4] Hungry for diversion, DPs flocked to the theater.

DP troupes understood that they were waging a battle to reclaim the Jewish heritage, to revive the Jewish soul, and to imagine the Jewish future. H. Perlmutter, the so-called Showman of Auschwitz and later director of Feldafing DP camp's "Amcho" troupe, was struck by the tremendous responsibility he had to rebuild Jewish cultural life and to prove Jewish productivity after the Holocaust.[5] Ruth Minsky Sender's brother-in-law founded a Yiddish theater in Leipheim DP camp. She recalls his excitement about the audiences' reception of the performances: "We bring them the voices of the past, the good and the evil. We remind them that we, the remnants of our people, must carry on. … It is up to us to rise from the ashes and build a new life."[6] For these former victims of Nazi persecution, survival meant more than physical existence; it meant the revival of Jewish cultural life.

Memorializing the past

DP performers frequently portrayed their recent suffering through song, dance, and drama. The lack of scripts, costumes, scores, and other resources combined with the desire for light entertainment resulted in the staging of revues, reminiscent of ghetto cabarets. Even this light fare often included songs or skits from the Holocaust period and songs from wartime exile in the Soviet Union, alongside Hebrew songs and folk songs.[7] The narratives the troupes enacted emphasized the suffering of mothers and children alongside heroic resistance. The plays honored the martyred dead, and at the same time they presented new coping strategies of armed resistance and Zionist politics.

Music was an integral part of the revues and Yiddish theater. Both melodies and lyrics expressed the experiences, sorrows, and yearnings of the performers and audiences. A song frequently featured in DP shows was *Dos elente Kind* (*The Lonely Child*) from the Vilna ghetto, about a child separated from her mother who had given her to a Christian family for safekeeping. The song concludes with the command for the daughter to tell later generations about her parents' suffering. The founder of an amateur troupe in the Föhrenwald DP camp, Jacob Biber reports of the song's first performance there, "The lengthy applause [following this song] showed our need to cry, to demonstrate our collective pain."[8] The separation of mother and child symbolized universal grief and suffering, and the final verse reminded survivors to bear witness on behalf of the dead.

The first concert of the Katzet-Teater in Belsen demonstrated the symbolic importance of song. The excited audience sang along to the opening number, *S' brennt* (*It's Burning*). Written by Mordechai Gebirtig in response to a 1936 pogrom, the song calls Jews to action: "Don't stand there brother/Douse the fire!" During the Holocaust, the Jewish resistance in Krakow adopted the song, and it was popular in the ghettos and concentration camps. After the war, the call to action still resonated with survivors since there were pogroms in postwar Poland and the Jewish community in Palestine was waging battle for an independent state.

The musical conclusion to the Belsen evening was no less fraught with meaning. The troupe had debated what to sing. Traditionally the national anthem would be played at the conclusion. Given that they were in the British zone of occupied Germany, the British anthem would seem to be the appropriate one, but some members argued in favor of the Zionist anthem *Hatikvah* and others for the socialist *International*. Finally, they decided to conclude with the partisan song by Hirsh Glik, *Zog nit keynmol* (*Never Say* or *Hymn of the Partisans*). Sami Feder rewrote the final scene of the revue so that the entire ensemble would be on stage to sing the song in place of the traditional anthem. The audience joined in, moved by the connection that the song made between them and the partisans. In the end, they also sang *Hatikvah* and followed it with *God Save the King*. In the future, the Belsen ceremonies commemorating the day of liberation would begin with *S' brennt* and conclude with *Zog nit keynmol*, calling the survivors to action and to continue the partisan fight. In the American zone of occupied Germany, *Hatikvah* customarily ended performances, signifying the DPs' Zionist aspirations. The music reminded DPs not simply of their suffering but also of their defiant spirit. It expressed their resistance to their oppressors and called them to action.

Most scenes in the first Belsen revue portrayed life during the Holocaust.[9] One piece depicted concentration camp inmates keeping up morale with music after guards left them without food or light. Dolly Katz's "The Mother's Dance" expressed the suffering of a mother after her child's murder in a concentration camp. The artist performed in front of a swastika flag, wearing a striped dress reminiscent of concentration camp uniforms. The theme of the suffering mother that spoke so movingly to DP audiences later figured prominently in Israeli Holocaust memorials as a universal symbol of affliction.[10]

Later Belsen performances included the play *In Auschwitz* and Sonia Boczkowska's recital of the poem "Shoes from Majdanek." Boczkowska wore a stylized concentration camp uniform and stood before a mountain of shoes for the performance. DP performers and audiences did not shy away from representations of their recent suffering. Instead, they found emotional release through the retellings.

When looking at the recent past for subject matter, DP directors often focused on resistance fighters and partisans. For example, Feder wrote and directed a play called *Partisans* (see Figure 2.2 and 2.3). In one scene, a cabaret singer seduced German officers and stole their weapons to pass along to resistance fighters. In the Leipheim DP camp, a theater group director had a similar plot in mind for a skit,[11] and MIT would stage a play about resistance in a transit camp. These storylines were fantasies for the majority of DPs who had not been able or willing to participate in armed conflict during the war. And yet, the subject of resistance was not uncommon in survivor re-imaginings of the past at the same time as survivors sought to reassert their sense of agency and control over their own lives.

FIGURE 2.2 Scene from the Katzet-Teater play "Partisans" at the Belsen DP camp
Source: Yad Vashem, courtesy of Hadassah Rosensaft.

Simply staging the plays required determination and skills learned during the Nazi years. Material shortages posed great difficulties for troupes, and they took pride in their resourcefulness to acquire cosmetics, costumes, and props. For example, the cabaret singer required an elegant dress. Her costume was made from a curtain "organized" from a British officer's room. Feder writes,

> We "Katzetlers" who, under British administration, were still locked up for a long time after liberation in the same camps and could not move about freely, we had no other choice but to "organize" like in the Hitler-camps – i.e., to acquire that which one needs through all possible means – whether legal or illegal.[12]

Since the survivors remained in a camp and since the British authorities were responsible for keeping closed the gates to Palestine, DPs felt justified in using whatever means necessary to get what they needed. The cabaret singer's costume represented a symbolic blow against British power. The resistance to the Nazis portrayed in the play became linked to the struggle against the British in the present.

Making the connection to a Jewish homeland

When survivors' expectations that the world would open its arms to them were not met, a majority of DPs focused their hopes on immigration to Palestine. DP political and cultural life soon revolved around Zionist aspirations. Zionism offered an explanation of the past and hope for the future. In a world of continued anti-Semitic violence, the need for a Jewish homeland seemed clear to many. As historian Avinoam J. Patt wrote, "Zionism in the DP camps was thus not merely a monolithic Zionism geared solely to the requirements of the Yishuv; it filled the needs of many groups, productively, therapeutically, and diplomatically."[13] The survivors' determination to help create a Jewish state in Palestine stemmed both from political, ideological commitment and from psychological, emotional, and pragmatic impulses. DP actors shared these values. Both the Katzet-Teater and MIKT/MIT openly held Zionist positions. DP drama circles and theater troupes frequently connected the experiences of the recent past to the need for a Jewish homeland. They expressed the DPs' Zionist worldview on stage.

Like the Belsen performances, plays in Feldafing and Föhrenwald depicted wartime suffering but these productions continued the storyline into the post-liberation era, emphasizing the survivors' ties to Palestine. *Blood and Fire* was the first play produced by the Feldafing amateur ensemble that would become the acclaimed "Amcho" troupe. The action begins in prewar Poland in the home of a bourgeois Jewish family. One of the sons, a member of a kibbutz, urges his parents to sell their possessions and move the family to Palestine. The parents laughingly dismiss their son's advice and he leaves alone. With the arrival of the Nazis, the parents meet their end in the gas chamber. After the war, the Zionist son, now an officer in the Haganah, returns to Poland in an effort to find his family. The officer locates his sole surviving

FIGURE 2.3 Cabaret scene from the Katzet-Teater play "Partisans" at the Belsen DP camp. Note the dress made from an "organized" curtain.
Source: Yad Vashem, courtesy of Hadassah Rosensaft.

sister in a DP camp in Germany and takes her with him to Palestine. This play affirmed the foresight of prewar Zionists and drew a connection between the sufferings of the Shoah and the need for a home in Palestine. It also held out the comforting dream that somehow the survivors would be reunited with a family member who would rescue them from the DP camps.

The Föhrenwald play *Illegal Aliyah* explored the connections between the Shoah and the quest for a new Jewish home in a graphic and melodramatic fashion.[14] First performed on April 5, 1946, it used the Holocaust as a prologue to the main action, illegal immigration to Palestine. The curtain opens on one part of the stage to show pious Jews at prayer in Jerusalem. The audience's attention is then directed to the other side of the stage where a mother and child stand before the crematorium in a concentration camp. A camp guard grabs the child and throws it into the flames of the crematorium. As the guard continues to slaughter inmates, on the other side of the stage British soldiers enter the Palestine scene and begin beating the praying Jews. The Jews in the concentration camp cry, "They kill us here and beat us there! Where shall we go?" while the Jews in Palestine scream, "They kill us there and beat us here! What shall we do?"

The ensuing play focuses on bands of illegal immigrants to Palestine who meet and join forces. They are caught by a British border patrol and taken to court where a young Zionist defendant passionately explains why these survivors are determined to enter Palestine. One of the British judges recognizes two elderly defendants as his parents. The play concludes with the family's reconciliation and the judge's promise to serve the Jewish people. In this drama, the horrors of the Shoah were juxtaposed and even equated with the brutality of the British occupation of Palestine. Here, Jews were seen as paralyzed by their persecution at the time of the Shoah, but in its aftermath, they were filled by Zionist purpose. It was the survivors who awakened the judge, and the rest of the world, to the need for Jewish unity and for a homeland in Palestine. The DPs were thus called on to learn the lessons of the Holocaust and to devote themselves to the Zionist cause.

The question of aesthetics

Within the DP community, debates swirled around the appropriate way to stage wartime experiences. Some DPs agreed with the international aid workers that the best approach was to avoid the subject altogether. Others believed that more time needed to pass to allow proper perspective and the development of new artistic forms that could better convey the catastrophe. Most DPs accepted the need to portray the recent past but argued about how it should be artistically represented. Old debates about high (European) and low (*shund*) theater resurfaced.

On one level the debates over artistic forms appeared to be a discussion about the appropriateness of Holocaust themed plays. On another level, it was a continuation of prewar debates between high and lowbrow culture. *Shund*, popular theater, remained the bane of the cultural elite's existence with its melodramatic, scene-chewing stars and mixture of Yiddish dialects. Criticism that the DP theaters lacked repertoire and artistic sensibility reflected the continuing battle to raise the cultural level of the Jewish masses as well as the reality of the amateur nature of most DP theaters. Yiddish theater had been plagued by the lack of a uniform language before the war, and the demographic jumble in the DP camps only heightened this. Yiddish dialects from across eastern and southeastern Europe were spoken from the stage.

In his blistering critique of the prologue to the Föhrenwald production of *Illegal Aliyah*, the famous actor and director Jonas Turkow objected to the presence of a crematorium on stage:

> a crematorium, how a Jewish child, torn from its mother, was thrown into the oven … I could barely remain seated. How dare one offer such a profanity?! Our bloody wounds are still too fresh to allow them, in such a brutal form no less, to be exposed on the stage. Even veteran, talented artists must be careful when touching such painful problems that are so holy and dear to us. If one had simply alluded to the crematorium and not shown it in such a brutally realistic form, the effect would have been stronger. It is simply enough to talk about a crematorium to send a shudder through our limbs.[15]

That Turkow offered the alternative of alluding to the crematorium offstage suggests that he did not object to the subject matter but rather to the aesthetics of the staging. Attempts to realistically portray the tortures of the Holocaust could only fail, since the staging would be simultaneously too graphic and yet not realistic enough. This disdain for DP theater's excesses did not differ much from the prewar critiques offered by the "Europeanists" in the Yiddish theatrical world. "European" meant a modern, cosmopolitan style emphasizing ensemble work. In the American zone, the Jewish Professional Actors' Union and the Central Committee's officially sponsored MIT Theater both encouraged a more European approach to theater to differentiate themselves from the shund practiced by many of the amateurs. As cultural activity flourished among the Jewish survivors, professionalization of the theaters further emphasized the divide between popular and elite theater.

The European emphasis did not shield MIT from criticism, however. With American military government dignitaries in the audience, MIT premiered Moshe Pintschewski's *Ich leb* (*I am Living*) in Munich on November 6, 1946. Set in a transit camp, the play depicted Jewish leaders as intellectuals who comply with the Gestapo, while a young man seeks to organize an underground movement. He is captured and killed. His devoted fiancée, Miriam, pretends to assist the Gestapo in order to save her imprisoned, scholarly father. Ultimately, Miriam kills the commandant and escapes to the partisans. Meanwhile, a German officer, despairing of the bad news from the front and hoping to win their gratitude, releases Miriam's father and a violinist. The two intellectuals then join the partisans, reuniting with Miriam.[16] The emphasis in this play, as in *Partisans*, is on heroic action and self-sacrifice, not on passive victimhood. These plays enabled the audiences to feel that they too had participated in the victorious battle against the Nazis. The reenactment of the traumatic past with new coping strategies and new endings had therapeutic value for the survivors' recovery, aiding the integration of Holocaust experiences into the survivors' life stories.[17] Through the characters on stage, they, both men and women, became heroes rather than victims.

Some DP theater critics viewed Pintschewski's emphasis on resistance as a lack of respect for *Kiddush ha-Shem* – the term for traditional Jewry's willingness to accept martyrdom. One critic accused the author of cheap effects and suggested that Pintschewski, who had written the play in exile in Argentina and then the Soviet Union, did not have the experience necessary to write a successful play. Other critics emphasized that the play lacked perspective that the passage of time would allow.[18]

The MIT directors had anticipated the reactions of the critics. The program acknowledged that the play's content was too shocking for those who had not experienced German captivity and too tame for those who had. In the program the artistic director, Israel Segall, recognized that there were those who for artistic reasons opposed treatment of the recent past. In justifying his choice of material, Segall emphasized the didactic function of the theater. The troupe was portraying behaviors from the past that could inspire action in the present. The bright lights of resisters and partisans were to inspire the survivors to heroic action in the postwar era. The stage director, Israel Beker, argued that the survivors had a responsibility to tell about the "gruesome tragedy" and not permit it to be forgotten.[19]

In 1947 MIT reorganized to pursue a Jewish yet European artistic mission. In this cause it staged three major productions: first, *Shlomo Molcho*, about "a national [Jewish] question in search for its solution" in fourteenth century Portugal; second, *Der Ojcer*, a folk play that with "much music, color and movement made this an entertaining piece, in contrast to the first performance, that carried a serious, monumental character;" and third, *Die Haffnung*, a truly European play about a Dutch fishing village with no specifically Jewish character whatsoever. Satisfied with its efforts MIT reported:

> The greatest accomplishments of this theater are: the maintenance of an interesting and valuable repertoire, the well-balanced ensemble work, a skilled endeavor that on the one hand works with the actors, on the other hand makes the effort to bring the "inner substance" into harmony with modern staging and costumes.[20]

MIT's emphasis on European aesthetics did not mean that the artists would avoid the subject of the Shoah. Principal individuals from MIT would apply this aesthetic to a 1948 feature film about the Holocaust.[21]

Reinterpreting the classics

By 1946 improved material conditions enabled theaters to stage Yiddish classics. In the American zone, the Central Committee established a collection of scripts that were made available to representatives of camp committees for copying. Before, troupes had had to rely on the memories of its members in order to reconstruct an old standard. Popular authors included Anski, Goldfaden, Peretz, and Sholom Aleichem. During the Shoah, amateur theaters in the ghettoes had performed parts of their works, mostly in revue form. The Nazis had discouraged serious theater in favor of cabaret, perhaps to promote moral degeneracy among the Jews.[22] In the DP camps, full-scale productions were now possible, as was highbrow theater. These plays represented a connection of DPs with the theater of their parents, of their childhoods. At the same time, DPs used these classics to interpret their place in Jewish history and to strengthen their ethnic identity.

The staging of Yiddish classics encouraged the identification of recent sufferings with those of previous generations. For example, the Bamberg drama studio put on a performance of Sholem Asch's *Kiddush Ha-Shem*, about seventeenth-century pogroms. A reviewer found the play quite appropriate for the DP stage:

> When we see the shadow of Asch's masterwork on the camp stage, we are as if elevated and it seems to us as if we are organically bound together with the martyrs of our people from Chmielnicki's time. That is the long, holy, golden chain, in which we are bound and put into the context of the generations.[23]

The chain did not stop with the Shoah but continued to a future in Palestine, when the next night the same troupe performed a revue, *Tel-Aviv*. In the skit "Haganah" illegal immigrants swam to shore just as described in the newspapers, and for added drama, an old mother recognized her son on shore.[24] Yiddish classics helped to make sense of the Holocaust by placing it within the cycles of Jewish history. At the same time, DPs sought to break the cycle of martyrdom by promoting Jewish ethnic identity and demands for a Jewish state.

Sholem Aleichem remained a popular playwright, and DP theaters found ways to link his works to their own experiences. On the first anniversary of the founding of the Katzet-Teater in Belsen, the troupe performed *The Jackpot*, Aleichem's play about a tailor swindled out of his lottery winnings. Connecting the play to the recent past, director Sami Feder dedicated the performance to those he had directed in a 1939 production in Poland and who had not survived the war.

On August 3, 1946 MIKT premiered *The Bloody Hoax*, its version of Sholem Aleichem's novel by the same name. The story was a Yiddish version of *The Prince and the Pauper*: a Russian nobleman trades places with a Jewish classmate, David Shapiro, and learns about the daily discrimination Jews faced in Czarist Russia. When the disguised nobleman is put on trial for blood libel charges, Shapiro returns to rescue him and to reclaim his Jewish identity. Emphasizing the nationalist implications, the performances concluded with the Zionist anthem, *Hatikvah*.

The play won accolades in the DP press for the professional production and for the psychological depth of the treatment.[25] One critic wrote that the play had a

> powerful effect, the audience applauded approvingly and spontaneously (like at a rally) in the middle of a scene and were transported, together with David Shapiro, in the moment when he emphasizes his national dignity and consciousness of belonging to a persecuted people.[26]

Another reviewer used the opportunity to profess Zionist goals:

> Never has our heart been so heavy, alone and mournful as now when we, the Saving Remnant, stand with eyes open and see the big world that should open

the doors to the Land of Israel and let us in there so that we should be able to live our lives culturally and nationally as do all peoples on this earth.[27]

Sholem Aleichem's national consciousness made his texts relevant to Holocaust survivors. When DP theaters performed classic Yiddish works, they emphasized the connections to the persecution the DPs had experienced and to the importance of Jewish ethnic identity.

Re-imagining trauma for psychological health

Theater could alleviate the monotony of life in the camps, transporting the audience from Germany to one or more of three places: the world of their childhood, the Shoah itself, and their future in Palestine. Sender recalled watching her brother-in-law perform in Leipheim, "The people around me cry and laugh. Shout their anger. Burst into song as they wander with him from yesterday to today, to tomorrow."[28] The prewar past offered comforting nostalgia and a momentary connection with parents and community. The period of the Holocaust expressed the torment of loss but also rewrote the immediate past into a story of partisan resistance to Nazi power, giving the former victims a sense of control over their destiny. The imagined future enacted the Zionist dream of redemption in Palestine.

At a time when UNRRA workers and other international observers discouraged survivors from discussing their recent past, these productions acknowledged the survivors' experiences in the concentration camps, ghettoes, and forests, validating their preoccupation with their recent past. Through the plays, performers and audiences alike were able to experiment with new roles and to relearn the rules of social interaction.[29] It is interesting to note that research on trauma survivors has demonstrated that imaginal exposure therapies can play an important role in recovery.[30] Converting intense emotions into narratives about a traumatic experience can result in improved health and a reduction in the effects of post-traumatic stress syndrome.[31] In fact, contrary to the assumptions of postwar psychologists and educators, reenactments and creative expressions of the trauma could facilitate the survivors' recovery by suggesting new endings and new coping strategies.

Evidence indicates that some surviving Jews believed in the psychological benefits of discussing the recent trauma. DP teachers debated the value of recording children's testimonies. Some asserted the benefits of "opening a wound and extracting the pus."[32] The emotional release that came through retelling could facilitate healing. Theater troupes throughout the DP camps seemed to embrace a similar perspective on the role of theater in rehabilitation, allowing survivors to revisit past trauma while focusing attention on the "bright lights" of the recent past with an emphasis on resistance.[33]

Audience reactions to the graphic portrayal of Holocaust experiences within the relative safety of the DP community suggest that DP theater did function as a form of therapy. Sender comments on the catharsis that survivors experienced when they saw their lives depicted on stage:

I watch Mala, dressed in black and sitting on the darkened stage amid rubble. I know it is my sister, but on that stage she is every one of us who returned to the ruins of our homes, found rubble or strangers where our families once lived. Her pain-filled voice is the voice of all who survived and found only ashes. ... She cries bitterly. We all cry with her. The score is too big.[34]

Denied the luxury of expressing, or even of feeling, emotion during the Shoah, the performances permitted survivors to weep and grieve. The emphasis on resistance allowed DPs, the majority of whom had not been resistance fighters, to imagine themselves taking action against their tormentors, alleviating the terror of helplessness. Within the DP community, concentration camp survivors came to see partisans and resistance fighters as their alter egos who had expressed their will to resist when they had been unable to do so themselves.[35] DPs were drawn to artistic expressions of their suffering that enabled them to confront and reinterpret their traumatic past. By emphasizing the importance of resistance fighters, DP theater participated in rewriting the Holocaust experience from one of victimization into one of heroic resistance and a legitimation of Zionist goals.

Mala had survived the war in exile in the Soviet Union, yet through her performances she portrayed the collective experience of loss. By 1948 a significant number of Jewish DPs were those who had spent the war years in Soviet exile. They were neither concentration camp survivors nor partisans. They could honor the memory of the martyrs in the concentration camps and extol the heroes of the resistance. Through the theater they could imagine the fate of their loved ones who had come under German control, the fate they would have shared had they not fled eastward. They could imagine that they would have been partisans had they had the opportunity. DP theater helped integrate these DPs into the memory community of survivors.

Conclusion

Far from remaining silent, survivors recounted and retold their experiences. The myth of silence developed not from their unwillingness to speak but from the unwillingness of others to hear.[36] This myth has had profound consequences. Not only does it obscure the creative efforts of survivors to cope with their trauma, but it also leads scholars to misread the past, casting DPs as passive and malleable pawns in the hands of others. In Israel, the "new historians," such as Tom Segev, Idith Zertal and Yosef Grodzinsky, have argued that Zionists manipulated and exploited survivors for their own political purposes.[37] The voices of the survivors are muted in these histories, and DPs remain without agency.[38]

Idith Zertal, for example, has argued that Israeli Zionists distinguished between the heroic resistance fighters of the Warsaw Ghetto Uprising and the ignoble masses of Jewish victims in order to co-opt the resistance fighters as representatives of Zionist Palestine.[39] She also argues that the triumph of the Zionist heroic narrative in Israel is evidence of the "coercive, engulfing ideologic pressure exerted over newcomers by the prevailing Israeli discourse of the first years of statehood."[40] She assumes that since most of the survivors had not been active in the resistance that they must have been forced to accept a narrative that privileged the resistance over their own lived experiences. In fact, the narratives created by the survivors themselves in DP theaters, that is, before their arrival in Palestine/Israel, strongly connected the resistance fighters to the Zionist battle for Palestine. Rather than view the resistance as separate from themselves, the DPs re-imagined *themselves* as fighters and partisans. Before they had arrived in Israel, many survivors had identified themselves with the resistance and with the Zionist cause.

The assumption that survivors had remained silent about their wartime trauma allowed scholars to read their own agendas into that void. Rediscovering the survivors' words, therefore, is a crucial step in correcting the historical record. Important recent studies that focus on the internal workings of the DP community have begun recovering the survivors' voices and have demonstrated that DPs had very clearly defined interests and argued vigorously on their own behalf. These works refute the suggestions of DP passivity and victimization.[41]

An examination of DP theater demonstrates the important role reenactment of the Holocaust played in survivors' immediate postwar experiences. The plays constructed narratives out of the traumatic past, helping survivors to articulate their own experiences while shaping collective memories. Within the relative safety of the DP camps, survivors re-lived their past trauma, not to wallow in it, but to gain some control over it and to imagine new endings, new coping mechanisms. The narratives they constructed led to Zionism, linking the wartime resistance against the Nazis to the fight for a Jewish state in Palestine. By looking at what the survivors themselves said, we can avoid the error of putting words into their mouths or of accusing others of doing the same.

Notes

1 Greta Fischer, "D.P. Children's Center, Kloster Indersdorf Kreis Dachau," pp. 37–38, United States Holocaust Memorial Museum, Greta Fischer Papers, RG-19.034★01.
2 Various *Fragebogen*, YIVO Archive, Microfilm, Roll 94, Folder 1308.
3 Information about the Katzet-Teater given in this chapter comes primarily from Sami Feder, *Farzeichenishn zum Tag-Buch fun "Kazet-teater" in Bergen-Belsen*, esp. pp. 9–12, Yad Vashem Archives (YV) O-70/31.
4 J. Beker, ",Mikt' un, Mit,'" *Ibergang* 6(8), p. 5, YV M-1/P-85.
5 H. Perlmutter, *Bine-Maskes Bay Katsetlekh* (Tel Aviv: Hamenorah, 1974), p. 26.
6 Ruth Minsky Sender, *To Life* (NY: Macmillan Publishing, 1988), p. 143.
7 "Program von 'Bunten Abend,'" 28 October 1945, YIVO, Microfilm Roll 2, Folder 16.
8 Jacob Biber, *Risen from the Ashes* (San Bernardino, CA: The Borgo Press, 1990), p. 27.
9 Muriel Knox Doherty, letter dated 18 September 1945 in *Letters from Belsen 1945: An Australian Nurse's Experiences with the Survivors of War*, edited by Judith Cornell and R. Lynette Russell (St. Leonards, NSW Australia: Allen & Unwin, 2000), p. 121.
10 Judith Tydor Baumel, "Rachel Laments Her Children: Representation of Women in Israeli Holocaust Memorials," in *Double Jeopardy: Gender and the Holocaust* (London: Vallentine Mitchell, 1998), esp. pp. 214 and 224.
11 Sender, *To Life*, p. 148.
12 Feder, *Farzeichenishn zum Tag-Buch*, p. 10.

13 Avinoam J. Patt, "Living in Landsberg, Dreaming of Deganiah: Jewish Displaced Youths and Zionism after the Holocaust," in *"We Are Here": New Approaches to Jewish Displaced Persons in Postwar Germany*, eds. Avinoam J. Patt and Michael Berkowitz (Detroit: Wayne State University Press, 2010), p. 123.

14 "Di Ensztejung fun Dramkrajz 'Maapilim' in Föhrenwald: Ojfgenumen durch di Historisze Komisie in Föhrenwald d. M. Schamroth," YV M-1/P-81.

15 Jonas Turkow, "Dram-Krajzn un zajere Aufgabn," [no date], p. 18, YV M-1/P-81. Also printed as Jonas Turkow, "Dram = krajzn un zejere ojfgabn," *Unzer Hofenung*, 1 November 1946, p. 4.

16 M. Pinezevski, "I am Living," YV M-1/P-85.

17 See, Lenore Terr, *Too Scared to Cry: Psychic Trauma in Childhood* (New York: Harper & Row, 1990), p. 301.

18 Assorted newspaper reviews, November 1946, YV M-1/P-85.

19 Israel Segall, "Repertoire" (in Yiddish) and Israel Beker, "Our New Production" (in Yiddish), in program of "Ich leb," November 1946, YV M-1/P-85.

20 Kurzbericht von der Taetigkeit der Theater "Mit", YIVO 94/1319.

21 In *Lang ist der Weg* (*Long is the Road*) Israel Beker played David, the assimilated son of traditional parents. During the war and joins the partisans, while his parents continue to a concentration camp where the father is murdered. Rather than a realistic scene of brutality, we surmise the father's fate, as ever thickening smoke slowly obscures his heavenward-turned face. After the war David marries a German-Jewish survivor and reunites with his mother in Germany. At the conclusion, the former partisan labors on a DP agricultural training farm, preparing for a life in Palestine. The film answered Israel Segall's call for a work that would reflect the recent past and also the present while spurring survivors to take control of their fate.

22 Nahma Sandrow, *Vagabond Stars: A World History of Yiddish Theater* (Syracuse, NY: Syracuse University Press, 1977), pp. 343–44.

23 "'Kidusz Haszem' Ojsgefirt fun Bamberger dramatiszer studje," *Bamidbar*, 4 June 1946, p. 7.

24 "Tel-Awiw," *Bamidbar*, 4 June 1946, p. 7.

25 Various newspaper reviews, August/September 1946, YV M-1/P-85.

26 "'Der blutiker szpas' fun Sholem Aleychem," *Unzer Welt*, 23 August 1946, YV M-1/P-85.

27 Frank, "Der blutiker szpas," *Unzer Weg*, 16 August 1946.

28 Sender, *To Life*, p. 143.

29 Shamai Davidson, "Encounter," in *Holding on to Humanity – The Message of Holocaust Survivors: The Shamai Davidson Papers*, ed. Israel W. Charny (New York: New York University Press, 1992), p. 213.

30 Neuroscientist Daniel Schacter reports, "Repeated reexperiencing of a traumatic memory in a safe setting can dampen the initial psychological response to trauma." Most effective for the reduction of intrusive memories, flashbacks, and related symptoms of Post-Traumatic Stress Disorder are "imaginal exposure therapies" that repeatedly expose patients to stimuli associated with the trauma, prompting them to recall and reexperience vivid images of the experience. Daniel L. Schacter, *The Seven Sins of Memory: How the Mind Forgets and Remembers* (Boston: Houghton Mifflin, 2001), p. 177.

31 Schacter, *The Seven Sins of Memory*, p. 171.

32 Quoted in Boaz Cohen, "The Children's Voice: Postwar Collection of Testimonies from Child Survivors of the Holocaust," *Holocaust and Genocide Studies* 21 (Spring 2007), p. 86.

33 In 1947 survivors in Lodz, Poland filmed *Undzere Kinder* in which two actors ask Jewish children in an orphanage to dramatize their wartime experiences. The director of the orphanage encourages the actors: "If we don't deal with these memories during the day, they will suffer them at night as terrible nightmares. The only way [to dispel the nightmares], for children as well as adults, is to express their experiences creatively." An actor replies, "That's something we understand. What is the purpose of theatre, if not to provide a release for tragedy in a creative manner?" Recognizing that recreating the experiences of the Holocaust would not be useful without the introduction of new

coping mechanisms, the assistant director of the orphanage points out, "I believe that the greatest healing for our children is to help them understand how Jews finally resisted and fought!" My thanks go to Boaz Cohen for suggesting that I look at this film.

34 Sender, *To Life*, pp. 143–44.
35 Zeev W. Mankowitz reaches a similar conclusion in *Life between Memory and Hope: The Survivors of the Holocaust in Occupied Germany* (Cambridge: Cambridge University Press, 2002), pp. 211–12.
36 A former DP leader reported from New York that the American Jewish community did not want to know about the DPs' sufferings and that the DP film *Lang ist der Weg* had played to empty theaters. Abraham J. Peck, "'Our Eyes Have Seen Eternity'": Memory and Self-Identity Among the She'erith Hapletah," *Modern Judaism* 17 (1997): 70. For more on survivors' decisions to fall silent when they felt Americans were unwilling or unable to listen to them, see Beth B. Cohen, *Case Closed: Holocaust Survivors in Postwar America* (New Brunswick, NJ: Rutgers University Press, 2007), esp. Chapter 8.
37 Tom Segev, *The Seventh Million: The Israelis and the Holocaust* (New York: 1993); Idith Zertal, *Israel's Holocaust and the Politics of Nationhood* (Cambridge: Cambridge University Press, 2005) and *From Catastrophe to Power: Holocaust Survivors and the Emergence of Israel* (Berkeley: University of California Press, 1998); Yosef Grodzinsky, *In the Shadow of the Holocaust* (Monroe, Maine: Common Courage Press, 2004).
38 On the "new history" and its approach to the DPs, see Yechiam Weitz, "Dialectical versus Unequivocal: Israeli Historiography's Treatment of the Yishuv and Zionist Movement Attitudes toward the Holocaust," in *Making Israel*, edited by Benny Morris (Ann Arbor: University of Michigan Press, 2007), pp. 278–98, esp. pp. 286–87 and 293; Derek J. Penslar, *Israel in History: The Jewish State in Comparative Perspective* (London: Routledge, 2007), pp. 37–38.
39 Zertal, *Israel's Holocaust*, pp. 25–44, esp. p. 40.
40 Zertal, *Israel's Holocaust*, p. 40f.
41 Margarete Myers Feinstein, *Holocaust Survivors in Postwar Germany, 1945–1957* (Cambridge: Cambridge University Press, 2010); Hagit Lavsky, *New Beginnings: Holocaust Survivors in Bergen-Belsen and the British Zone in Germany, 1945–1950* (Detroit: Wayne State University Press, 2002); Mankowitz, *Life Between Memory and Hope*; Avinoam J. Patt, *Finding Home and Homeland: Jewish Youth and Zionism in the Aftermath of the Holocaust* (Detroit: Wayne State University Press, 2009).

3

NO SILENCE IN YIDDISH

Popular and scholarly writing about the Holocaust in the early postwar years

Mark L. Smith

The claim that Holocaust survivors were largely silent during the early postwar years neglects the internal culture of the Yiddish-speaking survivors. Debates regarding the emergence of Holocaust awareness in the early postwar period have focused primarily on the broad public sphere of American Jewry, not on the survivors' own cultural context. To the extent that such debates have considered the role of survivors, it has been to assess or explain their relative absence from that sphere.

For the worldwide community of Yiddish-speaking survivors, there was no "silence" and no "myth of silence." As will be seen, Yiddish-speaking survivors exhibited a striving for self-expression that was realized within their own public sphere. Their internal dialogue, conducted almost entirely in Yiddish, has been preserved for examination today in the books and articles they published throughout their postwar dispersion. Evidence of their vigorous "non-silence" is now also provided by recent research in related fields, such as studies of publishing in the Displaced Persons camps,[1] the literature of postwar Poland,[2] and the writings of specific populations such as child survivors.[3]

I propose, however, to explore the internal dialogue of the survivors through the perceptions of their own historians. These historians, whom I describe as the "Yiddish Historians of the Holocaust," were perhaps the most prolific of all survivors. Each of the five historians to be considered here produced an average of one hundred Yiddish works on Holocaust themes, ranging from monographs to single-page essays, many reprinted across decades and continents. Their works appeared in the leading Yiddish publications of Poland, Israel, France, Argentina, and the United States, and, on occasion, Brazil, Canada, and South Africa.[4]

Continuing a prewar tradition of Yiddish scholarship that regarded the educated lay public as both informants and recipients of historical writing, the postwar Yiddish historians created a form of "lay-professional partnership" with their fellow survivors. They assumed the interrelated functions of documenting the popular urge for self-expression, giving exposure to the testaments of those who had perished, supporting commemorative efforts by survivors, incorporating the voices of both survivors and victims into their works, and making available the results of their research to the Yiddish-reading public.[5]

Each of these historians worked within multiple contexts and may be viewed from more than one perspective. Neglected among these perspectives is that of the Yiddish-speaking world, with which they identified most directly. These historians published in many languages and have been viewed by recent scholars as participants in, variously, the continuum of Polish-Jewish historiography,[6] the phenomenon of early postwar Holocaust documentation centers,[7] and the internal conflicts at Yad Vashem.[8]

These historians' Yiddish works are simultaneously participants in, and reflections upon, the internal conversation of Yiddish-speaking survivors. Both have been neglected in studies of Holocaust representation. Today, the works of the Yiddish historians serve as a point of entry into the decidedly verbal, which is to say "non-silent," world of the survivors, and it is my purpose here that the former should illuminate the latter.

No silence in Yiddish

Among the first to recognize the survivors' urge for self-expression was Philip Friedman, the acknowledged leader of the Yiddish historians of the Holocaust. Had Emanuel Ringelblum survived, this role would surely have been his, but when Friedman emerged from hiding in his hometown of Lvov in 1944, he was the senior survivor among the prewar Polish-Jewish historians remaining in Europe. In August of that year he formed the Jewish Historical Commission in Lublin, the temporary capital of postwar Poland. In December, he was invited to direct the Central Jewish Historical Commission (CJHC), where he served until his departure from Poland in June 1946 in response to increasing anti-Semitism and Soviet domination. Following positions in education and research in Munich and Paris, he lived the remainder of his life from 1948 to 1960 in New York, where he lectured in Jewish History at Columbia University and was regarded as one of the pioneers of Holocaust research.

Roads to Extinction, the well-known posthumous collection of Friedman's Holocaust essays, is diminished by the omission of his seminal Yiddish essays of 1948–50 on the writing of Holocaust historiography. These present not only the early maturity of his thinking but also the immediacy of his responses to contemporary events. As early as 1948, in "From Anti-Historicism to Super-Historicism," Friedman describes, as an "elemental spiritual force," the "mighty folk movement by which the folk-instinct seeks to eternalize the most severe catastrophe to befall us in 2,000 years."[9] He refers to the "flood" of publications by ordinary people "who never in their lives dreamed of becoming writers." And the writers whom he counts as "hundreds" in this 1948 essay become "thousands" in his expanded version of 1950. There, Friedman reports the creation of more than 10,000 books and articles on "our recent catastrophe," which he declares "is already a whole literature."[10]

It is also in Friedman's early Yiddish works that the urgency of Holocaust representation, both among historians and the public, is expressed through turns to biblical allusion that are rare in the writings of secular Yiddish scholars. In one of his first public statements as director of the CJHC in 1945, he declares that the obligation of the commission is to realize in the present day the ongoing Jewish commandment, "And you shall tell your son. ... "[11] In the 1950 essay cited above, he extends to the survivors the metaphor of a divine imperative to speak, saying, "All have become prophets, all have encountered God's burning fire and have brought speech to their mute lips."[12]

Three other Yiddish historians were Friedman's principal associates at the CJHC: Yosef Kermish, Nachman Blumental, and Isaiah Trunk.[13] Kermish served as founding director of the CJHC archives; Blumental succeeded Friedman as director of the (renamed) Jewish Historical Institute; and Trunk concentrated on original research. In 1953, Kermish and Blumental were among the initial scholars at Yad Vashem, where Kermish founded and directed the archives, and Blumental was a research associate. Trunk settled in New York and became director of the archives at the Yiddish Scientific Institute (YIVO), succeeding Friedman in 1960 as chair of the YIVO Historians' Circle.[14]

Each of these historians echoes the urgency indicated by Friedman. Kermish argues that "the great cataclysm penetrated deeply into the mood and feeling of our people," and it "impels us to record, to describe, to revivify that which so tragically disappeared."[15] Blumental speaks of returning from his wartime refuge in Russia to his town of Borszczów in Eastern Galicia to find that fewer than 100 of the town's 2,000 Jews had survived. "Day and night we sat together, listening to tales of the last three years. Everyone had an endless story to tell about his personal experiences, and no one ever tired of hearing it." He continues, "we passed from house to house, inquiring into the fate of former residents,"[16] which led to surveys of surrounding towns, and the reader may observe that here commenced Blumental's Holocaust research. Trunk, who avoided self-reference in his writing, places in a footnote to his 1948 study of Jewish labor camps the news that he has already completed a manuscript on "the history of the destruction of the Jewish community of Kutno," his hometown.[17]

The fifth of the Yiddish historians, Mark Dworzecki, was unique among survivors in converting the mission of postwar writing into a second career as a Holocaust historian. He had served as a medical doctor in Vilna before the war, then survived the Vilna Ghetto and seven concentration camps. Within a month of his escape from the Nazis in the spring of 1945, he arrived in Paris and began to publish. In June, he wrote an article entitled, "Remain Silent – or Tell the Whole Truth?" in which he concludes that every detail of the Jewish experience under the Nazis, both uplifting and degrading, must be told.[18] By September, he resolves to dedicate his "second life, the one after the camps, the one that is a gift of fate" to recounting that whole truth.[19] He settled in Israel in 1949, where he lobbied for Holocaust instruction at Israeli universities, and in 1959, was installed in the world's first chair of Holocaust studies at Bar-Ilan University.

Quantitative evidence for the "non-silence" of the Yiddish-speaking survivors and also for the predominance of Yiddish as the survivors' language of internal discourse is found in Friedman's contemporaneous accounts. In mid-1948, Friedman reviewed the publishing activities of the DP camps in the American Zone of Germany, where he served as Educational Director for the Joint Distribution Committee, and indicated that Hebrew was the language of instruction for youth in preparation for life in the Land of Israel but that Yiddish was the language of the adult survivors. Specifically, 68 out of 83 textbooks appeared in Hebrew, while 68 out of 84 newspapers appeared in Yiddish.[20] A decade later, he recounted that the joint Yad Vashem-YIVO Bibliographical Series, which he directed from its formation in 1954 (and to which all of the Yiddish historians contributed), had identified 310 periodicals worldwide as richest in Holocaust materials as of January 1955, and that 170 of these were in Yiddish and 35 in Hebrew.[21]

A specific example of the growth and reception of Holocaust writing in Yiddish is the *Poylishe yidntum* series of books published by the Central Union of Polish Jews in Argentina. The series published 175 titles on predominantly Holocaust themes between 1946 and 1966,[22] including one from each of the Yiddish historians except Dworzecki. The public celebration of the twenty-fifth volume in Buenos Aires in 1947 was greeted in the official Yiddish press in Poland with the statement that the series "has called forth great recognition and very warm appraisals from the whole world of Yiddish culture."[23] In its first four years, 100,000 copies of volumes 1–65 were reported to have been sold.[24] With the publication of volume 75 one year later, the publisher reported 200,000 copies in circulation, and a press run of 2,000 to 5,000 per title. He also singled out Mordecai Strigler, Chaim Grade, and Philip Friedman as examples of authors without whose works the publishing house would have no justifiable existence.[25]

The continuity of Jewish self-expression

The desire for self-expression among those who experienced the Holocaust did not begin with the survivors but with those who lived in the ghettos and camps under Nazi occupation. Friedman notes that for some, "the urge to record for eternal memory was literally as strong as the instinct to save one's life,"[26] to which Kermish added that postwar writing "is no doubt a continuation of that urge to record."[27] The continuity of Jewish expression was at times evoked through the metaphor of the "golden chain" traditionally applied to Yiddish literature. Blumental notes that the "golden chain of Jewish literary creativity was not interrupted in the Lodz Ghetto, even in the worst living conditions,"[28] and Friedman asserts that "to extend further the golden chain, to extend the chain between our past and our new future," was one of the great historic tasks of the CJHC.[29]

Before the extent of literary creativity in the Warsaw Ghetto was revealed through recovery of the first portion of the Ringelblum Archive in September 1946, the CJHC had already retrieved a large number of written materials from the ruins of the Lodz Ghetto. Blumental had personally discovered a Yiddish verse cycle of ironic protest in the debris of the Chelmno extermination camp.[30] He declared that "in no epoch did there arise such a great number of works, and such a great number of writers!"[31] On behalf of the CJHC, Friedman announced in the spring of 1946 that the commission had assembled "hundreds of songs of the ghettos, of partisan life, of the forests, of the camps" and "folk-sayings, folk-stories, fables," as well as sculptural works in all media.[32]

The attempt by captive Jews to record and communicate their struggle was given renewed expression by the Yiddish historians, each of whom responded according to his own experiences and interests. Dworzecki, who had been acquainted in the Vilna Ghetto with Hirsh Glik, the author of the Partisan Hymn (*Partizaner lid*), thereafter prepared a monograph on Glik's life and work.[33] The essay by Dworzecki in appreciation of Yitskhok Katzenelson was inspired by his stay, on his last night in France before leaving for Israel, at the same Hotel Providence in Vittel in which Katzenelson had been interned by the Nazis and had written his well-known "Song of the Slaughtered Jewish People."[34] The recollection by Trunk of the prominent folklorist Shmuel Lehman, and of his efforts in the Warsaw Ghetto to collect songs and stories from arriving refugees, was founded on his prewar acquaintance with Lehman and the support that he and other leading Yiddish intellectuals had given to Lehman's work.[35] In a similarly personal manner, Trunk's eulogy of Shmuel Zygelboym, the leader of the Polish Bund (General Jewish Workers' Union), whose inability to mobilize Allied opposition to the Nazi murder of Polish Jews led to his protest suicide in London in 1943, derived from Trunk's lifelong allegiance to the Bund and his admiration for Zygelboym.[36]

Blumental, who had specialized in Jewish literary history before the war, devoted his postwar Yiddish work primarily to literary expression during the Holocaust. At the early date of 19–20 September 1945, the CJHC held its *second* academic conference in Lodz,[37] and Blumental presented his "Introduction to the History of Literary Creativity in Yiddish at the Time of the German Occupation."[38] He reported that the desire to "eternalize the most frightful act of violence in the world," as well as "to capture the everyday," had inspired Jews of every class and occupation. He discussed the literary salons and theaters of the Warsaw Ghetto and, by contrast, the "return to the Middle Ages" seen in reversion to spoken literature among street singers and news criers.[39]

In their respective works, Blumental and Dworzecki both remarked on the striving by Jews under Nazi occupation for internal communication. Blumental reported on messages of farewell and revenge in the margins of books and on the walls of homes.[40] In "Ghettos and Concentration Camps Seek Contacts," Dworzecki recounts the sending of "news" between concentration camps in the form of names of murdered Jews written on the walls of trains and on shipments of raw lumber. He describes the ghettos as "Jewish islands in a Nazi Ocean" (at the very time of the Berlin Airlift in early 1949, when Berliners saw themselves as "islanders"), and he provides one of the earliest appreciations of the emissaries, mostly women, who risked their lives to smuggle messages and calls to revolt along a network of secret routes in Poland.[41]

The Yiddish historians' recognition of the many forms of "non-silence" among the victims soon led to their shared imperative to publish wartime materials. At first, Friedman proposed a measured pace for the publishing activity of the CJHC, outlining a two-year plan for collecting and publishing at the September 1945 conference. However, the consensus of those assembled was that "it is already high time to display the fruits of our efforts so far" and to publish as quickly as possible.[42] Friedman later ascribed this difference to conflicting academic-versus-propagandistic views between the central and regional historical commissions,[43] but in his final report on the work of the CJHC he concludes, "Seeking out and imparting to our people these creative works is one of the most important tasks" of the CJHC.[44] Under his successor, Blumental, the JHI emphasized that its obligation was not only to preserve materials for use by researchers but also to "make them available for the widest mass readership."[45]

Of first importance was the *Oyneg Shabes* archive, which Ringelblum had intended to publish as soon as possible after the war, and within it, Ringelblum's own *Notes*. Yet the publishing of wartime Yiddish documents in Poland was delayed, in the early years, by a shortage of funds and Yiddish type, and under the Soviet domination that became complete in mid-1949 by the emigration of leading historians and ideological constraints on those who remained. The portions of Ringelblum's *Notes* that did appear in Warsaw in 1952 were criticized by Kermish and Blumental as tendentious selections, edited to advance the communist agenda.[46] As late as 1965, Trunk lamented that "20 years after the death of our historian-martyr, the materials from the Ringelblum Archive lie in the cupboards of the Jewish Historical Institute in Warsaw, and no redeemer for them has yet been found."[47]

The Yiddish historian most dedicated to "redeeming" the materials of Jewish self-expression was Kermish, who specialized in Jewish documentary history before and after the war. Many of his larger works are critical editions in Hebrew or English of materials from the Ringelblum Archive, and his essays are often discussions in Yiddish of those materials. As director of the Yad Vashem archives, Kermish declared in 1954 on the front page of the (Hebrew) *News of Yad Vashem* that it was the institution's "obligation to publish source-materials from the ghetto archives," a position that figured in the internal conflict of 1958–60 between the East European immigrants and established Israelis. His ultimate success may be credited to his long-evity and perseverance (the latter reflected in the decades-long plot lines of his cor-respondence with Trunk in New York).[48] An early project that follows the typical trajectory of his works is "The Testament of the Warsaw Ghetto," in which he analyzes the answers of leading intellectuals to an *Oyneg Shabes* questionnaire on life after two-and-a-half years in the Warsaw Ghetto. His original Yiddish essay of 1951 was excerpted in English in 1951 and 1957 and serialized in Hebrew in 1956–57,[49] but the documents themselves did not appear until 1986 with their inclusion in his English-language anthology of the Warsaw Ghetto, *To Live with Honor, To Die With Honor!*

All of the Yiddish historians participated in advocating or assisting the publication of wartime Jewish writings, and their imperative to publish was based on two perceived obligations. The first, as seen, was to the demand inherent in the victims' writings for public exposure. The second was the obligation to the survivors that they be included in the process of historical assessment.

The lay-professional partnership

As early as 1935, the founding father of Eastern European Jewish historiography, Simon Dubnov, had recognized a distinction in the choice of audience between the scholarly publications of YIVO and the Hebrew University, both founded in 1925. At the conference in Vilna celebrating the tenth anniversary of YIVO, he praised the YIVO scholars for including an educated lay audience among their intended readers, while also praising the University scholars for their more academically oriented work.[50] At the same conference, Friedman spoke of the need to "popularize Jewish history" through publishing "historical books for the people."[51] Friedman's last prewar publication was a review of the collected works of Saul Ginsburg (arguably the first Yiddish historian), in which he notes with approval that "most of the articles combine research based on primary sources with a popular form and a remarkable literary style."[52] After the war, he praises Leo Schwarz, in whose "cabinet" he had served in Munich, for presenting his account of the DP camps, *The Redeemers* (1953), as a "people's book capable of penetrating the masses."[53]

By their choice of publishing venue, all of the Yiddish historians demonstrated their concurrence with Friedman's emphasis on popular scholarship. Each published one or more books in Yiddish for an educated lay audience. They contributed hundreds of articles to the leading Zionist, socialist, Bundist, communist, literary, and general Yiddish journals in the United States and Israel from 1945 to 1988 (usually, but not always, in accordance with their political allegiances).[54] The Yiddish academic journals in which they appeared, the *Bleter far geshikhte* of the JHI in Warsaw and the *YIVO bleter* in New York, also had a largely non-academic circulation.[55]

The Yiddish historians' relationship with their survivor public may be described as a "lay-professional partnership" that developed from their recognition of the survivors' and victims' striving to communicate. They encouraged, promoted, and then drew upon, the survivors' works of self-expression. The historians addressed these works at three levels of survivor authorship – the lay historian, the personal author, and the memorial society. At each level, they found the opportunity to discuss their own particular areas of interest in Holocaust history.

The "lay historians" were the small number of authors who drew on materials from multiple sources to write general accounts of Jewish life under the Nazis in a given town or ghetto, not limited to personal experience. Support was expressed by Friedman for three such works in 1948 in the form of laudatory forewords to books by Joseph Gar and Benjamin Orenstein on Kovne and Czenstochow, respectively, and in his review of Dworzecki's book on the Vilna Ghetto. Friedman, whose chief interest in Holocaust studies was historiography itself, discussed each author's stance and method, and praised Dworzecki's as the outstanding work on Vilna and of its genre (the Hebrew translation of 1950 earned Dworzecki the first Israel Prize in social science).[56] When Dworzecki later transitioned from "lay historian" to academic, he in turn encouraged such works by others. An example is his foreword to Toni Solomon-Ma'aravi's 1968 history of the Holocaust in Romania, in which Dworzecki's interest in passive resistance engendered praise for her depictions of solidarity and mutual aid.[57]

Works by survivors at the personal level of authorship – memoirs, poetry, fiction, and drama – also carried contributions by Yiddish historians. Blumental and Kermish each provided approving forewords to M. Balberyszski's account of the Vilna Ghetto, in which Blumental describes the author's personality, and Kermish focuses on the value of quotations from ghetto documents that were later destroyed.[58] Most prolific was Blumental, who contributed not fewer than ten forewords to works by lay authors, commencing with the first Yiddish book printed in postwar Poland, in 1945,[59] and continuing until at least 1982. In each foreword, he gives further development to the author's treatment of a topic that coincides with his own particular interests, such as the dilemma of choosing whether to flee or stay during the German invasion; the differing experiences of West and East European Jews in occupied Poland; the dangers of life on the "Aryan side"; and the inner life and language of the Warsaw Ghetto.

The largest, and perhaps least known, contribution by the Yiddish historians to the public sphere of the Yiddish-speaking survivors was their work on behalf of the *yizkor* books, the memorial volumes published by representatives of destroyed communities. Their contribution included both recognition and participation. Each of the Yiddish historians published discussions of the *yizkor*-book phenomenon, which was described by Kermish as a "far-reaching folk movement,"[60] by Friedman as a "new distinct genre,"[61] and by Blumental as a "new literary form."[62] Blumental suggests that "if each survivor – except the small number who 'want to forget' – had had the means to do so, he would have published a book" of his own experiences, but lacking the means "he joins as a 'partner' in a *yizkor* book." By the end of the 1950s, Friedman counts 270 such books, with 160 in Yiddish,[63] and Blumental finds 200 in Yiddish and 90 in Hebrew,[64] declaring that he has read them all.[65]

In their reviews of *yizkor* books, the Yiddish historians regard most highly the books with greater concern for historical development, but their own participation in *yizkor* books has received little attention. Kugelmass and Boyarin, for example, note only that some books "contain substantial essays by Jewish academic historians."[66] It is true that a great number of *yizkor* books have been thought by historians, including the Yiddish historians, to provide no more than raw materials for future researchers, but this is due only to the shortage of surviving historians. As Friedman notes, in assessing the tasks of survivor-historians (paraphrasing R. Tarfon), "The day is short, the work is great, and the workers … few."[67] Nevertheless, each of the Yiddish historians did, in fact, contribute articles to *yizkor* books, including a Holocaust history of his own ancestral town or region. There are at least 35 books to which they contributed, several with pieces by more than one Yiddish historian.[68] The respect accorded the historians' contributions is evident from their frequent placement at the start of a book or division.

Not only did the Yiddish historians include their fellow survivors among their intended audience, they also actively sought the participation of survivors in their historical research. When Friedman returned to Lodz in 1945 as director of the CJHC, he posted the notice: "Dr. Philip Friedman has returned. Persons who possess memoirs, documents, photographs, or other materials about the Jewish destruction, are invited to come," followed by his address and hours.[69] In addition to receiving such materials, he and his colleagues at the CJHC also conducted thousands of interviews of survivors. Their research methods continued the prewar YIVO tradition of soliciting documents, memoirs, and answers to questionnaires from the Jewish public.

The Yiddish historians were aware of the difficulties of relying on survivor accounts, however, and they often acknowledged the issues of inaccuracy or exaggeration. Friedman specified that it was the historian's obligation to analyze contradictions in eyewitness accounts and, in one instance, praised the literary historian Shlomo Bikl for doing so as editor of the Kolomey *yizkor* book of 1957.[70] Nevertheless, as early as 1948, Friedman declares, "Apart from official sources (archives) there are – and these are the very most important – living sources, quivering reality with traces of the 'historical process' on their bodies and in their hearts."[71] In Blumental's foreword to the Sarny *yizkor* book, he notes that, because of the destruction of Jewish documents, the book brings forth "a great quantity of facts and information that only those who were there know and remember."[72] A negative example is given by Friedman in the Vitebsk *yizkor* book, in which he discusses the rare problem of writing the Holocaust history of a city for which there was not a single surviving Jewish eyewitness (and only one non-Jewish witness).[73]

The reciprocal aspect of the "lay-professional partnership" is the use by Yiddish historians of survivor accounts in their own works. As director of the CJHC, Friedman was a member of the official Polish investigating commission to visit Auschwitz in 1945. One of the earliest uses of eyewitness testimony was Friedman's incorporation of testimony gathered during this visit into his monographs on Auschwitz.[74] By contrast, an early use of published accounts is Trunk's 1949 essay on the Jewish Councils, in which he cites information on Czenstochow from Orenstein and on Lodz from Israel Tabaksblat.[75] The increasing availability and usefulness of published accounts is seen in Trunk's research notes for his 1972 *Judenrat* (which received the National Book Award). The notes indicate his methodical compilation of materials on various Jewish Councils from a number of memoirs and *yizkor* books.[76]

Dworzecki's first major work, his 1948 *Yerusholayim d'lite*, has itself become one of the most ubiquitously cited sources of historical information on the Vilna Ghetto. His last major work, a history of the Nazi camps in Estonia (for which he received his Ph.D. from the Sorbonne in 1967), is notable for its reliance on 174 eyewitness testimonies and dozens of published accounts by survivors, as well as official German and Russian documents.[77] The works furthest along the spectrum of survivor inclusion are those consisting almost exclusively of survivor accounts. An example is Friedman's first major book in English, *Martyrs and Fighters* (1954), which presents the experience of the Warsaw Ghetto in the form of substantial quotations from survivors' published works.[78]

A concluding example of the "lay-professional partnership" is Blumental's final book, a collection of words and expressions used by Jews under Nazi rule. Blumental relates that he began to gather material immediately upon returning to Poland in 1944 because he "almost could not understand" the Yiddish of the survivors he met, although "every one of them very willingly related [his story], as if to be rid of the heavy load that weighed on him."[79] Blumental drew first on conversations, and then primarily on the published accounts of living and deceased writers to preserve thousands of elements of Jewish speech from the Nazi era. From 1956 to 1963, he serialized the entries for the first seven letters of the alphabet. In his introduction to the series, he explains that the language of the time "provides a key to the folk-spirit. It helps us understand the life of our martyrs. Each expression is saturated with blood. Each word is literally a symbol, an entire world."[80] Blumental's collection became a lifelong project, and he continued to gather material until the completed book was published in 1981.

The engagement of the Yiddish historians with the survivors' and victims' words was not limited to encouraging, publicizing, utilizing, or even expressing empathy. Deeper reading of the historians' works leads to their observations on the emotional involvement of the survivor writers and readers, the separation of the survivor's and historian's voice within their own works, the transformation of historical events into the legends and symbols of national memory, and the popular preference for literary over historical representation of the holocaust. But all of these are topics for further discussion. Their point of departure is that the Yiddish historians recognized the survivors' compelling desire for self-expression and provided works that serve as contemporary witnesses to the "non-silence" of the Yiddish-speaking survivors.

Notes

1 T. Lewinsky, "Dangling Root? Yiddish Language and Culture in the German Diaspora," in A. Patt and M. Berkowitz (eds) *"We Are Here": New Approaches to Jewish Displaced Persons in Postwar Germany*, Detroit: Wayne State University Press, 2010, pp. 308–34.

2 J. Nalewajko-Kulikov, "The Last Yiddish Books Printed in Poland," in E. Grözinger and M. Ruta (eds) *Under the Red Banner: Yiddish Culture in the Communist Countries in the Postwar Era*, Wiesbaden: Harrassowitz, 2008, pp. 111–34.

3 Boaz Cohen, "Representing the Experiences of Children in the Holocaust," in Patt and Berkowitz, pp. 74–97.

4 To conserve space, only first publications are cited here.

5 The present work derives from my forthcoming dissertation, "The Yiddish Historians and the Struggle for a Jewish History of the Holocaust." Major themes include their internal approach to Jewish life under Nazi occupation, the continuity of Jewish and Holocaust history in their work and careers, their attachment to Yiddish, mutual relations, and adumbrations of others' works in their early research agenda.

6 N. Aleksiun, "The Central Jewish Historical Commission in Poland, 1944–47," *Polin* 20, 2007, pp. 74–97.

7 L. Jockusch, "Chroniclers of Catastrophe: History Writing as a Jewish Response to Persecution Before and After the Holocaust," in D. Bankier and D. Michman (eds), *Holocaust Historiography in Context: Emergence, Challenges, Polemics and Achievements*, Jerusalem: Yad Vashem, 2008, pp. 135–66.

8 Boaz Cohen, "Setting the Agenda of Holocaust Research: Discord at Yad Vashem in the 1950s," in Bankier and Michman, pp. 255–92.

9 Friedman, "Fun antihistoritsizm tsum superhistoritsizm," *Kiem*, March 1948, pp. 30–31.

10 Friedman, "Unzer khurbn-literatur," *Idisher kemfer*, 31 March 1950, p. 87.

11 Friedman, "Unzer historishe oyfgabe," *Dos naye lebn*, 10 April 1945, p. 6 (Exodus 13:8).

12 Friedman, "Unzer khurbn-literatur," p. 87.

13 Their biographies, available from multiple sources, are omitted here to conserve space.

14 Not included here are Shatzky, Mahler, and Gelber, who left Europe before the war and did not become Holocaust historians; Mark, Datner, Eisenbach, and Brustin-Berenstein, who remained behind the Iron Curtain and constitute a separate chapter; and Auerbach, a close associate but not, strictly, a historian.

15 Kermish, preface to Kermish, preface to *Ta'aruhat Sifre-Zikaron le-kehilot Yisra'el sheharvu*, Tel Aviv: Agudat shohare YIVO be-Yisra'el u-Muze'on Geniza le'omanut yehudit amamit, 1961, p. 5.

16 Blumental, "Spinka, the Shabbes-Goy," *Yad Vashem Bulletin* 18, April 1966, p. 31.

17 Trunk, "Yidishe arbet-lagern in 'varteland,'" *Bleter far geshikhte* i:1, January-March 1948, p. 116n6; *Sefer Kutnah veha-sevivah*, Tel Aviv: Irgun yotse Kutnah, 1968, pp. 340–53, 243–45.

18 Dworzecki, "Farshvaygn – oder dertseyln dem gantsn emes?" *Undzer vort*, 22 June 1945, p. 3.

19 Dworzecki, "Oyf fir vegn veln mir fanandergeyn," *Undzer vort*, 21 September 1945, p. 2.

20 Friedman, "Dos gedrukte yidishe vort bay der sheyris ha-pleyte in daytshland," *Di tsukunft*, March 1949, p. 153.

21 Friedman, "A fertl-yorhundert 'khurbn-literatur,'" *Di tsukunft*, September 1959, p. 358. Extracting statistics from the 14 language-specific volumes is frustrated by their coverage of disparate periods and publication types.

22 158 distinct titles, including 17 double or triple volumes.

23 Anon. [B. Mark, ed.], "25 bikher 'dos poylishe yidntum,'" *Dos naye lebn*, 14 December 1947, p. 4.

24 *American Jewish Yearbook 1951*, p. 221.

25 A. Mitelberg, "Bikher-monument," *Oyfn shvel*, January 1952, p. 15.

26 Friedman, "Unzer khurbn-literatur," p. 87.

27 Kermish, *Ta'aruhat*, p. 5.

28 Blumental, foreword to Sh. Shayevitsh, *Lekh-lekha*, Lodz: CJHC, 1946, p. 12.

29 Friedman, "Unzer historishe oyfgabe," p. 6.

30 Blumental, "Vegn a literarisher shafung beys der daytsher okupatsye," *Kiem*, February 1948, pp. 45–49.

31 Blumental, "Yidishe literatur unter der daytsher okupatsye," *Dos naye lebn*, 14 September 1945, p. 5.

32 Friedman, "Di yidishe historishe komisye in poyln," *Aynikayt*, June 1946, p. 11.

33 Dworzecki, *Hirshke glik: der mekhaber fun partizaner-himn*, Paris: Unzer kiem, 1966.

34 Dworzecki, "Dort vu s'iz geshribn gevorn 'dos lid fun oysgehargetn yidishn folk,'" *Ilustrirte literarishe bleter*, September 1953, pp. 3, 12, 16.

35 Trunk, "Shmuel lehman, z'l," *Lebns-fragn* 10, February 1952, p. 6.

36 Trunk, *Geshtaltn un gesheyenishn*, Buenos Aires: Tsentral-farband, 1962, pp. 51–55.

37 The first, August 12, 1945, was devoted primarily to the work of the regional commissions.

38 A. Shedletsky, "Tsveyte visnshaftlekhe baratung," *Dos naye lebn*, 13 October 1945, p. 5.

39 Blumental, "Di yidishe literatur unter der daytshisher okupatsye," *Yidishe kultur* 8:1, January 1946, p. 10.

40 Blumental, "Oyfshriftn oyf vent, ksovim un bikher," *Lebns-fragn* 145/146, January/February 1964, pp. 10, 7.

41 Dworzecki, "Getos un kontsentratsye-lagern zukhn kontaktn," *Kiem*, April 1949, p. 899.

42 Shedletsky, "Tsveyte," p. 5.

43 Friedman, "The European Jewish Research on the Recent Jewish Catastrophe in 1939–45," *Proceedings of the American Academy for Jewish Research* 18, 1948–49, p. 197.

44 Friedman, "Di yidishe historishe komisye," p. 21.

45 *Prospekt fun oysgabn fun der tsentraler yidisher historisher komisye in poyln*, Warsaw-Lodz-Krakow, 1947, p. 7.

46 Kermish, "In Varshever Geto," *YIVO bleter* XXXVII, 1953, pp. 282–96; Blumental, "Di yerushe fun emanuel ringelblum," *Di goldene keyt* 15, 1953, pp. 235–42.

47 Trunk, "Emanuel ringelblum – der historiker 1900–1944," *Di tsukunft*, April 1965, p. 161.

48 YIVO archive, RG483, F29.

49 Kermish, "Di tsavoe fun varshever geto," *Di goldene keyt* 9, 1951, pp. 134–62.

50 Sh. Dubnov, "Der itstiker tsushtand fun der yidisher historiografye" in N. Maisel (ed.), *Tsum hundertstn geboyrntog fun shimen dubnov*, New York: YKUF, 1961, pp. 73–75.

51 Friedman, "Di oyfgabes fun undzer historisher visnshaft un vi azoy zey tsu realizirn," *YIVO bleter* XIII:3–4, 1938, p. 310.

52 Friedman, review of Ginsburg's *Historishe verk*, *Jewish Social Studies* iii:1, 1941, p. 95.

53 Friedman, "Di sheyris hapleyte un yisker-literatur," *Di tsukunft*, April 1956, p. 168.

54 All were anti- or non-communist.

55 The *Argentiner iwo-schriftn* published exclusively Argentine Jewish history.

56 Friedman, review of *Yerusholayim d'lite in kamf un unkum*, *Kiem*, June 1948, 406–7.

57 Dworzecki, foreword to Toni Solomon-Ma'aravi, *Teg fun tsorn*, Tel-Aviv: Hamenora, 1968, p. 9.

58 Blumental and Kermish, forewords to M. Balberyszski, *Shtarker fun ayz*, Tel-Aviv: Hamenora, 1967, pp. 12–19.

59 Blumental, foreword to Mendl Man, *Di shtilkeyt mont*, Lodz: Borokhov-farlag, 1945, pp. 3–4.

60 Kermish, *Ta'aruhat*, p. 5.

61 Friedman, "Khurbn hosht," *Kultur un dertsiung*, October 1958, p. 19.

62 Blumental, "A nayer literarisher min – yisker-bikher," *Lebns-fragn* 99, January 1960, p. 7.

63 Friedman, "A fertl-yorhundert," p. 361.

64 Blumental, "A nayer literarisher min," p. 7.

65 Blumental, "Pro domo sua," *Lebns-fragn* 110, December 1960, p. 7.

66 J. Kugelmass and J. Boyarin, *From a Ruined Garden*, Bloomington: Indiana University Press, 1998, p. 40.

67 Friedman, "Fun antihistoritsizm," p. 32 (ellipsis his).

68 Articles by deceased historians were also often included, including Balaban, Shiper, and Ringelblum.

69 R. Oyerbakh, "D"r filip fridman z"l (dermonung un gezegenung)," *Di goldene keyt* 38 (1960), 178.

70 Friedman, "Kolomey – di hoyptshtot fun pokutye un ire yidn," *Di tsukunft*, September 1958, p. 355.

71 Friedman, "Di forshung fun unzer khurbn," *Kiem*, January 1948, p. 49.

72 Blumental, preface to *Sefer yizkor le-kehilat Sarny*, Jerusalem: Yad Vashem, 1961, p. 11.

73 Friedman, "Umkum fun vitebsker yidn," *Vitebsk amol*, New York, 1956, pp. 603–26.

74 Friedman, *This Was Oswiecim*, London: United Jewish Relief Appeal, 1946; *Oshventsim*, Buenos Aires: Tsentral-farband, 1950.

75 Trunk, "Sotsyale antagonizmen in geto un di rol fun di yudenratn," *Yidishe shriftn*, June 1949, p. 6.

76 YIVO archive, RG483, F54.

77 Dworzecki, *Vayse nekht un shvartse teg*, Tel-Aviv: Y.L. Perets, 1970.

78 The largest number are quoted from Yiddish texts.

79 Blumental, *Verter un vertlekh fun der khurbn-tkufe*, Tel-Aviv: Y.L. Perets, 1981, p. 7.

80 Blumental, "Verter un vertlekh fun der khurbn-tkufe," *Yidishe shprakh*, January-March 1956, pp. 25–26.

4

BREAKING THE SILENCE

The Centre de Documentation Juive Contemporaine in Paris and the writing of Holocaust history in liberated France

Laura Jockusch

In October 1944, Jean-Paul Sartre penned a sociological and historical analysis of French anti-Semitism. Published in excerpts on the pages of *Les Temps Modernes* in 1945 and in its entirety in the following year, *Réflexions sur la question juive*[1] displeased both Jewish and non-Jewish readers alike: the non-Jews for being taken to task for their anti-Jewish sentiments, the Jews for Sartre's ignorance of their history and culture.[2] The essay reflected Sartre's dismay that just weeks after the liberation non-Jewish Frenchmen not only continued their prewar animosities towards their Jewish compatriots but responded with silence to the tragic cataclysm that the Jews had suffered during the war.

> Today those Jews whom the Germans did not deport or murder are coming back to their homes. [...] Now all France rejoices and fraternizes in the streets; social conflict seems temporarily forgotten; the newspapers devote whole columns to stories of prisoners of war and deportees. Do we say anything about Jews? Do we give a thought to those who died in the gas chambers at Lublin? Not a word. Not a line in the newspapers.

This was all the more discomforting for Sartre, because Jews had made a fundamental contribution to France's liberation since "[m]any were among the first members of the Resistance" or "had sons or cousins in Leclerc's army." Sartre summarized common justifications for the silence over the Jewish fate, such as the wish not to stir up anti-Semitism or to destroy the national unity urgently needed after a devastating war.

> Well-meaning journalists will tell you: "In the interest of the Jews themselves, it would not do to talk too much about them just now." For years French society has lived without them; it is just as well not to emphasize too vigorously the fact that they have reappeared.

While Sartre held non-Jews responsible for the absence of public discourse on the distinct Jewish victimhood, he believed however that some Jews approved and hence vanished from the public arena, reckoning "'[t]he less we are noticed, the better.'" He argued that they had arrived at this "resigned wisdom, at this policy of self-effacement," after years of exposure "in their own country" to their gentile compatriots' "hostility, ugly looks always watching, indifference always ready to turn into bitterness". Consequently, Sartre noted, Jews "made a clandestine return, and their joy at being liberated is not part of the nation's joy."[3]

The problematic nature of the essay's analysis of French anti-Semitism and its suggested solutions notwithstanding, Sartre's post-liberation observations on the "strange silence" with which the French public encountered recent Jewish suffering correspond with the findings of historical research that was undertaken decades later. Historians of postwar France have demonstrated that up until the 1970s and 1980s the nation's non-Jewish citizens maintained a celebratory self-perception, according to which Vichy had been a temporary aberration of France's republican traditions, forcibly imposed by German invaders and revoked through the population's collective engagement with the Résistance in an act of national self-liberation. Obscuring the inconvenient truth of Vichy's shared responsibility for the Holocaust in France, this vision of the past left little to no room for the voices of the Jewish victims.[4] In turn, historians of the French Jewish community emphasized that in the early postwar years Jews eagerly merged with their non-Jewish environment, be it in fear of anti-Semitism or as a continuation of prewar patterns of secularization and acculturation. While some segments of the community strengthened their ethnic and religious Jewish identities, the majority maintained a low public profile as Jews and kept their stories of racial persecution to their own circles.[5] Recent research has stressed that Jews had not been silent about their pasts to begin with, rather that in searching for "normalization" and the return of rights, jobs, apartments, and property, they adjusted to their non-Jewish compatriots' silence and unwillingness to listen to stories of distinct Jewish victimhood.[6]

This essay seeks to shed further light on how French Jews dealt with their past in the first postwar decade. Using new source material, it explores the history of the Centre de Documentation Juive Contemporaine (CDJC) in Paris, a Jewish documentation center founded by Holocaust survivors to bring the Holocaust—or rather *le cataclysme* or *der khurbn* to use the language of the day—to public consciousness, commemorate its victims and reintegrate Jews into their French surroundings.[7]

Preparing the ground: the Jewish Documentation Center from clandestine to public institution

The project to capture the Jewish tragedy in France by collecting documentary evidence began sixteen months before the liberation. In late April 1943, under the impression of the German defeat at Stalingrad and in anticipation of the war's end, the Russian-born Jewish entrepreneur Isaac Schneersohn gathered 40 representatives of various official and underground Jewish organizations representing both French-born and immigrant Jews in his apartment in Grenoble, then under Italian occupation. The group included prominent religious and communal leaders: René Hirschler, formerly chief rabbi of Strasbourg, then chief chaplain to Jews in internment camps in the south of France; Léon Meiss, future vice-president of the Consistoire Central, and André Weill, its treasurer; Raul-Raymond Lambert, secretary general in the Southern Zone of the Union Général des Israélites de France (UGIF)—the central Jewish body created by the Vichy authorities—and André Baur, vice-president of that body in the Northern Zone; Léo Glaeser, Ruven Grinberg, and Nahum Herman of the immigrant organization Fédération des Sociétés Juives de France (FSJF); and the Alsatian-born Zionist writer Henri Hertz, among others. The Jewish documentation center to be founded would gather a great variety of documents attesting to crimes that the German occupiers and Vichy committed against the Jews of France and its North African colonies. This material, Schneersohn hoped, would help to prepare the postwar reconstruction of the Jewish community, facilitate the return to civic equality and lay the foundation for material compensation and legal redress after the war.[8] The group developed a multifaceted program to collect materials on anti-Jewish legislation, measures of economic deprivation, anti-Semitic propaganda and public opinion about Jews, Jewish responses to persecution, as well as Jewish contributions to fighting the enemy. However, once German forces occupied all parts of the Southern Zone in November 1943, the activists' energies were primarily consumed by their struggle for survival.[9] While six of the founding members were murdered, most of the remaining activists survived in hiding in the countryside in the south. The actual documentation work could only begin after the liberation, when Schneersohn and his surviving collaborators reunited and established the documentation center as *Centre de Documentation Juive Contemporaine* in Paris in December 1944.

Most of the 30–50 coworkers of the documentation center were lawyers, journalists, and writers untrained in the historical profession. Most of the initiators and staff of the CDJC, most prominently its director Isaac Schneersohn, and Léon Poliakov, its research director, as well as coworkers Wladimir and Eugène Schah, Ruben Grinberg, Jacques Szeftel, David Knout, Don Aminado, Jacques Ratner, Léon Czertok, Joseph Billig, and Marcel Livian among others, were Jews of east European origin who had come to France before or after the First World War. For the most part they had received academic training at French universities and engaged in the social, political, cultural and philanthropic networks of Jewish immigrants, mainly in the FSJF but also in the immigrant aid agency HICEM, the vocational training association ORT, and the child welfare organization OSE. By the time of the German occupation, they had undergone a process of integration into French society, had fully adopted the French vernacular and had become French citizens. Their traumatic experiences in the war years had not shattered their belief in the French model of emancipation, nor had it undermined their conviction that their future was in France. They collaborated closely with a number of prominent individuals from established French-Jewish families affiliated with the central institutions of French Jewry, among them Léon Meiss, Pierre Paraf, Maurice Moch, Gaston Kahn, and Henri Hertz. Together they concentrated on collecting documentation from government agencies and Jewish organizations and began to prepare monographs on the cataclysm of French Jewry which had cost the lives of approximately 80,000 French Jews, one-fourth of the prewar community.[10]

The 200,000–250,000 Jews in liberated France received conflicting messages from government and society as they struggled to rebuild their communities and reclaim civic rights, property, and jobs.[11] The provisional French government, eager to correct the wrongs of the recent past, revoked Vichy's racial legislation as early as August 1944 and three months later passed legislation for the return of despoiled property. Nonetheless Jews faced anti-Semitism on a daily basis, and when it came to the distribution of jobs and apartments, victims of racial persecution had to stand in line behind Résistance fighters and released political prisoners, who had a much stronger public presence than the Jewish deportees, barely 3 percent of whom had returned. Apart from the difficulties of coping with the physical, material, and psychological repercussions of persecution, Jews had to come to terms with the profound shock that the society with whose egalitarian and democratic ideals they identified had generated an authoritarian regime which in collaboration with the Germans had participated in the disfranchisement, expropriation, internment, deportation, and mass murder of French Jews. Despite this betrayal of republican principles, however, the fact that 75 percent of the French Jewish community had survived the war showed that the anti-Jewish policies of the Nazi and the Vichy regimes had not found the broad support of the French population. The Fourth Republic's resumption of prewar democratic traditions suggested that Vichy had merely been a historical error caused by a minority of collaborators and that France was now returning France to its true, republican path.[12] The CDJC activists saw their contribution to this process as bringing the cataclysm of French Jews under the Germans and Vichy to public consciousness.

Balancing the particular and the universal: documenting, writing and remembering Jewish suffering in liberated France

Schneersohn and his coworkers were drawn into action because they clearly sensed that the society into which they sought to reintegrate was reluctant either to acknowledge that Jews had suffered particular injustices and horrors or to admit its share of responsibility. Six months after the liberation the CDJC activists realized they would have to break the "blockade of silence"[13] over Jewish suffering which they attributed to suppressed shame and guilt on the part of their non-Jewish compatriots. "France knows what it did to the Jews and to what extent the French administration was tied to the persecution, for that reason the Jewish question in France is regarded as a shameful disease," claimed CDJC coworker Jacques Ratner at an internal meeting in February 1945. "France must purify itself," he further noted. "There is no need for false shame, we simply have to admit that the French administration consciously did wrong. to the Jews." By gathering and disseminating documentary evidence of these wrongs, the CDJC would assist Charles de Gaulle's government in its "work of purification" of French society and in bringing the "criminals of Vichy to justice," and do a service to "both the Jews and France."[14]

Yet despite this belief in the ultimate benefit of the documentation work, internal debates among the coworkers suggest their apprehensions: how could they tell a story of distinct Jewish suffering, yet acclaim a civic equality that did not discriminate according to religious or ethnic bonds; how could they criticize France without jeopardizing their fragile reintegration into French society? The CDJC activists deployed a four-pronged strategy to meet these challenges.

First, the CDJC activists generally restricted their criticism of France to internal debates and took moderate and reconciliatory positions in public. They focused on the deeds of the Germans and on a minority of French collaborationists without collectively accusing the French; indeed they emphasized that large segments of the population had helped the Jews to survive the occupation.[15] For example, in February 1945, when CDJC activists met to discuss how to write about French anti-Semitism, they agreed that anti-Semitism had been a central component of France's past and present. Some advocated relentless confrontation with France's anti-Semitic traditions in order to demonstrate that historically-rooted French anti-Semitism had enabled the German occupiers to carry out their anti-Jewish polities.[16] Others warned, however, that such direct confrontation might nurture the prevailing anti-Semitic climate rather than combating it.[17] Against this latter position, one of the CDJC affiliates objected: "It is not only the right but also the duty of the Jews to expose what non-Jewish Frenchmen said or wrote against us, in order to show what level of moral decadence those who follow the enemy can reach."[18] The CDJC activists ultimately agreed that they would openly criticize anti-Semitism; yet rather than exposing its historical roots, they emphasized the German influence on French public opinion during the occupation. After all, Schneersohn reminded his colleagues: "We do not want to accuse the French people [...] our mission is to settle a score with Vichy and the Germans."[19]

Second, the CDJC based its inquiries into the recent past on its collections of solid documentary evidence, including materials left behind in France by the Gestapo, the SS, the general staff of the German Military command and the German foreign office in Paris, as well as records of the Commissariat Général aux Questions Juives and holdings of various French Jewish organizations.[20] The Center thus viewed it as a sign of official recognition by the French government when its delegation at the International Military Tribunal in Nuremberg utilized its archives during the trial against the major war criminals of the Nazi regime from November 1945 to October 1946. In return, the CDJC coworkers Léon Poliakov and Joseph Billig gained access to the tribunal's own archives and were able to acquire more than three tons of copied documents for the Center.[21] To make these sources accessible to the wider public in France, beginning in March 1945 the CDJC launched a comprehensive publication program of annotated documents[22] and carefully researched studies covering anti-Jewish legislation under the Vichy regime and the Third Reich,[23] internment and deportation,[24] propaganda and French public opinion on the Jews,[25] the responses of French Jews to the persecution, and Nazi ideology more generally.[26] With the generous support of American Jewish organizations, most notably the American Jewish Joint Distribution Committee (AJDC), the CDJC published twenty works in the first five years after the war, along with the monthly *Bulletin du Centre de Documentation Juive Contemporaine*, which began to appear in April 1945 and a year later continued as *Le Monde Juif.* Since the CDJC's intended audience was primarily non-Jews, in particular France's political and intellectual circles, the publications were exclusively in French.[27]

The Center's third strategy focused on the contributions Jews had made to the liberation of France. In a society which celebrated the Résistance and honored victims of political persecution while largely excluding those who had been persecuted because of their Jewish origin, addressing the participation of both French-born and foreign Jews in fighting the Germans provided a niche for integrating the Jews into the public discourse on the recent war.[28] Moreover it countered the widespread image of passive Jewish victimhood and showed that Jews' contribution to liberating France from Vichy and the Germans merited their inclusion into postwar society. By presenting a positive and unified picture of the Jewish community under the occupation, a picture that emphasized communal solidarity but ignored internal conflicts that divided the Jewish population in the face of persecution, the CDJC's works presented a multifaceted image of the armed and unarmed, collective and individual resistance of Jews.[29] At the same time, in its public self-representation, the Center propagated its work of documenting the Holocaust as a contribution to the Résistance, describing its Grenoble activists as *"maquis documentaires."*[30]

A fourth strategy to bring the Jewish cataclysm into public consciousness was linking the documentation center with a public memorial site. In fall 1950, Isaac Schneersohn developed the idea of a memorial, consisting of a crypt housing ashes from the extermination camps and a memorial book with the names of the victims. Initially, Schneersohn's idea met with skepticism from some coworkers who feared that the use of ashes and their transport from Poland to France conflicted with the traditions of Judaism and would be seen as disrespecting the dead. Others demanded that a central memorial be located in Israel, not France. The argument that French Jews needed a centralized and representative memorial site in their country, bolstered by the potential that a memorial in the heart of Paris might have for integrating the survivors into their surrounding society, ultimately won the Center activists for Schneersohn's project.[31] A prominent location for the memorialization of the Jewish cataclysm was assured when the municipality of Paris made available a site in the fourth *arrondissement* near the Hôtel de Ville. The *Tombeau du Martyr Juif Inconnu*, as the memorial was officially named in 1951, would serve as a Jewish equivalent to the *Arc de Triomphe* and translate the European tradition of the grave of the unknown soldier into a Jewish context.[32] In order to avoid the impression that the memorial was "sectarian," the CDJC emphasized that the public commemoration of the distinct Jewish suffering also served the transmission of universal lessons. In the context of growing Cold War antagonisms, the CDJC stressed that commemoration of the Holocaust played a crucial role in the fight for "western values" and against anti-Semitism, racism, dictatorship, and totalitarianism.[33] The CDJC activists also stressed that France, not Israel or eastern Europe, was the obvious location for the memorial because to them this country, more than others, represented humanitarian and democratic ideals.[34] Not least, it had to be located in Paris because the CDJC activists deemed that city "the spiritual capital of the civilization of the free world,"[35] where the "Emancipation of the Jews had been announced and where once again [...] light had triumphed over the shadows of Barbarianism."[36]

Despite its initial rejection by the French Jewish community, the memorial opened its doors in October 1956, thanks to donations from across Europe and the U.S. and with the help of the French government and the Conference on Material Claims against Germany.[37] As indicated by its name–*Tombeau du Martyr Juif Inconnu*–the memorial sent out the message that the Jewish tragedy meant not only that Jews were the "first victims" of the Nazi genocide which ultimately targeted all humanity, but also that the Jewish victims were in fact "martyrs" in a universal fight for a liberal and democratic anti-totalitarian system. By emphasizing these universal lessons of the Jewish tragedy and by choosing a secular republican memory cult that stood in the tradition of the grave of the unknown soldier, the CDJC sought to integrate the memory of the Holocaust into the topography of the French memory of the Second World War.

Joining forces: the CDJC in the context of other Jewish documentation projects in Europe

The phenomenon of Jewish Holocaust documentation and research was not specific to France. Similar initiatives arose in over a dozen European countries in the immediate aftermath of the war or even before it came to an end.[38] Prominent examples included the Central Jewish Historical Commission in Lodz, which had its origins in Lublin in August 1944, and the Jewish historical commissions founded by survivors in the Jewish Displaced Persons (DP) camps of Germany, Austria, and Italy in the years 1945–47.[39] Despite the differences in their goals and the circumstances under which they worked, these projects shared a number of common characteristics. In all countries, they manifested as bottom-up initiatives by civilians without the backing of a government. With few exceptions, those who provided the impetus to document the recent catastrophe were Jews of eastern European, particularly Polish origin, men as well as women, from various social and educational backgrounds and diverse wartime experiences. Some of the activists—for example, Philip Friedman and Joseph Kermisz—had been professional historians before the war; others, such as Léon Poliakov and Joseph Wulf, made careers as historians following their engagement in Holocaust documentation. However, the vast majority of the estimated 1,000–2,000 individuals who constituted the core of activists in the first years after the war, were untrained in the historical profession, but deemed chronicling the cataclysm a moral imperative and a "holy duty" towards the dead and the generations to come. This urge to document the catastrophe was the result of a rationalization process in which the survivors worked through their traumatic experiences; they had not survived by accident, but rather in order to fulfill a duty to expose the historical truth of the German atrocities against the Jews of Europe. The activists also regarded documentation as a way of mourning and commemorating the dead, and the act of collecting and recording in itself assumed the function of a symbolic gravestone or memorial for millions of victims who had received no proper burial. Not least, the activists chose to dedicate their lives to the meticulous and painful reconstruction of the tragic events because they believed that it was an indispensable tool for rebuilding their lives: it helped them to fulfill their moral obligations towards the dead and the generations to come; the historical truth exposed was the most powerful charge that the survivors could bring against the perpetrators and the most poignant appeal to the "conscience of the world." Moreover, the data collected could serve as evidence in war crime trials and claims for compensation.

The activists in the respective countries were well aware that the sheer magnitude and Europe-wide scope of the Holocaust necessitated that the respective Jewish documentation initiatives collaborate across national borders. For that purpose, the CDJC hosted the first European conference of Jewish historical commissions and documentation centers in Paris in 1947.[40] From November 30, a day after the U.N. decision to establish a Jewish and a Palestinian state, through December 9, 32 delegates representing Jewish historical commissions, documentation centers, and communal organizations in 13 countries discussed their documentation work. Delegates included: Dr. Joseph Kermisz, vice-director of the Jewish Historical Institute in Warsaw (which had replaced the Central Jewish Historical Commission in Lodz a few weeks earlier); Simon Wiesenthal and Tuvia Frydman, the directors of the Jewish historical documentation centers in Linz and Vienna; Dr. Nella Rost, the head of the Jewish historical commission in Stockholm; Dr. Alfred Wiener, director of the Central Jewish Information Office (Wiener Library) in London; Moses Joseph Feigenbaum, the secretary of the Central Historical Commission in Munich; Michał Borwicz and Joseph Wulf, the heads of the Centre d'Études d'Histoire des Juifs Polonais in Paris; Dr. Philip Friedman, former director of the Central Jewish Historical Commission in Lodz and currently the director of the AJDC's education and culture department in the U.S. Zone of Germany; Massimo-Adolpho Vitale, the director of the Center for Research on Jewish Deportees in Rome; Fred Herz of the Office of the Chief of Counsel for War Crimes of the American National Military Tribunal at Nuremberg; delegates of Jewish communities and research institutes in Algeria, Bulgaria, Greece, Romania, Switzerland, as well as representatives of the Jewish Agency and the American Jewish Committee. The conference met in the Salle des Centraux, a city mansion in the eighth arrondissement near the Elysée Palace and foreign embassies— ironically the same venue where two years earlier Jean-Paul Sartre had given his public lecture "L'existentialisme est un humanisme." Participants hoped that the conference would result in standardizing research methods, coordinating the exchange of documentation, and organizing a central Holocaust archive in Europe. Some also expected to pave the way for comparative historical studies which would illustrate the European dimension of the Jewish cataclysm.

After singing both Hatikva and the Marseillaise and paying tribute to the dead in a memorial service, the conference began in a sense of unity among the delegates based on their shared experiences of persecution and survival and their common goal of documenting the catastrophe. Yet it became increasingly clear that they were divided on various issues and found themselves in a pecking order over who was entitled to leadership over the "community of victims" and its documentation. The French hosts claimed leadership, arguing that their country represented democratic values and human rights and was the political center of a Europe freed from Nazism. The Polish delegates, by contrast, made their claim for leadership on the basis of the numerical strength and cultural significance of the prewar Jewish community and the fact that Polish Jewry had suffered much higher numbers of victims than had other Jewish communities in Europe. While the French acknowledged that Jews in some countries had been hit harder than others, the conference's overall agenda remained focused on France. Almost half of the delegates represented French Jewish institutions, and their wartime experiences received disproportionate coverage.[41] This discrepancy caused a rift between the delegates, with the Polish guests feeling particularly under-represented.

Conflicts also revolved around the methodology and language of Holocaust documentation. Whether researchers should rely more on victim or perpetrator sources remained a matter of debate, although there was a general consensus that Nazi sources were unreliable because they did not adequately reflect, indeed they purposefully distorted, the experience of the victims. Some demanded that Yiddish—as the language formerly spoken by most of the victims—rather than Hebrew, French, or English, be the primary language of research on the catastrophe.[42] Another deep divide among delegates was the question whether the ultimate goal of Holocaust documentation should be historical scholarship or political struggle. Most delegates were not interested in historiography per se. For them, the purpose of documentation was to fulfill the present and future political needs of the survivors, namely, to fight for justice and restitution, and against anti-Semitism.[43] A number of delegates, however, strictly opposed the mixing of scholarship and politics, arguing that any political use of the material could only discredit the documentation efforts of survivors.[44]

Another divisive issue was the overall ideological positioning of delegates on the future of the Jews, namely whether it should be in the Diaspora or in Israel. The French delegates expressed their deep sympathy for the Jewish state in the making, but they did not question that their future was in France: the most suitable place to document, research, and commemorate the catastrophe. Not only was France the center of the "free world," but it also embodied a new world order of tolerance, democracy, and anti-totalitarianism. Thus the French hosts proposed the building of a World Documentation Center in Paris, analogous to Yad Vashem in Jerusalem but with a special focus on the Diaspora.[45] Many non-French delegates subscribed to the idea of concentrating the documentary evidence in a centralized European institution, but they were divided whether it should be located in Paris or elsewhere in Europe.[46] Some of the eastern European delegates who were optimistic regarding the future of their communities under the new communist regimes suggested the creation of a central memorial and research institution in Poland, where most of the victims of the Holocaust had been murdered.[47] Yet others warned that current manifestations of anti-Semitism in Poland would jeopardize such a project and its holdings. These opponents included delegates from the Jewish DP camps in Germany and Austria, most of whom were Polish Jews who had left Poland because they had concluded that there was no future for Jews in that country. For them, a sovereign Jewish state would be the most appropriate place for a central Jewish memorial and research institute; hence materials should be transferred from Europe to Yad Vashem.[48] Other delegates advised that multiple copies of the documentation should be stored in different places, preferably in Jerusalem, New York, and Paris, to protect the material from destruction.[49]

Despite these disagreements, the conference established a Paris-based European Coordination Committee to coordinate the documentation work.[50] Due to a chronic lack of funds and growing Cold War antagonisms that rendered cooperation between the documentation centers in east and west increasingly difficult, the Committee ultimately proved ineffective. With the dissolution of the Jewish historical commissions in the DP camps, the closing of the Jewish Historical Institute behind the "Iron Curtain," and the further migration of many activists, the CDJC, along with the Wiener Library in London, emerged as a central Jewish Holocaust research institution in western Europe, becoming the Diasporic counterweight to Yad Vashem.

Conclusion

The history of the CDJC demonstrates that some survivors in postwar France made a conscious effort to resist the silence with which their non-Jewish compatriots encountered the Jewish tragedy: Jews trying to rebuild their lives in liberated France should not acquiesce in that silence. The CDJC's documentation work stemmed from a genuine wish to reintegrate into a nation where they felt they belonged. By uncovering the crimes and injustices committed against the Jews, they sought to bring the Holocaust into public consciousness and to show that Jews in France—both French and foreign-born—had deep connections with France and French culture, had made a significant contribution to the liberation of France, and deserved to be fully recognized and accepted as equal citizens. Or, to echo Sartre's words, the CDJC activists sought to prove that their joy of being liberated was indeed also the nation's joy.

The Vichy years had not destroyed the activist's commitment to France's republican ideals, or they had remained what Pierre Birnbaum called "fous de la République,"[51] even after the war. It is not accidental that Jews of immigrant backgrounds spear-headed the initiative. Not only did they come from a cultural milieu of communal activism and self-help which might have led them to establish the documentation center as grassroots effort to serve rebuilding of the Jewish community after the war. More so, Jews of immigrant backgrounds—who had been particularly vulnerable during the war and made up two-thirds of the Jews deported from France—knew particularly well that civic equality and rule of law were precious goods that needed to be cherished and fought for since they were not to be taken for granted. Through documenting the wrongs they suffered they sought to strengthen the republican France which they had known before the war and which they had never ceased to see as the true, the actual France in spite of their traumatic experiences.

Certainly, in the immediate wake of the war, the CDJC did not elicit the large-scale attention and following which it had actually hoped to attract from both Jews and non-Jews. It would take decades until the French Jewish community grew more self-confident and rendered writing and commemorating the Holocaust in France a major public communal endeavor. This occurred in a non-Jewish environment that had become ready to question crude narratives of collective resistance and self-liberation. It should not be underestimated in the light of later activities that survivors in the immediate wake of the war laid the groundwork for writing and commemorating the history of the Holocaust in France and that French Jews had never been utterly silent about their past.

Notes

1 Jean-Paul Sartre, *Anti-Semite and Jew: An Exploration of the Etiology of Hate*, preface by Michael Walzer (New York: Schocken Books 1995).
2 Thus Sartre asserted that Diaspora Jews had no history, culture or achievements of their own but were condemned to passivity and suffering. To Sartre the problem of anti-Semitism would ultimately be solved if Jews vanished as a collective in a society liberated from the existence of classes and religious or racial groups.
3 Ibid., 71–72.
4 See for example Eric Conan and Henry Rousso, *Vichy: An Ever-Present Past* (Hanover and London: University Press of New England, 1998); Richard J. Goslan, "The Legacy of World War II in France: Mapping the Discourses of Memory," in Richard Ned Lebow et al., eds., *The Politics of Memory in Postwar Europe* (Durham, London 2006), 72–101; Julian Jackson, *France: The Dark Years 1940–1944* (New York 2001), 6–20; Tony Judt, *Postwar: A History of Europe since 1945* (New York: Penguin Press, 2005), 815–20, and idem, "The Past is Another Country: Myth and Memory in Postwar Europe," in István Deák, et al., eds., *The Politics of Retribution in Europe: World War II and Its Aftermath* (Princeton: Princeton University Press, 2000), 293–323; Pieter Lagrou, *The Legacy of Nazi Occupation: Patriotic and National Recovery in Western Europe, 1945–1965* (Cambridge: Cambridge University Press, 2000); Renée Poznanski, "Vichy et les Juifs. Des marges de l'histoire au coeur de son écriture," in Jean-Pierre Azéma and François Bédarida, eds., *Vichy et les Français* (Paris: Fayard, 1992), 57–68; Henry Rousso, *The Vichy Syndrome: History and Memory in France since 1944* (Cambridge, Mass.: Harvard University Press, 1991).
5 Esther Benbassa, *The Jews of France: A History from Antiquity to the Present* (Princeton: Princeton University Press, 1999), 182–83; Anne Grynberg, "Après la tourmente," in Jean Jacques Becker and Annette Wieviorka, eds., *Les Juifs de France de la Révolution française à nos jours* (Lourai: Editions Liana Levi, 1998), 249–86; Ido de Haan, "Paths of Normalization after the Persecution of the Jews: The Netherlands, France, and West Germany in the 1950s," in Richard Bessel and Dirk Schumann, eds., *Life After Death: Approaches to a Cultural and Social History of Europe During the 1940s and 1950s* (Cambridge: Cambridge University Press, 2003), 65–92; Paula Hyman, *The Jews of Modern France* (Berkeley and Los Angeles: University of California Press, 1998), 185–91; Maud Mandel, *In the Aftermath of Genocide: Armenians and Jews in Twentieth-Century France* (Durham, NC: Duke University Press, 2003),162–77; David Weinberg, "Between America and Israel: The Quest for a Distinct European Jewish Identity in the Postwar Era," *Jewish Culture and History* 5, 1 (Summer 2002): 91–120; idem, "France," in David Wyman, ed., *The World Responds to the Holocaust* (Baltimore and London: Johns Hopkins University Press, 1996), 3–44; and idem, "The Reconstruction of the French Jewish Community After World War II," in Israel Gutman and Avital Saf, eds., *Shearit Hapleta 1944–1948: Rehabilitation and Struggle* (Jerusalem: Yad Vashem, 1990): 168–86; Annette Wieviorka, *Déportation et génocide: entre la mémoire et l'oubli* (Paris: Plon, 1992), esp. 361–68.
6 Renée Poznanski, "French Apprehensions, Jewish Expectations: From a Social Imaginary to a Political Practice," in David Bankier, ed., *The Jews Are Coming Back: The Return of the Jews to their Countries of Origin after WWII* (Jerusalem: Yad Vashem, 2005), 25–57, and

her *Propagandes et Persécutions: La Résistance et le "problème juif" 1940–1944* (Paris: Fayard, 2008), 551–92.

7 For valuable previous research on the CDJC after 1945, none of which made extensive use of the CDJC's administrative archives, which until recently were not open to the public, see Georges Bensoussan, "The Jewish Contemporary Documentation Center (CDJC) and Holocaust Research in France, 1945–70," in David Bankier and Dan Michman, eds., *Holocaust Historiography in Context: Emergence, Challenges, Polemics and Achievements* (Jerusalem: Yad Vashem, 2008), 245–54; Jacques Fredj, "Le Centre de Documentation Juive Contemporaine (CDJC)," in Annette Wieviorka et al., eds., *Storia e memoria della deportatione: modelli di recerca e di communicazione in Italia ed in Francia* (Florence: La Giuntina, 1996), 151–64; Annette Wieviorka, "Du Centre de documentation juive contemporaine au Mémorial de la Shoah," *Le Monde Juif. Revue d'histoire de la Shoah* 181/2 (2004), 11–36; idem, *Déportation et génocide*, 412–31; idem, *Il y a 50 ans: aux origines du Mémorial de la Shoah* (Paris: CDJC, 2006).

8 There is virtually no documentation on the CDJC's pre-Liberation activity, except for a number of undated documents in the wartime archives of the Consistoire Central; see Renée Poznaski, "La création du centre de Documentation Juive Contemporaine en France (Avril 1943)" in *Vingtième Siècle* 63 (July–September 1999), 51–63, and her "Hakamat ha-merkaz le-ti'ud yahadut zmanenu be-tsarfat. Mitos u-metsiyut," in Israel Gutman, ed., *Me-genizah le-tsiyune derekh historiyim: Arkhiyonim yehudiyim me-tekufat ha-milhama ve-ha-sho'ah* (Jerusalem: Yad Vashem, 1997), 161–80. For an early mission statement of the group see: Archives of the Alliance Israélite Universelle, Paris, Archives du Consistoire Juif pendant la guerre (hereafter ACC), microfilm reel 1, folder 4, "Voici quelques mots en ce que nous voulons" [1943].

9 See ACC, "Ordre du Jour" and the outline of nine research areas to be studied by the group, no date, reel 1, folder 4, French.

10 France's prewar Jewish population numbered 300,000–330,000, of whom 190,000–200,000 were French citizens (55,000 naturalized in the interwar years), and 130,000–140,000 were foreign citizens or stateless Jews. German and Vichy authorities deported 75,721 Jews between 1942 and 1944; an additional 4,000 Jews perished in France. Of a total of some 80,000 wartime deaths among Jews living in France, 56,500, that is two-thirds, were of foreigners. See Serge Klarsfeld, *Vichy-Auschwitz. Le rôle de Vichy dans la "solution finale" de la question juive en France, 1943–1944* (Paris: Fayard, 1983), 2: 179–80.

11 Accounts of the Jewish population in liberated France vary. David Weinberg estimates a total of 180,000–215,000 Jews, including 160,000 who had lived in France before the war and 20,000 refugees from central and eastern Europe, in addition to 35,000 Jewish Displaced Persons who settled in France between 1945 and 1948. See Weinberg, "The Reconstruction of the French Jewish Community After World War II," 169. Annette Wieviorka estimates between 150,000 and 200,000 Jews in France right after the war; see her *Déportation et génocide*, 337.

12 On these conditions, see André Kaspi, *Les Juifs pendant l'Occupation* (Paris: Éditions du Seuil, 1997), 375–93; Poznanski, "French Apprehensions, Jewish Expectations: From a Social Imaginary to a Political Practice," 45–52, and idem, *The Jews in France During World War II* (Hanover and London: University Press of New England, 2001), 462–73.

13 Archives of the Centre de Documentation Juive Contemporaine in Paris (hereafter ACDJC), "Procès-verbal de la Réunion de la Commission des Camps," February 22, 1945, p. 3. The administrative archives of the CDJC have not yet been catalogued and are not accessible to the public. I wish to thank the archive's director, Karen Taïb, for allowing me to use these materials.

14 Ibid.

15 ACDJC, "Procès-verbal de la Réunion de la Commission de Presse," April 26, 1945, p. 1–2; "Procès-verbal de la Réunion de la Commission de la Presse," May 31, 1945, p. 3; Jacques Ratner, "Les travaux de la Commission des Camps. Contre la Conspiration du Silence," *Bulletin du Centre de Documentation Juive Contemporaine* 3 (June 1945), 2.

16 ACDJC, "Procès-verbal de la Réunion de la Commission de Presse," February 26, 1945, p. 5.

17 Ibid., 2–3.

18 Ibid., 4.

19 ACDJC, "Procès-verbal de la Réunion de la 5e Commission," March 22, 1945, 3.

20 On the Center's post-liberation acquisitions, see Léon Poliakov, *Mémoires* (Paris: Jacques Grancher Éditeur, 1999), 186f, and Isaac Schneersohn, "Der yidisher dokumentatsye-tsenter in Frankreykh," *YIVO bleter* 30, 2 (Winter 1947): 249–57, here 251f.

21 See Claudia Moisel, "Resistance und Repressalien. Die Kriegsverbrecherprozesse in der französischen Zone und in Frankreich," in Norbert Frei, ed., *Transnationale Vergangenheitspolitik. Der Umgang mit deutschen Kriegsverbrechern in Europa nach dem Zweiten Weltkrieg* (Göttingen: Wallstein Verlag 2006), 247–82, here 259, and Annette Wieviorka, *Le Procès de Nuremberg* (Caen: Éditions du Mémorial de Caen, 2005), 114. The CDJC published some of the materials as source editions: Henri Monneray, ed., *La persécution des Juifs en France et dans les autres pays de l'Ouest presentée par la France à Nuremberg* (Paris: Éditions du Centre, 1947), and idem., ed., *La persécution des Juifs dans les pays de l'Est presentée à Nuremberg* (Paris: Éditions du Centre 1949).

22 These included, for example, Jean Cassou, *Le Pillage par les allemands des œuvres d'art et des bibliothèques appartenant à des Juifs en France* (Paris: Éditions du Centre, 1947); CDJC, ed., *La Bataille du Ghetto de Varsovie: vue et racontée par les Allemands* (Paris: Éditions du Centre, 1946); Léon Poliakov, *La condition des Juifs en France sous l'occupation italienne* (Paris: Éditions du Centre, 1946); idem, *L'Étoile Jaune* (Paris: Éditions du Centre, 1949).

23 For example Joseph Lubetzki, *La condition des Juifs en France sous l'occupation allemande, 1940–1944. La législation raciale* (Paris: Éditions du Centre 1945); Raymond Sarraute and Jacques Rabinovitch, eds., *Examen succinct de la situation juridique actuelle des Juifs* (Paris: Éditions du Centre, 1945); Raymond Sarraute and Paul Tager, *Les Juifs sous l'occupation* (Paris: Éditions du Centre, 1945).

24 For example, Joseph Weill, *Contribution à l'histoire des camps d'internement dans l'Anti-France* (Paris: Éditions du Centre, 1946) and George Wellers, *De Drancy à Auschwitz* (Paris: Éditions du Centre 1946).

25 Jacques Polonski, *La presse, la propagande et l'opinion publique sous l'occupation* (Paris: Éditions du Centre, 1946).

26 Joseph Billig, *L'Allemagne et le génocide: plans et réalisations nazis* (Paris: Éditions du Centre, 1950). Although a Center coworker, Léon Poliakov chose an outside imprint to publish his important work, *La bréviaire de la haine* (Paris: Calmann-Lévy, 1951), published as *Harvest of Hate: The Nazi Program for the Destruction of Jews of Europe* (Syracuse, NY: Syracuse University Press, 1954). This decision, made in order to attract a larger readership, led to a break between Poliakov and Schneersohn and to his leaving the CDJC. See Poliakov, *Mémoires*, 199–203.

27 The only Yiddish and English translations of CDJC works in the early postwar years were Léon Poliakov, *Yidn unter italyenisher okupatsye* (Paris: Éditions du Centre, 1952) or *French Jews under the Italian Occupation* (Paris: Éditions du Centre, 1954) and idem, *Di gele late* [The Yellow Badge] (Paris: Éditions du Centre, 1952).

28 On the cult of the Resistance see Jackson, *France*, 570–612, and Pieter Lagrou, "Victims of Genocide and National Memory: Belgium, France and the Netherlands 1945–65," in *Past and Present* 154/1 (February 1997), 181–222, here 194–205.

29 ACDJC, "Procès-verbal de la Réunion de la Commission de Presse," April 26, 1945, pp. 3–5; "Procès-verbal de la Réunion de la Commission de la Lecture," November 16, 1945, p. 3; "Procès-verbal de la Réunion de la Commission de la Presse," June 7, 1945, pp. 1–4. In 1947 the CDJC published three major works on Jewish resistance, in the sense of both unarmed resistance or self-help and armed combat: CDJC, ed., *Activité des organisations juives en France sous l'occupation*; David Knout, *Contribution à l'histoire de la résistance Juive en France, 1940–1944* (Paris: Éditions du Centre, 1947); Jacques Lazarus, *Juifs au combat: témoignage sur l'activité d'un mouvement de résistance* (Paris: Éditions du Centre, 1947).

30 André Spire, "Méssage," *Le Monde Juif*, No. 63–64 (March–April 1953), 25; see also Schneersohn, "Der yidisher dokumentatsye-tsenter," 250; "Le Centre de Documentation Contemporaine a Quatre Ans," in *Le Monde Juif*, No. 9–10 (May–June 1947), 20, and Henri Hertz, "Les débuts du Centre de Documentation Juive Contemporaine," in *Dix années d'existence du Centre de Documentation Juive Contemporaine*, Paris 1953, 1–2, 24.

31 ACDJC, "Procès-verbal de la Réunion du Comité Directeur," November 8, 1950, 2–3. A memorial site with ashes from the death camps was not Schneersohn's idea. Already in October 1947, with the help of the French foreign ministry and the Consistoire Central, Jewish Communist groups had arranged the distribution of twenty urns with ashes from Auschwitz-Birkenau among Jewish communities and associations of deportees. Nevertheless, French Jews lacked a central memorial site to commemorate their dead. Without an official memorial, since September 1944 various Jewish groups had returned to the Drancy transit camp to commemorate the victims. In February 1949 the first Jewish memorial was established in the synagogue in Rue de la Victoire in Paris. See Wieviorka, *Déportation et genocide*, 391–411. Similar ideas for memorials using ashes were also discussed in the first postwar decade in New York and in Palestine/Israel; see Hasia Diner, *We Remember with Reverence and Love: American Jews and the Myth of Silence after the Holocaust, 1945–1962* (New York: New York University Press, 2009), 24–44.

32 ACDJC, "Note on the Project to erect the Tomb of the Unknown Jewish Martyr," [1951/1952], 2.

33 Ibid., and ACDJC, undated memorandum on memorial project.

34 ACDJC, Isaac Schneersohn to Nachum Goldmann, September 9, 1953.

35 ACDJC, "Note pour mémoire," February 21, 1952.

36 ACDJC, Isaac Schneersohn to Robert Schuman, May 15, 1951.

37 On the polemics against the memorial from within the Jewish community, see Abraham Rudy, *Emes vegn sheker* (Paris: Imprimérie Moderne de la Presse, 1956). The critical Jewish press rejected the memorial mainly for Halakhic and financial reasons. Some voices demanded that money raised for the memorial instead be used to support the French Jewish community or Israel. See Annette Wieviorka, "Un lieu de mémoire et d'histoire: le mémorial du Martyr juif inconnu," in *Pardès* 2 (1985), 80–98, here 83 f. On the history of the CDJC after 1956, see Simon Perego, *Histoire, justice, mémoire: le Centre de Documentation Juive Contemporaine et le Mémorial du Martyr juif inconnu 1956–1969* (MA thesis, École Doctorale de Sciences Po, 2007).

38 For an overview see Philip Friedman, "The European Jewish Research on the Recent Jewish Catastrophe in 1939–45," *Proceedings of the American Academy for Jewish Research*, 28 (1949): 179–211.

39 On these initiatives see: Natalia Aleksiun, "The Central Jewish Historical Commission in Poland, 1944–47," *Polin* 20 (2008), 74–97; Laura Jockusch, "A Folk Monument to Our Destruction and Heroism: Jewish Historical Commissions in the Displaced Persons Camps of Germany, Austria and Italy," in Avinoam Patt and Michael Berkowitz, eds., *"We Are Here": New Approaches to Jewish Displaced Persons in Postwar Germany* (Detroit: Wayne State University Press, 2010), 31–73; idem, *Collect and Record! Jewish Holocaust Documentation in Postwar Europe, 1943–1953* (Oxford University Press, forthcoming 2011); idem, "*Khurbn-Forshung*: Jewish Historical Commissions in Europe 1945–49," in *Simon Dubnow Institute Yearbook* 6 (2007), 441–73; Ada Schein, "'Everyone can hold a pen,' – The Documentation Project in the DP Camps in Germany," and Feliks Tych, "The Emergence of Holocaust Research in Poland: The Jewish Historical Commission and the Jewish Historical Institute (ZIH), 1944–89," both published in Bankier and Michman, eds., *Holocaust Historiography in Context*, 103–34 and 227–44.

40 Two other Jewish Holocaust conferences had already taken place in 1947. The first conference was held in January by the YIVO Institute in New York. The July conference, hosted in Jerusalem by Yad Vashem and the Hebrew University, was seen as competition to the Paris event, since some of its organizers, above all the historian Ben Zion Dinaburg, viewed it as an attempt to establish the hegemony of Yad Vashem over the European

documentation initiatives and establish Palestine/Israel as the center of Holocaust research and commemoration. On the Jerusalem conference, see Boaz Cohen, "Ha-ve'ida ha-olamit le-heker ha-sho'ah ve-ha-gvura shel tekufatenu, jerushalyim 1947," in: *Cathedra* 125 (2007): 99–108. On the beginnings of Yad Vashem see Roni Stauber, *The Holocaust in Israeli Public Debate in the 1950s* (London and Portland, OR: Valentine Mitchell, 2007).

41 See CDJC, ed., *Les Juifs en Europe (1939–1945). Rapports présentés à la première conférence européenne des commissions historiques et des centres de documentation juifs* (Paris: Éditions du Centre, 1949), 22–24 and the list of participants and conference program, 247–53.

42 ACDJC, protocol, December 8, 1947, morning session, pp. 2–3 and *Les Juifs en Europe*, 174–75.

43 ACDJC, protocol, December 7, 1947, morning session, p. 9; protocol, December 8, 1947, morning session, pp. 7, 9–10.

44 ACDJC, protocol December 7, 1947, p. 12; protocol December 8, 1947, p. 7, and *Les Juifs en Europe*, 78–79.

45 See *Les Juifs en Europe*, 88.

46 ACDJC, protocol, December 7, 1947, morning session, p. 9; *Les Juifs en Europe*, 32–33, 176–77.

47 ACDJC, protocol, December 8, 1947, morning session, p. 8.

48 Ibid., p. 3, and Yad Vashem Archives, AM.1; Feigenbaum's speech of December 8, 1947, folder 128, frame 0642.

49 See *Les Juifs en Europe*, 82 and ACDJC, protocol, December 8, 1947, morning session, p. 6.

50 See the resolutions of the conference in *Les Juifs en Europe*, 185–89.

51 Pierre Birnbaum, *Jewish Destinies: Citizenship, State and Community in Modern France* (New York: Hill and Wang, 2000), 4.

5

DIVIDING THE RUINS

Communal memory in Yiddish and Hebrew

David G. Roskies

Cast in bronze and set in Swedish granite, the monumental Warsaw Ghetto Memorial of Nathan Rapoport was erected on the ghetto ruins in 1948.[1] There were two sides to the memorial. The ceremonial side facing the empty plaza is where wreaths were to be laid in front of larger-than-life iconic figures redolent of "Liberty Leading the People" and of Polish insurrections past and present. The muscular figure with one hand bandaged and the other clutching a Molotov cocktail, as befitted the stand-in for Mordecai Anielewicz, once the most feared and respected person in the ghetto, was flanked on the left by a woman with one breast bared, by a youthful, slightly effeminate fighter on the right reminiscent of Michelangelo's David, and a bearded Herculean figure below—altogether a defiantly secular, vital, vibrant and heroic tableau. No matter that the "real" Anielewicz had been described as slight, pale and unpre-possessing,[2] or that Rachel Auerbach who represented Jewish womanhood had not taken part in the uprising. (Proud of this rendering, Auerbach used it at the beginning of her ghetto memoir in lieu of a photograph.[3]) The bronze statues stood for the heroes, each of whom would be remembered by name and political affiliation.

The side panel, a bas relief etched in stone, paid homage to the nameless martyrs. They represented the parochial side of the past, the recurrent specter of Jewish Exile, as first depicted in the Arch of Titus and as recently reimagined by Samuel Hirszenberg.[4] Clutching their children, their few belongings and a Torah scroll, they were led by a bearded man with the legendary wander staff in his hand, only instead of a bare and desolate backdrop, they were guarded by German soldiers, their helmets and bayonets protruding from behind the procession. The dark side of the past was patriarchal, pious, and passive.

Rapoport's Warsaw Ghetto Memorial gave public shape to Holocaust memory in the postwar era: The dead were divided between the named heroes and the nameless martyrs; the heroes were rooted in time and place, while the martyrs were but the most recent incarnation of an eternal past. Rapoport then exported the same mix of romantic realism to the nascent State of Israel, where the uprising of the doomed was seen as the prelude to the war of national liberation, allowing for a statue of Anielewicz alone to go up at the entrance to Yad Mordechai, the kibbutz built in his memory, and for a desexualized reproduction of the Warsaw Ghetto Memorial to be installed at the entrance to Yad Vashem.

Rapoport successfully negotiated the treacherous postwar terrain by means of manageable eclecticism. Drawing on familiar Western and Jewish iconography in equal measure, he fashioned a public consensus in two such vastly different settings as Poland and Israel. He also had the advantage of having spent the war in the free Soviet zone. For survivors of the Jew-Zone, with a Holocaust-specific story to tell, the odds against going public were much greater, as they encountered linguistic and ideological divisions even within the same postwar community.

Leyb Rochman was one among thousands of survivors and refugees who made their way to Paris and while en route to permanent homes elsewhere turned Paris into a Yiddish Mecca and a hub of Holocaust memory. Rochman arrived there after a lengthy recuperation in Switzerland with a story to tell, transcribed from the diary-cum-journal that he had kept while in hiding with his wife, his sister- and brother-in-law and a friend, from 17 February 1942 until their liberation by the Red Army on 8 August 1944. First serialized in the Yiddish press, *Un in dayn blut zolstu lebn* (And In Your Blood Shall You Live) portrayed a world both familiar to its readers and utterly strange.[5] The setting was Minsk Mazowiecki, 35 kilometers from Warsaw: the final liquidation of its ghetto on Black Friday, 21 August 1942, and the struggle to survive while in hiding among Polish villagers, each Jew armed with Aryan papers and assumed Polish identities, but essentially living by their wits and on the strength of relationships with members of the Polish underclass and underworld. Yiddish readers everywhere still remembered these peasants, with their passions, superstitions and pagan blood lust. No one, however, could remember a time when the Jews were the hunted, the peasants the hunters, and even children took part in the Jew-hunt; when the mewing of a cat, an unstifled cough, or a drunken brawl on the other side of the partition could give you away; and no one had yet divided time in precisely the way it was divided here: Survival Time in the various hideouts, one more primitive than the next, rendered slowly, the durational time of the diary, measured with painstaking effort and self-awareness, simultaneous with but opposed to the Time of the Slaughter, broken up into four long episodes and recorded out of sequence, since Black Friday was the heart of darkness, which those in hiding tried to keep buried, lest it overwhelm their ability to persevere. Rochman's chronicle, in short, was the first authentic confessional diary to appear after the war, a genre so new that it didn't have a name, and so emotionally wrenching that readers and critics would describe it as "novelistic."[6] Indeed, the partition in Aunty's and Felek's cottage was a perfect novelistic device, for it allowed the narrator to be a *roye ve-eyno nir'eh*, a magical Unseen Seer, and provided a voyeuristic lens through which to view the chamber of horrors. "We don't really count as people," the chronicler explained, "we're just part of the wall"[7].

The diary format made this work perfectly suited to be serialized, simultaneously, in the New York daily *Der tog* and the Buenos Aires daily *Yidishe tsaytung*, for Yiddish was still the universal Jewish language and the Yiddish press was to remain for decades the main purveyor of Holocaust memory. The title, a quotation from Ezekiel 16:6–7, was meant to be understood both metonymically and mythically, for just as the Polish soil was steeped in Jewish blood, the Hebrew words *"Bedamayikh hayyi, bedamayikh hayyi!"* (In your blood shall you live!) were the climactic formula of the Jewish circumcision ceremony, proclaiming the blood-bond between the God of Israel and those who entered into His covenant. The Scriptural reference, in turn, was of a piece with the traditional values shared by those in hiding, which included a fervent hope of someday returning to Zion. And finally, because Rochman's personal saga was enmeshed in the destruction of his entire community, the Paris branch of Friends of Minsk Mazowiecki underwrote the book publication and paid for a modernist cover design by the Bialystok-born artist, Bencjon Benn (born Rabinowicz).

Rochman, then, succeeded in producing a Holocaust classic by making fact read like fiction and by filtering the unassimilable horrors through a Jewish folk-sensibility—Rochman being both the last of his generation born in the shtetl and the first to negotiate the Polish landscape with utter fearlessness. The revelatory power of Rochman's wartime diary was widely acknowledged, by readers as diverse as the conservative critic S. Niger and the radical nonconformist, Isaac Bashevis Singer.[8]

In 1950 Rochman immigrated to Israel, where he continued to maintain an international profile through his columns in the New York Yiddish daily *Forward* and his Yiddish broadcasts on Kol Yisrael. Then one day in 1960, armed with a Hebrew translation of his celebrated work and in the company of his translator, Rochman appeared in the Tel Aviv offices of a young independent publisher named (as usually happens only in a novel) Nathan Rapoport. Like his namesake, this Rapoport believed that he could harness the memory of the Holocaust to negotiate between the New Jew and the Old, so he published a cheap paperback edition, placed advertisements in the Israeli press, offered discounts to distributors and did a mass mailing of flyers complete with blurbs and favorable reviews. The result? Most of the 3,000 copies were returned unsold, Rapoport sustained a considerable loss, and swore off Holocaust literature for the remainder of his career.[9]

If statues could speak, the heroic side of the Warsaw Ghetto Memorial would speak to us in Polish-accented Israeli Hebrew and the tragic side would speak in Yiddish—authentic, Old World Yiddish. Each language, as it were, claimed opposite sides of the memory bank: Resistance on one side, Martyrdom on the other. The postwar landscape, our tale of two Nathan Rapoports teaches us, was fraught with multiple roadblocks, making it almost impossible to cross from one side to the other. Nathan Rapoport the Sculptor had to dispense with the martyrs if he wished to export his art to Israel, and despite his outlay of capital, Nathan Rapoport the Publisher could not make a chronicle of mere survival marketable to an audience schooled in tales of Jewish resistance. Barely a decade before, Rochman and his fellow survivor-refugees were taunted in the streets of Israel by children yelling *"Sabon! Sabon!"*—based on the belief that the Germans had turned the fat of the Jewish dead into soap; and although the Eichmann Trial coincided with the Hebrew publication, Rochman's diary failed to whet the reader's appetite for a new kind of narrative. Works of authentic wartime experience could cross over from the Jew-Zone to the Liberated Zone only if published in their original languages in limited editions. The rich and unique body of wartime writing that had survived by dint of extraordinary collective and clandestine effort, and sometimes just by chance, was rooted in a different time, place, and circumstance, which often required decrypting. Simply put: Its natural audience had perished, or was too scattered to stand up and be counted. While the postwar ruins were divided between East and West, Left and Right, wartime writing – the bedrock of Holocaust memory, the source for everything that followed—languished in obscurity. What followed, therefore, had to be reinvented.

★★★

That reinvention began with a story "written especially for *Di yidishe tsaytung*" of Buenos Aires and published on 25 September 1946 in honor of the High Holiday season. Its author was Zvi Kolitz, who happened to be in town as part of his fund-raising mission on behalf of the Revisionist Zionist movement. The story was called "*Yosl Rakovers vendung tsu got*" (Yosl Rakover's Appeal to God). "In one of the ruins of the ghetto of Warsaw," a prefatory note explained, "among piles of charred rubble and human bones, there was found, concealed and stuffed in a small bottle, the following testament, written during the Warsaw Ghetto's last hours by a Jew named Yosl Rakover."[10] Apart from the hackneyed device of a found document and the by-now standard use of the Warsaw Ghetto uprising as the pivotal event of the Holocaust, Kolitz cast a Gerer Hasid in the title role; this, to proclaim his faith in a seemingly absent God on the High Holidays. Rakover, implausibly, was also portrayed as an independent ghetto fighter; this, to espouse the need for armed resistance and the absolute dichotomy between the merciful God of Israel and the merciless God of Love. A theologically expurgated version of the story appeared a year later in an English-language collection of Kolitz's *Stories and Parables of the Years of Death*, the changes apparently made by the translator without Kolitz's knowledge.[11]

Yosl Rakover was a fraudulent figure, a figment of the postwar Jewish imagination that wanted to have it all: a fighter who was also a religious martyr; a model of heroism at once physical and spiritual. The efforts of wartime writers like Huberband, Katzenelson, Shayevitsh, and Sutzkever to distinguish between religious and secular forms of resistance and to define heroism downwards were irrelevant to a postwar community hungry to harness the past to further its agenda for the future. Even the survivor community was taken in when, in 1954, an anonymous typescript of the original Yiddish story arrived in the Tel Aviv office of the literary quarterly *Di goldene keyt*, under the editorship of Abraham Sutzkever. "*Yosl Rakover redt tsu got*" ("Yosl Rakover Speaks to God," as it was renamed) was published as an authentic document from the Warsaw ghetto, but with stylistic improvements, as per Sutzkever's usual practice. Jacob Glatstein, among many others, hailed the newly discovered testament as "a part of our monumental Holocaust literature [*khurbn-literatur*], which will remain for all the generations." This caught the eye of the poet, former ghetto fighter, and Holocaust historian Michel Borwicz (born Maksymilian Boruchowicz). Disappointed that Sutzkever provided him with so poor an explanation of the manuscript's provenance, Borwicz decided to expose the story's manifold historical inaccuracies and obvious literary gildings. In the face of public protest, Borwicz proclaimed it a fake, and published his findings in a Paris-based literary journal.[12]

The public protested because, as Borwicz understood, the need to believe was simply too great. The Yiddish-reading public had responded viscerally to a "sacred testament" that fully met its expectations and slaked its spiritual thirst. Since, by the time the issue went to press, the truth of Kolitz's authorship had already come to light, Borwicz appended an afterword in which he expressed the hope that the public would soon develop a hermeneutics of reading that would distinguish between the literature **of** the Holocaust and the literature **on** the Holocaust.

"Our monumental Holocaust literature" refused to honor such distinctions, least of all when it came to texts that purported to be true but defied historical analysis; that could be excerpted, edited, anthologized, translated, performed, and retranslated. In the major centers of postwar Jewry, Holocaust-specific anthologies became a reader's first exposure to the subject. Thus, in 1948, Shmuel Niger, the preeminent Yiddish literary critic of his day, published *Kidesh hashem*, subtitled *A collection of selected, oftentimes abbreviated reports, letters, chronicles, testaments, inscriptions, legends, poems, short stories, dramatic scenes, essays, which describe acts of self-sacrifice in our own days and also in days of yore*.[13] That year, the former Vilna partisan Shmerke Kaczerginski published the definitive edition of *Songs of the Ghettos and Concentration Camps*: definitive by virtue of size, H. Leivick's imprimatur, and inspirational chapter headings.[14] Only a handful of these songs were deemed performable at memorial gatherings; just enough to establish the genre of Holocaust song as lyrical, communal, sanitized, and vaguely historical.[15] The signature song at such gatherings was "*Es brent!*" (Fire!) by Mordecai Gebirtig (1877–1942), a stirring hymn written in response to a prewar pogrom in Poland that was universally understood to have prophesied the Holocaust.[16]

To sanctify the memory of the dead, the Holocaust was read backwards in time. Everyone who perished was deemed holy and everything they had created was rendered holy, too. No effort, therefore, was spared to collect their sacred remains. In New York, Machmadim Art Editions published *Kdoyshim* (Martyrs): *Poetry of Those Tortured to Death* (1947) on blue-gray stock in a numbered edition with each selection from the work of a Polish-Yiddish poet set to music by the modern composer Henech Kon and illustrated with paintings by Isaac Lichtenstein. In Paris, H. Fenster anthologized the artistic legacy of *Undzere farpaynikte kinstler* (Our Martyred Painters), a numbered folio-size volume that commemorated eighty-four east European Jews who had hoped to become world-class artists in the art capital of the world and perished instead as Jews. Introduced by an homage to the martyred artists by Marc Chagall in his own handwriting, this magnificent volume concluded with just the names of several hundred Jewish artists murdered in other parts of the Jew-Zone.[17] In the Orthodox sector, regrouped and incubating in Brooklyn, NY, Lakewood, NJ, Jerusalem, and B'nai B'rak, the anthological project was led by the indefatigable Moshe Prager, a Hebrew-Yiddish journalist and the great grandson of the first Gerer Rebbe. No sooner had Prager escaped from occupied Warsaw and made his way to

Palestine than he began documenting the slaughter, producing four Hebrew collections of factual evidence between 1941–45.[18] After the war, he too began sifting through the ruins. With the support of the Conference on Jewish Material Claims Against Germany, established in 1951 to underwrite just such projects and active until this very day, Prager published a 640-page *Anthology of Yiddish Poems, Stories and Essays Written by Religious Authors, Victims of Nazi Persecution*.[19] To distinguish the authentic voice of religious Jewry from the neo-Romantic ventriloquists and the study house rebels—from the likes of Peretz and Asch, Glatstein and Grade—Prager defined his subject as *emune-dikhtung*, the poetry of true faith[20], in the hope of rehabilitating a severed branch of east European Jewry.

No surprise, then, that the Jewish anthological imagination included Yosl Rakover among the martyrs. He appeared in *Ani ma'amin*, a Hebrew compilation of *Testimonies on the Life and Death of Believers at the Time of the Holocaust* and in *Out of the Whirlwind: A Reader of Holocaust Literature*, where a postscript identified Rakover as a real person whose tragic fate was known to the author.[21] Through the art of anthologizing, it was possible to erase the terrible divide between the living and the dead, to sacralize the lost culture of European Jewry, and to harmonize the martyrs with the fighters.

Kolitz seduced his readers into believing that they were privy to an authentic piece of wartime writing "rescued from the ruins." In point of fact, little of that corpus made it into the postwar canon of "our monumental Holocaust literature," for what Yiddish and Hebrew readers regarded as Holocaust-specific genres were written or rewritten mostly after the war, with their concerns in mind. While the Black Book Committees, one in the United States and the other in the Soviet Union, collected direct eyewitness testimonies from every place on the Holocaust compass to form the documentary evidence of a crime against humanity defined in 1943 as "genocide," the survivors and former residents of the martyred communities turned inward to produce a different kind of testimonial: a comprehensive yizkor book in their own collective voice. The first to do so was the United Emergency Relief Committee for the City of Lodz, whose *Lodzer Yiskor Book* appeared in December 1943 and took three years to assemble. It opened with a split-screen illustration by the Lodz-born artist Artur Szyk of a German bayonet thrust through the Lodz municipal coat of arms above the grieving heads of three Polish Jews: an elderly bearded man, his kerchiefed wife and their very young son. Then came greetings to President Roosevelt and ex-Governor Herbert H. Lehman on behalf of the former residents of Lodz in America, whose immediate goal was to bring relief to their coreligionists in the Jew-Zone – just how great their suffering they gleaned from a single source, *Dos blut ruft tsu nekome* (The Blood Cries Out for Revenge), a collection of eyewitness accounts of Polish-Jewish refugees published in Moscow in 1941. Were they to have known about the mass deportations from the ghetto, the last section of the yizkor book filled with souvenir ads and ending with photographs of Lodzer offspring serving in the US Army would not have achieved the desired balance of remembrance, celebration, and fund raising.

Eventually to number well over a thousand, the bulk of these memorial books appeared long after there was anyone left to rescue, or any desire to exact retribution.[22] Each routinely opened with an off-scale memory map of the town, drafted in Yiddish or Hebrew to complement an idealized, harmonized image of the Jewish life that was destroyed, and devoted its last, lengthy and terrifying section to a description of the slaughter. Those volumes produced in Israel sometimes included photographs of the native-born offspring in IDF uniform. The stated purpose of the yizkor book was to leave a lasting memorial for future generations. The real purpose was to close the chapter on the tragic past and to move on to other concerns, now that the survivors had successfully rebuilt their homes elsewhere. The Book of Lamentations, recent scholarship has argued, was not written in the immediate aftermath of the Temple's destruction but in the midst of its rebuilding.[23]

The most prominent of Holocaust-specific genres in the first decades after the war were memorial volumes compiled by those with a living link to the dead. Their size and claim to comprehensiveness testified to the staying power of the survivor community. But that community was now dispersed and divided. As the Jewish deportation community in Paris banded together to commemorate the martyred painters, the surviving members of the Yiddish secular school movement in New York pooled their memories to produce the *Lerer Yizkor Book*, an alphabetical lexicon of murdered men and women who had dedicated their lives to raising a proud new generation of Polish Jews.[24] In Israel, the heroic self-image of the emerging state was greatly enhanced by the visible and vocal presence of survivors who had been active in the Jewish armed resistance.[25] The means of memorial production, however, were virtually controlled by the kibbutz movements and the political parties of the left. What got published and by whom was determined by the political affiliation of the fighters, both living and dead.[26] Three massive memorial projects resulted from the new political alignment: *Sefer milhamot haget'aot* (1954), which showcased the members of the Zionist underground who had died as ghetto fighters, *Sefer Hashomer Hatsa'ir* (1956), which commemorated the Holocaust as an episode in the history of this pro-Soviet Zionist youth movement, and the two-volume *Sefer hapartizanim hayehudim* (1958), which celebrated as no less heroic and patriotic the Zionist youth who had fought in the forests, either alone or as part of Soviet partisan brigades. Each of these volumes required the mobilization of scarce resources in a difficult period of nation building, and was published by a different arm of the labor movement. The religious wing of the Zionist movement, meanwhile, had its own publishing house called Mosad Harav Kook, which expended great effort to produce *Arim ve'imahot beYisrael*, seven volumes chronicling twenty *Major Jewish Cities … Annihilated by the Tyrants and the Impure in the Last World War* (1946–50)—yizkor books by any other name.[27]

In one massive, meticulously edited and comprehensive volume, *Sefer milhamot hageta'ot* provided readers with the Holocaust Complete, the martyrs all treated as combatants in the *Wars of the Ghettos* and the full sweep of the eastern Jew-Zone—*Between the Walls, in the Camps, in the Forests*—included within its compass.[28] Two pull-out maps told the feature story in graphic form: one of "The Jewish Underground in Poland, the Ghettos and Camps," with color-coded lines to distinguish between the secret communication routes of the underground as a whole and those of the Zionist youth movements in particular, and one of the Warsaw Ghetto, color-coded to highlight the battles fought in January and April, 1943. Through testimony, diary, reportage, last letters, battle bulletins, calls-to-arm, memoir, documentary fiction, poetry, and song from across the eastern Jew-Zone, written by both the living and the dead, the editors Yitshak Zuckerman and Moshe Basok constructed a heroic master narrative in loose chronological and tight geographical order. While among the fighters, obvious priority was given to the Zionist underground, the roster of martyrs drew from across the social and generational spectrum. Janusz Korczak rubbed shoulders with Reb Mendl of Powianec; fifteen-year-old Yitskhok Rudashevsky from Vilna with seventy-year-old Hillel Zeitlin from Warsaw. So too the rich selection of Yiddish, Hebrew, Polish and German poetry and prose, much of it translated here for the first time. Whosoever studied its dense pages—hardly the stuff of leisure reading—came away with the conviction that in the war against the Jews, the Jews had emerged victorious.

Among Jews, a sefer was designed for study, for permanence, and was considered holy. Like the editors and publishers, the intended audience of these memorial tomes to the poets and partisans, the teachers and ghetto fighters, the Parisian artists and east European communities, were first-generation rebels from traditional Judaism, separated from the dead by only one degree. During the immediate postwar period, all private memory was communal, for reasons both practical and existential. Without political or institutional backing, no Holocaust testimony or text got published, and in order to go public, Holocaust memory had to obey the habits of the Jewish heart. That heart was now divided between Right and Left, sacred and profane. So the medium of Holocaust memory was key to its message; not only who sponsored its publication but also where it appeared: whether as a memorial volume created for all eternity or in the daily press; whether enshrined as an emblem of the severed past or enmeshed in the messy, contentious business of creating a new life. Through diverse media and to a different degree in both Jewish languages simultaneously, the two competing sides of Rapoport's memorial were gradually naturalized into the postwar Jewish landscape.

In Poland, as throughout the Communist Bloc, Holocaust memory became a pawn of the Cold War. After the Communists seized power, their loyal servant, Ber Mark, was appointed director of the Jewish Historical Institute in Warsaw, the memory bank of Polish Jewry and the repository of the two surviving parts of the Oyneg Shabes Archive. Mark dutifully placed the Party imprimatur on everything he published: from the story of the ghetto uprising, revised to put the Communist underground in charge, to the fiction and reportorial prose written in the ghetto.[29] Printed on cheap paper with identical covers, the literary legacy of the Oyneg Shabes Archive contained no negative mention of the Soviet Union.[30] All the more reason to defend the authenticity of Yehoshue Perle's chronicle of the Great Deportation by turning Perle into a hero of the Cold War.[31] When surveying and evaluating *The Jewish Tragedy in Polish Literature*, Mark ranked the over thirty writers and poets by order of their political correctness. Tadeusz Borowski, whose naturalist style "distorted reality … and essentially leads to fatalism" he dismissed in three pages.[32] Only in the privacy of a Paris hotel room in 1956, on the occasion of the official opening of the Centre de Documentation Juive, did Mark confess his sins before two members of the Israeli delegation, and in exchange for their forgiveness arranged to have millions of historical documents microfilmed and secretly sent to Israel.[33]

Because of his familial and ideological links to the kibbutz movement, the poet and playwright Yitshak Katzenelson became the commanding voice of the martyrs. When the surviving members of the Zionist youth movement Dror established a new kibbutz in Western Galilee and pledged to turn Kibbutz Lohamei Hageta'ot into "a living memorial to the ghetto revolt," they named the archive that opened in April 1950 after the man who had been both their mascot and moral compass.[34] Highest priority was given to publishing Katzenelson's monumental *Song of the Murdered Jewish People* in both Yiddish and Hebrew. But when it came to the *Vittel Diary*, the editors eliminated the names of the poet's ideological foes who were still living.[35] Sacred memory required that one protect both the living and the dead. That notwithstanding, Katzenelson's long day's journey into the ghetto night made maximal demands of the reader and would never have appeared were it not for its institutional sponsor.

Abraham Sutzkever was one of the few survivors who negotiated between East and West without compromising his integrity. Even before he was airlifted to safety by the Red Army, in March 1944, Sutzkever was recast to fit the heroic Soviet mold of a partisan-poet.[36] There, in Soviet Russia, his memoir of the Vilna ghetto was published in 1946, and it was from there that his first two volumes of wartime verse, *Di festung* (The Fortress, 1945) and *Lider fun geto* (Poems from the Ghetto, 1946), were sent to the United States, where they were published by YKUF, the publishing arm of the International Workers' Order. The first Jew to give testimony at Nuremberg, on 27 February 1946, Sutzkever testified in Russian, one of four official languages, with the blessings of the Soviet prosecutor, a testimony that would be preserved in vol. 8 of the official protocols of the International Military Tribunal and highlights thereof (many decades later) on YouTube.[37] His heart and mind focused all the while on the destruction of Jerusalem of Lithuania, over the course of three years (1945–47) and in three cities (Moscow, Lodz, Paris) the poet composed *Geheymshtot* (Secret City), an epic about ten symbolic survivors living beneath the ruins of the Vilna ghetto, which he managed to have published within months of securing passage to his new home in Palestine.[38] By the time Jewish Palestine became the State of Israel, Sutzkever convinced the Histadrut Labor Federation to underwrite the publication of *Di goldene keyt*, the gold standard of Yiddish literature and a main purveyor of Holocaust memory, which it continued to support from 1949–95.

A very different kind of writing flourished in the rough-and-tumble world of the Yiddish press. With Nazi killers on the loose, honor courts settling the score with suspected Jewish collaborators, and the scandal of reparations—German blood money—erupting in Israel and spilling over onto the Yiddish-speaking street, the Holocaust remained front page news. Featured in the Yiddish press were the writings of talented young Holocaust survivors in serialized form. The postwar art of reportorial fiction provided just the right mix of history and emotion, Jewish idiom and journalese, the communal and the personal. Written in sound-bites, each segment was just long enough to fit into one's favorite (ideologically compatible) daily newspaper.

Mordecai Strigler emerged from the war looking "like a slum-bred thirteen-year-old boy," in the words of war correspondent Meyer Levin: "He had an intellectual face, widening upward from a delicate chin to a broad forehead; he wore glasses."[39] All his copious wartime notes and manuscripts were lost, and reconstructing them from memory was neither feasible nor desirable. In order for his experiences in Majdanek, in Factory C., the infamous munitions factory at Skarżysko-Kamienna, and in Buchenwald to reach a wider audience, Strigler decided to adopt a thin fictional cloak, and he defended this decision in a tedious, three-part introduction to his cycle of documentary novels.[40] Fiction, he argued, would mitigate some of the horror, while a literary approach to his real-life protagonists would help deepen their psychological profile. To ensure that the reader not mistake this as mere "literature," historical documentation preceded and punctuated the story.

Thus the concept of *khurbn-literatur* was born; true tales of the ghettos and camps that employed modes of enhanced authenticity, such as confessions, autobiographies, memoirs, and diaries, lest, as Strigler worried, they be read as "mere" fiction.[41] Rochman, Strigler, and their cohort each adopted fictional and journalistic techniques to make their story not only more readable, but also more relevant. The most effective way of engaging the reader was through breaks in the narrative, flashes of introspection and voice-over commentaries addressed to the reader directly, punctuated by Biblical quotations and Rabbinic phrases that together turned the unassimilable record of German atrocity, Christian betrayal and Jewish cowardice into a species of history "written with anger and with bias."[42]

Strigler's *Majdanek* opens with the imminent liquidation of his labor camp, located just outside his native town of Zamość. All the inmates, male and female, are headed for Majdanek, to certain death. The narrator, acting on some ill-conceived plan of escape, tries to leave the barracks to take a leak but is stopped at gunpoint. "The rifle, clearly, is in no mood to argue," he writes, personifying the SS guard through his weapon. "So he throws one word at me, that carries with it the warning of all four death penalties meted out by the Beit Din: *Zurück!*" In the two seconds that it takes to read this sentence, the reader is expected to see the disjuncture between ancient Rabbinic justice, which carried out the death sentence with fear and trembling, and the Nazi penal system, which targeted an entire people for annihilation. All this, compressed into the juxtaposition of the liturgical phrase, *arba mises besdin*, and the brutal German command, *Zurück!* Get back![43]

The Yiddish press was—and remains—a school for scandal, so there were no strictures on what aspects of the Holocaust could be described in its columns. Also serialized was the work of an eyewitness chronicler who was intent upon intensifying, not mitigating, the horror, by situating the Holocaust within its own geography, representing real personal experience through the veil of hallucination and nightmare, and rendering the historical transtemporal. Enter: Ka-Tzetnik 135633 who, when asked his name by his Red Army liberators replied: "My name was burned along with all those others in the Auschwitz crematorium." Ka-Tzetnik defined himself solely in terms of his experience of absolute extremity. The public would learn only decades later of one Yekhiel Fajner-Dinur, an

Expressionist poet of middling talent, who had emerged from the ranks of Polish Orthodoxy.[44]

With literary ambitions even greater than Strigler's, Ka-Tzetnik set out to write *The Chronicles of a Jewish Family in the Twentieth Century*. The first three volumes— *Salamandra* (1946; trans. as *Sunrise over Hell*, 1977), *House of Dolls* (1955), and *They Called Him Piepel* (1961)—concerned the fate of that family in the Holocaust. Although Ka-Tzetnik invented very little, "Kongressia" being a (thin) fictional cloak for Lodz, "Metropoli" for Sosnowice in Upper East Silesia, and Monyek Matroz for Moshe Merin, head of the Sosnowicz Judenrat; and although the most horrific episodes could be historically corroborated, the poetics of horror rendered reality into nightmare and history into myth.[45] The authorial self was a cipher. The ghetto and *Lager* were a closed system. The branding of Jews, both male, and especially female, marked a new and demonic covenant, a permanent defilement that could never be eradicated. The world was split between good and evil: Jews vs. Germans, Vevke the Saint vs. Monyek the Devil, Fella the Survivor vs. Daniella the Victim, and so on. When Daniella threw herself on the electrified barbed wire at the conclusion of *House of Dolls*, questions of causality were suspended. Since no human initiative made any difference, her fate was preordained. The train that had whisked her off on her last summer vacation pre- figured the train that would transport her to Auschwitz. If there existed a metonymy for Auschwitz, it was pure womanhood defiled. Fella the *Feldhure* would never birth again.

Ka-Tzetnik's Holocaust trilogy was preoccupied with sexual abuse and sadomaso- chism. He evinced an almost insane obsession with depravity.[46] The Nazi guards and their underlings indulged every possible perversion and sexual fantasy. All three of his protagonists, as *Prominenten*, camp functionaries, existed outside the pale of humanity. Harry Preleshnik, Ka-Tzetnik's fictional stand-in, began his camp career as a member of the paramedical staff in the camp infirmary, but was later inducted into the Sonderkommando. Daniella, his sister, was sterilized (without an anaesthetic) before being inducted into the Joy Division, and Moni, their kid brother, served as a homosexual sex-servant of the Block Aelteste.

It was the press, above all, that helped normalize the Holocaust, mainstreaming it within Jewish communal memory. Judenräte, ghettos, Aktions, and the Umschlagplatz; crematoria, selections, kapos, and the Sonderkommando; Buchenwald, Sobibor, Treblinka, and Majdanek: within a decade these Holocaust-specific terms had become standard in the Yiddish lexicon. In Yiddish, the war-specific lexicon and the terminology of mass destruction never became a thing of the past. In Yiddish alone, moreover, there appeared a popular library whose focus was the civilization of Polish Jewry, its achievements, its destruction, and its living heritage. Published in Buenos Aires and free of political patronage, *Dos poylishe yidntum* was an ambitious and well- edited series of reprints and original works, a kind of portable library of Polish Jewry in exile. Appearing at the rate of almost ten books a year, these black-bound volumes, each with an illustrated jacket and book review section, were distributed in twenty-two countries, even reaching Holocaust survivors in Poland and the DP camps.[47] Among the most prominent titles were Strigler's multivolume *Farloshene shtern* (Extinguished

Lights), comprising *Majdanek* (1947), *In di fabrikn fun toyt* (In the Death Factories, 1948), *Werk C* (Factory C; 2 vols., 1950), and *Goyroles* (Destinies, 2 vols., 1952). The youngest author to be included in the Argentinean series was a rookie Yiddish-Hebrew journalist named Eliezer Wiesel. Wiesel's ... *Un di velt hot geshvign* (... And the world was silent, 1956) appeared as volume 117, two down from Ka-Tzetnik's *The House of Dolls*. Until Wiesel, Hungarian Jewry had not yet been heard from.

Because the medium was the testimonial message, the same work could assume a different meaning if it appeared in more than one medium. Readers who first encountered Rochman's chronicle in the Yiddish press responded as to a work of fiction: they couldn't wait for the next installment. Once enshrined in a book with a covenantal title and striking cover, which memorialized the names of the dead and was sponsored by the home-town society of Minsk Mazowiecki, *In Your Blood Shall You Live* would double as a yizkor book until such time as a proper yizkor book appeared.[48] When stripped of both communal functions, however, and published in Hebrew translation as a free-standing work of Holocaust literature, Rochman's finely wrought narrative failed to engage a new reader. His most lasting impact on Israeli culture would come through his protégé, Aharon Appelfeld.[49]

Documentary fiction of the Holocaust, a species of the new journalism, was produced by survivors who had either just begun their literary careers on the eve of the war and whose wartime experience changed their writing forever, or by those who became writers by virtue of their wartime experience. Ka-Tzetnik, Rochman, Strigler, Wiesel and their cohort introduced Yiddish readers to the landscape and chronology of the Holocaust, differentiated by place and fateful setting, sometimes broken down hour-by-hour. Together, they established the precise and allowable boundaries of *khurbn-literatur*, grounded in the survivor's lived experience, but carefully mediated for a non-survivor audience.

***

Who spoke for the Holocaust were not only authentic eyewitnesses, those with tattooed numbers on their arm. The chair of the Yiddish Writer's Union in Paris between 1946 and 1948 was Chaim Grade, a different kind of survivor, who had fled eastward into the Soviet Union, abandoning his mother and wife. The crucible of memory, loyalty, and guilt for Grade the poet, essayist, and novelist would henceforth be Vilna, not only its secular Yiddish culture, but also its great Torah sages and radical asceticism. These two sides of his personal past were brilliantly pitted against each other in his first work of autobiographical fiction, "My Quarrel with Hersh Rasseyner," the lion's share of which takes place in postwar Paris.[50]

Here, in the cradle of the Enlightenment, someone like Chaim Vilner, who broke away from the strictures of Jewish law to embrace the religion of secular humanism, would seem to enjoy a strategic advantage over Hersh Rasseyner, who cut himself off from the secular world and its seductions. Yet Grade keeps the sides evenly matched, for Hersh, while an inmate in Auschwitz, dabbled in Western philosophy. The war, he tells Chaim, presented him with such irrefutable proof of the need for Jewish law in the face of barbarism, that he is astounded by Chaim's unrepentant humanism.

In the end, each side refuses to despair, the one of God, the other of humankind,[51] and when Vilner embraces his old adversary, he thereby signals that this internal Jewish dialogue will continue as before—answerable to the past but not crushed by it.

Another vicarious survivor was Isaac Bashevis Singer. Like Grade, who used Paris as a city of refuge for his Yiddish-speaking refugees, Singer's circle of misfits ended up in Hertz Dovid Makover's smoke-filled living room on New York's Upper West Side; and later, his "Last Demon" found shelter in an attic in the Juden- and Devil-rein shtetl of Tishevitz. Even "The Cafeteria" would do, for close Yiddish encounters of the third kind.[52] Inspired by Rochman's chronicle of Polish-Jewish relations *in extremis*, Singer wrote *The Slave* (1960), a tale of Polish captivity in the time of Chmielnicki, which Yiddish readers understood to be a prelude to the time of Hitler.

Singer's great contemporary, S. Y. Agnon (né Czaczkes), went a parallel route. Let us assume that when he wrote "The Lady and the Peddler," a Gothic tale about Jewish self-betrayal in the European Diaspora, the tale of a hapless Jew named Joseph who is almost devoured by a vampire named Helen, Agnon did not yet know the full extent of the catastrophe. But by 1944 he knew for certain that the Jewish community of his native Buczacz had been annihilated, the shock of which produced *"Hasiman"* (The Sign), a semi-mystical tale in which the narrator is consecrated to become the memorial and liturgical crucible of his martyred community. When Agnon returned to this story some two decades later and expanded it tenfold, he began a massive, unfinished project of retelling tales in praise of Buczacz. *'Ir umlo'ah* (The City in Its Fullness) became what is perhaps the first personal yizkor book.[53]

Thirty poets were included in Zuckerman's and Basok's compendium-sefer of *The Wars of the Ghettos*, eight of them appearing in a separate liturgical coda. Missing was the commanding voice of the Holocaust in postwar Hebrew poetry, that of Uri Zvi Greenberg. Greenberg had been ostracized for two decades both by the Hebrew literary establishment and the left-wing kibbutz movement for his Revisionist views. No matter that in 1945, when he broke his vow of silence, Greenberg was immediately acclaimed as "the Jeremiah of our generation," his poems were mainstreamed in the influential daily *Ha'aretz*, and a nation-in-the-making hung on to his every word.[54] The left-wing kibbutz movement refused to forgive and forget, and in any event, could hearken instead unto Katzenelson, a jeremiah from within its own ranks.

Greenberg was anathema for fundamental reasons as well. In *Rehovot hanahar, Streets of the River* (1951), the first and only book of Holocaust poetry designed to be a sefer, all the secular props were discarded. The poet-prophet abjured the term Shoah, which implied a natural disaster unrelated to its root cause—Christian Jew-hatred—and he refused the easy consolation of coupling *shoah* with *gevurah*, the martyrs with the fighters. The destruction of a people was a catastrophe of cosmic proportions, requiring a new poetic language—"No Other Instances!" he proclaimed—a new accounting with God, a last encounter with the dead, and a final reckoning with the goyim.[55]

Greenberg endowed the murder of Europe's Jews with cosmic and, ultimately, redemptive significance. It was a *Book of Dirges and Power*, which is to say, a poetry at once bardic, encompassing the sweep of Jewish time and space, and lyric, addressed to the poet's murdered family.[56] Speaking throughout in the first-person singular, "as one of the many beheaded of father and mother" ("I'll Say to God"), the poet saw a universe riven in two. "A lying poet can poeticize," he said to God in Europe, "that after entering Your heaven / Your useless shepherd staff will shine, a rainbow in the sky. / Not I—who sees within the vision the divided body of the [sacrificial] bird." At precisely the moment when Sutzkever and Celan, still within the Jew-Zone, engaged their murdered mothers in lyric dialogue, Greenberg began imagining hallucinatory encounters with *his* mother; so childish, regressive, and raw, that they forced Hebrew readers to confront their own loss and guilt and utter helplessness.[57] Whatever consolation might yet be won from witnessing "the great palace of power," Greenberg's code for the miracle of Jewish political sovereignty, "the crown-of-the-universal kingdom" in "the returning time of greatness" was predicated on facing an abyss, an unbridgeable divide, which would forever separate Jew from Gentile. Little wonder the left-wing kibbutzim wanted no part of it.

Inasmuch as Greenberg's poetry of personal bereavement and national consolation stood in opposition to the heroic self-image of a young nation state, it was of a piece with the response to the Holocaust in Yiddishland. Glatstein's first postwar collection of poems, which launched his career as a theologian, not merely a poet of the Holocaust, was called *Radiant Jews* (1946). "We accepted the Torah on Sinai," says the poet in the name of the surviving People Israel, "And in Lublin," in the shadow of the Majdanek death camp, "we gave it back." Quoting Scripture back at God, the poet continues: "The dead don't praise God [Ps. 115:17]— /The Torah was given for Life. / And just as we stood together / At the giving of the Torah, / So indeed did we all die in Lublin."[58] "O God of Mercy," says Kadia Molodowski in her first postwar collection of verse, "Choose— /another people. / We are tired of death, tired of corpses, / We have no more prayers."[59] Only when the Jewish body politic, still grievously wounded, faced off against a diminished, intimate, Yiddish-speaking God, did it feel itself empowered.

By the early 1950s, readers of Yiddish and Hebrew had two very different literary responses to the Holocaust to choose from. Enshrined as sacred memory in yizkor book, sefer, and liturgical volumes of secular verse, the Holocaust became part of a new metanarrative of destruction and rebirth. Through the alchemy of the Jewish anthological imagination, passive martyrs were melded together with armed resisters. One side of Rapoport's monument merged into the other. Prose writers and poets alike restored human agency by transposing the brute struggle for survival onto a metaphysical plane. Instead of dwelling on the chronology and terminology of mass murder, they returned to a conceptual vocabulary encoded in the ancient texts. Kolitz, in Yosl Rakover's name, spoke of *hester-panim*, God's momentary, mysterious lapse. The other approach—newsworthy, raw, and scandalous—focused on the assault to the body. Rochman, Strigler and Ka-Tzetnik were unsparing in their attention to bodily detail. The men who made it through the first selection in Buchenwald were seen sifting through their own shit to locate the diamonds and precious metals they had swallowed the day before. Oh, how the narrator lamented the loss of his Polish banknotes, which were biodegradable and therefore could not have been salvaged.[60] In a fairly straightforward, chronological manner, these writers inducted the reader into a new order of reality, centered on brute survival, a world of choiceless choice.

At one pole of response were the liturgists, secular humanists who, in the face of such a catastrophe, become guardians of the sacred flame. Occupying the other were young men raised in traditional homes who for the same reason turned to naturalism, becoming radical realists. These two sides of EveryJew could no sooner be reconciled than the two sides of everysoul, living (as we all do) in the aftermath.

★★★

If Holocaust memory could be brought home, only then could it speak to a native-born generation with no direct link to the murdered millions. In Israel, theater was the main stage for national identity formation. Original Hebrew productions on contemporary themes were as closely watched as the establishment of each new agricultural settlement and municipality. So who would speak on stage for the destruction of European Jewry? In Leah Goldberg's *Lady of the Castle* staged at the Cameri Theater in 1955, those who spoke for the war were: (implausibly) a coura-geous German aristocrat, two emissaries from Palestine, and a Jewish girl rescued from captivity.[61] Drawing on Goldberg's Symbolist poetics of indirection, the play was as much about the eclipse of the old Europe as about survivors and rescuers struggling to respond to the eclipse of European Jewry. Since no one on stage was "really" speaking Hebrew, no one spoke with an accent.

A more popular choice by far was that of Hannah Szenes, a young Jewish–Hungarian girl who immigrated to a kibbutz and soon after joined the British army, parachuting into the Jew-Zone with thirty-one others in order to try and save as many Hungarian Jews as possible.[62] Inspired by a recent Hebrew production of George Bernard Shaw's *St. Joan*, Aharon Megged created the first Israeli drama about the capture, trial and execution of this Palestinian Jewish martyr-and-resistance-fighter.[63] Megged's timing could not have been better, for his play was staged by the prestigious Habimah Theater when the trial, conviction, exoneration and assassination of another Hungarian Jew named Rezső or Israel Kasztner were still very fresh in the public mind. Indeed, Megged's brother Matti had given the Israeli public a choice: either a female Palestinian paratrooper who died heroically, or your typical Diaspora bureaucrat, who saved 1,684 Jews by entering into a pact with Adolph Eichmann, the Devil. The public resoundingly chose Szenes, with but one dissenting voice, that of the poet Natan Alterman, who rejected the false dichotomy between resistance and negotiation, the fighters and collaborators.[64]

The scandal of Jewish passivity was greatly mitigated once the focus of Holocaust memory shifted to women and children. Especially children. How did one mourn, let alone understand, the murder of 1.5 million Jewish children? Their annihilation through deprivation, disease, deportation, and mass death threatened the moral equilibrium of the adult world they left behind. By focusing instead on the narrative of rescue. The fate of the *Kindertransport*, to begin with, was a tale of individual rehabilitation under the most humane of wartime conditions. The few who were reunited with their parents after the war and the many who learned to speak English without an accent could pass as unexceptional citizens and resume an outwardly normal life. To enter public memory, however, their private success and silent struggle would have to wait until the 1990s. The fate of those traumatized, brutalized children inside the Jew-Zone who had somehow beaten the odds presented an altogether different challenge. They were *Undzere kinder* (Our Children), the name of a Yiddish docudrama filmed on location in Poland with a screenplay written by Rachel Auerbach.[65] Here the adults, led by the famous comedians Dzigan and Shumacher, had much to learn from the children, before they, the child-survivors, could be taught how to laugh.

The way children performed authentic ghetto songs and the way they narrated their own wartime experience would change the course of Holocaust memory, first in Yiddish and Hebrew, and later, in other languages. Meeting face-to-face with these children and being the first to collect their eyewitness testimonies, both Noah Gris and Binyamin Tenenbaum (later: Tene) were struck by a qualitative difference in word and deed. Gris marveled at their seeming indifference to death, their matter-of-fact tone, their "moral equilibrium and stoic calm." While adults were at a loss to find some analogy to the monomaniacal evil of Nazism and the untrammeled sadism of the German Master Race, children were emancipated from the need to analogize, so they could describe the atrocities with primitive directness.[66] After collecting a thousand child testimonies throughout Poland and in seventeen DP camps in Germany, Tenenbaum concluded that they were free of the self-blame and self-consciousness that bedeviled the construction of adult lives. The simplicity and directness with which children recalled their wartime experience reminded him of "an ancient saga or pages of the Hebrew Bible," where events were recounted without elaboration or pathos.[67] Gris's *Kinder-martirologye* (The Martyrology of the Children) appeared as volume 16 of The Library of Polish Jewry, while Tenenbaum's *Ehad me'ir ushnayim mimishpaha* (One From Each City and Two from Each Family) appeared as part of a series published by the left-wing Sifriat Poalim devoted to "The Evil Decrees of 1939–45." Arranged spatially, both anthologies placed the ghettos first and the death camps last. Communal sponsorship and anthological design bespoke a measure of continuity. The actual content set a new standard for solidarity, heroism, and truth.

When, a decade later, the first of these rescued children produced his own unmediated story, he further challenged the communal master narrative under the guise of simplicity. Yurik and his kid brother Kazik, the two protagonists of *Hayalei oferet* (The Lead Soldiers, 1958), a semi-autobiographical novel by Uri Orlev (né Jerzy Henryk Orlowski), were just plain children, who peed in their pants, screamed in their sleep, and had no idea what a Jew was.[68] The only heroics to speak of were the fantastically elaborate exploits they themselves invented. Like Anne Frank, who transformed her Secret Annex into a site for high adventure, fantasy for these children was a means of both escaping from reality and transmuting it. Orlev, who went on to become the most celebrated Israeli children's writer, boldly entered the zany, irreverent, capacious mind of his child protagonists, who were capable of turning everything they saw, heard, and suffered into a source of play. They had to, because the reality they entered defied the imagination.

★★★

One generation begat another. In a short story ironically titled "*Yad Vashem*" (The Name), Megged senior depicted an intergenerational conflict over the naming of a newborn child after someone who perished in the Holocaust.[69] The native-born parents refused to burden their son with any relic of the Diaspora. Neither side of the ghetto monument was of any use to them. So of all that was rescued, recorded, anthologized, translated, and published in Yiddish and Hebrew; of all the poets who eulogized and survivor-witnesses who fictionalized; from the whole communal memory bank created in the first fifteen years after the liberation, two figures were chiefly responsible for bringing the Holocaust home to the next generation: Yosl Rakover, the legendary martyr-fighter-and-challenger-of-God, and Ka-Tzetnik, whose sadomasochistic Nazi women in tight pants and riding boots, not to speak of the virginal Jewish maidens forced into prostitution, provided a whole generation of adolescent readers with forbidden reading material.[70] It was the old division of the sacred and profane played out against a rarefied and reconfigured Holocaust landscape.

Notes

1 James E. Young, *The Texture of Memory: Holocaust Memorials and Meaning* (New Haven, CT: Yale University Press, 1993), 155–84.
2 Emanuel Ringelblum, *Ksovim fun geto*, ed. A. Eisenbach et al. and Yosef Kermish (Tel Aviv: Y. L. Perets, 1985), vol. II: *Notitsn un ophandlungen*, 141.
3 Rachel Auerbach, *Behutsot Varshah: 1939–1943* (Tel Aviv: Am Oved, 1954).
4 David G. Roskies, *Against the Apocalypse: Responses to Catastrophe in Modern Jewish Culture* (Cambridge, MA: Harvard University Press, 1984), 276–80.
5 Leyb Rochman, *Un in dayn blut zolstu lebn: togbukh 1943–1944* (Paris: Fraynd fun Minsk Mazowieck, 1949); the quotation is from *The Pit and the Trap: A Chronicle of Survival*, trans. Moshe Kohn and Sheila Friedling (New York: Holocaust Library, 1983).
6 Jan Schwarz, "Blood Ties: Leib Rochman's War Diary," in *Memorial Books of Eastern European Jewry: Essays on the History and Meanings of Yizker Volumes*, ed. Rosemary Horowitz (Jefferson, NC: McFarland Press, 2011), 163–79.
7 Rochman, *Un in dayn blut zolstu*, p. 15.
8 Schwarz, "Blood Ties."
9 Anat Livneh, "The Cry of the Desperate and the Fortitude of the Remaining will Suffice": Commemorative Literature, Documentation and the Study of the Holocaust," *Dapim: Studies on the Shoah* 24 (2010): 177–78.
10 Zvi Kolitz, "Yossel Rakover's Appeal to God" (a new translation with afterword by Jeffrey V. Mallow and Frans Jozef van Beeck), *Cross Currents* (Fall 1994): 362–77.
11 Ibid., 373–74; Zvi Kolitz, *Tiger Beneath the Skin: Stories and Parables of the Years of Death*, trans. Shmuel Katz (New York: Creative Age Press, 1947).
12 Michal Borwicz, "Der apokrif u.n. 'Yosl Rakover redt tsu got'," *Almanakh* (Paris) (1955): 193–203.
13 *Kidesh hashem: a zamlung geklibene, oft gekirtste barikhtn, briv, khronikes, tsavoes, oyfshriftn, legendes, lider, dertseylungen, dramatishe stsenes, eseyen, vos moln oys mesires-nefesh in undzere un oykh in frierdike tsaytn*, ed. S. Niger (New York: CYCO Farlag, 1948).

14 Shmerke Kaczerginski, ed., *Lider fun di getos un lagern*, ed. H. Leivick (New York: CYCO Bicher Farlag, 1948).

15 Gila Flam, *Singing for Survival: Songs of the Lodz Ghetto, 1940–45* (Urbana: University of Illinois Press, 1992), 4.

16 Mordecai Gebirtig, "Fire!" (1936) in *The Literature of Destruction: Jewish Responses to Catastrophe*, ed. David G. Roskies (Phila.: Jewish Publication Society, 1989), 371–73.

17 *Kdoyshim*, melodies by Henech Kon and paintings by Isaac Lichtensten (New York: Machmadim Art Editions, 1947); *Undzere farpaynikte kinstler*, with a foreword by Marc Chagall (Paris: H. Fenster, 1951).

18 Livneh, "The Cry of the Desperate," 180.

19 Moshe Prager, *Antologye fun religyeze lider un dertseylungen: shafungen fun shrayber, umgekumene in di yorn fun yidishn khurbn in Eyrope* (New York: Research Institute of Religious Jewry, 1954); Conference on Jewish Material Claims Against Germany, *History of the Claims Conference: A Chronology* (New York, 2001).

20 Prager, *Antologye fun religyeze lider un dertseylungen*, p. 15.

21 *Ani ma'amin*, ed. Mordecai Eliav (Jerusalem: Mosad Harav Kook, 1965); *Out of the Whirlwind: A Reader of Holocaust Literature*, ed. Albert H. Friedlander (New York: Union of American Hebrew Congregations, 1968).

22 Jack Kugelmass and Jonathan Boyarin, eds., *From a Ruined Garden: The Memorial Books of Polish Jewry*, with bibliography and geographical index by Zachary M. Baker, 2nd ed. (Bloomington: Indiana University Press, 1998). The earliest yizkor books were written a generation earlier, in response to the Ukrainian pogroms. See David G. Roskies, *The Jewish Search for a Usable Past* (Bloomington: Indiana University Press, 1999), 57–64.

23 Edward L. Greenstein, "The Book of Lamentations: Response to Destruction or Ritual of Rebuilding?" in *Religious Responses to Political Crisis*, Library of Hebrew Bible/Old Testament Studies 444, ed. Henning Graf Reventlow and Yair Hoffman (New York: T & T Clark, 2008), 52–71.

24 Chaim S. Kazdan, ed., *Lerer-yizker-bukh: di umgekumene lerer fun Tsisho shuln in Poyln* (New York: Komitet tsu fareybikn dem ondenk fun di umgekumene lerer fun di Tsisho shuln in Poyln, 1954).

25 Boaz Cohen, "Holocaust Heroics: Ghetto Fighters and Partisans in Israeli Society and Historiography," *Journal of Political and Military Sociology* 31 (2003): 197–213.

26 Livneh, "The Cry of the Desperate," 177–222.

27 Ibid., 211.

28 *Sefer milhamot hageta'ot: ben hahomot, bamahanot baye'arot*, ed. Yitshak Zuckerman and Moshe Basok (Tel Aviv: Hakibbutz Hameuchad and Bet hageta'ot 'al shem Yitshak Katsenelson, 1954).

29 Yehudo Feld[wurm], *In di tsaytn fun Homen dem tsveytn*, ed. L. Olicki (Warsaw: Yidish bukh, 1954); *Tsvishn lebn un toyt*, ed. Leyb Olicki (Warsaw: Yidish bukh, 1955); Zelman Skalow, *Der haknkrayts (di hak on krayts)*, ed. L. Olicki (Warsaw: Yidish bukh, 1954)—all under the general editorship of Ber Mark.

30 The longest of Peretz Opoczynski's *Reportages from the Warsaw Ghetto* is "House No. 21" (1941), which tracks the push-and-pull between staying in Warsaw under German occupation or seeking one's fortunes across the new German-Soviet border. Gone from Mark's edition is the trade in wristwatches that the boys from Wołynska Street discover are "worth their weight in gold on the Other Side." By eliminating the last half of the reportage, Mark spared his readers the cruelty of the Russian border guards who began to behave no differently from the Germans. Cf. Peretz Opoczynski, *Reportazhn fun varshever geto*, ed. Ber Mark (Warsaw: Yidish bukh, 1954), 9–24 and Opoczynski, "House No. 21" trans. Robert Wolf in Roskies, ed., *Literature of Destruction*, 415–16, 419–24.

31 Ber Mark, "Yudenratishe 'ahves-yisroel' (an entfer afn bilbl fun H. Leyvik)," *Bleter far geshikhte* 5, no. 3 (1952): 63–115.

32 Ber Mark, *Di yidishe tragedye in der poylisher literatur* (Warsaw: Yidish bukh, 1950), 138–41.

33 Khone Shmeruk, "A briv in redaktsye," *Di goldene keyt* 140 (1995), 214–16.

34 Boaz Cohen, "Holocaust Heroics."

35 Cf. the censored version of Yitzhak Katzeneslon, *Vittel Diary*, trans. Myer Cohen (Israel: Ghetto Fighters' House, 1964) with *Ktavim aharonim: begeto Varsha uvemahane Vitel*, vol. 5 of *Ktavim*, ed. Menahem Dorman (Israel: Beit Lohamei Hageta'ot and Hakibbutz Hameuchad, 1988). Even in the latter, however, the names of Shloyme Mendelson, Artur Ziegelbojm and other Bundist leaders excoriated by Katzenelson are not identified in the biographical appendix.

36 Hannah Pollin, "*Geheymshtot* and the Construction of Avrom Sutzkever's Public Persona" (Senior thesis, Columbia College, 2004).

37 Abraham Sutzkever, "Mayn eydes-zogn farn nirnberger tribunal: togbukh-notitsn" (1966), in *Baym leyenen penimer: dertseylungen, dermonungen, eseyen* (Jerusalem: 1993), 161–64; YouTube, Nuremberg Day 69 Sutzkever, http://www.youtube.com/watch?v=cMDa 7OcXthw&feature=related

38 Abraham Sutzkever, *Geheymshtot: poeme* (Tel Aviv: Ahdut, 1948); excerpted in Abraham Sutzkever, *Selected Poetry and Prose*, trans. Barbara and Benjamin Harshav (Berkeley: University of California Press, 1991), 185–97.

39 Meyer Levin, *In Search: An Autobiography* (New York: Horizon Press, 1950), 241.

40 Mordecai Strigler, *In di fabrikn fun toyt* (Buenos Aires: Tsentral-farband fun poylishe yidn in Argentine, 1948), 7–67.

41 James E. Young, "Holocaust Documentary Fiction: The Novelist as Eyewitness," in *Writing and the Holocaust*, ed. Berel Lang (New York: Holmes & Meier, 1988), ch. 13.

42 Jan Schwarz, "A Library of Hope and Destruction: The Yiddish Book Series *Dos Poylishe Yidntum*, 1946–66," *Polin:* 20 (2007):185; quoting Y. Shatzky, "Problemen fun yidisher historiografye" (1955), *Shatski-bukh: opshatsungen vegn Yankev Shatski*, ed. E. Lifschutz (New York and Buenos Aires: YIVO, 1958), 248.

43 Mordecai Strigler, *Maydanek*, with a preface by H. Leivick (Buenos Aires: Tsentral-farband fun poylishe yidn in Argentine, 1947), 20–21.

44 Dan Miron, "Bein sefer le'efer," in *Hasifriya ha'iveret: proza me'urevet 1980–2005.* (Tel Aviv: Yedioth Ahronoth and Chemed Books, 2005), 147–83; Yehiel Szeintuch, *Salamandra: mitos vehistoria bekitvei Ka. Tzetnik*, ed. Carrie Friedman-Cohen (Jerusalem: Magnes Press, 2009).

45 Szeintuch, *Salamandra*.

46 Miron, "Bein sefer le'efer"; Omer Bartov, "Kitsch and Sadism in Ka-Tzetnik's Other Planet: Israeli Youth Imagining the Holocaust," *Jewish Social Studies*, ns 3(1997): 42–76.

47 Schwarz, "A Library of Hope and Destruction," 173–74.

48 *Seyfer minsk-mazovyetsk*, ed. Ephraim Shedletzky (Jerusalem: Minsk Mazowiecki Societies in Israel and Abroad, 1977).

49 Aharon Appelfeld, introduction to Rochman, *The Pit and the Trap*, 7–9.

50 Chaim Grade, "My Quarrel with Hersh Rasseyner" (1952), trans. Milton Himmelfarb in *When Night Fell: An Anthology of Holocaust Short Stories*, ed. Linda Schermer Raphael and Marc Lee Raphael (New Brunswick: Rutgers University Press, 1999), 161–84.

51 Ruth R. Wisse, *The Modern Jewish Canon: A Journey through Language and Culture* (New York: Free Press, 2000), 139.

52 Issac Bashevis Singer, *Shadows on the Hudson* (1957), trans. Joseph Sherman (New York: Farrar Straus and Giroux, 1998); "The Last Demon," trans. Martha Glicklich and Cecil Hemley; "The Cafeteria," trans. by the author and Dorothea Straus, in *The Collected Stories of Isaac Bashevis Singer* (New York: Farrar Straus and Giroux, 1983), 179–87, 287–300.

53 Shmuel Yosef Agnon, "The Lady and the Peddler" (1943), trans. Robert Alter in *Modern Hebrew Literature*, ed. Robert Alter (New York: Behrman House, 1971), 201–12; "The Sign" (1944, 1962), trans. Arthur Green in Roskies, *The Literature of Destruction*, 585–604; *'Ir umlo'ah* (Jerusalem: Schocken, 1973).

54 Dan Miron, *The Prophetic Mode in Modern Hebrew Poetry* (Milford, CT: Toby Press, 2010), 230–37.

55 Uri Greenberg, "To God in Europe," (1951), trans. Robert Friend in Roskies, *The Literature of Destruction*, 571–77; Miron, *The Prophetic Mode*, 237–46.

56 Alan L. Mintz, *Hurban: Responses to Catastrophe in Hebrew Literature* (New York: Columbia University Press, 1984), 181.

57 Miron, *The Prophetic Mode*, 246.

58 Jacob Glatstein, *Shtralndike yidn* (New York: Farlag Matones, 1946)*; I Keep Recalling: The Holocaust Poems of Jacob Glatstein*, trans. Barnett Zumoff with an intro. by Emanuel S. Goldsmith (Hoboken: Ktav, 1993), 92.

59 Kadia Molodowsky, "God of Mercy" (1945), trans. Irving Howe in *The Penguin Book of Modern Yiddish Verse,* Irving Howe, Ruth R. Wisse and Khone Shmeruk, eds. (New York: Penguin Books, 1988), 330–33.

60 Strigler, *Maydanek*, 42–44.

61 Leah Goldberg, "Lady of the Castle" (1955), in *Israeli Holocaust Drama*, ed. Michael Taub (Syracuse: Syracuse University Press), 21–78.

62 Judith Tydor Baumel, *Giborim lemofet: tsanḥane hayishuv bemilḥemet ha'olam hasheniyah vehazikaron hakolektivi hayisre'eli* (Sdeh-Boker: Ben Gurion Institute for Israel Studies and the Legacy of Ben Gurion and Ben Gurion University Press, 2004).

63 Dan Laor, "How Are We Expected to Remember the Holocaust? Szenesz versus Kasztner," in *On Memory: An Interdisciplinary Approach*, ed. Doron Mendels (Oxford and Bern: Peter Lang, 2007), 195–213; Aharon Megged, "Hanna Senesh" (1958) in Taub, *Israeli Holocaust Drama*, 79–126.

64 Natan Alterman, 1954. "Yom hazikaron vehamordim," in *Hatur hasvi'i* – vol. 2; as cited in Laor, etc.

65 *Undzere kinder*, dir. Natan Gross, prod. Shaul Goskind (Poland, 1948); J. Hoberman, *Bridge of Light: Yiddish Film between Two Worlds* (New York: Museum of Modern Art and Schocken Books, 1991), 330–31.

66 *Kinder-martirologye: zamlung fun dokumentn*, ed. Noyekh Gris (Buenos Aires: Tsentral-farband fun poylishe yidn in Argentine, 1947; vol. 16 of Dos poylishe yidntum), 57–62.

67 *Ehad me'ir ushnayim mimishpaha,* ed. Binyamin Tenenbaum (Tel Aviv: Sifriat Poalim, 1948), vi.

68 Uri Orlev, *The Lead Soldiers*, trans. Hillel Halkin (New York: Taplinger Publishing Co, 1980).

69 Aharon Megged, "The Name" (1950), trans. Minna Givton in *Facing the Holocaust: Selected Israeli Fiction*, ed. Gila Ramras-Rauch and Joseph Michman-Melkman (Philadelphia: Jewish Publication Society, 1985), 21–36.

70 Bartov, "Kitsch and Sadism in Ka-Tzetnik's Other Planet." *Dos hoyz fun di lyalkes* (The House of Dolls) was the first Yiddish novel I read on my own, far from my mother's watchful eye.

6

"WE KNOW VERY LITTLE IN AMERICA"

David Boder and un-belated testimony

Alan Rosen

Silence in relation to the Holocaust has many faces. "If my family is famous," declares the primordial victim in a poem of Dan Pagis, "not a little of the credit goes to me. My brother invented murder/my parents invented grief, I" – apparently the hapless victim – "invented silence."[1] Another prominent survivor, Elie Wiesel, tells of his ten-year vow of silence following the war's end.[2] This kind of deliberated silence is not likely that which constitutes the questionable historical assumption under review in this volume. But the integrity of this form of silence may bear nevertheless on the myth of silence that we are investigating, and I'll plan to return to it at the end of my essay.

The myth of silence surrounding postwar survivor testimony is certainly well established. Most assume that because survivors were reluctant to speak, or relatives and acquaintances were not interested in listening, little survivor testimony was heard in a public venue until the time of the Eichmann trial.[3] According to this view, testimony made headway in the 1970–90s, spurred onwards with the advent of videorecording, the medium used by Yale University's Fortunoff Video Archive for Holocaust Testimonies, Steven Spielberg's Survivors of the Shoah Visual History Foundation, and other such projects. Survivor testimony was thus understood to have emerged belatedly, deferred until survivors had fashioned new lives, until interest in the Holocaust had accelerated, until the denialists had reached new heights of cruel sophistication, and until it was deemed that popularization of the Holocaust was immeasurably distorting the truth.

But by no means all Holocaust survivor testimony was voiced belatedly. From 1944–49, Holocaust survivor testimony gathered in Europe by individuals and institutions numbered in the thousands: some 7000 interviews in Poland, 3500 in Hungary, 2500 in Germany and numbers more in Austria, France, Italy and Czechoslovakia.[4] Chicago-based psychologist David Boder contributed to this trove of testimony by interviewing over 100 DPs in Europe in the summer of 1946. He was one of the few, however, who had in mind the particular contribution of survivor testimony to the education of America. My essay examines how Boder attempted to carry through this pedagogy, the nature of and response to his efforts, and the significance for revising the myth of American silence in the aftermath of the Holocaust.

Boder himself arrived in North America in his mid-thirties and immigrated to the United States right around his fortieth birthday. Born in Libau, Russia (today Latvia) in 1886, Boder had arrived in the United States (via Mexico) in 1926, and a year later joined the faculty of the Chicago-based Lewis Institute (precursor of the Illinois Institute of Technology). During nine weeks in Europe – from July 29 to October 4, 1946 – Boder carried out approximately 130 interviews in nine languages and recorded them on a state-of-the-art wire recorder.[5]

The interviews were among the earliest (if not *the* earliest) audio recorded testimony of Holocaust survivors.[6] They are today the earliest extant recordings, valuable for the spoken word (that of the DP narrators and of Boder himself) and also for the song sessions and religious services that Boder wire recorded at various points through the expedition. Copies of the wire recordings were initially shipped to the National Institute of Mental Health, but were shunted from there to the Motion Picture and Sound Division of the Library of Congress. This is one of the sites where tape recorded copies can be found today; the other is the Archives of the United States Holocaust Memorial Museum. The original wire recorder spools have disappeared.

For more than a decade following the European expedition, Boder was tireless in transcribing, disseminating, publicizing, analyzing and lecturing on the material he had collected. Eighty of the interviews were eventually transcribed into English, most of which were included in a self-published manuscript of over 3100 pages comprising sixteen volumes. The volumes all appeared under the title *Topical Autobiographies of Displaced People*; they formed Boder's own library of catastrophe. Boder published two other major contributions based on the interviews: one, a 1949 book entitled *I Did Not Interview the Dead*; the other, a lengthy 1954 article, "The Impact of Catastrophe."[7] Another long article analyzing a single interview remains in manuscript.[8] By the time of his death in December, 1961, almost exactly fifteen years after returning from the DP "shelter houses" of postwar Europe, Boder had accomplished much, if not all, of what he set out to do with the interview project.

Foreign-born and bred, conversant in a number of European tongues (including Yiddish), Boder nevertheless identified himself as an American and hence as an outsider to the experience endured by the majority of his interviewees. In some respects, this was natural. By the time he set out to interview the DPs, he had been living in the United States for nearly twenty years. He was employed and funded solely by US institutions and most of his professional contributions – articles, lectures, research – were written in English and directed toward an American audience.

This American identity is important to note because when Boder in the spring of 1945 conceived the interview project and set about trying to realize it as soon as possible, he turned to hundreds of Americans, some of whom were well known and powerfully connected. Over the course of the fourteen months of preparation and planning, he conferred with dozens of prominent figures who were eagerly supportive.

He did not work in isolation but was rather in dialogue with members of the American Jewish and non-Jewish communities. Indeed, this support reflects American interest in the Holocaust at this time and came as a consequence of Boder's industry in making known the psychological dimensions of its aftermath.

There was interest but less knowledge of what had actually happened. In fact, Boder fashioned the interviews as a tool to teach Americans the basics. "We know very little in America about the concentration camps" was the phrase he used to set the interview agenda. In narrating wartime experience, the interviewees' task was to assume nothing. Terms, sites, procedures had to be spelled out. And this was the case in each and every interview. In one of the earliest interviews, Polia Bisenhaus described the grueling routine in Bergen-Belsen:

POLIA: We slept on the ground, and it was … all day we were sitting on the ground, on the same straw, and afterwards at night we slept on the same place. It was very dirty there. Many died from the dirt that was there.
BODER: What did the Germans say? Why were you held there?
POLIA: They told us nothing about why they held us there. They did not tell us but we knew that they held us because they wanted to annihilate us, but they did not succeed.

Boder didn't let up:

BODER: All right. Did they annihilate there other people?
POLIA: /two words not clear/ When the people were weak, and were becoming weaker from day to day because they were not given any food, so they annihilated them. There was … well a chamber where they gassed /gas-killed/ them, and afterwards they burned … well that all is known what the Germans have done.
BODER: How come you say it is well known? In America they know very little.
POLIA: Oh, they know in America. The periodicals have written a lot. Don't they know?
BODER: Oh yes, some people know, some people don't.[9]

What was basic information for those who were on the scene was not for at least "some people" in America. It was for these people that Bisenhaus was telling her story.

Throughout the interviews, Boder regularly reminded the narrator, in this case Jacob Minski, of the nature of this American audience and why that mattered:

MINSKI: For two years we could relatively … That is, we wore the Jew-star – were "tagged"; we had to buy in designated stores …
BODER: Yes.
MINSKI: And it is self-understood that we had no right to go to theaters and other /public/ places …
BODER: Don't make that so "self-understood"; we in America don't know that. You were not permitted to go to theaters, to movies … ?[10]

This broad pedagogical task comes through emphatically in Boder's prompting of Mendel Herskovitz:

BODER: All right. Good. Now, would you tell me with the best details, what happened in the few days before the Germans came, and when they came, and all that? Tell me everything the way you remember it. We want later to tell it to the American children.

For Boder to envision the children of America as a necessary part of the audience is not surprising, since it parallels his attention to children and youth as both potential and actual interviewees in Europe. Boder had his eye constantly fixed on America, estimating who might be the preferred audience and what piece of information couldn't be passed up. After soliciting from Roma Tcharnabroda a graphic and terrible account of a women camp prisoner being hanged, he asks, with apparent naïveté, about funeral rites:

BODER: Did you not have there a clergyman, a rabbi?
TCHARNABRODA: Where?
BODER: ... to give the woman the last rites?
TCHARNABRODA: Oh God, the SS does not recognize, did not recognize any clergy. They had torn down from the Polish women all the medallions, and all such objects; they said, "Here one needs no God any more."
BODER: Nu ...
TCHARNABRODA: God won't help you anyway.
BODER: You see I do know it, to be sure; but I am asking it for my American friends ...
TCHARNABRODA: /laughing/ Yes, they know very little about this /laughter/
BODER: Now continue.[11]

If America couldn't help but regard what happened in the camps with misplaced assumptions, Boder worked together with his narrators to provide a sobering corrective. America, then, was the main target. But this was because America – apparently in Boder's mind distant and ignorant regarding the victim's harrowing experience – needed to learn from the bottom up.

For all of its importance in giving a context, audience, and purpose to the interviews, the introductory phrase – "we know very little in America" – is not to be heard on the recorded interviews or read in the transcripts. Stated before the recording was under way, it served as something the narrator needed to hear but the listener – the audience in question – did not. For later researchers who hope to reconstruct the context of the interviews, the exclusion of this introductory material feels conspicuous. That it was left out shows how much Boder, though having in mind scholars who would eventually use the recordings, focused his efforts on overcoming American ignorance. The audience needed to hear the story, not to be instructed in the particulars of the interview process.

America knew little in spite (or because) of the wide circulation of newsreels depicting the liberation of the camps with the attendant grim scenes of corpses and starved survivors.[12] Graphic though these newsreels were, these "images of witness" were thought by some, including Boder, to have inherent limitations in conveying knowledge of what took place. "The present writer," Boder set forth in his 1945 memorandum, "could not help observing the enormous discrepancy between the abundance of visual material collected on subjects of the war and the meagerness of first-hand auditory material available on the same subject."[13] Boder's effort to rectify this discrepancy was what led to his recorded interviews, a kind of imageless testimony that sought to augment – and, perhaps, to challenge – the camera's work.

To his mind, there had been little in-depth testimony, little in the way of a story told by those who had gone through the experience. He wanted to produce what in the social science vocabulary of his day was called a "human document." Because of the problems presented by multiple languages and because of his psychological interest in traumatized language, recording the interviews offered the best possible option.

Boder saw himself offering a service that others working on behalf of the DPs could not. His authority on the matter came from the top: "It seems to me," Boder wrote in June, 1945, "to be the express desire of the Commander of the Army, General Eisenhower,

> that the proper organizations should be as completely informed through personal contact and their own specific methods of the human factors involved in the European tragedy and especially the tragedy of displaced persons. A group of motion picture producers have been flown to Europe only a few days ago. I think at least one psychologist should be entitled to facilities and cooperation for a survey with psychological methods and corresponding tools.[14]

The inadequacy of film newsreels to do justice to the victims affected others similarly. Renowned Buchenwald survivor Jorge Semprun's account of watching in December, 1945 newsreels of the liberation of concentration camps reads as if it came directly from Boder's notebook:

> Even though [the newsreel images] showed the naked obscenity, the physical deterioration, the grim destruction of death, the images, in fact, were silent. Not merely because they were filmed without live sound recording, which was standard practice at the time. They were silent above all because they said nothing precise about the reality they showed, because they delivered only confused scraps of meaning. … What was really needed was commentary on the images, to decipher them, to situate them not only in a historical context but within a continuity of emotions. And in order to remain as close as possible to the actual experience, this commentary would have had to be spoken by the survivors themselves: the ghosts who had returned from that long absence, the Lazaruses of that long death.[15]

Spurred by the silent newsreel images, Semprun's epiphany leads to a strategy for dealing with his Buchenwald experience: "One would," Semprun surmises, "have had to treat the documentary material, in short, like the material of fiction," a strategy he has carried out in his memoirs.[16] Boder was similarly impressed by the lack of "commentary," the lack of a meaningful story told by survivors. But the strategy he chose was to assemble a collection of "commentary spoken by the survivors themselves."

For both Semprun and Boder, the visual implied silence; it produced images lacking narrative and in need of deciphering. The images showing the "grim destruction of death" had to be situated, in Semprun's arresting phrase, in a "continuity of emotions." For both, it fell to the survivor to narrate and decipher. Strikingly, the often-referred to silence following liberation, frequently attributed to survivors themselves, is here directed back to the images. In this formulation, the technology itself is at fault. In contrast to the usual formulation, the survivors come to release the meaning that lies inert in (or behind) the silent images. In this case, the silence is to be found neither in a public's lack of interest or aversion to dealing with the Holocaust, nor in the survivor's refusal or inability to testify. Silence – the lack of commentary, the absence of a continuity of emotions – neutralized the very images of witness, short-circuiting the testimony they were meant to convey.

Focusing on personal wartime stories, Boder also hoped to revise America's distorted view of displaced persons. The fact that the DPs had been imprisoned often led a general public to think the worst of them, taking them for criminals.[17] This played into the hands of conservative forces pitted against DP immigration to the United States. The aforementioned newsreels, moreover, indirectly reinforced the unpalatable image of the survivor. Before being released, the raw newsreel footage from the camps was edited to underscore death and destruction and to eliminate the DPs' signs of life and recovery – a strategy apparently taken in order to justify the all-out war against an enemy that would commit such atrocities.[18]

Boder used the material from the interviews as a platform to redress this distorted view: the DP's, writes Boder, "are not riffraff, not the scum of the earth, not the poor devils who suffer because they don't know their rights, not idlers who declaim that the world owes them a living. They are uprooted people."[19] Boder echoes the harsh terms in circulation at the time in order to counter them. In doing so, he dignifies the DPs with the title, "uprooted people," nomenclature then increasingly in vogue to refer to migrants of all kinds. In this vein, Oscar Handlin, noted scholar of American history, published a few years later his bestseller, *The Uprooted*, a tribute to the essential role played by immigrants in forging the special ethos of the United States. Boder's renaming performed a similar act of rehabilitation.[20]

Giving a portrait of catastrophe by means of the "human document," Boder's book, *I Did Not Interview the Dead*, book was widely cited in the literature on displaced persons and concentration camps as well as in studies of psychology, sociology, and political science.[21] Some of the authors and publications who drew on it during the 1950s and early 1960s include Cornelius Krahn, *Mennonite Life* (1951); *Social Change: Latvian Society at Home and in Migration* (1952); David Reisman, *Individualism Reconsidered* (1955); H.G. Adler, *Theresienstadt* (1955); Joseph Tennenbaum, *Race and Reich: The Story of an*

Epoch (1956); *Social Problems* (1957); *Yad Vashem Bulletin* (1957); Martha Wolfenstein, *Disaster: A Psychological Essay* (1957); *Books for College Students' Reading* (1958); Donald Ray Cressy and Johan Galtung, *The Prison* (1961); and Seymour Martin Lipset, ed., *Culture and Social Character* (1961). Boder's DP interviews thus had ongoing relevance for any number of disciplines and kinds of readers, from the scholar to the student.

A decade or so after publication it was still being read by some important readers, including pioneering American sociologist Erving Goffman. Goffman's 1961 book, *Asylums: Essays on the Social Situation of Mental Patients and Other Inmates*, deals with the Holocaust only as it pertains to Goffman's broader inquiry into "the social situation of mental patients and other inmates."[22] *Asylums* nonetheless draws on examples from concentration camps to document its case. References to this literature appear throughout the book, yet Goffman limits his pool of sources to three books on concentration camps: Eugen Kogon, *The Theory and Practice of Hell*, Elie Cohen, *Human Behavior in the Concentration Camp*, and Boder, *I Did Not Interview the Dead*. Boder is here in distinguished company. The books by Kogon and Cohen are regarded as classics, both of them being systematic studies of concentration camps penned by social scientists who were also prisoners.[23] It is thus no surprise that Goffman should single them out. Inclusion of *I Did Not Interview the Dead* with these two suggests that, in 1961, Boder's interview collection, a different kind of book from the others, was held in high regard for what it too could convey through victims' voices. And Goffman's volume, saturated with references to the Holocaust even while focusing on a general sociopsychological phenomenon, shows how his mandate was to filter the Holocaust not out but in.

One of the most powerful professional validations of Boder's work came by way of the ongoing support of the National Institute of Mental Health. The NIMH had its origins in Franklin Roosevelt's New Deal policies, where it was deemed that the United States government, along with the sponsorship of other aggressive social programs, should play an active role in promoting the health of United States citizens. One avenue toward this goal was establishing a series of research and training institutions.[24] In 1937, the first such center, the National Cancer Institute, was established. In Truman's postwar administration several other institutes would follow: the National Heart Institute, the National Institute for Dental Sciences, the National Institute for Neurological Diseases and Blindness, and the National Institute of Mental Health, all of which subsisted under the umbrella of the National Institutes of Health.

The National Institute of Mental Health was itself formally established by law in 1946 but began to be funded only in 1948. Boder got in on the ground floor, having applied for support in 1948 and having corresponded with the administration of the program while it was still under the Mental Hygiene Division.[25] Boder's funding varied only slightly over the years, with a drop in the second and third years and a modest increase in the latter stages:

1949–50 $9400
1950–51 $6912
1951–52 $6000

1952–53 $7776
1953–54 $7776
1954–55 $10000
1955–56 $10649[26]

That Boder ended up not having enough funds to complete the transcriptions has distorted the views of the NIMH's role, leaving an impression that, because Boder's funding came to term with a number of interviews still not fully transcribed, the NIMH did not appreciate the significance of Boder's work and was parsimonious toward that which deserved better.[27] This estimation seems far from the truth.

Boder's funding from the NIMH was substantial in several respects.[28] To begin with, he received continuous funding during the NIMH's first nine years. Few of Boder's colleagues who were funded by the NIMH in these formative years, even those from premier research universities, were funded for a comparable span of time. Moreover, even once the NIMH was an established institution boasting a substantially more robust budget, few colleagues were funded for as many years. And if Boder's actual grant allocation was far lower than the amount supplied to the most prestigious names in American academia, the $70,000 was nevertheless greater than that given to the majority of those funded.[29]

To be sure, the funds turned out to be less than were needed to complete the transcriptions (though Boder transcribed more than has generally been thought). Yet Boder blamed himself for falling short. He felt he had not been able to foresee the extraordinary labor that the project would require and thus had been too modest in his requests.[30] He, in other words, got what he asked for – which, in the long run, simply wasn't enough. But the duration of the funding was exceptional and the amount respectable.

Noteworthy when compared to grantees at large, Boder's success looks even better when taking stock of those who did not receive funding during this period. Included in this group is one of the preeminent psychologists of the late 1940s, Carl Rogers, who among other notable contributions to the profession developed the nondirective interview technique that Boder had adopted. Professor at the University of Chicago and president of the American Psychological Association, Rogers was nevertheless turned down in numerous bids to receive NIMH grants. Only when he was able to put together the right constellation of supporters was he successful.[31] Funding was thus not at all a foregone conclusion, especially in the NIMH's early years. The institution's ongoing commitment to Boder's project conveys its belief that Boder's work would make a difference in American life. It was understood that Boder had collected a wealth of primary sources that needed to be preserved and rendered accessible.

On multiple levels, Boder's interviews found an engaged lay and scholarly American audience. While it is true that his book was not a best seller and that it was not easy for him to get it published, its fortunes were due less to its subject matter than to its uneven quality of presentation. That said, it was read, cited, and drawn on by many important readers.

The myth of silence is not only challenged by reviewing Boder's contributions and the response to them. It has also played a role in distorting the reception of his work. Because it has been presumed that there was little American response to the Holocaust before the 1960s, the context of Boder's DP interviews has disappeared. Rather than his 130 or so interviews being seen as representing a small sample within a huge crop of DP interviews, Boder's have been deemed the only ones of their kind. And rather than being correctly viewed as emerging from an intersection of various streams of American social science research in the 1940s, they are seen to have come out of the blue.

The myth has similarly eclipsed the career of the Boder interviews during the 1950s. Having influenced a wide range of writing and research in this period, the interviews are treated as something lost and then discovered, on the order of the buried-and-then-unearthed Warsaw Ghetto Oyneg Shabes archives and other war-time writings. "In 1998," notes one summary of the project, "a sixteen-volume set of typescripts from these recordings were discovered."[32] "Although his work produced the only recorded oral histories of survivors from that time," reads a second, "Boder's efforts attracted little interest and were nearly lost before the Galvin Library [at the Illinois Institute of Technology] rediscovered his work after more than 50 years." This account doubles the "discovery" motif when it explains the recent attention: "When a story about the recordings was found in an old university newsletter, the [IIT] library ... embarked on a grand restoration project in 1998 ... "[33]

In order to dramatize the alleged discovery, Boder's contemporary achievements are muted, minimizing the dissemination of the interviews both during his lifetime and in its aftermath:

> Despite the groundbreaking nature of his work, Dr. David P. Boder was largely unsuccessful in his efforts to publish the displaced persons (DPs) interviews. Before his death in 1961 though, he did submit a set of seventy interview transcripts to a select number of libraries and historical foundations across the U.S. (including Illinois Institute of Technology), though few volumes remain today.[34]

Historian Donald Niewyk, who may be the source of the above conjecture, strangely speaks in his abridged edition of the interview transcriptions of Boder depositing his "mimeographed and microcard copies in a handful of large research libraries."[35] Yet Boder posted the transcripts to some 45 libraries worldwide;[36] and, contra the inaccessibility implied in both accounts, the volumes of *Topical Autobiographies* can be found today in at least 23 libraries in America alone, with a number of others located in research centers worldwide.[37]

The myth of silence organizes the facts to suit its purposes. And, in this case, it fashions an idiom of loss/discovery to reinforce it. Indeed, the rhetoric of "discovery" of what was lost shadows postwar responses to the Holocaust, with the unearthing of a portion of the Oyneg Shabes archives in Warsaw in 1946 and 1950 establishing the litmus test of authenticity.[38] Some authors have deliberately used the found manuscript or book topos to give their fictional stories a patina of authenticity.[39] The complicated history of Boder's materials can easily be made to fit this paradigm, partially because there is a degree of discovery associated with the wire recordings – a saga I have elsewhere chronicled.[40]

But that said, the story has been slanted for several reasons. First, Boder's interviews took place near enough to the war so that they themselves take on the aura of wartime material. Second, historiography has by and large drawn on the documentation of the perpetrators, consigning troves of victim testimony to the periphery. And third, Boder's transcriptions were monumental in size, clumsy in organization and, until recently, mainly available only in translation. Historians were seemingly reluctant to try to negotiate the cumbersome materials. Indeed, in recent years a number of premier historians have chosen to use the abridged version of the interviews rather than investigate Boder's originals.[41] All in all, the myth of silence undergirds the rhetoric of discovery, making it seem that there was little interest in such primary sources until decades later.

Although exaggerated, the topic of postwar silence has at least one dimension that is apparently not a myth. Even though the testimonies of displaced persons in the late 1940s number, as I mentioned, well over ten thousand, this number was itself but a small proportion of the DPs, roughly 2–3 per cent.[42] Most seemingly did not testify, were not interviewed. According to the protocols of the German Historical Commission, for example, who were in charge of conducting interviews and obtaining testimony in the American zone in Germany, most DPs were reluctant to step forward. Indeed, in order to gain a larger contingent, the Commission was compelled to try various strategies to convince the DPs to set outside their desire to put the past behind them.[43] Silence was, then, the norm in this community, at least in terms of public expression; it was the gateway to forgetting a tortuous past, the means to go forward in rebuilding lives. Not all followed this path. But for the majority that did, silence was not a myth, but a way to live.

Admittedly, this European-based testimonial silence does not bear directly on America. But the reluctance to bear witness among many European DPs does suggest that the specter of postwar silence, however overextended and underresearched, played a role as well. The silence we are investigating thus has at least two faces, one a distorted myth, the other a necessary strategy of coping. Perhaps then it is better to speak, following the haunting strains of Pagis' primordial victim, of the invention of silence, but also of its uses and abuses.

Notes

1 Dan Pagis, *The Selected Poetry of Dan Pagis*, trans. Stephen Mitchell, intro. Robert Alter (Berkeley: University of California Press, 1996).
2 Elie Wiesel, "An Interview Unlike Any Other," *A Jew Today*, trans. Marion Wiesel (New York: Vintage, 1979), 18–19.
3 On the reluctance to speak and the refusal to listen, see William Helmreich, *Against All Odds: Holocaust Survivors and the Successful Lives They Made in America* (New Brunswick, NJ: Transaction, 1996), 38; Tony Kusher summarizes (and endorses) this view by stating

that the survivors spoke little in "the postwar world that was largely indifferent or hostile to their memories." "Holocaust Testimony, Ethics, and the Problem of Representation," *Poetics Today* 27 (2006), 276. On the path breaking nature of the Eichmann trial for survivor testimony, see Shoshana Felman, "Theaters of Justice: Arendt in Jerusalem, the Eichmann Trial, and the Redefinition of Legal Meaning in the Wake of the Holocaust," *Critical Inquiry* 27 (2001); on the evolution of survivor testimony after the trial, see Annette Wieviorka, *The Era of the Witness* (Ithaca, NY: Cornell UP, 2007); for a similar but more complex view of the evolution of survivor testimony in Israel, see Anita Shapira, "The Holocaust: Private Memories, Public Memory," *Jewish Social Studies* 4 (1998): 40–58.

4 For Poland, see *Holocaust Survivor Testimonies Catalogue, Jewish Historical Institute Archives, Record* (Warsaw: 1998–2002); for Hungary, Rita Horvath, "'A Jewish Historical Commission in Budapest': The Place of the National Relief Committee for Deportees in Hungary [DEGOB] among the Other Large-Scale Historical-Memorial Projects of *She'erit Hapletah* After the Holocaust (1945–48)," *Holocaust Historiography in Context*, eds. David Bankier and Dan Michman (Jerusalem: Yad Vashem, 2008), 475–96; and for Germany, Ada Schein, "'Everyone Can Hold a Pen': The Documentation Project in the DP Camps in Germany," *Holocaust Historiography in Context*, eds. David Bankier and Dan Michman (Jerusalem: Yad Vashem, 2008), 103–34; and, more generally, on the collection of victim testimony in early postwar Europe, Phillip Friedman, "European Jewish Research on the Holocaust," in *Roads to Extinction: Essays on the Holocaust*, ed. Ada June Friedman (New York and Philadelphia, 1980) 500–524 (Friedman's essay originally appeared in 1949 in the *Proceedings of the Academy*); Shmuel Krakowski, "Memorial Projects and Memorial Institutions Initiated by She'erit Hapletah," *She'erit Hapletah, 1944–1948*, eds. Yisrael Gutman and Avital Saf (Jerusalem: Yad Vashem, 1990) 388–98; Laura Jockusch, "'Collect and Record., 1943–1953," diss., New York University, 2007; Laura Jockusch "*Khurban Forschung*: Jewish Historical Commissions in Europe, 1943–49," *Simon Dubnow Institute Yearbook* 6 (2007): 441–73.

5 I address the puzzling indeterminate number of interviews in Alan Rosen, *The Wonder of Their Voices: The 1946 Holocaust Interviews of David Boder* (NY: Oxford, 2010), in appendix II, "The Disputed Number of Boder Interviews," 239–40.

6 The historical commission based in Munich recorded survivors singing songs, but it apparently did not record them recounting their wartime experiences.

7 David Boder, *I Did Not Interview the Dead* (Urbana: University of Illinois Press, 1949); David Boder, "The Impact of Catastrophe: I. Assessment and Evaluation," *Journal of Psychology* 38 (1954): 3–50.

8 "The Tale of Anna Kovitzka: A Logico-Systematic Analysis or an Essay in Experimental Reading." The essay can be found at several locations, including the David Boder Museum file, Archives of the History of American Psychology/M16; and the David P. Boder Papers, Special Collections, Charles Young Research Library, UCLA/Box 6.

9 "Polia Bisenhaus," *Topical Autobiographies*, vol. 5, chap. 19 (Chicago and Los Angeles: 1950–57); "David Boder Interviews Polia Bisenhaus," *Voices of the Holocaust*, Paul V. Galvin Library, Illinois Institute of Technology, 2009, October 19, 2010, Available at: http://voices.iit.edu/interview?doc=bisenhausP& display = bisenhausP_en

10 Jacob Minski, *Topical Autobiographies*, vol. 8, chap. 31; "David P. Boder Interviews Jacob Minski," *Voices of the Holocaust*, October 20, 2010, http://voices.iit.edu/interview? doc=minskiJ& display = minskiJ_en

11 Roma Tcharnabroda, *Topical Autobiographies*, vol. 5, chap. 18; "David P. Boder Interviews Roma Tcharnabroda," *Voices of the Holocaust*, October 20, 2010, http://voices.iit.edu/interview?doc=tcharnabrodaR& display = tcharnabrodaR_en

12 On newsreel images and the predominant role of the "image as witness" in the United States in the months following the war's end, see Jeffrey Shandler, *While America Watches: Televising the Holocaust* (New York: Oxford University Press, 1999), pp. 5–22; on the photographic image, see Barbie Zelizer, *Remembering to Forget: Holocaust Memory Through the Camera's Eye* (Chicago: University of Chicago Press, 1998).

13 Boder also incorporates these words in his "Addenda" to *Topical Autobiographies*, 3161.

14 Letter to Dael Wolfle, June 19, 1945.UCLA/Box 1.

15 Jorge Semprun, *Literature or Life* (New York: Viking, 1997), 200–201.

16 *Le Grand Voyage* (The Long Voyage) and *Quel beau dimanche!* (What a Beautiful Sunday).

17 Michael Berkowitz details this cruel perception in *The Crime of My Very Existence: Nazism and the Myth of Jewish Criminality* (Berkeley: University of California Press, 2007), particularly in the chapter, "Lingering Stereotypes and Jewish Displaced Persons."

18 Shandler, pp. 16–17.

19 David Boder, *I Did Not Interview the Dead*, p. xviii.

20 Maurice Hindu's 1929 volume, *Humanity Uprooted*, is one of the first to use the term in this manner. Oscar Handlin, *The Uprooted: The Epic Story of the Great Migrations That Made the American People* (Boston, Little, Brown, 1951). Several authors preceded Boder in using the term to refer to World War II displaced persons.

21 From the 1960s onward, books and journals have continued to cite Boder's interview project. See Albert Biderman, *March to Calumny: The Story of American POWs in the Korean War* (1963); Stephen Spitzer and Norman Denzin, *The Mental Patient* (1968); Polsky, Claster, and Goldberg, *Social System Perspectives in Residential Institutions* (1970); Kurt Wolff, *Trying Sociology* (1974); Earl Rubington and Martin Weinberg, eds., *Deviance: The Interactionist Perspective* (1978); Jerome Manis and Bernard Meltzer, eds., *Symbolic Interaction* (1978); Reeve Brenner, *The Faith and Doubt of Holocaust Survivors* (1980); Jehuda Reinharz, *The Jewish Response to German Culture* (1985); Richard Harvey Brown, *Society as Text: Essays on Rhetoric, Reason, and Reality* (1987); Steven Weine, *When History is a Nightmare* (1999); Ewa Geller, *Warschauer Jiddich* (Niemeyer, 2001); and Phillip Bean, *Crime: Critical Concepts in Sociology* (2003).

22 Erving Goffman, *Asylums: Essays on the Social Situation of Mental Patients and Other Inmates* (New York, Anchor, 1961).

23 Eugen Kogon, *The Theory and Practice of Hell: The German Concentration Camps and the System Behind Them*, trans. Heinz Norden (New York: Farrar, Straus, 1950); Elie Cohen, *Human Behavior in the Concentration Camp*, trans. M.H. Braaksma (New York, Norton, 1953).

24 See Wade Pickren, "Science, Practice and Policy: An Introduction to the History of Psychology and the National Institute of Mental Health," in *Psychology and the National Institute of Mental Health: A Historical Analysis of Science, Practice and Policy*, ed. Wade E. Pickren and Stanley F. Schneider (Washington, DC: American Psychological Association, 2004).

25 See Boder's correspondence with Lawrence Kolb, Research Projects Director, Mental Hygiene Division, U.S. Public Health Service, June 8, 16, and 21, 1948. AHAP/M11.

26 Boder's summary of funding is corroborated by NIMH's listing of its grants. See *Mental Health Research Grant Awards, Fiscal Years 1948–1963,* (Washington, 1964).

27 See Donald Niewyk, "Introduction," Fresh Wounds: Early Narratives of Holocaust Survival (Chapel Hill: University of North Carolina Press, 1998); Carl Marziali, "Uncovering Lost Voices: 1946 David Boder Tapes Revived," February 1, 2003; and the *Voices of the Holocaust* website http://voices.iit.edu.

28 For the context of the discussion that follows, see Charles Rice, "The NIMH Research Grants Program and the Golden Age of American Academic Psychology," in Pickren and Schneider (eds.) *Psychology and the National Institute of Mental Health*. Wade Pickren generously provided me with a longer unpublished version of Rice's paper. Professor Rice elaborated on the issues discussed therein in a telephone interview, August, 2005.

29 His association with IIT likely did not hurt his chances but neither did it help them; most of the NIMH's grants flowed to researchers at the major universities. Boder's eventual move to Los Angeles and affiliation with UCLA probably helped his cause, even though the psychology department at UCLA in the early 1950s was not yet considered a major research center. I am indebted to Wade Pickren for his assessment of Boder's affiliations.

30 Letter from Boder to Philip Sapir, Chief, Research Grants and Fellowship Branch, NIMH, April 26, 1956; "Addenda," *Topical Autobiographies*, 3160.

31 Charles Rice, "Early NIMH Funding of American Psychology," American Psychology Association Conference Paper, 2003.

32 Karen Kring, "David Boder Recorded Earliest Holocaust Survivors Testimonies [sic]," 2009, *SkokieNet*. October 13, 2010, http://www.skokienet.org/node/3761.

33 Carl Marziali, "Uncovering Lost Voices: 1946 David Boder Tapes Revived," February 1, 2003.

34 "Project History," *Voices of the Holocaust*. 2009, Paul V. Galvin Library, Illinois Institute of Technology, October 18, 2010 http://voices.iit.edu/voices_project.

35 Niewyk, "Introduction," *Fresh Wounds*, 5.

36 David P. Boder Papers, Archives of the History of American Psychology. A number of lists from the mid-1950s show the institutions and individuals that were sent copies of the mimeographed and microcard transcriptions. These included the British Museum, the University of Malaya, and the National Library of Hebrew University.

37 See *Topical Autobiographies*, on WorldCat, which lists 19 libraries, but doesn't include the copies in the holding of the United States Holocaust Memorial Museum, the Simon Wiesenthal Center, the Library of Congress, and Harvard University.

38 See Samuel Kassow, *Who Will Write Our History? Emanuel Ringelblum, the Warsaw Ghetto, and the Oyneg Shabes Archive* (Bloomington: University of Indiana Press, 2007), 1–2, 215–16.

39 See for example John Hersey's *The Wall* and Anne Michael's, *Fugitive Pieces,* and my discussion of the two in *Sounds of Defiance: The Holocaust, Multilingualism and the Problem of English* (Lincoln: University of Nebraska Press, 2005), 184–85.

40 *The Wonder of Their Voices*, 165–70.

41 See for example Christopher Browning, *Collected Memories: Holocaust History and Postwar Testimony* (Madison, WI: University of Wisconsin Press, 2003), 62–63 and notes thereon. Despite citing Boder's interview and transcript in tandem with Niewyk's edited version, Browning clearly uses the latter's rendition – a strategy that leads to a misreading of some of the testimony in question. See also Saul Friedländer, *The Years of Extermination: Nazi Germany and the Jews, 1939–1945* (New York: Harper Perennial, 2007), 145, where his invocation of a few Boder interviews cites only Niewyk's abridged edition.

42 On DP numbers and postwar predicament, see Eugene Kulischer, *Europe on the Move: War and Population Changes, 1917–1947* (New York: Columbia University Press, 1948); Jacques Vernant, *The Refugee in the Post-War World* (New Haven: Yale University Press, 1953); Malcolm Proudfoot, *European Refugees, 1939–1952: A Study in Forced Population Movements* (Evanston: Northwestern University Press, 1957); Michael R. Marrus, *The Unwanted: European Refugees in the Twentieth Century* (New York: Oxford University Press, 1985); Mark Wyman, *DP: Europe's Displaced Persons, 1945–1951* (Philadelphia and London: Balch Institute Press and Associated UP, 1989); Anna Holian, "Between National Socialism and Soviet Communism: The Politics of Self-Representation among Displaced Persons in Munich, 1945–51," unpublished dissertation, 2005; Tony Judt, *Postwar* (New York: Penguin, 2006). Essential studies of Jewish DPs, focusing mainly on DP camps in Germany, include *She'erit Hapletah, 1944–1948*, eds. Yisrael Gutman and Avital Saf; Michael Brenner, *After the Holocaust: Rebuilding Jewish Lives in Postwar Germany* (Princeton: Princeton University Press, 1997); Ze'ev Mankowitz, *Life between Memory and Hope: The Survivors of the Holocaust in Occupied Germany* (Cambridge: Cambridge University Press, 2002); Hagit Lavsky, *New Beginnings*; Ruth Gay, *Safe Among the Germans: Liberated Jews After World War II* (New Haven: Yale University Press, 2002); Atina Grossman, *Jews, Germans, and Allies: Close Encounters in Occupied Germany* (Princeton: Princeton University Press, 2007); Avinoam Patt and Michael Berkowitz, eds., *"We Are Here": New Approaches to Jewish Displaced Persons in Postwar Germany* (Detroit: Wayne State University Press, 2010).

43 Jockusch, "'Collect and Record'"; Jockusch, *"Khurban Forschung"*; Laura Jockusch, personal communication, summer, 2009.

7

DAVID P. BODER

Holocaust memory in Displaced Persons camps

Rachel Deblinger

In 1946, Latvian-born psychologist David P. Boder traveled from Chicago, Illinois, to Displaced Persons camps in France, Switzerland, Italy, and Germany to record the memories and experiences of those who lived through what later became known as the Holocaust. Armed with a wire recorder and 200 spools of wire, Boder recorded 109 interviews in over seven languages with Displaced Persons including Jewish concentration camp survivors, Baltic workers, and Mennonites escaping from Soviet Russia. Eight of the interviews, six of Jewish victims and two of other witnesses, were translated, transcribed, and published in 1949 as *I Did Not Interview the Dead*.[1] Boder continued to translate the interviews and, between 1950 and 1957, he privately distributed copies of 70 transcripts in a five-series collection entitled *Topical Autobiographies of Displaced People Recorded Verbatim in Displaced Persons Camps*.[2]

Boder's collection is only one challenge to the idea that silence followed the Holocaust. The hours of eyewitness accounts he collected confirm the ability and eagerness of survivors to speak about their experiences, and his published work proves that there was at least some market for books to be published about the subject in America. Yet, Boder's collection does more than just prove that people were talking about the persecution of Jews in Nazi Europe in the immediate postwar period; his work allows us to examine how survivors talked about the Holocaust in this period.

This essay will rely on Boder's collection to illustrate the diversity of early testimony in Displaced Persons (DP) camps and examine the limitations of recording Holocaust memory in such spaces, recognizing how the constraints of postwar life framed survivor narratives and marked the narratives Boder collected. I will first explore the liminality of DP space and the challenges that both Boder and the survivors faced in communicating with one another. I will then focus on how Boder's collection serves as an example of the open and candid recollection of the Holocaust preserved in early testimonies that confirm the varied behavior and experiences of victims under Nazism. Here, the paper will address how early Holocaust testimony cuts against the grain of later taboos and complicates our understanding of the survivor experience. Finally, I will consider how the DP camps fostered early collective memory and how these accounts anticipated what later became central motifs in more recent Holocaust culture.

In many ways, recording Holocaust memory in DP spaces was the most obvious place to do so in postwar Europe, as they were home to most DPs and the majority of Jewish Holocaust survivors. Victims from different concentration camps, work camps, and non-camp experiences jointly formed communities and worked together to organize DP life. In the summer of 1946, Boder visited over fifteen such camps and homes in three months. Most of these spaces, even those outside organized camps, had been part of the war effort. Camps like Bergen-Belsen and Landsberg were established in former concentration camps, while others were organized in spaces that had formerly held the German Army or Nazi Youth. Thus, the survivors of the Holocaust were rebuilding their lives in spaces that were no longer part of the war but still remnants of the German war effort. As evident in the testimonies, such spatial realities prolonged the feeling of victimization for many survivors and complicated the emotional recovery survivors faced in the postwar period.

Boder's interview with Anna Kaletzka demonstrates the emotional contradictions of the survivors, who were trapped between the past and future.[3] Kaletzka, a Jewish survivor from Poland who spoke of her time in Auschwitz, the separation from her husband, and the death of her daughter, alternately wept and laughed during the interview. Towards the end, her emotion and despair intensified. Kaletzka said,

> After work, to come alone to my room – today is a holiday. Where are all mine, who used to celebrate the holidays with me? Thank God! There are Jews staying with me on this holiday. There was never a holiday in Auschwitz. But my own people are no more. I am alone.[4]

Kaletzka conflated her sadness and loss with the relief of being able to celebrate the holiday. The duality of her emotional state reveals the lasting impact of the war years in the DP period and how the DP experience became part of the early record about the Holocaust.

Kaletzka's interview also shows the contradiction of DP spaces – they were not only a space of continued struggle but also of renewed Jewish life and communal practice. The interview ends as above in *I Did Not Interview the Dead*, but in *Topical Autobiographies* there is one additional paragraph. Boder wrote,

> Now I don't find a little episode which she told me, apparently after I had stopped the machine. It is not on the wire, but here it is, written from memory: 'Last night /and that means on the first evening of Rosh Hashona/* we, like at home, prepared the holiday meal, and as was customary at home, we invited a soldier to share it with us. But this time it was *not a poor soldier*, away from home, who had to be fed, but an American Jewish soldier, who, accepting the invitation, brought us an armful of gifts, all kinds of American food and delicacies.[5]

This continued story underscores Boder's collection as a documentation of DP life. The interaction of a group of young DP women and an American soldier sharing Rosh Hashanah dinner is specific to the DP experience and reveals the tension between moving forward and thinking back. There is obvious joy in sharing with the American soldier and in celebrating the holiday at all. But, Anna explained that this act reminded her of home – twice the home of Anna's past and once the present home of the American soldier. While the women here are trying to make the space they were in as home-like as possible, they had no home at that time. This story reveals one historian's assessment that the refugees were "a unique community that had abandoned its past and was yet to find its future."[6]

As Kaletzka expressed, DP life was defined by the same in-between-ness as their postwar spaces. Boder's collection must be read with this physical and psychological liminality in mind. While survivors were rebuilding their lives, any sense of relief was still tenuous. In 1947, Leo Srole, the Welfare Director of Landsberg camp, wrote, "Twenty months later, [the DP] is still captive and still in jeopardy ... The victims still await final rescue."[7] Srole explained that despite a fierce determination to live and a deep longing to return to normalcy, the DPs were trapped, still waiting for their futures, which would begin elsewhere. This frustration, which Boder preserved, framed the way survivors spoke about the Holocaust and was often expressed as bitterness toward liberation. Such bitterness was voiced enough that Boder noted, "One feels that by not having taken the immediate impressions in 1945 we have lost a number of enthusiastic stories full of hopes which by 1946 have proved empty illusions."[8] Boder's note here is telling. In Holocaust testimony collections from the 1980s and 90s there is a sharp break between wartime and postwar. This kind of chronological delineation was not present in 1946.

Nor was there a clear sense of when the survivor's story should start or stop. Boder often asked his interviewees to begin by talking about where they were when the war began. For interviewees from Poland, their story started in 1939 or earlier. For some living in France, their story began in 1940. Lacking chronological consistency, the interviews highlight the differences between survivor experiences but also pre-suppose that a survivor "story" began with the direct interruption of their lives by the Nazis. In fact, many survivors had to go back before the war to make their narratives clear. The stories jump through time to explain a point or clarify family structure or other relationships and to include what the interviewee considered most important.

In particular, the narratives lack resolution. Survivors were often unable to con-clude their narratives because their struggle for freedom continued and their attempt to assimilate their experience into a story was not complete. Most did not know where or when they would be able to emigrate. Israel had not yet been created as a state, British immigration restrictions denied Jews refuge in Palestine, and the US retained strict immigration quotas. Additionally, in the early postwar period, those who survived were still learning about what happened to their families and friends. Lists were circulated by American Jewish organizations and the DP administrations in an effort to reunite survivors and DPs sought any information they could find about their relatives.

Boder's interview with Henja Frydman articulates how survivors were only just learning the details of their own family stories. Frydman spoke at length about her brother, who had been detained in Drancy. At one point, she explained that her family received a letter stating that the brother had been deported.

QUESTION: Where was he deported? Do you know?

MISS FRYDMAN: We didn't know where he was deported.

QUESTION: Was it found out later?

MISS FRYDMAN: Afterwards, when I was deported to Auschwitz, I asked around everywhere among the men. Possibly someone knew, but nobody had seen him. /Her speech here is still interrupted by repeated blowing of her nose./ Why he wasn't seen I know; because my brother had died of typhus, right at the beginning.

QUESTION: Who informed you about that?

MISS FRYDMAN: One of our acquaintances who has now returned. He had seen him in the lager Auschwitz in 1942, that my brother fell, that he got sick with typhus, and died immediately afterwards.[9]

Many of Boder's interviewees were still running into such acquaintances and fitting together the elements of their own narratives.

The particularities of DP life also contributed to the truncated narratives. Boder had trouble finding quiet, private spaces in which to conduct the interviews, and the recordings were marred by interruptions like airplane noises, dogs barking, and other DPs.[10] Additionally, technical problems disrupted the narratives; each wire lasted about twenty-seven minutes and then had to be changed, the microphone sometimes needed to be adjusted, and the electricity was inconsistent in postwar Europe so power shortages would often shut down the wire recorder. Such interruptions constrained the flow of conversation, and most interviews failed to construct a fluid narrative.

Most often, however, the narratives were interrupted by Boder's own questions. He regularly interrupted his interviewees to clarify terminology, time line, and important elements of the survivor's account. While part of his need to interrupt might have been due to a lack of available knowledge at that time, it was more than just confusion. In an unpublished interpretive essay Boder wrote in response to Anna Kaletzka's interview, he said,

> I have a feeling that every time I interrupted the story to clarify a point, I have lost a no less important item which would have been told spontaneously. Nevertheless, it had to be done from time to time, if for no other reason than to assure the interviewee of my interest in his narrative.[11]

As he explained, the interruptions did more than clarify confusion, and the transcripts reveal tension between his methodological intention to act as a trained psychologist and the reality of recording Holocaust memory in 1946.[12] He was occasionally shocked and repeated clarifying questions, regularly delaying the progression of the survivor's account. In this way, Boder's interruptions and confusion point to the incomprehensibility of Holocaust testimony – one that was especially acute in the immediate aftermath of the war when basic terms were not yet clear and a lack of historical understanding prevalent.

Boder's interview with Kalman Eisenberg included many moments when Boder lost track of the narrative and interrupted.[13] While the interruptions derail the fluid narrative, they also lead to discussions about the specifics of Eisenberg's experience and record in detail what might have been missed if the interviewer had not voiced his confusion. Near the middle of the interview, Eisenberg explained that he was deported to a work camp. Boder became confused by the term "Nagan" used by Eisenberg and asked for clarification.

EISENBERG: I go once to a "chief" whose name was … eh … what was his name? Altoff. A chief Von /?/ Altoff. His name was Altoff. He was a "leader" of the … of a factory, a German. He took us, eight boys, to him … to work for him, to work for him. We would work very diligently. He would stand and watch. All at once he comes over, gives us a Nagan in the hand and says, "Beat your comrade!" I take /it/ and beat him. He says, "that is not how one beats," takes that Nagan out of my hand, and gives me such a hard blow that I could not lift my hand any more. He says to me, "That is how one beats. Now will you know? Now beat your comrade." In such a … in such a way they tried to liquidate us in the quickest manner. And afterwards he took … and said …

BODER: What is a "Nagan"? /Nagan is the make of a revolver. He may confuse it with the term Nagaika, a short, heavy horse whip used by the cossacks/.

EISENBERG: That is a rubber, a special … a special rubber … a thick one that with one blow …

BODER: Yes?

EISENBERG: One blow with it, then there shows … there is immediately a mark on that place, a black mark. There is immediately a black welt on that place.

BODER: Yes.

EISENBERG: That is a terrible thing which the Germans used a lot against the Jews.[14]

This exchange over the meaning of the word "Nagan" highlights Boder's confusion, but his interruption also slowed down the narrative and invited Eisenberg to explain how the Nagan was used and what the consequences were. As a result, the interview included more detail about the physicality of the beating and the particulars of the Nagan. The recorded confusion thus preserves the initial difficulties of interviewing Holocaust survivors before any historical narrative had been established.

In 1998, Donald Niewyk edited 34 of Boder's interviews and published them in the collection *Fresh Wounds: Early Narratives of Holocaust Survival*.[15] He included Eisenberg's interview among those published, but his edited version skipped over this confusion. Niewyk simply added a parenthetical explanation that a Nagan is a "rubber truncheon."[16] He may have assumed that his reader was familiar with the narrative of the Holocaust and accepted that the camp prisoners were forced to beat each other with some kind of tool. To Niewyk, the detail of the beating was not the essential part of the story or a moment that required additional meditation. However, Boder's original transcript allows the reader to be confused, just as he was when confronted by terms he didn't know and the jarring reality of the camps. Returning to the original reimbues the account with the power to provoke readers into thinking about the conditions under which these prisoners were beaten and required to beat their comrades.

This interview exemplifies the challenge outsiders faced in understanding the universe of the Nazi concentration camps. Boder's expectations were confounded and the recordings reveal how he tried to make sense of the stories he heard. Later in the interview, Eisenberg told Boder about his arrival at the Starachowice camp; upon arrival, an SS man gave an order to execute ten people. Eisenberg started to explain that ten people were selected at random when Boder interrupted:

BODER: How were the ten people selected?
EISENBERG: He passed through. Whoever he pleased, whoever caught ... whoever struck his fancy. He made a sign with the revolver in his hand. And he had to step out in spite of knowing that he is going to a certain death.
BODER: Did he pick older people, younger people /words not clear/?
EISENBERG: Whoever ... whoever caught his eye. Whoever was standing near him. Whoever struck his fancy he took. There was no difference whether young or old. The burned offering could have been any one, whoever stood there.[17]

Boder assumed that there was a logical reasoning for the order and for the selection. Eisenberg tried to explain that there was no logic in the decisions, that decisions were made randomly, based on the whim of the SS. The gap between Boder's understanding and that of the DP is repeated again and again when Boder asked his interviewees, "Why were you beaten?" In one particular example, Jürgen Bassfreund responded, "Why? Most people didn't know why."[18] Even after weeks of listening to these eyewitness accounts, Boder could not overcome the need to make sense of what happened.[19]

The various types of interruptions point to the challenge of recording Holocaust memory in DP camps and in postwar Europe. In particular, the confusion that pervades Boder's collection is a stark reminder that those who initially sought to document survivor memory of the events later known as the Holocaust were often working without a clear understanding of what was to be documented and how best to undertake that project. Survivors, too, were experimenting with how best to communicate what they had lived through, struggling to find narrative structure for their own stories.

Boder's collection, then, serves as a case study for early Holocaust memory and reveals the result of recording Holocaust memory in a transitional period, between the events of the Holocaust and the moment when Holocaust memory became cemented into a well-known narrative. Although survivors had begun to share their experiences with one another, there was not yet a larger historical understanding or interpretation that defined the scope and progression of events under the Third

Reich that led to the "Final Solution." In that period, no institutions prioritized specific narrative modes or organized individual storytelling. In 1946, it was not clear that any one part of a survivor's wartime experience should be either highlighted or minimized. Without such constraints, the survivors interviewed by Boder openly shared stories that later became shameful or controversial. Specifically, Boder's collection includes conversations about violence between Jews, personal depravity, and revenge.

Many historians, including Christopher Browning, have argued that sensitive topics like revenge and rape were not present in survivor testimony until very recently.[20] Yet, Naomi Seidman and Henry Greenspan argue that anger and the impulse for revenge were present at first and later minimized.[21] Boder's collection includes numerous references to Jewish violence and revenge, as well as expressions of personal depravity that have been underplayed as Holocaust testimonies became central to a larger historical narrative meant for wide audiences.

As Eisenberg's "Nagan" story above depicts, the demands of the Nazis often forced violence between Jews. Henja Frydman expressed this behavior more clearly. She told Boder, "They made Jews responsible for management of the work … And that is why we saw Jews beating Jews … A Jew would beat a Jew because Germans were strict, and the German would beat the Jew who did not want to beat another Jew."[22] She pointed specifically to the Jews who worked in the crematoria and burned their own kind. It was these Jews, she believed, that led to her hearing in postwar France that "bandits have come out of the lagers."[23] Her interview suggests that Jews were initially villanized for such work and speaks to the reality of the DP period in which Jews were already being blamed for complacency in their own destruction.

Yet, Boder's collection includes many stories of violence between Jews and for reasons other than Nazi orders. Israel Unikowski explained that violence was often a result of hunger and greed. He told Boder about his time in the Lodz ghetto and explained, "There were cases of murder where people killed one another." In particular, he says, "There was a case when a young girl was killed. She was seen leaving /the store?/ with two loaves of bread." Boder clarifies by asking if a Jew did it. Unikowski responds, "Yes. Then a Jew followed her and with an iron /bar/ he killed them both in the house."[24] The murderer killed not only the young Jewish girl who took the two loaves of bread but also her mother, the intended recipient of the second loaf. Stories of violence in these contexts have not been widely discussed in recent testimony collections.

Taboos established in later years also served to filter out moments of personal shame so that stories of physical depravity were minimized. Some details of Boder's collection might have provoked concerns of decency and audience – would people be interested in hearing stories of personal shame? Boder's interview with Nechama Epstein-Kozlowski provides a salient example. She detailed the lack of water and intense heat of the railroad car journey to Auschwitz. On the train, she explained, "There lay a little girl of four years. She was calling to me, 'Give me a little bit of water. Save me.' And I could do nothing. Mothers were giving the children urine to drink." Boder seemed unwilling to believe this. He asked her if it was really true. And she replied, "/Screaming/ I saw it. I did it myself, but I could not drink it.

I could not stand it any more. The lips were burned from thirst."[25] She continued to describe the scene in even more detail:

EPSTEIN: So I saw that the mother is doing it, and the child said, "Mama, but it is bitter, I cannot drink it."

BODER: Yes?

EPSTEIN: So she said, "Drink, drink." And the child did not want to drink it because it was bitter. And I myself imitated it, but I was not able to drink it, and I did not drink it.[26]

Although the terrible thirst in the rail cars continued to be a common theme in Holocaust survivor narratives, the details recorded here predate a taboo that might have made testimonies more palatable for large audiences.

The question of vengeance in the postwar period has been one of the more well discussed taboos. Naomi Seidman has demonstrated that the French translation of Elie Wiesel's *Night* removed the anger and impulse for revenge that were in the original Yiddish version.[27] She detailed the transformation of Wiesel's memoir and asserted that Wiesel recognized that in order to be respected and widely read, he had to hide his anger. The legacy thereafter was of a passive and forgiving survivor. Boder's interviews support Seidman's findings that survivors were angry in the postwar period and felt or sought vengeance. Actual stories of revenge were still rare, but the interviews confirm intense anger and emotion. One example of a revenge story comes when Unikowski mentions briefly that he and other inmates at Buchenwald chased after SS guards when they abandoned the camp, captured them, and beat them.[28]

Benjamin Piskorz, however, was more explicit. He explained to Boder that after the end of the war, while he was in the Czech countryside, "There I took a bit of revenge on the Germans." Boder pushed him further and Piskorz explained:

PISKORZ: For instance, I struck down people. I, too, tortured.[29]

BODER: Killed dead?

PISKORZ: Yes, killed dead. I, too, tortured a few people. And I also did the same things with the German children as the SS men did in Majdanek with the Po- ... with the Jewish children.

BODER: For instance?

PISKORZ: For instance, they took small ... small children by the little legs and beat the head against the wall so long until the head cracked and /the child/ was killed.

BODER: Did you do the same thing?

PISKORZ: I did the same to the German children, because the hate in me was so great ... [30]

This is not to say that these stories represent widespread Jewish violence or revenge. In fact, these types of stories are rare, even in Boder's collection. Yet, the violence Piskorz expressed here speaks to the impulse for revenge and the open expression of violence in the early postwar period.

Niewyk included both Unikowski and Piskorz among the witnesses in his collection. He acknowledged the uniqueness of their revenge narratives and that these circumstances are rarely mentioned in subsequent memoirs. As he writes, "It was, perhaps, easier to talk about them with a sympathetic American in the immediate aftermath of the war."[31] This comment suggests that there was already a taboo against discussing revenge, one which Boder allowed his witnesses to overcome. In fact, the taboos that prevent these types of stories from being discussed later were not yet in place. So the witnesses were not overcoming any shame to tell Boder these stories but relating their experiences as they perceived them.

The taboos and shame that accompanied a later acceptable narrative of Holocaust history and of the Jewish role within that story were not fixed in 1946. As a result, these themes challenge some aspects of what has become a standard and fixed narrative of Holocaust history and the conception of Jewish victimization. The unfiltered content of these narratives preserve the complexity of the actions taken by Jews during the war.

Indeed, what makes the complexity of individual memory all the more important here is that Boder's collection also recorded early expressions of communal memory and suggests at least one way in which a survivor identity was first defined. Sometimes Boder brought his wire recorder to services or events held in the camps. These non-interview segments of his recordings were never published, but the original recordings include small groups of children singing traditional songs, Mennonite prayer tunes, and Greek Orthodox Hymns. Boder also recorded concentration camp and resistance group songs. By preserving these expressions of communal memory, Boder's collection suggests how unique experiences like resistance and lager life were shared with DPs who had come back from Soviet Russia or out of hiding and how a survivor identity based on survival of concentration camps was first favored.

Even among the transcripted interviews, the collection gives early voice to many of the powerful images later canonized in Holocaust narratives and representations. Although these accounts break with some later established taboos, they also reaffirm the central place of many Holocaust tropes. Many of Boder's interviewees recall their arrival at Auschwitz or their perpetual fear of selections. These experiences, perhaps particularly the ramp at Auschwitz, have become iconic images. Yet, before references like *Schindler's List* or Elie Wiesel's *Night* popularized the moment of arrival at Auschwitz, Boder's collection recorded how survivors articulated these memories. Unikowski explained that when he got off the train at Birkenau there were Jewish prisoners on the ramp instructing all the young people to say they were older and all the older people to say they were younger.[32] The inclusion of these popular references in postwar memory illuminates the roots of such iconic images in the immediate postwar world.

By recording eyewitness testimony before a canonical narrative of the Holocaust was determined, these interviews serve both to anticipate later themes and to complicate the historical narrative by recalling themes that have since been filtered out. As such, these interviews, while unique in structure, tone and candor, do not altogether challenge Holocaust historiography or undermine the central images of Holocaust memory. Rather, they reinvigorate traditional tropes and confirm the varied and complex behavior and experience of victims under Nazi Rule. Although scholars are beginning to recognize that the immediate postwar period was a time of intense memory creation, these testimonies have not received the attention of later testimony collections and demand renewed study both for what they tell about the Holocaust and for how they portray DP life.

Examination of the relationship between the DP space and the memory created there reveals that the impermanence of the space was reflected in the emotional state and varied expression of Holocaust survivors. Boder's collection captured an immediate response of witnesses and now stands as a key source for understanding how survivors began to express their own experiences while also developing a communal memory and early survivor identity. Reading these early accounts in their particular historical context brings a more exacting eye to the development of Holocaust memory and reinserts the uncertainty of DP life into early narratives about the Holocaust.

Notes

1 David P. Boder, *I Did Not Interview the Dead* (Urbana: University of Illinois Press, 1949).
2 David P. Boder, *Topical Autobiographies of Displaced People Recorded Verbatim in Displaced Persons Camps with a Psychological and Anthropological Analysis* (Chicago: D.P. Boder, 1950–57).
3 Kaletzka's interview was published twice by Boder: first in *I Did Not Interview the Dead* as "I Am Alone" under the name Anna Kovitzka, then in *Topical Autobiographies* under her real name Anna Kaletzka. He also wrote an interpretive essay in response to her interview entitled, "Tale of Anna Kovitzka: A Logico-Systematic Analysis or an Essay in Experimental Reading." The essay was never published, but Boder continued to edit and refine the essay throughout the 1950s. Numerous copes of the essay exist. I will quote from a bound copy dated November 15, 1956. David P. Boder's Papers, 1938–57 (DPB Papers), UCLA YRL Special Collections, Box 6, Folder: Kovitzka Interpretation.
4 Boder, *I Did Not Interview the Dead*, 25.
* The "/" indicate Boder's notes in *I Did Not Interview the Dead* and *Topical Autobiographies*.
5 DPB Papers, Box 3, Folder: The Tale of Anna Kovitzka, Manuscript, "The Tale of Anna Kovitzka," 31.
6 Zeev W. Mankowitz, *Life Between Memory and Hope: The Survivors of the Holocaust in Occupied Germany* (New York: Cambridge University Press, 2002) 3.
7 Leo Srole, "Why the DPs Can't Wait," *Commentary* 3 (1947): 13–24, 13.
8 DPB Papers, Box 15, Working Notebook (97–98), in response to the interview with George Kaldore.
9 Boder, *Topical Autobiographies*, Henja Frydman (First Series, 1950, Volume 4, Chapter 13) 585.
10 In his interview with Nachama Epstein-Kozlowska, Boder included a note about the following interruption: "The interviewer apparently pleads with people who, in spite of his many requests, continue to eavesdrop under windows and behind the door. 'Are you not ashamed of yourselves? Don't you really understand … '" Boder, *Topical Autobiographies*, Nechama Epstein-Kozlowska (Fourth Series, 1956, Volume 14, Chapter 54) 2631.
11 DPB Papers, Box 6, Folder: Kovitzka Interpretation, "Tale of Anna Kovitzka," 14.
12 Boder explained in *I Did Not Interview the Dead* that he tried to apply the most advanced psychological interview methodologies by sitting behind the interviewee and denying them view to his responses. His tone and language reflects his formal demeanor, but he was often less professional than intended.
13 Boder, *Topical Autobiographies*, Kalman Eisenberg (Series 4, 1956, Volume 14, Chapter 52). Eisenberg's interview was somewhat problematic. The tone of his interview suggests

a lack of spontaneity and Boder noted, "The style of the interview *appears* especially full of somewhat artificial pathos" (2534). Boder also notes later that due to problems with the recorder the interview was delayed a day, giving Eisenberg time to prepare set language (2544).

14 Boder, *Topical Autobiographies*, Eisenberg, 2540–41.

15 Donald L. Niewyk, *Fresh Wounds: Early Narratives of Holocaust Survival* (Chapel Hill: University of North Carolina Press, 1998).

16 Niewyk, *Fresh Wounds,* 88.

17 Boder, *Topical Autobiographies,* Eisenberg, 2546–47. Eisenberg, who speaks in Yiddish throughout his interview with Boder, used "die khurbn" to indicate the victims in his story. *Khurbn* is literally translated as "catastrophe," but Yiddish speakers, including the majority of Holocaust survivors, used and continue to use, the term *Khurbn* to indicate the Holocaust as an event. Here, Eisenberg employs the term to indicate specific victims. Boder translated the word as "burned offering," perhaps linking the idea to that of the term "holocaust" which is traced back to the Bible to mean "burnt offering." Although the word "holocaust" was used to refer to the treatment of Jews in Nazi Europe at that time, it became the signifying term in America later in the postwar period and was cemented as the defining title in the 1970s and 80s. The translation suggests that the theme of martyrdom was present in discussing the Jewish victims of Nazism from the earliest postwar period on. For a discussion of the etymology of "Holocaust" as it is linked to the idea of a burnt offering and martyrdom, see Giorgio Agamben, *Remnants of Auschwitz: The Witness and the Archive* (New York: Zone Books, 2002) 28–31.

18 Boder, *I Did Not Interview the Dead,* Jürgen Gastfreund, 37. (Boder gave Jürgen Bassfreund the name Jürgen Gastfreund in the book.) This exchange seems to anticipate Primo Levi's famous passage in *Survival in Auschwitz* when a prison guard tells Levi, "There is no why here." Primo Levi, *Survival in Auschwitz* (New York: Simon and Schuster, 1996) p. 29.

19 In *Holocaust Testimonies: Ruins of Memory*, Lawrence Langer identified a gap in moral universes between the interviewer and interviewee. He argued that the distance between now and then was not only the temporal distance of 40 years and the spatial distance of America to Europe, but the moral distance from our world, in which we are "trained in the necessity of moral choice to preserve the integrity of civilized behavior" to the moral universe of the Holocaust that upended logical expectations. In Boder's collection, Langer's argument of a moral gap is not dependent on any temporal or spatial distance from the events. Boder still approached the survivors with different assumptions and expectations. Lawrence Langer, *Holocaust Testimonies: The Ruins of Memory* (New Haven, CT: Yale University Press, 1991), p. 33.

20 In *Remembering Survival*, Browning wrote, "Events of rape and revenge killing – obviously known to all Starachowice survivors but openly hinted at only by some and denied by others – began to become public memory some forty-five years after the event." Christopher Browning, *Remembering Survival: Inside a Nazi Slave-Labor Camp* (New York: W.W. Norton & Company, 2009) 11.

21 Naomi Seidman, "Elie Wiesel and the Scandal of Jewish Rage," *Jewish Social Studies*, New Series, 3:1 (Autumn 1996): 1–19, 8; Henry Greenspan, "The Awakening of Memory: Survivor Testimony in the First Years after the Holocaust, and Today," Monna and Otto Weinmann Lecture Series, 17 May 2000, 19. Available at: http://www.ushmm.org/research/center/publications/occasional/2001–2/paper.pdf.

22 Boder, *Topical Autobiographies*, Henja Frydman (First Series, 1950, Volume 4, Chapter 13) 623.

23 Boder, *Topical Autobiographies*, Frydman 623. Frydman said, "Jews worked in the crematories, which means that Jews have been burning their own kindred."

24 Boder, *Topical Autobiographies,* Israel Unikowski (Fourth Series, 1956, Volume 10, Chapter 38) 1805.

25 Boder, *Topical Autobiographies,* Nechama Epstein-Kozlowski (Series 4, 1956, Volume 14, Chapter 54) 2608.

26 Boder, *Topical Autobiographies*, Epstein 2609. Benjamin Piskorz also notes that he asked a friend to urinate in his mouth as a way to alleviate the terrible thirst. He said, "And also during the ride I was terribly thirsty. So there was an acquaintance, a comrade of mine whom I begged, from the terrible thirst, /that/ he should for me even … nu … I don't know how to say it, because … urine … he made urine into my mouth … This wasn't the first case, because all the people drank this way." Boder, *Topical Autobiographies*, Benjamin Piskorz (Series 4, 1956, Volume 12, Chapter 48) 2270–71.

27 Naomi Seidman, "Elie Wiesel and the Scandal of Jewish Rage," *Jewish Social Studies*, New Series, 3:1 (Autumn 1996): 1–19.

28 Boder, *Topical Autobiographies*, Unikowski 1836. Unikowski says that they did not kill the guards because the German Communist prisoners who had taken control of the camp forbade them from killing.

29 Piskorz fought in the Warsaw Ghetto Uprising and was then tortured by the Germans following the Warsaw Ghetto uprising. Boder, *Topical Autobiographies*, Piskorz 2267–68.

30 Boder, *Topical Autobiographies*, Piskorz 2292–93. Piskorz's interview has a different structure than most of the others. Towards the end of his trip, Boder tried to record only shorter interviews with witnesses in what he called "special episodes" (2256). Instead of recording a whole interview, Boder focused his questions to the Warsaw Ghetto resistance activities and other out of the ordinary experiences.

31 Niewyk, *Fresh Wounds*, 19.

32 Boder, *Topical Autobiographies*, Unikowski 1827.

8

AUTHORITARIANISM AND THE MAKING OF POST-HOLOCAUST PERSONALITY STUDIES

Michael E. Staub

I

It can no longer be considered noteworthy to argue that in the aftermath of the Second World War there was no special silence in the United States surrounding the events which came eventually to be known as the Holocaust. The myth that there was silence has been undermined by Jewish studies scholarship for more than a decade, as scholars have documented how the Holocaust almost immediately earned a prominent place in American (and American Jewish) discussions and debates. In 1997, Stuart Svonkin observed how Jewish professionals active in the intergroup relations agencies (like the American Jewish Committee, American Jewish Congress, and Anti-Defamation League) "were profoundly influenced by the cataclysmic events of the 1930s and 1940s," and that "the Holocaust, as it eventually came to be known, was arguably the touchstone of their identities as Jews."[1] In 1999, in a study of the Holocaust on American television, Jeffrey Shandler wrote that

> although generally characterized as a period of American Jewish silence on the Holocaust, the immediate postwar years saw a considerable amount of activity in response to this as-yet-unnamed subject: pioneering historical scholarship, the writing of the first of hundreds of personal and communal memoirs, the establishment of the earliest memorials.[2]

In 2002, I also proposed that "far from being silent, either out of horror at the magnitude of the Nazi crimes or out of respectful sensitivity toward the trauma of survivors, commentators of all political persuasions made analogies to the mass murder of European Jewry," and that while "there was never any agreement on what the lessons for the American context were," nonetheless "all agreed that there were lessons, and that the Nazi genocide was a logical reference point from which to draw conclusions about the situation in the U.S. as well."[3] And in 2003, Lawrence Baron concluded that although "the term 'Holocaust' did not become common in American parlance until the 1960s, a sense of what it denoted had become widespread in the fifteen years after World War II."[4] In other words, we might benefit from asking not whether the Holocaust was remembered and memorialized in the first fifteen years after 1945, but why and through what precise historical processes these many diverse acts of memory came subsequently to be suppressed and "forgotten" for so many decades afterwards.

In a book on postwar American Jewish history, I explored how the purported lessons of the Holocaust for the American Jewish political scene had traveled already by the early 1960s through a series of at least three contested and negotiated stages with respect to Jewish attitudes toward African American civil rights activism. I argued that it was only against the background of these earlier debates over black-Jewish relations that we might appreciate what was at stake in the conflicted – and conflicting – fashions in which the Holocaust came subsequently also to be invoked in arguments over American Jews' appropriate stances on the war in Vietnam or the state of Israel. And I also argued that when commentators from the 1970s onward began to repeat the quickly conventional view that Holocaust consciousness in the U.S. only flourished in the aftermath of the Six-Day War in 1967, they were not solely serving to erase the presence of various earlier and more progressive ways to interpret the possible lessons of the Holocaust with respect to racial justice. They were choosing to neglect as well early *anti*progressive versions of the Holocaust's supposed lessons and the specific context of discomfort with black civil rights activism within which these versions were first articulated.

This question, then, of how a plethora of historical acts of remembrance were erased and forgotten in new narratives about the evolution of memory politics also motivates the inquiry of the present essay. If we can agree – as the scholars cited above appear to, and as Hasia Diner more recently reiterated – that when Jews in the postwar moment contemplated the Holocaust, they "differed among themselves as to how best to narrate the catastrophe and what lessons should be derived from it," then we also need to ask by what mechanisms, and in the context of what ideological conflicts, certain memories or lessons gained the aura of legitimacy – while other memories and lessons slipped into historical oblivion.[5] This is not to propose that the lessons and memories which were erased from the subsequent retrospective narratives were superior to the memories and lessons which came to dominate later discussions and debates, nor vice versa. Rather it is to suggest that processes of remembrance and forgetting are rather complexly intertwined with ideological processes, and that interrelationships between politics and memories need careful reconstruction and analysis.

This essay examines the emergence of authoritarianism as a concept employed with intense regularity in postwar "personality studies" – a subfield sitting at the intersection of social psychological and sociological investigation and psychoanalytic research as well as in psychoanalytic reflections on the presumed personality structures of the perpetrators and the bystanders of Nazi genocide. I am especially interested in the attempt to draw lessons from the German case for the American context, and I see this psychoanalytically inclined body of scholarship as strongly saturated by – indeed animated by – what we would now call Holocaust consciousness. A stark term of opprobrium, "authoritarianism" was represented as a scientific *and* social scientific concept quantifiable through medical knowledge and with statistical data. Authoritarianism could be measured and charted, and its embeddedness in and enmeshment with other anti-democratic tendencies analyzed. In effect, the aspiration to analyze authoritarianism was to make reason out of unreason. Significantly, moreover, and quite dissimilar from the model for understanding perpetrator mentality which came to dominate popular discourse in the early 1960s in conjunction with Hannah Arendt's coinage of the term "banality of evil," the authoritarianism model placed special emphasis on hatred and prejudice. Intriguingly, scholars in this school explored and promoted the idea that antisemitism and racism might be thought of as indicators of mental illness; at other times (or sometimes at the same time) they proposed that antisemitism or racism was a "social disease." As emigré psychoanalyst Ernst Simmel wrote already in 1946, the hatred of Jews which swept through Nazi Germany had been a "mass psychopathology."[6] Such a position became popular commonsense in the half-decade following the end of World War II. Yet its usefulness as a model for thinking through the relations between psychology and politics came soon to be displaced – and judged untenable – only a few short years later, and with the displacement this particular form of more immediate postwar Holocaust consciousness would also come to be forgotten. How did this happen?

II

That there were political lessons for the American situation to be drawn by psychiatrists and social psychologists in the immediate wake of the mass murder of European Jewry was largely taken as self-evident. The psychic dilemmas and temptations experienced by citizens during the Third Reich were not specific to Nazi Germany; comparable problems might easily develop also for individuals living in the United States. It was hardly surprising, then, that medical doctors and social scientists who were interested in politics sought to extrapolate from an examination of the Nazi enemy. Attention focused on the possible relationships between individual psychological development and adherence to political ideologies. If the psyche of the individual was vulnerable especially while young, and if there existed a decisive link between the development of personality and the evolution of ideological values, then environment (particularly within families) required closest scrutiny.

By the time sociologist Theodor W. Adorno and social psychologists Else Frenkel-Brunswik, Daniel J. Levinson and R. Nevitt Sanford, a research team based in Berkeley, published *The Authoritarian Personality* (1950), a project dedicated to the unraveling of the relationship between personality and political values, the idea that personal psychological development and political values and identities were deeply intertwined had been in wide circulation within psychiatric and psychoanalytic circles already for several years. A main trend in psychoanalytic and social psychological studies of both antiblack racism and antisemitism was to argue that racism functioned as a compensatory or defense mechanism, an unconscious means to manage deep feelings of humiliation which were too awful and difficult consciously to contemplate. For instance, it had been theorized since the 1930s that when routinely frustrated, human beings responded with acts of aggression – even though this aggression was often displaced onto a scapegoat, especially against individuals or groups deemed lesser or worthless.[7] Quite a few psychoanalytic studies of antisemitism and the personality of the anti-semite in Nazi Germany emerged even before the full extent of the horrors perpetrated during the Holocaust had been revealed; these included Wilhelm Reich's *The Mass Psychology of Fascism*, Otto Fenichel's "The Psycho-analysis of Anti-Semitism," Erik H. Erikson's "Hitler's Imagery and German Youth," and Abraham H. Maslow's "The Authoritarian Character Structure."[8] Additionally, social psychologist Erich Fromm had proposed in 1941 that social conditions which squelched individual self-expression offered rich soil for the nurturance of an "authoritarian character" which displayed "the simultaneous presence of sadistic and masochistic drives."[9] Such persons sought to surrender themselves to a master (not least so as to avoid responsibility for their own aggressive actions) even as they sought also to dominate others and to inflict pain upon them. And psychoanalyst Ernst Simmel had contributed the insight that also the "relatively normal, well-adapted person" "regressed" at moments of social panic or crisis.[10]

Did persons who harbored resentments and hostilities towards minorities share a specific character structure that might be labeled "authoritarian"? Was it possible to extrapolate from an individual case study to the population as a whole? What was the link between the individual who possessed an "authoritarian" personality and the ability of states to carry out policies whose aim was to scapegoat so-called undesirable groups? And did the presence of authoritarian personalities within a society not only make fascism possible, but also ensure that fascistic policies could be carried by popular consent? Integrating an innovative array of social psychological methods, the Berkeley researchers sought to make sense of these questions through the collection of a mass of empirical and statistical evidence. They interviewed more than two thousand subjects and took their life histories. They devised elaborate questionnaires. They showed their subjects dramatic images and asked them to invent stories about these pictures. (This technique first introduced in the mid-1930s was known as the Thematic Apperception Test.)[11] And they developed several scales to quantify their findings. There was the "A-S scale" (for "antisemitism") and the "E scale" (for "ethnocentrism"); there was the "PEC scale" (for "politico-economic conservatism") and – most famously – the "F scale" ("f" for "fascist"), each of which was intended to measure an individual's tendency towards prejudiced and undemocratic values as a corollary of personality factors. The result was the most comprehensive study ever undertaken on how political attitudes related to personality traits. And what the Berkeley researchers finally argued was that there did in fact exist "the potentially fascist individual, one whose structure is such as to render him particularly susceptible to anti-democratic propaganda."[12]

Several points bear emphasis. For one thing, there can be no question that this project in its nearly one thousand pages was haunted throughout by the mass murder of European Jewry. Published a half-decade after the defeat of Nazi Germany, the opening page of the book's foreword asserted – in an interesting endorsement of the idea that silence reigned, but also clarifying that specifically the Judeocide and not "just" antisemitism motivated their inquiry – that "today the world scarcely remembers the mechanized persecution and extermination of millions of human beings only a short span of years away in what was once regarded as the citadel of Western civilization."[13] For another thing, and although it left unclear whether pathological personality traits were innate or produced by early parent–child interaction, while at the same time it certainly did also attend to the impact of the wider social environment, *The Authoritarian Personality* definitely took the view that there were strong correlations between character structure and ideological attitudes. Additionally, while the book was framed principally as an inquiry into the nature of prejudice, and the subjects were tested to measure the extent of their ethnocentrism, racism and antisemitism, it also had much to say about the combination of ambivalent submission to authority figures and cruelty and aggression towards those more vulnerable that the authors identified as characteristic of anti-democratic and even incipiently fascistic impulses.

Finally, and despite the reams of seemingly objective scientific data marshaled, the book was without a doubt intended as a political – and even deeply evocative and emotional – intervention into discussions about what Americans should value. It sought especially to position prejudice as antithetical to democracy. In pursuit of this cause, the authors unfortunately – although tellingly – did not hesitate strategically to portray the prejudiced person as both latently homosexual and mentally disturbed (even while the study had also tested for homophobia as an indicator of potentially fascist traits). Indeed, the authors of *The Authoritarian Personality* did not – or perhaps could not – resist casting the bigot in the most unflattering terms. The bigot was a sexually frustrated and pathetic wimp. Unloved as a child, he suffered as his authoritarian parents doled out their affections in tiny spoonfuls. This led him to grow to adulthood in pitiful search of tenderness, while masking his erotic attraction to other men by acting macho. He hated himself for being weak, and he turned that hatred against scapegoats. For the authors of *The Authoritarian Personality* – and in this way strongly again echoing the arguments advanced by Fromm and Simmel, among others – the person who hated was psychologically deficient and emotionally damaged. At the same time, and by contrast, the Berkeley researchers gave the unbiased individual a clean bill of mental health.

III

The Authoritarian Personality quickly emerged as one of the most significant and widely-critiqued texts published in the postwar era.[14] It was both a landmark text in the field of social psychology and a major contribution to an emerging postwar discussion about the fortitude and resilience of American democracy. Yet far from finding it gratifying and useful that so many unpleasant aspects of human nature were being made explicable, critics quickly savaged *The Authoritarian Personality* on both methodological and substantive grounds. The reasons for the almost instant umbrage taken were several.

First, *The Authoritarian Personality* pointed an accusatory finger at American society as a whole, deeming the phenomenon of vulnerability to anti-democratic attitudes to be far more pervasive than had been previously assumed. Already a 1946 study by social psychologists Gordon W. Allport and Bernard M. Kramer had ventured the view that "it would seem a safe estimate that at least four-fifths of the American population lead mental lives in which feelings of group hostility play an appreciable role."[15] Here now was a blockbuster book that, while reducing the estimate of the proportion of Americans afflicted, raised the stakes by redirecting the conversation away from the rather mundane phenomenon of "feelings of group hostility" to the far more dramatic tendency to "authoritarianism." A feature piece in the *New York Times Magazine* in 1950 promoting the conclusions of *The Authoritarian Personality* flatly asserted "it can be said that about 10 per cent of the population of the United States probably consists of 'authoritarian men and women' while as many as another 20 per cent have within them the seeds that can grow into authoritarianism."[16] Having just defeated German and Italian fascism, Americans were not eager to learn that it *could* happen here – that the U.S. also possessed the potential for fascism.

Second, *The Authoritarian Personality* insulted those with traditionally conservative values, expressly tarring conservatism as both an incipient form of authoritarianism and fascism *and* a sign of mental disorder. The book also suggested that many conservatives were "phony" or "pseudo" in their patriotism, waving the flag while hating the democratic institutions they claimed to honor. Authoritarian individuals often appeared well-adjusted, but that was only because they externalized their seething resentments onto others (rather than being able to reflect self-critically). Notably, then, while prior studies (not incidentally produced in the wake of the Great Depression) had emphasized the tendencies toward prejudice especially among the lower-class and economically vulnerable, *The Authoritarian Personality* cast aspersions on mainstream, also prosperous Americans.

In addition, a number of scholars found serious flaws with personality studies as a methodological enterprise. In 1950, sociologist Nathan Glazer expressed irritation both at what he took to be the tautological quality of the Berkeley team's approach and at its political implications. "When the researcher, on the basis of a subject's agreement or disagreement with a series of statements composed by the researcher himself, proceeds to determine the nature of the subject's thought-processes," Glazer rhetorically inquired, "is he not moving in a circle?" (Glazer was especially huffy about Adorno et al.'s "rather simple and simple-minded assumptions about what is progressive or liberal," and "their assumption that opposition to intermarriage can only be a sign of prejudice.")[17] In 1954, in an anthology dedicated to assessing the strengths and (above all) weaknesses of *The Authoritarian Personality*, one contributor also made the telling critique that Adorno and his associates had neglected utterly to explore "Leftist authoritarianism."[18] Other contributors decried the Berkeley team's disregard for social conditions and overemphasis on individual character.[19] By the later 1950s, a perspective that prejudiced attitudes could be linked to mental illness was in the process of being actively repudiated.[20]

Finally, and related, was how essentially pessimistic and despairing about human nature the entire social psychological field of personality studies in the immediate postwar years had been. Well-publicized and coordinated attempts to combat bigotry with accurate information about minority groups had initially been presented by leading social psychologists as the best weapon against intolerance, but after 1945, the conviction that such attempts really might work dimmed considerably. "Can We Fight Prejudice Scientifically?" inquired two leading social psychologists in an early issue of *Commentary* magazine from 1946; their answer here was already ambivalent at best.[21] And in 1947, Marie Jahoda, who had co-authored the *Commentary* essay, clarified her own negative position when she documented how bigoted individuals typically remained unmoved by "anti-prejudice propaganda." As Jahoda wrote, the same weak personality structure that caused a person to become prejudiced in the first place was also a personality structure which, "as a defense mechanism," evaded efforts to reeducate it – a defense mechanism which came into play "whenever an individual senses a danger to his ego structure – that is, whenever his self-confidence hangs in the balance."[22]

By the early 1950s, however, new Cold War ideological parameters required a revised (and less gloomy) theory of white racism. As America claimed its postwar place as a beacon for democracy in the world, the dirty linen that had been slavery and remained as racial segregation above all required both political and intellectual redress.[23] It was not palatable by the mid-1950s to argue within social psychological circles that a good number of American citizens could easily succumb to political values which were potentially fascistic.

Social progress and individual reform were presented by the early 1950s as eminently achievable. For instance, a significant contribution to the emphatically upbeat direction in child clinical studies was sociologist Mary Ellen Goodman's *Race Awareness in Young Children* (1952). Drawing her analysis from data collected in three nursery schools, Goodman rejected the disquieting argument that people could not change their natures. Also notable was the work of prominent social psychologist Marian Radke-Yarrow and her team at the Philadelphia Early Childhood Project. Radke-Yarrow's project tested over two hundred children in six Philadelphia public schools, con-cluding that any child might be educated to racism – but also that any child could be educated to tolerance. As Radke-Yarrow and co-author Helen G. Trager announced in the indicatively-entitled *They Learn What They Live: Prejudice in Young Children* (1952), their ambitious aim was nothing less than to offer parents a guidebook for how to raise children who could "learn to live democratically."[24] (It was fitting, therefore, that the findings from Radke-Yarrow's Philadelphia Early Childhood Project were entered as evidence for the plaintiffs in the Brown v. Board of Education case as a means of dramatizing how children might unlearn prejudiced attitudes in integrated social environments.)[25]

A new model was quickly emerging, one which offered a far more optimistic read of human nature. Thus it was reiterated that a reduction in the social distance between groups that feared or hated one another could likely reduce a perpetuation of stereotypes held by members of both groups.[26] It was also argued that the degree of social alienation or anomie tended to define a person's political values – but that the anomie could be reduced.[27] And it was argued that prejudiced feelings were the result of weak egos, but that weak egos could be effectively bolstered.

The argument that persons raised racist were immune to later social forces went out of fashion in the course of the 1950s, and was rapidly replaced with an argument that racists were really quite capable of attitude improvements – given adjustments in their social circumstances. Clinical studies of children's racial attitudes conducted in the early 1950s began overwhelmingly to reject the analysis that children were predisposed innately to particular political attitudes, favoring instead a far more open-ended and hopeful interpretation that democratic (and non-authoritarian) values could be schooled effectively into the ignorant and the very young. In short, and even though these studies with children were not about Jewishness or antisemitism, it is precisely my argument that it was the combination of Cold War imperatives and liberal optimistic antiracist efforts that helps to explain the displacement of a distinctly post-Holocaust conceptual framework for personality studies.

IV

It would not be until the war in Vietnam that the concept of authoritarianism would appear relevant all over again. Revelations in the late 1960s that American soldiers in Vietnam had committed atrocities effectively brought the psychological insights concerning an "authoritarian" personality out of exile. It again became acceptable – even urgently so – to use social psychology to understand how events like the My Lai massacre in 1968 – in which "ordinary" American men had engaged in the rape, torture and mass killing of unarmed South Vietnamese citizens – could possibly have taken place.[28]

By the late 1960s research into the psychological roots of violence and cruelty recaptured a place of central importance both in the academy and in the public imagination. Prominent among these efforts was psychiatrist Joel Kovel's *White Racism: A Psychohistory* (1970), which took *The Authoritarian Personality*'s desolate message about human nature and refashioned it for the antiwar movement. Kovel wrote:

> When the Marine officer described the American obliteration of a city in Vietnam by explaining that "we had to destroy the city in order to save it," was he not expressing in the succinct form given by such an extreme situation, the pure, nuclear fantasy underlying Western history – to save and destroy, include and extrude? And what of the prime means of our warfare: bombing? Is this not also the external, societally mobilized, endlessly rationalized enactment of an immemorial infantile, anal-sadistic fantasy: the efficient, rational, distant (no pilot sees his victim) operation of a machine ...[29]

And in the following year, psychologist Nevitt Sanford published papers from a symposium on "the legitimization of evil" organized in specific response to the My

Lai massacre. Robert Jay Lifton contributed a paper on "existential evil," and Stanley Milgram's experiments on obedience to authority and *The Authoritarian Personality* were both repeatedly cited. For instance, one contribution – pointedly entitled "It Never Happened and Besides They Deserved It" – noted derisively that the public comments of President Richard Nixon and Vice President Spiro Agnew (who had labeled anti-war activists "parasites" and "goats") reflected "a text book manifestation of modern totalitarianism" as outlined in the Berkeley study.[30] And Sanford used the occasion to rehearse and refine arguments he and his associates had originally presented in *The Authoritarian Personality* – arguments Sanford presented as remaining both highly relevant and extremely productive.[31]

On the one hand, then, antiwar and anti-militarist activists were effectively resurrecting the theory of the potentially fascistic personality which had been developed initially in the 1940s and early 1950s in direct response to the rise of Nazism and the Holocaust. On the other hand, however, and in yet a further twist, the concept of authoritarianism was about to become a bad object all over again – this time for an entirely new generation of psychologists, psychiatrists and social theorists. It was a backlash which began within a moderate brand of liberalism – but which in the decades to follow would slide quite demonstratively to the extreme right. It was also a backlash which appeared to reserve a special place in hell for Adorno and his associates – blaming them in essence for a whole raft of unconscionable sins. The authors of the Berkeley study were elitist; they were guilty of a supreme condescension towards the very same Americans they claimed better to understand. By the 1980s and 1990s and into the twenty-first century, the increasingly vitriolic case against *The Authoritarian Personality* argued that Adorno and his colleagues had launched the nation on a downward ethical and spiritual spiral – one epitomized by the catastrophic mess of the 1960s.[32] In short, attacks on *The Authoritarian Personality* became a short-hand method to turn against the 1960s, as if Adorno and his colleagues had worked so assiduously on prejudice and personality studies in the late 1940s only in order to hatch an execrable Frankenstein monster twenty years later. This proved a durable and persistent means of right-wing ideological line of attack – one which (not incidentally) elided the text's obsession with the nature of human cruelty.

Conclusion

For a particular postwar generation of social psychologists and psychoanalysts – many of whom were Jewish, and a good number of whom had also been forced into exile by Nazism – the concept of authoritarianism came to serve as a means to express both anguish and rage at the genocidal and antisemitic policies of Hitler's Germany. Theirs was a flawed, if intensely felt, mission to express their sorrow that a civilized nation could turn against the vulnerable in its midst – targeting these persons for extermination and proceeding to carry out these aims with the willing assent of the populace. These influential intellectuals searched for meaning in this madness and, in this search, they found the concept of authoritarianism especially useful – as a way to portray the Nazi perpetrator and the Nazi bystander in the most unflattering psychological terms they could muster *and* as a cautionary tale which warned that American citizens were also hardly immune to the social diseases of hatred and prejudice which had so powerfully taken hold in Germany. That such lessons did not sit well with many Americans cannot in retrospect be particularly surprising. Yet the recognition that these lessons were themselves a form of Holocaust remembrance – and that they deserve to be included in any accounting of how Americans (and American Jews) sought almost immediately to come to terms with the trauma of the mass murder of European Jewry – remains crucial to restore to the historical record.

Notes

1 Stuart Svonkin, *Jews Against Prejudice: American Jews and the Fight for Civil Liberties* (New York: Columbia University Press, 1997), 17.

2 Jeffrey Shandler, *While America Watches: Televising the Holocaust* (New York: Oxford University Press, 1999), 46–47.

3 Michael E. Staub, *Torn at the Roots: The Crisis of Jewish Liberalism in Postwar America* (New York: Columbia University Press, 2002), 9–10.

4 Lawrence Baron, "The Holocaust and American Public Memory, 1945–60," *Holocaust and Genocide Studies* 17 (Spring 2003): 63.

5 Hasia Diner, *We Remember with Reverence and Love: American Jews and the Myth of Silence after the Holocaust, 1945–1962* (New York: New York University Press, 2009), 366.

6 Ernst Simmel, "Anti-Semitism and Mass Psychopathology," in *Anti-Semitism: A Social Disease*, ed. Ernst Simmel (New York: International Universities Press, 1946), 34.

7 The classic text is John Dollard, Leonard W. Doob, Neal E. Miller, O. H. Mowrer, Robert R. Sears, *Frustration and Aggression* (New Haven, CT: Yale University Press, 1939). Also see the highly influential study, *Caste and Class in a Southern Town* (1937) in which psychologist John Dollard noted that economically insecure Southern whites displaced their aggression onto African Americans, while African Americans, unable to express their own frustration towards whites directly, often turned against one another – in black-on-black criminality and cruelty. John Dollard, *Caste and Class in a Southern Town* (New Haven, CT: Yale University Press, 1937), 267.

8 Wilhelm Reich, *The Mass Psychology of Fascism* (German orig. 1933; English trans. New York: Orgone Institute Press, 1946); Otto Fenichel, "The Psycho-analysis of Anti-Semitism," *American Imago* 1 (March 1940): 24–39; Erik H. Erikson, "Hitler's Imagery and German Youth," *Psychiatry* 5 (November 1942): 475–93; and Abraham H. Maslow, "The Authoritarian Character Structure," *Journal of Social Psychology* 18 (November 1943): 401–11.

9 Erich Fromm, *Escape from Freedom* (New York: Avon, 1969), 246. The book was first published in 1941. In 1951, Adorno would elaborate on Fromm's conception when he argued that the "sadomasochistic character" of fascists might be compared to the actions of bicyclists: "Above they bow, they kick below." T. W. Adorno "Freudian Theory and the Pattern of Fascist Propaganda," in *Psychoanalysis and the Social Sciences vol. 3*, ed. Géza Roheim (New York: International Universities Press, 1951), 291.

10 Ernst Simmel, "Anti-Semitism and Mass Psychopathology," 39, 43. Simmel concluded as well that "the process of civilization itself *produces* anti-Semitism as a pathological symptom formation, which in turn tends to destroy the soil from which it has grown." Ibid., 34.

11 See Christiana D. Morgan and Henry A. Murray, "A Method for Investigating Fantasies: The Thematic Apperception Test," *Archives of Neurological Psychiatry* 34 (1935): 289–306.

12 T.W. Adorno, Else Frenkel-Brunswik, Daniel J. Levinson, and R. Nevitt Sanford, *The Authoritarian Personality* (New York: Harper & Row, 1950), 1.

13 Adorno et. al, v.

14 See especially Richard Christie and Peggy Cook, "A Guide to Published Literature Relating to the Authoritarian Personality Through 1956," *Journal of Psychology* 45 (April 1958): 171–99; and the chapter on "The Authoritarian Personality and the Organization of Attitudes" in Roger Brown, *Social Psychology* (New York: Free Press, 1965), 477–546. Also see John T. Jost, Jack Glaser, Arie W. Kruglandski, and Frank J. Sulloway, "Political Conservatism as Motivated Social Cognition," *Psychological Bulletin* 129 (May 2003): 339–75.

15 Gordon W. Allport and Bernard M. Kramer, "Some Roots of Prejudice," *Journal of Psychology* 22 (July 1946): 9.

16 Samuel H. Flowerman, "Portrait of the Authoritarian Man," *New York Times Magazine* (April 23, 1950): 9.

17 Nathan Glazer, "The Authoritarian Personality in Profile: Report on a Major Study of Race Hatred," *Commentary* 4 (June 1950): 576–77.

18 Edward A. Shils, "Authoritarianism: 'Right' and 'Left,'" in *Studies in the Scope and Method of "The Authoritarian Personality,"* eds., Richard Christie and Marie Jahoda (Glencoe, IL: Free Press, 1954), 39. Also see Paul Kecskemeti, "Prejudice in the Catastrophic Perspective," *Commentary* 11 (March 1951): 286–92.

19 Herbert H. Hyman and Paul B. Sheatsley, "'The Authoritarian Personality' – A Methodological Critique," in *Studies in the Scope and Method of "The Authoritarian Personality,"* 60.

20 See also Arnold M. Rose, "Intergroup Relations vs. Prejudice: Pertinent Theory for the Study of Social Change," *Social Problems* 4 (October 1956): 173–76; Melvin M. Tumin, "Sociological Aspects of Desegregation," *American Journal of Orthopsychiatry* 29 (January 1959): 180–85; and Earl Raab and Seymour M. Lipset, *Prejudice and Society* (New York: Anti-Defamation League, 1959).

21 See Samuel H. Flowerman and Marie Jahoda, "Can We Fight Prejudice Scientifically?" *Commentary* 2 (December 1946): 583–87.

22 Eunice Cooper and Marie Jahoda, "The Evasion of Propaganda: How Prejudiced People Respond to Anti-Prejudice Propaganda," *Journal of Psychology* 23 (January 1947): 15–25. Also see Herbert H. Hyman and Paul B. Sheatsley, "Some Reasons Why Information Campaigns Fail," *Public Opinion Quarterly* 11 (Fall 1947): 413–23.

23 See Mary L. Dudziak, *Cold War Civil Rights: Race and the Image of American Democracy* (Princeton, NJ: Princeton University Press, 2002).

24 Helen G. Trager and Marian Radke Yarrow, *They Learn What They Live: Prejudice in Young Children* (New York: Harper, 1952), xi. Also Marian J. Radke and Helen G.Trager, "Children's Perceptions of the Social Roles of Negroes and Whites," *Journal of Psychology* 29 (January 1950): 3–33.

25 See Richard Kluger, *Simple Justice: The History of Brown v. Board of Education and Black America's Struggle for Equality* (New York: Random House, 1977), especially 318–19.

26 This was an older concept introduced by sociologist Emory S. Bogardus in the 1920s. See Emory S. Bogardus. "Social Distance and Its Origins," *Journal of Applied Sociology* 9 (1925): 216–26; and Emory S. Bogardus, *Immigration and Race Attitudes* (Boston: D. C. Heath, 1928). The Bogardus "social distance" scale continued to be tested and revised through the 1950s. See Michael Banton, "Social Distance: A New Appreciation," *Sociological Review* 8 (December 1960): 169–83. Also see the 1946 "change experiments" of social psychologist Kurt Lewin which explored how "basic skill training groups" (or T-groups) might reduce individuals' racial prejudices and resolve social conflicts. See Kurt Lewin, *Resolving Social Conflicts: Selected Papers on Group Dynamics* (New York: Harper, 1948).

27 See Leo Srole, "Social Integration and Certain Corollaries: An Exploratory Study," *American Sociological Review* 21 (December 1956): 709–16; and Leo Srole, Thomas S. Langner, Stanley T. Michael, Marvin K. Opler, and Thomas A. C. Rennie, *Mental Health in the Metropolis: The Midtown Manhattan Study* (New York: McGraw-Hill, 1962). Also see Edward L. McDill and Jeanne Clare Ridley, "Status, Anomia, Political

Alienation, and Political Participation," *American Journal of Sociology* 68 (September 1962): 205–13.

28 See Joanna Burke, *An Intimate History of Killing: Face-To-Face Killing in Twentieth-Century Warfare* (New York: Basic Books, 2000), especially 159–203.

29 Joel Kovel, *White Racism: A Psychohistory* (New York: Pantheon Books, 1970), 164–65. Kovel directly invokes the theories concerning "authoritarian prejudice" on 56–58.

30 Edward M. Opton, Jr., "It Never Happened and Besides They Deserved It," *Sanctions for Evil: Sources of Social Destructiveness*, eds. Nevitt Sanford and Craig Comstock (San Francisco: Jossey-Bass Inc., 1971), 57–58.

31 Nevitt Sanford, "Authoritarianism and Social Destructiveness," in *Sanctions for Evil: Sources of Social Destructiveness*, 136–54.

32 See for instance the hostile discussions of *The Authoritarian Personality* in: Brigitte Berger and Peter L. Berger, *The War Over the Family: Capturing the Middle Ground* (Garden City, NY: Anchor Press, 1983), 173; Allan Bloom, *The Closing of the American Mind* (New York: Simon and Schuster, 1987), 225; Christopher Lasch, *The True and Only Heaven: Progress and its Critics* (New York: W. W. Norton & Co., 1991), 453–55; Charles J. Sykes, *A Nation of Victims: The Decay of the American Character* (New York: St. Martin's Press, 1992), 53–58; Patrick J. Buchanan, *The Death of the West: How Dying Populations and Immigrant Invasions Imperil Our Country and Civilization* (New York: MacMillan, 2002), 82; and Jonah Goldberg, *Liberal Fascism: The Secret History of the American Left from Mussolini to the Politics of Meaning* (New York: Doubleday, 2008), 227–28. For the wider context of the backlash, see Michael E. Staub, *Madness is Civilization: When the Diagnosis was Social, 1948–1980* (Chicago: University of Chicago Press, 2011), especially the chapter "A Fashionable kind of Slander."

9

IF GOD WAS SILENT, ABSENT, DEAD, OR NONEXISTENT, WHAT ABOUT PHILOSOPHY AND THEOLOGY?

Some aftereffects and aftershocks of the Holocaust

John K. Roth

> … You will sooner or later be confronted by the enigma of God's action in history.
> Elie Wiesel, *One Generation After*[1]

Religion was not a sufficient condition for the Holocaust, but it was a necessary one. What happened at Auschwitz is inconceivable without beliefs about God first held by Jews and then by Christians. Holocaust and genocide scholars have explored the similarities and differences between the Holocaust and other genocides. Although the field of comparative genocide does not often make the point, one aspect of the Holocaust that is qualitatively different from all other programs of extermination and mass destruction in the modern period can be stated as follows: No example of mass murder other than the Holocaust has raised so directly or so insistently the question of whether it was an expression of *Heilsgeschichte*, that is, God's providential involvement in history. More than any other disaster in modern times, the Holocaust resonates and collides with the religio-mythic traditions of biblical religion, the dominant religious tradition of western civilization.

Breaking silence

Steeped in silence, which it also broke, Elie Wiesel's memoir, *Night*, abridged from the Yiddish version (1956), appeared in French (1958) and then in English (1960). One of its recollections focuses on the observance of Rosh Hashanah at Auschwitz in 1944. Amidst the congregation's sighs and tears, Wiesel heard the leader's voice, powerful yet broken: "All the earth and the Universe are God's!"[2] As the words came forth, Wiesel recalls that they seemed to choke in the speaker's throat, "as though he lacked the strength to uncover the meaning beneath the text."[3] *Night* does not explain that meaning, silently leaving readers to wonder about it.

Almost thirty years later, another Holocaust survivor, the philosopher Sarah Kofman, wrestled with silence when she spoke about smothered words, knotted words that "stick in your throat and cause you to suffocate, to lose your breath"; they "asphyxiate you, taking away the possibility of even beginning."[4] Expressing the dilemma she felt as a survivor trying to communicate with others, Kofman went on to ask, "How is it possible to speak, when you feel ... a strange *double bind*: an infinite claim to speak, *a duty to speak infinitely*, imposing itself with irrepressible force, and at the same time, an almost physical impossibility to speak, a *choking* feeling"?[5]

Wiesel and Kofman help to show that *silence*—the word and reality—is fraught with meanings. They can include a lack of interest, even indifference about events and ideas. Silence may reflect ignorance, humility, or shame; it may be a response to awesome beauty or immense destruction. It may signify, with special intensity and emotion, that even when one speaks, it is still possible to be speechless, for one may not know what to say or cannot find words that are appropriate, meaningful, and credible in relation to what is present, remembered, or yet to be faced.

It is one thing to remember that the Holocaust happened, to memorialize that disaster, to find ways to incorporate memory and memorialization into religious ritual, and to do so with reverence and love.[6] It may be something else, however, to deal with the philosophical and religious questions that continue to jar consciousness and conscience as those actions take place. Whatever silence(s)—mythical or otherwise—may have surrounded the Holocaust during and after that disaster, questions about God, justice, evil, and meaning reverberated in that chasm and continue to do so.[7] Theologians and philosophers have a long history of attempts to respond to versions of those dilemmas, but what responses did they make—and when did they make them—as awareness of the Shoah grew? In what ways did their encounters with the Holocaust make theologians and philosophers grapple not with myths of silence but with metaphysical and moral silences that still leave their traditions shattered and even reduced to silence when the Shoah penetrates them deeply? As post-Holocaust theology and philosophy attempt to salvage fragments of meaning from the Holocaust's devastation, the credibility of those efforts depends on reckoning with silences that remain even when they are broken.

Forty years after World War II, the Jewish philosopher and theologian Emil Fackenheim made an exaggerated but still valid point when he asserted that "philosophers have all but ignored the Holocaust."[8] Fackenheim prominent among them, notable exceptions to that judgment can be found in the relatively early post-war years.[9] Nevertheless, the Holocaust has never attracted as much philosophical and specifically ethical inquiry as might be expected after an event of such devastating proportions. Perhaps philosophy's reluctance to break silence about the Holocaust is an expression of humility, a profound puzzlement about what to say, but a stronger case can be made that much of philosophy in the second half of the twentieth century and on into the twenty-first has simply not attended to history as much as it might have done. In the meantime, while the impact of the Holocaust on religious thought and practice—within Jewish and Christian traditions in particular—was felt to a greater extent, and earlier too, it remains to be seen how deeply the Holocaust's reverberations have penetrated and to what lasting effect.

Especially among Orthodox Jews, whose eastern European communities were devastated by the Shoah, a great deal of theological reflection took place, as circumstances permitted, in German-occupied areas, ghettos, and camps or in places of refuge to which they had escaped while the Holocaust raged. Many of those who produced these wartime *Responsa* did not survive the Holocaust. According to Gershon Greenberg, a leading scholar on this *Responsa* literature, during the first two postwar decades, the wartime theological reflections, whether their authors survived or not, were "overlooked by the historians, even denied."[10]

In the anguished wartime reflections of those who wrestled with God and the catastrophe engulfing them, one finds versions of the themes and quandaries that remain key parts of post-Holocaust religious thought, except that the wartime *Responsa* are particularly poignant because they were made in the midst of the destruction. Some of the major issues, which can be put in five question-clusters, include the following: (1) How is the traditional covenant between God and the Jewish people to be understood in the light of that people's decimation? Will there be a saving remnant, and, if so, what is its destiny? (2) How, if at all, is God involved in the devastation? Is the destruction part of a redemptive plan? Does it signify the birth pangs of the Messiah? (3) Is something new and unprecedented taking place, or does the destruction fit within traditional interpretations of the tribulations that have befallen the Jewish people in the past? (4) How should God be identified in such crushing circumstances? As omnipotent? Hidden? Suffering? Beyond understanding? (5) What responses to God are appropriate? Rejection? Protest? Faithful waiting? Repentance? Martyrdom? Justification of God's ways—theodicy? Silence?

During and after the Holocaust—whether in the first two decades or those that followed—versions of these issues have remained central in post-Holocaust religious thought. As those efforts explore events and the meanings beneath words and texts, versions of Kofman's "double bind" are detectable. The Holocaust may make one feel a duty to speak, an obligation to state how the Shoah relates to religious traditions, but such work can produce a choking feeling, a sense that too much harm has been done for a good recovery to be made, a suspicion that religious convictions may be overwhelmed by the challenges they face. The bind is double because any attempts to overcome these difficulties remain hopelessly optimistic and naïve unless they grapple with the despair that encounters with the Holocaust are bound to produce. To be touched by that despair, however, scarcely encourages religious commitment and belief. Hasia Diner's study of postwar American Jewish life, for example, shows that the Holocaust produced a resurgence of Jewish identification in the United States, but she aptly cites Albert Gordon, rabbi and anthropologist, whose 1959 study concluded that while the suburban Jew

> believes that there must be a God who created this world, he cannot understand [God's] continuing association with the Jews or, for that matter, with mankind. He has seen so much misery and wretchedness.

The fate that recently overtook six million Jews in Europe has shaken what little faith was left in him.[11]

Fifty years later, the relevance of that judgment and its challenges still holds.

Whatever the silence(s) produced by the Holocaust, they were not absolute. In the English-speaking world, important Jewish thinkers such as Martin Buber, Abraham Joshua Heschel, and Chaim Grade early on raised agonizing questions concerning how traditional beliefs about God could be sustained in a world shadowed by the Holocaust. On the Christian side, the work done before, during, and after the Holocaust by the British scholar James Parkes forcefully documented the Christian roots of antisemitism and persistently made important contributions to postwar Christian-Jewish relations.[12] In the Anglo-American context, however, the most widely discussed and long-term influential theological writings by individual thinkers who focused explicitly and persistently on the Holocaust did not appear primarily in the late 1940s, the 1950s, or even the early 1960s. A longer gestation period seems to have been required, as writers struggled to figure out what most needed to be said and then sought the words to break difficult silences. The results were more challenging than comforting, a point that can be illustrated by attention to four significant thinkers—three Jews and one Christian—who have done much to sustain attention on issues that deserve to remain prominent in post-Holocaust religious thought.

The God of history

In the summer of 1961, a young rabbi named Richard L. Rubenstein planned to begin a research trip to West Germany on Sunday, August 13. That same day, the East Germans created a major Cold War crisis by hastily building a wall between East and West Berlin. Postponing his trip for two days, Rubenstein arrived in Bonn, the West German capital, and accepted an invitation from his hosts, the Bundespressamt (Press and Information Office) of the Federal Republic to fly to Berlin to see the unfolding crisis. In an atmosphere charged with fear that nuclear war might erupt, Rubenstein took the opportunity to interview Heinrich Grüber, a prominent German Christian leader who had resisted the Nazis, rescued Jews, and suffered imprisonment in Sachsenhausen.[13] Earlier in 1961, Grüber had been the only German to testify for the prosecution at the Jerusalem trial of Adolf Eichmann, a leading perpetrator of the Holocaust.

With American tanks rumbling through the streets of Dahlem, the West Berlin suburb where Grüber lived, Rubenstein interviewed him in the late afternoon of August 17. When their conversation turned to the Holocaust, this meeting became a turning point in Rubenstein's personal and intellectual life. Grüber affirmed a biblical faith in the God-who-acts-in-history. More than that, he held that the Jews were God's chosen people; therefore, he believed, nothing could happen to them apart from God's will. When Rubenstein asked Grüber whether God had intended for Hitler to attempt the destruction of the European Jews, Grüber's response was yes—however difficult it might be to understand the reason, he told Rubenstein, the Holocaust was part of God's plan.

Rubenstein was impressed that Grüber took so seriously the belief that God acts providentially in history, a central tenet of Judaism and Christianity. To Grüber, that belief meant specifically that God was ultimately responsible for the Holocaust. Although Grüber's testimony struck him as abhorrent, Rubenstein appreciated the consistency of Grüber's theology, and the American Jewish thinker came away convinced that he must persistently confront the issue of God and the Holocaust. The eventual result was Rubenstein's first and immensely important book, *After Auschwitz: Radical Theology and Contemporary Judaism*, which appeared in 1966. A second edition of *After Auschwitz*, so extensively enlarged and revised as to be virtually a new book, was published in 1992 with a different subtitle: *History, Theology, and Contemporary Judaism*.

After Auschwitz was among the first books to probe systematically the significance of Auschwitz for post-Holocaust religious life. Rubenstein's analysis sparked ongoing debate because it challenged a belief that many people have long held dear. After Auschwitz, Rubenstein contended, belief in a redeeming God—one who is active in history and who will bring a fulfilling end to the upheavals in the human condition—is no longer credible.

In the late 1960s, the stir caused by *After Auschwitz* linked Rubenstein to a group of young American Protestant thinkers—Thomas Altizer, William Hamilton, and Paul van Buren among them—who were dubbed "death of God" theologians. The popular media picked up the story. *Time* magazine's cover story on April 8, 1966, featured the topic, and the movement ignited public discussion for some time.[14] Although the spotlight eventually moved on, these thinkers' contributions—especially Rubenstein's—did not fade. Their outlooks posed questions and their testimonies raised issues too fundamental to disappear. Yet neither the labeling nor the clustering of these thinkers was entirely apt. None was atheistic in any simple sense. Nor were their perspectives, methods, and moods identical. What they loosely shared was the feeling that talk about God did not—indeed could not—mean what it apparently had meant in the past. In that respect, the term "radical theology" described their work better than the more sensationalistic phrase "death of God." Creating breaks with the past and intensifying discontinuities within traditions, they ventured to talk about experiences that were widely shared even though most people lacked the words or the encouragement to say so in public. Unlike his Protestant brothers, however, Rubenstein put the Holocaust at the center of his contributions to radical theology in the 1960s. *After Auschwitz* provoked Holocaust-related searches that continue to this day.

The 614th commandment

In 1968, Emil Fackenheim delivered the Charles F. Deems Lectures at New York University, which were published two years later as *God's Presence in History: Jewish Affirmations and Philosophical Reflections*.[15] About one hundred pages in length, this brief and often reprinted book contains one of the most powerful of the relatively early religious responses to the Holocaust. According to Fackenheim—he fled his native Germany in 1939 after imprisonment in the Nazi concentration camp at Sachsenhausen, taught for many years at the University of Toronto, and then immigrated to Israel, where he died in 2003—the Holocaust was the most radically disorienting "epoch making event" in all of Jewish history.[16] In contrast to Rubenstein, Fackenheim argued that the Jewish people must respond to this shattering challenge with a reaffirmation of God's presence in history. Fackenheim acknowledged that it is impossible to affirm God's saving presence at Auschwitz, but he did insist that while no "redeeming Voice" was heard at Auschwitz, a "commanding Voice" was heard and it enunciated a "614th commandment" to supplement the 613 commandments of traditional Judaism. The new commandment was said to be that "the authentic Jew of today is forbidden to hand Hitler yet another, posthumous victory." Fackenheim spelled out the 614th commandment, which he first articulated in 1967, as follows:

> We are, first, commanded to survive as Jews, lest the Jewish people perish. We are commanded, second, to remember in our very guts and bones the martyrs of the Holocaust, lest their memory perish. We are forbidden, thirdly, to deny or despair of God, however much we may have to contend with Him or with belief in Him, lest Judaism perish. We are forbidden, finally, to despair of the world as the place which is to become the kingdom of God, lest we help make it a meaningless place in which God is dead or irrelevant and everything is permitted. To abandon any of these imperatives, in response to Hitler's victory at Auschwitz, would be to hand him yet other, posthumous victories.[17]

Few, if any, post-Holocaust religious statements by a Jewish thinker have become better known.[18] For some time, Fackenheim's 614th commandment struck a deep chord in Jews of every social level and religious commitment. Much, but by no means all, of Fackenheim's writing was on a philosophic and theological level beyond the competence of the ordinary layperson. Not so this passage, which is largely responsible for the fact that Fackenheim's interpretation of the Holocaust arguably became for a time the most influential within the Jewish community. A people that has endured catastrophic defeat is likely to see the survival of their community and its traditions as a supreme imperative. By referring to a divine command, Fackenheim gave potent expression to this aspiration. Instead of questioning whether the traditional Jewish understanding of God could be maintained after Auschwitz, he implied that those who questioned God's presence to Israel, *even in the death camps*, were accomplices of the worst destroyer the Jews have ever known. The passion and the psychological power of this position are undeniable.

Nevertheless, Fackenheim's position could have unfortunate consequences. Not only were those Jews "who denied or despaired" of the scriptural God seemingly cast in the role of accomplices of Hitler, a serious and controversial allegation indeed. In addition, Fackenheim went so far as to suggest that those who did not hear the "commanding Voice" at Auschwitz were *willfully* rejecting God: "In my view," he wrote, "nothing less will do than to say that a commanding Voice speaks from

Auschwitz, and that there are Jews who hear it and Jews who *stop their ears*."[19] To stop one's ears is a voluntary act. Fackenheim seems to have either excluded or ignored the possibility that some Jews might honestly be unable to believe that God was in any way present at Auschwitz, no matter how metaphorically the idea was presented. Furthermore, in spite of its power, Fackenheim's position was not without difficulty even for the tradition he sought to defend. Given his conviction that revelation was inseparable from interpretation, it was not clear whether the commanding Voice was to be taken as real or metaphorical. Subsequently there was reason to believe that Fackenheim would reject both alternatives and would hold that the commandment would have been unreal absent an affirmative Jewish response. Taken literally, there does not appear to be any credible evidence that anybody heard the 614th commandment, as indeed Fackenheim's later description of how he came to write the passage indicates. In his 1982 book *To Mend the World*, Fackenheim told his readers that after he had come to the conclusion that the Holocaust was a radical challenge to Jewish faith, "my first response was to formulate a '614th commandment.'"[20] Clearly, as understood in traditional Judaism, one does not formulate a commandment. It derives from a divine source. In any event, whatever the psychological power of the 614th commandment, its status as commandment remains—perhaps unavoidably—ambiguous.

Fackenheim's critics also found considerable difficulty with his assertion that the commanding Voice had enjoined Jews to "survive as Jews." In the case of traditional Jews, no such commandment was necessary. They have always believed that Jewish religious survival was a divine imperative. They had no need of an Auschwitz to receive such an injunction. In the case of secularized Jews, the commandment appeared perhaps to be a case of pedagogic overkill. It hardly seemed likely that even a jealous God would require the annihilation of six million Jews as the occasion for a commandment forbidding Jews to permit the demise of their tradition.

Perhaps the most important aspect of the 614th commandment was the injunction not to deny or despair of God lest Hitler be given "yet other, posthumous victories." Here Fackenheim confronted the fundamental issue of Holocaust-related theology. He told his readers what God has commanded. Does this mean that Fackenheim perpetrated a fiction in order to maintain the theological integrity of his reading of Judaism? Given Fackenheim's faith in some sense of a Divine Presence, it was hardly likely that he could have thought of God as absent from Auschwitz. As Fackenheim came to realize that the real difficulty lay in formulating a view of God that took the Holocaust into account, he understood that one could no longer speak of a *saving* presence at Auschwitz. Yet, utter defeat and annihilation could not be the last word. A way out of the ashes had to be found. The 614th commandment expressed what most religious Jews regard as their sacred obligation in response to the Holocaust. In the language of Jewish faith, that response could most appropriately be communicated in the imagery of the commandments. Fackenheim's 614th commandment is religiously and existentially problematic. That, however, may remain beside the point. It is perhaps best to see Fackenheim's 614th commandment as a cry of the heart, transmuted into the language of the sacred. That would at least help to explain why it has touched so many Jews—and a lot of Christians, too—so deeply.[21]

A credibility crisis

Along with interest in Wiesel's *Night* and his early essays and fiction, the writings of Rubenstein and Fackenheim influenced some Christians as well as Jews.[22] One of them was Franklin Littell. On July 23, 1998, his friend the Holocaust historian Yehuda Bauer interviewed Littell at Yad Vashem in Jerusalem, where the two scholars frequently led seminars on the Holocaust. The interview provides an overview of Littell's primary concerns and concludes with remarks that succinctly capture his character, outlook, and aspirations. Underscoring that his motivation in writing and teaching about the Holocaust was above all to prevent "premature closure," Littell ended the 1998 interview by declaring his intent "to keep this thing [the memory of the Holocaust] irritating—you know, be the harpoon that the fish can't escape."[23]

Those who knew Littell may hear his voice in those words—a voice that was earthy and earnest, intense and impassioned, edged at times with laughter and humor, but one that cut to the chase as he expressed his conviction that the unredeemable atrocities of the Holocaust and of all genocides must provoke resistance against the injustice and indifference that produce them.

The catalog of the United States Library of Congress contains thirty-four Littell entries. The earliest titles, from the 1950s, suggest that this ordained Methodist minister, who held a doctorate in theology and religious studies, might have had a conventional professorial career. During this early period, he concentrated on church history in the United States, with an emphasis on Protestant Christianity and church-state relationships. However, much more was gestating. A visit to Nazi Germany in 1939 made an indelible impression on Littell—one that was deepened and intensified by his work in postwar Germany, where he served as the chief Protestant advisor for the U.S. occupation forces. These experiences honed the harpoon that Littell would thrust at multiple targets, including, first and foremost, his own Christian tradition.

Two books loom largest in Littell's body of works. Christian scholars James Parkes and Edward Flannery preceded Littell in documenting their tradition's culpability for antisemitism, but Littell's 1975 monograph *The Crucifixion of the Jews* was nonetheless ground-breaking in that it drove home Christian responsibility for and complicity in the Holocaust. Written in the aftermath of the military attacks on the state of Israel in 1967 and 1973, Littell's book also staunchly defended "the right of the Jewish people to self-identity and self-definition."[24]

Littell often referred to the Holocaust as an "alpine event," his way of identifying its unprecedented, watershed significance. In his view, the Holocaust constituted the most severe "credibility crisis"—one of his favorite terms—to afflict the Christian tradition. That tradition's "teaching of contempt" about Judaism and Jews had contributed mightily to genocide against the Jewish people, he believed. Only profound contrition and reform, including fundamental theological revision that tackled the New Testament's anti-Judaic themes, could restore integrity to post-Holocaust Christianity.

Littell's belief that Christianity faced a monumental credibility crisis was not based solely on his knowledge of the centuries-old history of Christian hostility toward Judaism and Jews. More immediately, his postwar experiences in Germany made him painfully aware that most German churches had embraced Adolf Hitler and Nazism. He recognized the complicity of German churches in the Holocaust, as well as the widespread indifference of the churches outside Germany when it came to the plight of Jews under the swastika. Yet, he understood that some Christians and churches in Germany had resisted Nazism and, at least to some extent, assisted Jews. Thus, even before Littell published *The Crucifixion of the Jews*, his pioneering work resulted in the other entry that looms largest among his works, the 1974 volume *The German Church Struggle and the Holocaust* (co-edited with his friend Hubert G. Locke).

Important in its own right—among other things it contains a memorable exchange between Richard Rubenstein and Elie Wiesel—this volume signaled the pivotal role that Littell played as an organizer and leader in both Holocaust studies and Christian-Jewish relations. *The German Church Struggle and the Holocaust* emerged from a conference that Littell and Locke convened at Wayne State University in 1970. Focused on Christians in Nazi Germany, their support for and resistance against Hitler's regime, and that conflict's implications for the future of Christianity and its relationship to Jews and Judaism, the meeting was the first in a series of conferences that would become the Annual Scholars' Conference on the Holocaust and the Churches. This interfaith, interdisciplinary, and international gathering of scholars, educators, clergy, and community leaders remains the longest continuously running initiative of its kind. The conference's work, including many publications, has significantly influenced and advanced the field of Holocaust and genocide studies, and stands as a tribute to Littell's influence and his persistent thrusting of a "harpoon that the fish can't escape."

No more theodicy

Influential contributions to post-Holocaust religious thought were also made relatively early by the Jewish philosopher Emmanuel Levinas. By the 1960s and 1970s, he was developing an important post-Holocaust ethical perspective, which drew extensively if not always explicitly on his Jewish heritage by arguing that previous ethical theory had failed to concentrate on something as obvious and profound as the human face.[25] Close attention to the face of the other person, Levinas affirmed, could produce a reorientation not only of ethics but also of human life itself, for our deepest seeing of the other person's face drives home how closely human beings are connected and how much the existence of the other person confers responsibility upon us.[26]

Levinas did not write explicitly about the Holocaust very often, but traces of that catastrophe do appear, and the overt emphases of his thought make plain that the Shoah is a powerful point of reference between the lines, in the silence—the void even—that shadows his philosophy. On some occasions, however, the Holocaust comes to the fore in Levinas's writing. One example is found in his brief but highly significant essay called "Useless Suffering," which did not appear early but in 1982. In that article, Levinas explicitly states a conviction that permeated his thought early and late. "The Holocaust of the Jewish people under the reign of Hitler," said Levinas, "seems to me the paradigm of gratuitous human suffering, in which evil appears in its diabolical horror."[27]

As a French prisoner of war, Levinas did forced labor under the Nazis, and almost all of his Lithuanian family perished in the Holocaust. It made a profound impact upon him. Calling the twentieth century one of "unutterable suffering," he emphasized that suffering of the kind that the Nazis and their collaborators inflicted on Europe's Jews was and is "for nothing." To try to justify it religiously, ethically, politically—as the Nazis did when they made the practice of useless violence, as Primo Levi identified it, essential to the German "superiority" that they envisioned—was what Levinas called "the source of all immorality."

When Levinas said that the useless suffering inflicted during the Holocaust was "for nothing," he did not overlook Nazi "logic" and what it meant. To the contrary, he took National Socialism to be about arrogant destruction, its grandiose rhetoric about a thousand-year Reich notwithstanding. The chief element in National Socialism's arrogance was that regime's resolve to deface the human face with remorseless determination. The Nazis did this not in some abstract way, but by useless suffering visited upon Jewish women, children, and men that made its antisemitic prerogatives dominant until overwhelming force stopped them from doing more of their worst.

Levinas thought that the twentieth century was one of "unutterable suffering." The evil in that suffering, and Levinas believed that "all evil relates back to suffering," was not confined to "persistent or obstinate" bodily pain but included "helplessness, abandonment and solitude," an abjection intensified when "a moan, a cry, a groan or a sigh" brought no relief but were swallowed up by silence. Levinas distinguished between "*suffering in the other*" and what he called "suffering *in me*." The latter's uselessness could have meaning insofar as it was "a suffering for the suffering (inexorable though it may be) of someone else." As for the uselessness of the suffering of the other, Levinas thought that striving to relieve it and to resist the forces that created it should be "raised to the level of supreme ethical principle—the only one it is impossible to question—shaping the hopes and commanding the practical discipline of vast human groups."

No sooner did Levinas write those words than he issued a caution about them. In no way should they be construed as a justification for suffering, as a mitigation of suffering's uselessness because such suffering could become the means to the good and the virtue of relieving it. Observing that its temptations should not be underestimated, Levinas rejected all forms of *theodicy*, the attempt to make suffering "comprehensible," to find "in a suffering that is essentially gratuitous and absurd, and apparently arbitrary, a meaning and an order." Noting that "Nietzsche's saying about the death of God" had taken on "the meaning of a quasi-empirical fact" in the Shoah and the paradox in Emil Fackenheim's allusion to the commanding voice at Auschwitz, namely that it entails "revelation from the very God who nevertheless was silent at Auschwitz," Levinas still affirmed that Fackenheim saw something of seminal importance not only for Jews but for humanity itself. Levinas put his point in the form of an extended question:

Must not humanity now, in a faith more difficult than before, in a faith without theodicy, continue to live out Sacred History; a history that now demands even more from the resources of the *I* in each one of us, and from its suffering inspired by the suffering of the other, from its compassion which is a non-useless suffering (or love), which is no longer suffering "for nothing," and immediately has meaning?

Levinas could not answer this question, at least not simply, because the response to it depends on how humanity breaks the silence that follows his asking.

Conclusion

Attempts to maintain traditional understandings of covenant and God's presence in history, analyses denying the credibility of providential divinity, searches that affirm the more-important-than-ever status of ethics and religion in times when traditions are in crisis and in contexts of atrocity and suffering that make every theodicy problematic—all of these perspectives and more emerged during the Holocaust and in its relatively early aftershocks. If it took time for some of these developments to unfold, if it is still taking time for them to find expression, that outcome should not be entirely surprising. What would be lamentable is failure to keep asking and pursuing the questions that the Holocaust raises—sometimes in word(s), sometimes in silence(s).

The Holocaust's place in history was not fixed at the time of its happening or in its short-term aftermath. The philosophical and religious quandaries evoked during and after the Shoah have no easy closure, if they allow closure at all. No defining terms encompass them all. Nor does a response made at one time suffice for all times. Inevitably, the Holocaust's place, its presence, is still in the making, with aftershocks that will continue to require the recognition and reconsideration, the contesting and breaking of silence, particularly with regard to God's death, reality, power, and relationship to history.

Notes

1 Elie Wiesel, *One Generation After*, trans. Lily Edelman and the author (New York: Random House, 1970), p. 215.
2 Elie Wiesel, *Night*, trans. Marion Wiesel (New York: Hill and Wang, 2006), p. 67.
3 Ibid. An earlier translation of *Night* nuances this quotation by referring to "the meaning beneath the words." See Elie Wiesel, *Night*, trans. Stella Rodway (New York: Bantam Books, 1982), p. 64.
4 Sarah Kofman, *Smothered Words*, trans. Madeleine Dobie (Evanston, IL: Northwestern University Press, 1998), p. 39. Kofman's book originally appeared in French in 1987.
5 Ibid., pp. 38–39.
6 Important reflections on and examples of liturgical responses to the Holocaust can be found in Marcia Sachs Littell and Sharon Weissman Gutman, eds., *Liturgies on the Holocaust: An Interfaith Anthology*, new and revised ed. (Valley Forge, PA: Trinity Press International, 1996). The examples of Holocaust liturgies in this volume come from civic and religious settings. They include texts, ritual acts, and music from the time of the Holocaust itself and from the early postwar years, but the editors also make the following observation:

"In the early 1970s, Yom HaShoah was observed by only a few dozen congregations in America. During the administration of President Jimmy Carter, observation of the Days of Remembrance grew rapidly and marked a permanent day on the calendar. Every American president since that time has supported this endeavor" (p. 1).

7 See, for example, Dan Cohn-Sherbok, ed., *Holocaust Theology: A Reader* (New York: New York University Press, 2002) and Steven T. Katz, Shlomo Biderman, and Gershon Greenberg, eds., *Wrestling with God: Jewish Theological Responses during and after the Holocaust* (New York: Oxford University Press, 2007).

8 Emil Fackenheim, "The Holocaust and Philosophy," *The Journal of Philosophy*, 82 (1985): 505.

9 See, for example, Albert Camus, *The Plague*, trans. Stuart Gilbert (New York: Modern Library, 1948); Karl Jaspers, *The Question of German Guilt*, trans. E. B. Ashton (New York: Dial Press, 1948); Hannah Arendt, *The Origins of Totalitarianism* (New York: Harcourt, 1951) and *Eichmann in Jerusalem: A Report on the Banality of Evil* (New York: Viking Press, 1963); Abraham Joshua Heschel, *Man Is Not Alone: A Philosophy of Religion* (New York: Farrar, Straus & Young, 1951); Martin Buber, *Eclipse of God: Studies in the Relation between Religion and Philosophy* (New York: Harper, 1952) and *On Judaism* (New York: Schocken Books, 1967); Theodor Adorno, *Prisms*, trans. Samuel and Shierry Weber (London: Neville Spearman, 1967) and *Negative Dialectics*, trans. E. B. Ashton (New York: Seabury Press, 1973); Emmanuel Levinas, *Totality and Infinity: An Essay on Exteriority* (Pittsburgh, PA: Duquesne University Press, 1969); Emil Fackenheim, *God's Presence in History: Jewish Affirmations and Philosophical Reflections* (New York: New York University Press, 1970); and Jean Améry, *At the Mind's Limits: Contemplations by a Survivor on Auschwitz and Its Realities* (Bloomington, IN: Indiana University Press, 1980).

10 See Katz, Biderman, and Greenberg, eds., *Wrestling with God*, p. 11.

11 Hasia R. Diner, *We Remember with Reverence and Love: American Jews and the Myth of Silence after the Holocaust, 1945–1962* (New York: New York University Press, 2009), p. 327.

12 Lawrence Baron helpfully discusses some of these early developments in "The Holocaust and American Public Memory, 1945–60," *Holocaust and Genocide Studies*, 17.1 (2003): 62–88.

13 Rubenstein's essay "The Dean and the Chosen People" depicts these events. See Richard L. Rubenstein, *After Auschwitz: History, Theology, and Contemporary Judaism*, 2nd ed. (Baltimore, MD: The Johns Hopkins University Press, 1992), pp. 3–13. See also Richard L. Rubenstein, *Power Struggle: An Autobiographical Confession* (New York: Scribner, 1974).

14 See Stephen R. Haynes and John K. Roth, eds., *The Death of God Movement and the Holocaust: Radical Theology Encounters the Shoah* (Westport, CT: Greenwood Press, 1999).

15 My discussion of Fackenheim is adapted from Richard L. Rubenstein and John K. Roth, *Approaches to Auschwitz: The Holocaust and Its Legacy*, rev. ed. (Louisville, KY: Westminster John Knox Press, 2003), pp. 348–52.

16 See Emil Fackenheim, *God's Presence in History: Jewish Affirmations and Philosophical Reflections* (Northvale, NJ: Jason Aronson, 1997), pp. 8–14 and *To Mend the World: Foundations of Future Jewish Thought* (New York: Schocken Books, 1982), pp. 9–22.

17 In traditional Judaism, the number of commandments given by God to Israel is said to be 613. The passage originally appeared in *Judaism* 16 (Summer 1967): 272–73. The text of Fackenheim's contribution to that journal's symposium on "Jewish Values in the Post-Holocaust Future" is reprinted in Emil L. Fackenheim, *The Jewish Return into History: Reflections in the Age of Auschwitz and a New Jerusalem* (New York: Schocken Books, 1978), 19–24. See also Fackenheim, *God's Presence in History*, 84–98. In the 1997 edition of the latter work, Fackenheim includes a new preface, "No Posthumous Victories for Hitler: After Thirty Years, the '614th Commandment' Reconsidered." Noting that the phrase "'no posthumous victories for Hitler' became a slogan, often poorly understood, and as such liked by some, disliked by others, mocked by a few," Fackenheim added that "what 'no posthumous victories for Hitler' asked of Jews was, of course, not to spite Hitler, but to carry on *in spite of* him" (xii, Fackenheim's italics).

18 One of the most noteworthy competitors for that distinction would be Irving Greenberg's "working principle," namely, that "no statement, theological or otherwise, should be made that would not be credible in the presence of the burning children." See Greenberg, "Cloud of Smoke, Pillar of Fire: Judaism, Christianity, and Modernity after the Holocaust," in Eva Fleischner, ed., *Auschwitz: Beginning of a New Era? Reflections on the Holocaust* (New York: Ktav, 1977), p. 23.

19 Emil L. Fackenheim, *The Jewish Return into History: Reflections in the Age of Auschwitz and a New Jerusalem* (New York: Schocken, 1978), p. 31. Italics added.

20 Fackenheim, *To Mend the World*, p. 10.

21 For further commentary on Fackenheim's thought, see David Patterson, *Emil L. Fackenheim: A Jewish Philosopher's Response to the Holocaust* (Syracuse, NY: Syracuse University Press, 2008).

22 Prominent among them would be: Robert McAfee Brown, Harry James Cargas, A. Roy and Alice Eckardt, Darrell Fasching, Eva Fleischner, David Gushee, Stephen Haynes, Elisabeth Maxwell, Johann Baptist Metz, John T. Pawlikowski, Carol Rittner, Dorothee Söelle, Paul M. van Buren, and Clark Williamson.

23 Bauer's interview with Littell is available online at: http://www1.yadvashem.org/odot_pdf/Microsoft%20Word%20-%203725.pdf.

24 Franklin H. Littell, *The Crucifixion of the Jews* (New York: Harper and Row, 1975), p. 3.

25 For evidence of Levinas's engagement with Judaism and Jewish tradition, see Emmanuel Levinas, *Difficult Freedom: Essays on Judaism*, trans. Sean Hand (Baltimore: Johns Hopkins University Press, 1990); *Nine Talmudic Readings*, trans. Annette Aronowicz (Bloomington, IN: Indiana University Press, 1990); and *New Talmudic Readings*, trans. Richard Cohen (Pittsburgh, PA: Duquesne University Press, 1999).

26 See Emmanuel Levinas, *Ethics and Infinity*, trans. Richard A. Cohen (Pittsburgh, PA: Duquesne University Press, 1985) and *Entre Nous: On Thinking-of-the-Other*, trans. Michael B. Smith and Barbara Marshav (New York: Columbia University Press, 1998).

27 "Useless Suffering" was published originally in the *Giornale di Metatisica* 4 (January–April 1982): 13–26. It is more readily found in Emmanuel Levinas, *Entre Nous: On Thinking-of-the-Other*, trans. Michael B. Smith and Barbara Harshav (New York: Columbia University Press, 1998), pp. 91–101. The quoted passage is on p. 97. The quotations in this paragraph are from Levinas, "Useless Suffering," in *Entre Nous*, pp. 94, 97, and 99.

10

TRIAL BY AUDIENCE

Bringing Nazi war criminals to justice in Hollywood films, 1944–59

Lawrence Baron

Until recently, most studies of Holocaust cinema dated the entry of the Holocaust into American feature films either to Edward Dmytryk's *The Young Lions* (1958) or George Steven's *The Diary of Anne Frank* (1959).[1] The public impact of the atrocity footage taken by Allied film crews and journalists when the concentration camps were liberated in 1945 and the revelations of crimes against humanity emanating from the Nuremberg Trials have been minimized as ephemeral. The scholarly consensus has maintained that the American movie industry paid little attention to a topic that would repel audiences, distract from the return to peacetime normalcy, embarrass the United States' new ally West Germany, overshadow the evils of Soviet communism, and substantiate charges that the Jewish movie moguls promoted a pro-Jewish political agenda.[2] In this regard the conventional wisdom about Hollywood's initial failure to depict Germany's genocidal crusade against European Jewry confirmed the prevailing silence about the subject in American society in general.[3]

Yet narrative and visual references to the decimation of European Jewry during World War Two appeared prior to the end of the war and through the 1950s in Hollywood movies, idealizing the American role in defeating the Third Reich, liberating the concentration camps, rehabilitating displaced persons, facilitating their immigration or repatriation, and apprehending and trying Nazi war criminals. Although these motion pictures placed what happened to the Jews in the broader context of the enormous toll of suffering and casualties incurred by the civilian populations in German occupied Europe, they made it equally clear that the Nazi animus towards Jews was particularly virulent.[4]

This essay focuses on a relatively neglected corpus of early postwar Hollywood films that dramatized the hunt for Nazi war criminals and their prosecution by international tribunals. Inspired by the Nuremberg Trials, these films established their verisimilitude by alluding to real events, citing historical sources in advertisements, credits, or prologues, employing eyewitness consultants and filmmakers, including clips from the atrocity footage taken by Allied camera crews or from newsreels of the Nuremberg Trials, and shooting scenes on location in the debris of war-ravaged Europe. The overt message of such movies glorified the United States for liberating the surviving remnant of groups incarcerated and oppressed by Germany and its accomplices and holding the perpetrators of inhuman policies criminally accountable by international tribunals. To be sure, the motion pictures analyzed here neither stressed the unique status of the Jews among Hitler's victims nor observed the scholarly taboo against imposing edifying endings on what is now considered an irredeemable chapter in human history. Nevertheless, they provide a portal to how Hollywood cumulatively contributed to forging an American memory of a European event. Stuart Liebman has warned against excluding such early representations of the aftermath of Nazi race warfare from surveys of Holocaust cinema: "Overlooking them would also compromise our understanding of the way the crimes against the Jews percolated into public discourse and consciousness during this crucial period."[5]

The first American films to grapple with crimes against humanity or genocide continued prewar and wartime government and industry guidelines for portraying Nazi outrages. Under considerable pressure from American isolationists, anti-Semitic demagogues, congressional critics of the film industry, the German government, and Hollywood's own self-censorship board, the major studios belatedly alerted audiences to the dangers of Nazi racism in feature films released between 1939 and 1941 that, with the notable exception of Chaplin's *The Great Dictator* (1940), generically referred to Hitler's persecution of non-Aryans or employed visual symbols like the identifying "J" on a concentration camp uniform, assuming audiences would make their own connections with news reports they had been reading about the plight of Jews under Hitler's rule.[6] Joseph Breen, the head of the Production Code Administration after 1934, demanded the deletion of scenes portraying anti-Semitic actions and attitudes out of fear they would incite, rather than inhibit, hatred of the Jews.[7] He opposed excessively graphic depictions of violence even in war movies documenting Nazi terror. The federal Offices of Censorship and War Information cautioned against singling Jews out as targets of Hitler's bigotry, anticipating that Germany would exploit this as proof of the pro-Jewish bias that Hollywood purportedly harbored.[8] The Office of War Information directed the media to publicize only verifiable atrocities like the Lidice massacre of 1942, which Germany officially acknowledged, rather than the incredible "rumors" about the mass murder of Jews.[9]

Filmed in 1943 and released the following year, *None Shall Escape* foreshadows Germany's defeat and imagines what an international tribunal convened by the United Nations to try Nazi perpetrators would look like.[10] The presiding judge accuses SS Reich Commissioner Wilhelm Grimm in Poland of "wanton extermination of human life, murder, unlawful detentions, degenerate atrocities, and common theft." The testimonies of witnesses segue into flashbacks of the biography of the ethnic German defendant. He had returned as an embittered and crippled World War One veteran to teach in his hometown of Litzbach, which has been incorporated into Poland. Though engaged to Maya, a beautiful Polish woman, Grimm predicts Germany will recover from the war and conquer Poland as part of its *Lebensraum*.

When she spurns him on account of his contempt toward Poles, he rapes a teenage pupil who drowns herself out of shame, a motif reminiscent of the Aryan woman "defiled" by the Jew in the notorious anti-Semitic Nazi film *Jud Süss* (1940). Grimm loses an eye when someone in an angry mob throws a rock at him, but he flees to Munich even though he was found innocent of the rape charge due to insufficient evidence. There he recovers his self- and national esteem by joining the SA and participating in Hitler's Beer Hall Putsch. The Nazi Party rewards him for his early loyalty in 1933 by appointing him the Deputy Chief of the Bureau of Living Space. When Grimm fails to persuade his socialist brother to jump on the Nazi bandwagon, he orders his arrest and imprisonment in a concentration camp and enlists his nephew Willy as his protégé in the Nazi cause. Grimm's brother and the eventually disillusioned nephew serve as the good German foils to Grimm's evil Nazi character.

On the heels of the victorious German invasion, Grimm returns to Litzbach as the tyrannical SS commissioner of the town. He confiscates food produced by Polish peasants, conscripts attractive women to be prostitutes for German officers, enslaves Polish workers, executes Polish resisters, and films German soldiers distributing bread to Poles who are commanded to smile gratefully until the charade is over. Jews fare even worse under Grimm's heavy hand. He burns the torah scrolls and desecrates the synagogue by turning it into a stable. In his racist logic, "horses are more important than Jews." In the most memorable scene of the film, German guards herd Jews onto cattle cars that will be coupled to trains transporting Jews from Warsaw. As Wilhelm and Willy drive up to the railroad station, Willy inquires why it is necessary to relocate the Jews. Grimm callously replies, "There's just so much food at our disposal. There must be fewer mouths to feed."

In a gesture of ecumenical cooperation, the village priest and rabbi implore Grimm to halt the deportation. Anticipating the nomenclature of the Nuremberg Principles, the priest exclaims, "Before God and man, I protest this crime against humanity!" The rabbi requests a chance to address his fellow Jews. Grimm consents thinking it will calm them down. Instead, the rabbi eloquently incites them to resist:

> Submission brought us rare moments in history when we were tolerated. Is there any greater degradation than to be tolerated, to be permitted to exist? We have submitted too long. If we want equality and justice, we must take our place alongside all oppressed peoples, regardless of race or religion. ... By our actions we will be remembered. This is our last free choice, our moment in history, and I say to you let us choose to fight here, now.

To quell the uprising, Nazi guards mow down the unruly Jews in bursts of machine-gun fire. Grimm personally shoots the rabbi. Visualizing the joint victimization of the Polish Catholics and Jews, the camera dwells first on a woman's body lying beneath a cruciform road sign and shifts over to the Jewish star on the armband worn by the prostrate rabbi. The priest rushes to help his dying friend, who uses his last breaths to recite the *Kaddish*. In an over-the-shoulder shot replicating the priest's gaze, the viewer stares at a mound of corpses blocking the entrance to a boxcar.

Producer Samuel Bishoff conceived of *None Shall Escape* upon hearing President Roosevelt announce on October 5th of 1942 that "the United Nations had decided that Nazi ringleaders and their brutal henchmen must be named and apprehended and tried in accordance with the judicial processes of criminal law." The incidents portrayed in the film drew from *The Black Book of Poland,* compiled by the Polish government-in-exile in 1941 and published in the United States in 1942. Though primarily documenting the travail of the Poles under German rule, it also devoted 37 pages to the persecution of the Jews.[11] Yet the movie evinced an awareness of the mass deportations of Polish Jews during 1942 and 1943 as is apparent in the aforementioned scene.[12] The émigré director Andre de Toth, a Hungarian filmmaker assigned to cover the invasion of Poland, vividly recalled how both Poles and Jews were oppressed by their German conquerors. He made *None Shall Escape* to reveal their mutual plight and illustrate how the civilized world pledged to deal with the perpetrators.[13]

Most reviewers applauded the rabbi's militant speech; though one condemned it as uncharacteristic of a pious Jew,[14] a view that may have stereotyped Jews as passive victims or perceptively detected an extraneous source. Lester Cole, the left-wing screenwriter, had borrowed some of the rabbi's fiery rhetoric from lines originally uttered by a communist leader during the Spanish Civil War.[15] Only the censorship

FIGURE 10.1 Rabbi David Levin, played by Richard Hale, looks in horror at the Jews shot down while boarding a deportation transport (*None Shall Escape*).
Source: Reproduced with permission from Photofest, Inc.

board of Ohio ordered that derogatory dialogue spoken by the indoctrinated Willy, saying Jews are not people, be cut from the version of the film shown in the state.[16]

None Shall Escape was both a commercial and critical success for the "poverty row" studio Columbia Pictures. The movie imparted mixed messages about the tragedy befalling Polish Jewry. The advertising campaign lured audiences into the theatre by intimating that the film was primarily about forced prostitution with the tagline: "Thank heaven your daughter wasn't there." Below this, however, ads mentioned that the movie was about the trial of war criminals or quoted the Moscow Declaration issued by Churchill, Roosevelt, and Stalin in November of 1943: "They will be brought back to the scene of their crimes and judged on the spot by the peoples whom they outraged."[17] The Communist *Daily Worker* praised *None Shall Escape* as "the most passionate, the most militant indictment of anti-Semitism in the history of Hollywood."[18] The film earned an Oscar nomination for best original screenplay. Only recently, however, have Holocaust film scholars like Annette Insdorf recognized *None Shall Escape* as "not only revelatory in its inclusion of the genocide of the Jews, but prescient in its postwar trial of an SS leader."[19]

Since it predated the liberation of the concentration and death camps, *None Shall Escape* lacked the atrocity footage and photographs which would become the iconic images of Nazi iniquities to Americans through their dissemination in contemporary newsreels, newspapers, magazines, and the Nuremberg Trials.[20] At the first International Military Tribunal, Allied prosecutors found the Third Reich guilty of engaging in a

FIGURE 10.2 Franz Kindler, played by Orson Welles, pulls a gun to avoid capture by Inspector Wilson, played by Edward G. Robinson (*The Stranger*).
Source: Reproduced with permission from Photofest, Inc.

campaign to exterminate the Jews throughout occupied Europe, but they subsumed this charge under the categories of war crimes and crimes against humanity.[21] While the trial was still in session, Orson Welles' *The Stranger* (1946) premiered.[22] It holds the distinction of being the first commercial movie to include atrocity footage from the newsreels and film entered as evidence at Nuremberg.

Welles modeled his sinister SS villain Franz Kindler after Martin Bormann, the highest ranking Nazi to elude capture by the Allies. As played by Welles, Kindler parlays his fluent English and forged credentials into an appointment as a German history professor at a New England college under the alias of Charles Rankin. Edward G. Robinson plays Detective Wilson of the Allied War Crimes Commission who tracks down Kindler, which hearkens back to his role as the FBI agent who exposes a Nazi espionage ring in *Confessions of a Nazi Spy* (1939).[23] Wilson tails an escaped SS camp commandant named Konrad Meinike to the town of Harper where Kindler resides. At a dinner party hosted by Kindler, Wilson listens to his host pontificate about the innate authoritarianism of the Germans and their lack of a philosopher who championed freedom. When Kindler's son-in-law cites Karl Marx to refute this generalization, Kindler scoffs at the notion that a Jew like Marx could be considered a German. Following the discovery of Meinike's body in the woods near Kindler's home, Wilson screens atrocity footage of naked corpses, a large gas chamber, and lime pits for Rankin's wife, appealing to her conscience to confirm that Meinike had contacted her husband. He reveals that Rankin is really Kindler, the Nazi mastermind who "conceived of the theory of genocide, the mass depopulation of conquered countries, so that regardless of who won the war, Germany would emerge the strongest nation in Western Europe, biologically speaking."[24]

In retrospect, the glaring inaccuracies of the *The Stranger*'s characterization of Nazi genocide, the gassing process (which Wilson mistakenly believes killed more quickly because the victims were forced to take hot showers first to open up their pores), and the failure to specify that Jews were targeted for extermination stand out. The latter flaw typifies the narration in postwar documentaries like *Nazi Concentration Camps* and *Night and Fog* (1955), which deliberately obscured the victimization of the Jews to accentuate the multinational scope of German crimes.[25] Despite Wilson's errors in describing the gassing process his overly broad definition of genocide, Rankin's anti-Semitic slip and the inclusion of concentration camp footage indicate an incipient awareness of what the Third Reich's racial policies entailed.[26] Most reviewers noted that Kindler was implicated in Nazi atrocities and mass murder.[27] A few commented on the anti-Semitic remark Kindler made.[28] Bill Krohn regards *The Stranger's* treatment of the Shoah as "part of a *danse macabre* of repression and revelation that went on throughout this period and didn't end when the war ended."[29]

Once the Allied nations instituted the International Military Tribunal at Nuremberg, seventy-five percent of Americans polled approved of it. While certain that the defendants were guilty, Americans believed the IMT would guarantee the defendants a fair trial.[30] These contradictory attitudes were apparent in the second American film about war crimes trials, Lewis Allen's *Sealed Verdict* (1948).[31]

FIGURE 10.3 Major Lawson, played by Ray Milland, cross-examines Themis DeLisle, played by Florence Marley (*Sealed Verdict*).
Source: Reproduced with permission from Photofest, Inc.

The opening credits and scenes of *Sealed Verdict* attest to its authenticity. The audience learns that all of the exterior scenes, including the first shots of the rubble and courthouse in Nuremberg, were photographed in Europe. Presumably within the court, the audience witnesses Justice Robert Jackson's opening statement at the Nuremberg Trials:

> The prisoners represent sinister influences that will lurk in the world long after their bodies return to dust. They are the living symbols of racial hatreds, of terrorism, and violence, and of the arrogance and cruelty of power. We must never forget that the record on which we judge these defendants today is the record on which history will judge us tomorrow.[32]

The camera pulls back to reveal that this is a newsreel film being screened to United States Army lawyers who will prosecute lower ranking Nazis in the coming months. The officer heading the team assumes his subordinates and the audience are familiar with the footage and the American commitment to international law: "I suppose you've all seen this film a dozen or so times. I have myself, but I don't know where you'll find a better summary of our mission than in Justice Jackson's address."

Ray Milland, in the role of Major Robert Lawson, fulfills this mission by arguing the case against General Otto Steigmann, who is charged with ordering the reprisal executions of hostages in the town of Leemach when he was its military governor. Though not spelled out in the film, the screenplay indicates that Leemach was in Bohemia.[33] The incident is modeled on the Nazi massacre of Czechs at Lidice as retaliation for the assassination of Reinhard Heydrich in 1942. Lidice had received much coverage in the American press and already had inspired two feature films, *Hangman Also Die* (1943) and *Hitler's Madman* (1943).[34] Indeed, a documentary film on Lidice was shown by the French prosecution team at the Nuremberg Trials.[35] Lawson's summation, however, implies that the evidence he had introduced in the trial implicated Steigmann in other crimes: "You have learned of the prison camps, the gas chambers, the crematory ovens, the mass graves heaped high with corpses." Like his real counterparts, Steigmann claims that he was only a good soldier who obeyed superior orders. The judges find Steigmann guilty and sentence him to death by hanging.

The only witness who spoke in Steigmann's behalf is Themis, the daughter of a French resistance leader whose life had been spared by Steigmann. Still believing in his innocence, she pleads with Lawson to reopen the case. Though he suspects her of having had an affair with Steigmann and collaborating with the Germans to save her father, Lawson has pangs of conscience since he had failed to produce two key pieces of evidence: a Night and Fog decree signed by Steigmann and a commendation letter from Hitler for the Leemach executions.

When Lawson learns Steigmann's mother might possess the missing documents, he locates her residing at the home of Meyersohn, a Hebrew teacher who survived a concentration camp. Lawson wonders how he could harbor the mother of a Nazi killer, but Meyersohn feels "only pity for those who persecuted me and my people." Personalizing the collective fate of his religious brethren, Meyersohn recalls his vain quest to locate his family after being liberated: "Day after day I searched, learning here and there what had happened. My poor Rachel, dead of starvation in Belsen; the three daughters killed at Buchenwald." He offered shelter to Frau Steigmann because she had been a friend of his wife. Mrs. Steigmann defends her son as just a good soldier descended from a Junker family.

Still believing in Steigmann's innocence, Themis visits him in prison where he instructs her to tell his mother to dispose of his "souvenirs." After receiving this message, Frau Steigman surmises that Themis has been dispatched by Lawson to recover the "souvenirs," namely the Night and Fog decree and commendation letter from Hitler. She orders Themis to leave the house immediately, and an argument ensues. Overhearing the ruckus, Meyersohn enters the room, infuriating Frau Steigmann who erupts in an anti-Semitic tirade, beginning in English, but ending in German: "You meddle too much, you and all your filthy kind, filthy (then slipping into German expressing what she had been suppressing), dirty, dirty pigs. Next time we will exterminate you."

To prove her anti-Nazi loyalties, Themis informs Lawson of the incident. He now believes her because he has fallen in love with her. By the time he arrives at Meyersohn's home, Frau Steigmann has burnt the incriminating documents, predicting that her son will be considered an "immortal" like Göring when Germany arises from the ashes. Feigning he has salvaged the two memoranda, Lawson confronts Steigmann in his cell. The latter defiantly admits his guilt,

> I killed as I had to kill, without fear, without remorse. I was a German of the elite Germany, of the Hitler Germans. I will die as I have killed your own airmen, ten of them. I had shot escaped English prisoners, Russians, Poles, and Frenchmen, on my orders. And we will rise again.

Then, like his mother, he shifts into German as he abandons his obedient soldier guise: "Throughout the world we will exterminate the sub-humans."[36]

Sealed Verdict has drawn criticism for its convoluted plot, portrayal of the rabbi as too forgiving, and unfaithful adaptation of the novel on which it is based.[37] Whatever its deficiencies, however, it inextricably linked Nazi reprisals against enemy civilians with racist rationalizations for the eradication of "inferior" groups like the Jews and played on American antipathy towards Germany by having Steigmann confess to executing Allied POWs, thereby evoking the bitter memory of the Malmédy Massacre of 1945.[38] The movie premiered several months after the Soviet Union had blockaded West Berlin and during the American, British, and French airlift to the city.[39] Despite speculation that Hollywood avoided the subject of the Holocaust to appease West German public opinion, the PCA's review of the script never censured it for broaching the topic of German war crimes.[40] Paramount vouched for the authenticity of the trial scenes by hiring Gordon Dean, Robert Jackson's press secretary, as a consultant. The studio's publicity campaign hyped the issue of fraternization with collaborationist and German women–a subplot concerns an American soldier killed by the German woman who is pregnant with his baby–but also mentioned the "dramatic war-crimes trials," "the mass murderer of Leemach," and the order legitimating "the murder without trial of countless Europeans."[41]

In the 1950s, ex-Nazis who evaded capture or trial remained menacing cinematic foes hatching plots to foment a Fourth Reich, inventing weapons of mass destruction, rationalizing evil with Nietzschean amorality, or trying to clone Aryan supermen and liquidate "inferior" ethnic and racial groups. Moreover, Nazi Germany manifested the same totalitarian attributes which the West now combated in the Soviet Union.[42] Thrillers about clandestine postwar Nazi activities discredited their villains by reminding audiences of the shameful record of the Third Reich. The vilification of the Nazi past and valorization of the democratic present could coexist in the Hollywood films about Germany which were produced in the 1950s.[43]

Andrew Marton's *The Devil Makes Three* (1952) draws on a true story of a gold smuggling operation conducted by former Nazis. Adhering to the aforementioned conventions for establishing historical verisimilitude, the movie opens with written and spoken statements attesting to its historical authenticity. The first is a notice of appreciation for the cooperation of the "Office of the High Commissioner of Germany, the US Army Military Police Corps, and the Munich City Police" in filming the picture on location in Austria and Germany. The second is a monologue delivered by an actor who plays the officer in charge of the investigation that is dramatized in the film. As he situates the plotline in Munich, footage of bombed out buildings juxtaposed with new housing projects in Munich flashes across the screen: "This is the same city where in a certain private house, later known as the Brown House, Adolf Hitler organized the Nazi Party thirty years ago." He contrasts the devastation wrought by the Allied powers in defeating Germany with the reconstruction of the country they are now mounting. Then he authenticates the source of the film's plot as "a composite of case histories taken from the Munich Headquarters' files, Criminal Investigation Division, Corps of Military Police, United States Army."[44]

The Devil Makes Three sympathizes with the plight of ordinary Germans eking out a living in the rubble of Munich but underscores that the ideologues responsible for plunging Germany into World War Two remain actively intent on restoring the country to Nazi rule. Lieutenant Eliot, played by Gene Kelly, returns to Munich in 1947 in search of the family that hid him after his plane was downed during the war. All of them perished during the bombardment of Munich except for their daughter Willie. He tracks her down to a bar where she solicits drinks and sex. She excuses her line of work as the only alternative to deprivation and starvation. The lyrics to a song performed by an entertainer in the club reinforce the dual theme of Nazi culpability and civilian suffering:

> First came the man with the little mustache,
> Quite without blinking an eye.
> The house will be standing for 1,000 years.
> Then came the bombs from the sky.
> Next came Marshall with promise of cash,
> Selling the sky full with pie.
> Still we are sitting with holes in the roof,
> Indoors, we can't even say why?

To earn extra money, Willie unwittingly abets a group of diehard Nazis. Wanting to repay his debt to her parents, Elliot offers to take her to visit close friends of her family who reside in Salzburg. To drive both of them there, she rents a car from the owner of the nightclub where she works. Border guards check the car and discover contraband medical and camera equipment, but do not arrest her because they suspect she may be involved in a more sinister smuggling ring. The Criminal Investigation Division of the U.S. Army recruits Elliot to infiltrate the operation. The CID chief informs him that surviving war criminals had stockpiled gold in Germany to fund a reorganization of the Nazi Party when the nation eventually recovers: "Some of it was gold melted down from church vessels and objects of art, but most of it came from the hands and mouths of victims of Nazi concentration camps, wedding rings and dental work." Now they were spiriting it out of Germany to Austria to wait for a more propitious time.[45]

The nightclub owner beats Willie into submission when she refuses to continue to carry packages from him to Germany. What Willie does not realize is that the cars she rents from him to cross the border are plated with gold camouflaged with a fresh coat of paint. Though there is no mention of Jews in the film, the ghosts of Hitler and his minions haunt the movement financed with the tainted loot. The disciples of the would-be Führer assemble for a motorcycle race held in Berchtesgaden. When Elliot witnesses his dramatic arrival in a Mercedes convertible, he exclaims, "It's all there but the Heils!" The final chase sequence climaxes at the Eagle's Nest which signs designate as Hitler's house. MPs and Elliot capture the neo-Nazi leader, and Elliot kisses his lover Willie who was wounded in the shootout. The brave American and decent German triumph over the Neo-Nazi "devil."

Samuel Fuller's *Verboten!* (1959) centers on the relationship between a wounded American GI named David and the German woman Helga who nursed him back to health at the end of the war.[46] Throughout the movie, Fuller intersperses on-location shots of postwar Germany with interior staged shots. David eventually marries Helga and takes a job with an occupation relief agency. Unbeknownst to either of them, Helga's brother Franz belongs to the Nazi Werewolves who assassinate American officials and disrupt the distribution of food and medicine. Ashamed of her brother's bigotry and subversive activities, Helga forces him to attend the Nuremberg Trials. The camera alternates between them sitting in the spectators' box and documentary footage of the trial with narration based on Robert Jackson's opening statement. This creates the impression that the characters from the film actually are at the proceedings.

A ten-minute excerpt of atrocity footage from *Nazi Concentration Camps* forms the core of the scene. The narrator, who is Fuller, describes how the Third Reich

FIGURE 10.4 The categories of Nazi war crimes posted on the walls (*Verboten!*).
Source: Reproduced with permission from Photofest, Inc.

persecuted Christian clergy, euthanized the physically and psychologically disabled, killed citizens of many European countries, and purged its political enemies. He declares, "Perhaps the greatest crime the Nazis committed was against the Jews whom they used as a scapegoat to make Hitler God and *Mein Kampf* the bible." and concludes, "This was genocide, the premeditated murder of entire peoples." As he hears the enumeration of Nazi crimes, Franz experiences superimposed flashbacks of relevant passages from the indoctrination speeches he heard at the meetings of his Werewolf cell. When he maintains he did not know, Helga responds, "You've got to look." Mortified by what he has seen, Franz disavows Nazism and assists David in locating safe houses used by the Werewolves to smuggle war criminals out of Germany.

Fuller, a combat veteran who served with the First Infantry Division in Europe during World War Two, had been assigned to film the burial of corpses strewn across the compound of Falkenau, a satellite camp of Flossenbürg, when it was liberated. Allied troops conscripted local townspeople to carry the bodies to mass graves and participate in their interment. In his autobiography Fuller disclosed the lifelong impact the liberation of Falkenau and burial of its victims had on him likening it to "a leaf in a fossil, never to fade away."[47] The policy of forcing local Germans to confront the carnage perpetrated by their government was intended to discredit claims that they were ignorant of Nazi crimes.[48] Fuller replicates this procedure in *Verboten!* with Franz as a proxy for all German civilians. Fuller obtained the atrocity and trial footage from special effects technician Ray Kellogg who had belonged to the team that had filmed the first Nuremberg Trial and selected the atrocity footage for *Nazi Concentration Camps*.[49] The cinematic strategy of recycling these hellish scenes in *Verboten!* and reenacting the liberation of Falkenau in color in his semiautobiographical *The Big Red One* (1980) transforms the audience into a vicarious witness to them.[50]

The film adaptation of Irwin Shaw's *The Young Lions* (1958) has provoked the ire of Holocaust scholars who inveigh against its apologetic portrayal of its German protagonist Christian Diestl, which they interpret as part of the trend to whitewash Nazi genocide for the diplomatic expediencies of the Cold War.[51] In the novel Diestl degenerates from an apolitical German attracted to Hitler's campaign promises of a restoration of national honor and social mobility into a ruthless killer who blindly obeys orders.[52] Director Edward Dmytryk and screenwriter Edward Anhalt felt that the "Nazi heavy" had become a "cliché" and changed Christian into a decent man who slowly becomes disillusioned with his nation's wartime brutality.[53] More specifically, Dmytryk indulged Marlon Brando's requests to redeem Christian at the culmination of the film. In the book and first draft of the screenplay, Diestl happens upon an inmate rebellion that has broken out in a concentration camp after most of the SS guards have retreated. Christian knocks out a prisoner and steals his uniform. To allay suspicions of his real identity, he cuts the throat of the camp commandant before fleeing into a forest where he ambushes two American soldiers who are the story's other main characters. In the final cut of the movie, Christian abhors what he discovers about the camp's malignant purpose from its commandant, smashes his rifle in disgust, and sacrifices himself to a barrage of bullets fired by the two GIs.[54] Assuaging Brando's vanity rather than exonerating West Germany resulted in this redemptive finale.

Shaw's and Dmytryk's outrage over German barbarism is displaced onto Captain Hardenberg, played by Maximilian Schell. He is as arrogant and brutal as Diestl is humble and humane. Hardenberg declines Diestl's petition to be relieved of his duty arresting "children" for the Gestapo in Paris by lecturing, "When you became a soldier, you contracted for killing in all its forms." Both serve on the North African front where Hardenberg presides over the massacre of British soldiers even though they have signaled their surrender. Disappointed by Diestl's refusal to execute a wounded Englishman, Hardenberg fires the fatal shot. During the 1950s, American movies like *The Desert Fox* (1951) and *The Desert Rats* (1953) differentiated between honorable German officers like Rommel and sinister Nazis.[55] Brando's Diestl has been cited as part of this trend, but Hardenberg's condoning of war crimes undercuts this apologetic thrust, particularly since some of them are committed on the North African front.

The concentration camp scenes implicitly indict Germany for crimes against humanity. Dmytryk watched unedited US Signal Corps footage to reenact what American troops saw when they liberated camps and rented an abandoned concentration camp for the set,[56] The SS commandant recounts his genocidal duties to Diestl, outlining how difficult it is to run such a facility "with all the gas chambers, target ranges, and doctors with their experiments." He proudly takes credit for exterminating his daily quota of 1,500 persons from among the "Jews, Poles, Russians, French, and political prisoners" incarcerated in his camp and predicts that the leaders of the Third

FIGURE 10.5 Liberated survivors in a concentration camp barrack (*The Young Lions*).
Source: Reproduced with permission from Photofest, Inc.

Reich will deny there "was a national policy to kill 12,000,000 people." The commandant's admission reveals more about the extent of Nazi criminality than what Shaw discloses in his novel or Anwalt in the original script.[57] (Citing a death toll higher than 6 million to encompass both Jewish and Gentile victims was a tactic employed by Fuller in *Verboten!* too.) Dmytryk apparently compensated for Brando's exculpation of Diestl by stressing the methodical nature of Germany's extermination of European Jews and repression of vanquished Gentile populations and the extent of its casualties.

After the Americans enter the camp and find emaciated survivors in a barrack, a rabbi in prisoner garb interrupts a meeting between the American captain and the mayor of a German village who has offered to "clean" the camp for upcoming visits by dignitaries. The rabbi asks for permission to conduct a memorial service for the Jews who perished there. The mayor advises against doing so since it would offend the Gentile prisoners. The captain sides with the rabbi and sternly warns the mayor to never return to the camp. Thus, Dmytryk's film incriminates ordinary Germans to a greater extent than Shaw's novel, where it is an interned Albanian diplomat who objects to the memorial service.[58] This scene serves the same didactic purpose as Franz attending the Nuremberg Trials in *Verboten!*. Noah, the film's American Jewish lead, who has literally engaged in fistfights to win the grudging respect of the anti-Semitic members of his platoon, witnesses the encounter between the captain and the mayor and stoically tells his buddy afterwards that his uncle had died in such a camp. Rather than being a "travesty" of Shaw's book, as Ilan Avisar has charged, the movie's anti-Nazism and philo-Semitism are consistent with Dmytryk's prior treatment of these topics in *Hitler's Children* (1943), *Cornered* (1945), *Crossfire* (1947) and *The Juggler* (1953).[59]

The body of films covered in this essay constituted one source of popular awareness of the Third Reich's brutalization of civilian populations, including the Jews. Rather than repressing the topic because it was diplomatically inconvenient or psychologically traumatic, Hollywood's early depictions of German war crimes and crimes against humanity reflected the perspective of a country that had defeated Germany, hunted Nazi fugitives, put them on trial, and recorded the evidence of their misdeeds. To be sure, Hollywood's initial approach to the Holocaust was neither as graphic nor as Judeocentric as subsequent movies about it would be. After all, this first wave of films was still subject to the Production Code's restrictive guidelines for portraying violence,[60] the Allies' inclusive definition of crimes against humanity, and the "melting pot" universalism that prevailed in the United States during the immediate postwar period.[61] Yet these motion pictures also laid the foundations for future cinematic conventions for representing the Holocaust by filming on location in Europe, intercutting clips of the iconic (and therefore permissible) images from the atrocity footage, invoking the credibility of their consultants, creators, or sources, and retaining a black and white documentary look even into the 1950s when color was being increasingly used for Hollywood productions.[62] Subsequent Hollywood productions would be freed of the limitations imposed by the Production Code and more attuned to the ethnic, racial, and religious politics that have informed minority group identity and depictions in the United States since the 1960s.[63]

Notes

1 Ilan Avisar, *Screening the Holocaust: Cinema's Images of the Unimaginable* (Bloomington, IN: Indiana University Press, 1988), 90–133; Judith E. Doneson, *The Holocaust in American Film* (Philadelphia, PA: Jewish Publication Society, 1987), 59–107; Trudy Gold, "An Overview of Hollywood Cinema's Treatment of the Holocaust," in *Holocaust and the Moving Image: Representations in Film and Television Since 1933* (London, UK: Wallflower Press, 2005), eds. Toby Haggith and Joanna Newman, 194; Annette Insdorf, *Indelible Shadows: Film and the Holocaust* (New York: Random House, 1983), 1–21; Alan Mintz, *Popular Culture and the Shaping of Holocaust Memory in America* (Seattle, WA: University of Washington Press, 2001), 3–21.

2 This consensus informs the interviews and viewpoint of *Imaginary Witness*, directed by Daniel Anker (USA: Anker Productions Inc, 2004). The documentary's emphasis on the deliberate dissociation of the Jewish movie moguls from the Holocaust draws heavily on Neal Gabler's interviews in the film and from his book, *An Empire of Their Own: How the Jews Invented Hollywood* (New York: Crown Publishers, 1988).

3 Peter Novick, *The Holocaust in American Life* (Boston, MA: Houghton Mifflin Company, 1999), 47–123.

4 Lawrence Baron, "The First Wave of American 'Holocaust' Films, 1945–59," *American Historical Review*, Vol.115, no.1 (February 2010), 90–114.

5 Stuart Liebman, "Historiography/Holocaust Cinema," in *Cinema and the Shoah: An Art Confronts the Tragedy of the Twentieth Century*, ed. Jean-Michel Frodon (Albany, NY: State University of New York Press, 2010), 207.

6 Lawrence Baron, "Picturing Prejudice in Hollywood's First Films about Anti-Semitism," *Studies in Jewish Civilization*, Vol.17 (2006), 17–37; Steven Alan Carr, "Hollywood, the Holocaust, and World War II," *Studies in Jewish Civilization,* Vol.17 (2006), 39–58; Felicia Herman, "Hollywood, Nazism, and the Jews, 1933–41," *American Jewish History,* Vol. 89, no. 1 (March 2001), 61–89; Bill Krohn, "Hollywood and the Shoah, 1933–45," in *Cinema and the Shoah*, ed. Jean-Michel Frodon, 149–60; K.R.M. Short, "Hollywood Fights Anti-Semitism 1940–45," in *Film and Radio Propaganda in World War II*, ed. K. R. M. Short (London, UK: Croom Helm, 1983), 149–55.

7 Thomas Doherty, *Hollywood's Censor: Joseph I. Breen and the Production Code Administration* (New York: Columbia University Press, 2007), 152–71, 199–224.

8 Thomas Doherty, *Projections of War: Hollywood, American Culture, and World War II* (New York: Columbia University Press, 1993), 36–59, 122–33;

9 Steven Casey, *Cautious Crusade: Franklin D. Roosevelt, American Public Opinion, and the War Against Nazi Germany* (New York: Oxford University Press, 2001), 56–72; Michaela Hoenicke Moore, *Know Your Enemy: The American Debate on Nazism, 1933–1945* (New York: Cambridge University Press, 2010), 131–52, 193–97.

10 *None Shall Escape*, directed by Andre de Toth (US: Columbia Pictures, 1944). The first proposal for this film is found in "Letter from Burt Kelly to Jeff Sherlock, 14 April, 1943. *None Shall Escape*," Special Collections, Margaret Herrick Library, Academy of Motion Picture Arts and Sciences (hereafter MHL-AMPAS). The film was originally entitled *The Day Will Come* and then *Lebensraum*.

11 "The Screen Anticipates Nazis at the Bar," *New York Herald Tribune*, 10 October, 1943; *The Black Book of Poland* (New York: G.P. Putnam's Sons, 1942), 217–53.

12 Bernard F. Dick, *The Star-Spangled Banner: The American World War II Film* (Lexington, KY: University of Kentucky Press, 1985), 207–8.

13 Andre de Toth cited in Robert Joseph, "The First Post-War Trials Are Staged in Hollywood," *San Francisco Chronicle*, 23 January, 1943," in Scrapbook #1, Manuscript Collection #U-304, Joseph Than Collection, MHL-AMPAS.

14 The positive reviews appear in Scrapbook #1 of the Joseph Than Collection as does the negative one written by WHM, "First Movie About War Guilt Trials Is Disappointing," *Tidings*, 14 April, 1944, *Tidings* Scrapbook #1, Manuscript Collection #U-304, Joseph Than Collection, MHL-AMPAS.

15 Lester Cole, *Hollywood Red: The Autobiography of Lester Cole* (Palo Alto, CA: Ramparts Press, 1981), 205–6. J. Hoberman notes that the Yiddish dubbing of the film also accentuated the rabbi's activism and Jewish resistance. J. Hoberman, *Bridge of Light: Yiddish Film between Two Worlds* (Philadelphia, PA: Temple University Press, 1995), 324–25.

16 "Confidential NSE," 8 February, 1944, *None Shall Escape*, Special Collections", MHL-AMPAS.

17 See the full-page advertisements as well as clippings of the box-office figures and reviews in Scrapbook #1, Manuscript Collection #U-304, Joseph Than Collection, MHL-AMPAS.

18 David Platt, "A New Powerful Anti-Nazi Film," *Daily Worker*, 8 April, 1944.

19 Annette Insdorf, *Indelible Shadows: Film and the Holocaust,* 3rd Edition (New York: Cambridge University Press, 2003), 252–54; Krohn, "Hollywood and the Shoah," in *Cinema and the Shoah*, ed. Jean-Michel Frodon, 164–68; Caroline Joan (Kay) S. Picart and David A. Frank, *Frames of Evil: the Holocaust as Horror in American Film* (Carbondale, IL: Southern Illinois University Press, 2006), 23; Sylvie Pierre, "A Propos of *None Shall Escape*, trans. Hillary Radner and Alistair Fox, http://archive.sensesofcinema.com/contents/03/26/none_shall_escape.html (accessed 16 October, 2010). Originally published in *Trafic*, no.35 (Autumn 2000).

20 Donald Bloxham, *The War Crimes Trials and the Formation of Holocaust History and Memory* (New York: Oxford University Press, 2001); 57–88; Lawrence Douglas, *The Memory of Judgment: Making Law and History in the Trials of the Holocaust* (New Haven: CT: Yale University Press, 2001), 11–37; Jeffrey Shandler, *While America Watches: Televising the Holocaust* (New York: Oxford University Press), 5–22; Janina Struk, *Photographing the Holocaust: Interpretation of the Evidence* (London, UK: I.B. Tauris and Co, 2004); Barbie Zelitzer, *Remembering to Forget: Holocaust Memory through the Camera's Eye* (Chicago: University of Chicago Press, 1998), 49–140.

21 Michael Marrus, "The Holocaust at Nuremberg," *Yad Vashem Studies* 26 (1998), 5–41.

22 *The Stranger*, directed by Orson Welles (USA: International Pictures, 1946).

23 *Confessions of a Nazi Spy*, directed by Anatole Litvak (USA: Warner Brothers Pictures, 1946); Steven Ross, "*Confessions of a Nazi Spy:* Warner Bros., Anti-Fascism, and the Politicization of Hollywood," http://www.learcenter.org/pdf/WWRoss.pdf (accessed 16 October, 2010).

24 Palmer R. Barton, "The Politics of Genre in Welles' *The Stranger*," *Film Criticism* 9, no. 2 (Winter 1984–85), 2–14.

25 Struk, *Photographing the Holocaust,* 150–58; Ewout van der Knaap, "The Construction of Memory in *Nuit et Brouillard*," in *Uncovering the Holocaust: The International Reception of Night and Fog*, ed. Ewout van der Knapp (London, 2006), 17–19.

26 Baron, *Projecting the Holocaust*, 27–28; Hubert Damisch, "A Cinema No Longer Silent," in *Cinema and the Shoah*, ed. Frodon, 45

27 Bosley Crowther, "*The Stranger*," *New York Times* (11 July, 1946), http://movies. nytimes.com/movie/review?res=9A06E2D7103AEE3BBC4952DFB166838D659EDE (accessed 13 September, 2008); "The New Pictures," *Time* (17 June, 1946), http:// www.time.com/time/magazine/article/0,9171,793120,00.html?promoid=googlep (accessed 13 September, 2008); ""Movie of the Week: *The Stranger*," *Life* Vol. 20: no. 22 (3 June, 1946), 78.

28 Jack D. Grant, "Welles, Young, and Robinson Score Hits," *Hollywood Reporter*, 21 May, 1946. Grant writes "This is the clue that trips a fellow who might otherwise have gone free."

29 Krohn, "Hollywood and the Shoah," in *Cinema and the Shoah*, ed. Frodon, 149–50.

30 Bosch, *Judgment on Nuremberg: American Attitudes toward the Major German War-Crime Trials* (Chapel Hill, NC: University of North Carolina Press), 90–112.

31 *Sealed Verdict,* directed by Lewis Allen (United States: Paramount Pictures, 1948)

32 Jonathan Latimer, "Sealed Verdict: Release Dialogue Script," (10 March, 1948) Special Collections, MHL-AMPAS.

33 Ibid., 4.

34 *Hangman Also Die*, directed by Fritz Lang (United States: Arnold Productions, 1943); *Hitler's Madmen*, directed by Douglas Sirk (United States: Producers Releasing Corporation, 1943); Edna St. Vincent Milay, *The Murder of Lidice* (New York, NT: Harper and Brothers, 942). Also see Casey, *Cautious Crusade*, 64–65, 70–71.

35 Helen Lennon, "A Witness to Atrocity: Film as Evidence in International War Crimes Tribunals," in *Holocaust and the Moving Image*, 67.

36 Latimer, "Sealed Verdict," Reel 4A-5A, MHL-AMPAS.

37 Bosley Crowther, "*Sealed Verdict*," *New York Times* (3 November, 1948), http://movies. nytimes.com/movie/review?res=9E05EED9153DE03ABC4B53DFB7678383659EDE (accessed 9 September, 2008). Herbert G. Luft, "The Screen and the Holocaust," in *Celluloid Power: Social Film Criticism from "The Birth of the Nation" to "Judgment at Nuremberg,"* ed. David Platt (Metuchen, NJ: Scarecrow Press, 1992), 378; Lester D. Friedman, *Hollywood's Image of the Jew* (New York: Frederick Ungar, 1982), 121.

38 James J. Weingartner, *Crossroads of Death: The Story of the Malmedy Massacre and Trial* (Berkeley, CA: University of California Press, 1979); James J. Weingartner, *A Peculiar Crusade: Willis M. Everette and the Malmédy Massacre* (New York: New York University Press, 2000); James J. Weingartner, "Americans, Germans, and War Crimes: Converging Narratives from the 'Good War'," *The Journal of American History* Vol.94, no.4 (March 2008), 1164–82.

39 "Release Dates," *Sealed Verdict*, Internet Movie Database, http://www.imdb.com/title/ tt0040764/ (accessed 7 September, 2008). The movie premiered in November of 1948. The blockade and airlift began in June of that year.

40 "Sealed Verdict," Production Code Administration File, Special Collections, MHL-AMPAS. Breen objected to the script primarily on the grounds that it implied an illicit sexual relationship between Lawson and Themis and that Themis might be a prostitute.

41 "*Sealed Verdict, Paramount Press Sheets-Releases Season 1948–1949*," Group A-8, Special Collections, MHL-AMPAS.

42 Hannah Arendt, *The Origins of Totalitarianism* (New York: Harcourt, Brace, and Company, 1951); Abbott Gleason, *Totalitarianism: The Inner History of the Cold War* (New York: Oxford University Press, 1995).

43 Lawrence Baron, "Holocaust Iconography in American Feature Films about Neo-Nazis," *Film and History* Vol. 32, no. 2 (2002), 38–40; Tony Barta, "Film Nazis: The Great Escape," in *Screening the Past: Film and the Representation of History*, ed. Tony Barta (Westport, CT: Praeger, 1998), 127–48; David Eldridge, *Hollywood's History Films* (New York, NY: I.B. Tauris, 2006), 189–94; Lester Friedman, "Darkness Visible: Images of Nazis in American Film," in *Bad: Infamy, Darkness, Evil, and Slime on the Silver Screen*, ed. Murray Pomerance (Albany, NY: 2004), 255–70; Picart and Frank, *Frames of Evil*, 22–28.

44 *The Devil Makes Three*, directed by Andrew Marton (US, 1952). See script by Jerry Davis, *The Devil Makes Three*, Special Collections, MHL-AMPAS.

45 For a history of Nazi confiscation, looting, and salvaging of gold extracted from concentration and death camp inmates, see Götz Aly, *Hitler's Beneficiaries: Plunder, Race War, and the Nazi Welfare State* (New York: Henry Holt and Company, 2008); Arthur Lee Smith, Jr., *Hitler and the Story of Nazi War Loot* (New York: Berg, 1989).

46 *Verboten!*, directed by Samuel Fuller (US, 1959); Christina von Hodenberg, "Of German Fräuleins, Nazi Werewolves, and Iraq Insurgents: The American Fascination with Hitler's Last Foray," *Central European History* Vol. 41, no. 1 (2008): 71–86. For more on Fuller's filmmaking career, see Lisa Dombrowski, *The Films of Samuel Fuller: If You Die, I'll Kill You* (Wesleyan, CT: Wesleyan University Press, 2008); Lee Server, *Sam Fuller: A Film is a Battleground* (Jefferson, NC: McFarland, 1994).

47 Samuel Fuller, *A Third Face: My Tale of Writing, Fighting, and Filmmaking* (New York: Alfred Knopf, 2002), 109–21, 213–18. Fuller's footage was subsequently edited into the documentary *Falkenau: The Impossible*, Directed by Emil Weiss (France: Michklan World Productions, 1988). *Falkenau* can be viewed at: http://invizuals.com/post/4869732598/ samuel-fuller-falkerau-the-impossible-full-movie-documen (accessed June 27, 2011).

48 Marsha Orgeron, "Liberating Images? Samuel Fuller's Film of Falkenau Concentration Camp," *Film Quarterly* Vol. 60, no. 2 (Winter 2006), 38–48.

49 Fuller, *A Third Face*, 354–74.

50 *The Big Red One*, directed by Samuel Fuller (USA: Lorac Productions and Lorimar Productions, 1980); Fuller, *A Third Face* 475–83. For an analysis of how viewing films and photographs of Nazi atrocities transforms the spectator into a vicarious witness, see Helen Lennon, "A Witness to Atrocity: Film as Evidence in International War Crimes Tribunals," in *Holocaust and the Moving Image*,65–73; Carol Zemel, "Emblems of Atrocity: Holocaust Liberation Photographs," in *Image and Remembrance: Representation and the Holocaust*, eds. Shelley Hornstein and Florence Jacobowitz (Bloomington, IN: Indiana University Press, 2003), 201–19.

51 Avisar, *Screening the Holocaust*, 111–16; Patricia Erens, *The Jew in American Cinema* (Bloomington, IN: Indiana University Press, 1984), 221–23; Deborah Lipstadt, "America and the Memory,"*Modern Judaism* Vol.16, no. 3 (1996), 200–201.

52 Irwin Shaw, *The Young Lions* (New York: Random House, 1948).

53 Edward Dmytryk, *It's a Hell of a Life, But Not a Bad Living* (New York, 1978), 219–30.

54 Edward Anhalt, "The Young Lions: First Draft," 25 April, 1957, Core Collection, MHL-AMPAS: 170–74.

55 Beverly Crawford and James Martel, "Representations of Germans and What Germans Represent: American Film Images and Public Perceptions in the Postwar Era," in David E. Barclay and Elisabeth Glaser-Schmidt, eds., *Transatlantic Images and Perceptions: Germany and America Since 1776* (Cambridge, UK: Cambridge University Press, 1997), 295–97.

56 Dmytryk, *It's a Hell of a Life*, 237–38.

57 Shaw, *The Young Lions*, 660–71; Anhalt, "The Young Lions: First Draft,"170–74.

58 Shaw, *The Young Lions*, 674–77.

59 Avisar, *Screening the Holocaust*, 114–16.

60 Leo Charney, "The Violence of a Perfect Moment," in *Violence and American Cinema*, ed. J. David Slocum (New York: Routledge, 2000), 49.

61 Judith E. Smith, *Visions of Belonging: Family Stories, Popular Culture and Postwar Democracy, 1940–1960* (New York: Columbia University Press, 2004).

62 Gloria A. Kindem, "Hollywood's Conversion to Color: The Techological, Economic, and Aesthetic Factors," in *Hollywood: Critical Concepts in Media and Cultural Studies*, Vol. 3, ed. Thomas Schatz (New York: Routledge, 2004), 51–65.

63 Matthew Frye Jacobson, *Roots Too: White Ethnic Revival in Post-Civil Rights America* (Cambridge, MA: Harvard University Press, 2006).

11

"THIS TOO IS PARTLY HITLER'S DOING"

American Jewish name changing in the wake of the Holocaust, 1939–57

Kirsten Fermaglich

In 1952, J. Alvin Kugelmass wrote an article for *Commentary* magazine entitled "Name-Changing—and What It Gets You." Basing his research on conversations with city court clerks, Kugelmass wrote that name change petitions had increased by 100 percent since World War II, and that 80 percent of those petitions were from Jews. Kugelmass argued that this upsurge in name changing was "partly Hitler's doing": while European Jews had been murdered by the millions, the American Jew "was sharply reminded of his identity and bore it with pride and militant defiance." Yet as soon as the war was over, he suggested, Jews' return to postwar comfort was accompanied by an abandonment of Jewish pride and identity. Kugelmass interviewed 25 men who had changed their names, and found that most of them were unhappy: "all twenty-five would like their old, comfortable names back."[1]

In retrospect, Kugelmass seems to have been mistaken in much of his description of name changing, at least in New York City. Name changing in New York actually rose to some of its greatest heights during World War II. Moreover, in New York's City Court, Jews were closer to 50 percent of name changers, not 80 percent. Kugelmass's piece is still significant, however, for its portrait of name changers as unhappy, pathetic people who separated themselves from the Jewish community, ignoring the lessons of genocide. His article reflects the degree to which name changing was in fact a phenomenon in the years after World War II; the piece also reflects the dominant way in which Jewish writers interpreted name changing in the years after the Holocaust.

The numbers of New Yorkers officially changing their names skyrocketed during the years of World War II, and they remained at high levels throughout the 1940s and 1950s. Throughout the 1930s, there were roughly 250 petitions in the New York City City Court each year. In 1940, official name-change petitions in City Court more than doubled to 664, and they climbed throughout the war, reaching a peak in 1946 at 1,127—four times the average of the previous decade, and the largest number of name changing petitions in one year in City Court for the entire twentieth century.[2]

A large percentage of the name-change petitions during and after the era of the Holocaust were submitted by petitioners with identifiably Jewish names—far out of proportion to the Jewish population of New York City.[3] To be sure, Jews had always been disproportionately represented in New York City's name-changing petitions—from the 1900s through the 1930s, Jews submitted roughly 65 percent of the City Court name-change petitions. But the numbers of petitions overall during these years had been quite small. Between 1939 and 1957, as the numbers of name-change petitions exploded, the percentage of Jewish petitioners declined somewhat, but they still equaled roughly 50 percent of the total pool of official name changers, at a time when the Jewish population in New York City was roughly between 25 and 30 percent. Taking account of the fact that most name-change petitioners at the City Court lived in Manhattan, the disparity was even greater, since the Jewish population of Manhattan was roughly between 15 and 20 percent during this era.[4]

No other ethnic groups came close to Jews' numbers in name changing during these years. Many individuals who petitioned the court to change their names in the first half of the twentieth century did so because of changes to their families such as divorce, remarriage, or abandonment. Jews were among these petitioners, though not in disproportionate numbers. But among those who sought to eliminate their ethnic names, those who claimed that their names were an embarrassment or a hindrance in social and work environments, Jews were disproportionately represented. Indeed, no other group came close to Jewish numbers in these sorts of petitions. In 1942, for example, the total number of petitions submitted by people with Slavic, German, Italian, and Greek names seeking to de-ethnicize their names equaled *altogether* about one half of the petitions submitted by people with Jewish names for the same purpose. The numbers of petitions and the percentage of Jewish names declined in the 1950s, but petition numbers remained higher than before the war, and Jews still outnumbered other ethnic groups every year. It was not until the 1960s that the numbers of name-change petitions declined substantially, and that the percentage of Jewish names in name change petitions came closer to their actual proportion in the New York City population.

Historians have not examined these petitions or the phenomenon of name changing in the United States in any detail. Scholars of race and ethnicity have occasionally mentioned name changing as a signal of assimilation into American culture, but they have not examined the significance of name changing in racial identity in the United States during and after World War II.[5] This gap in the literature is unfortunate, for the widespread phenomenon of name changing offers us a valuable window into both the racialization of Jews in the United States during the Holocaust and American Jews' understandings of the Nazi genocide in the years after the war.

The high numbers of name changers in New York City during and after World War II are striking, as was the large percentage of Jewish names among those name changers. There are a number of ways that these dramatic statistics can be explained. For one thing, the bureaucracy introduced during the war encouraged Americans of all ethnic persuasions to change their names officially and legally. Before World War II, most immigrant and second-generation Americans had changed their names casually and unofficially in large numbers, and those changes were generally accepted and unnoticed. But new concerns with security during World War II led many employers—particularly federal employers—to demand birth certificates from job applicants. In this environment, unofficial name changes from previous eras became suspect, and Americans rushed to make official their changed cognomens in order to get the military placement or the defense industry job they wanted.

Jews' position in the middle class also helps explain why they would be the ethnic group most likely to change their names officially. It was primarily members of the middle class who believed they needed to change their names legally. The United States has historically had flexible name-changing laws: a person generally need not change his name officially in order to take on a new name. It is only if an American is worried that his name might be scrutinized that he has changed that name officially. In the first half of the twentieth century, it was middle class Americans, much more frequently than working class Americans, who believed that their names might be scrutinized. Working class Americans would be more likely to find a job based on word of mouth, family connections, or an examination of their bodies. Middle class Americans, however, printed their names on application forms, business cards, and storefront signs, so as to impress potential customers, employers and school admissions officers. As the immigrant group most successful in attaining middle class status in the first half of the twentieth century, Jews were understandably heavily represented in name-change petitions.

There was, however, another, more poignant reason for Jewish overrepresentation in New York City Court petitions. Fears of antisemitism, experiences with discrimination, and even veiled references to the Holocaust recurred in New Yorkers' name-change petitions in the middle of the twentieth century. To be sure, almost no Jewish petitioners volunteered that they were changing their names because of antisemitism. But during World War II, they did note that they had had trouble finding jobs, that they feared entering the military bearing their current names, and that they wanted to abandon "foreign" names. After World War II, Jews made less mention of discrimination, but they continued to petition for name changes in large numbers and to cite their "foreign" surnames as the reasons for the changes.

Significantly, Jewish names were called "foreign" names even when they were easy to pronounce and spell in English. For example, the 1942 petition of Louis A. Friedman, Jr. and David Donn Friedman to change their last name to Freeman states that the

> petitioner desires to Americanize the name of Friedman, particularly in view of the conditions now existing and further in view of the fact that petitioner expects to make application for a commission in the United States Army, and therefore does not want a surname of foreign origin and sound.[6]

Milton Lefkowitz's 1942 petition to change his name to Martin Milton Lewis insisted that the name Lefkowitz was "Hungarian in origin," and that, as a native-born American, the petitioner wanted to bear a name "more in accord with his cultural and social background and in conformity with his heritage of democratic thought."[7] Clearly the nationalism of the war shaped these petitioners' desire to call their names "foreign," but it seems likely that other forces were at work as well: Lefkowitz's peculiar insistence that his obviously Jewish name was Hungarian suggests that fears of antisemitism played a role in his petition.

Louis and David Donn Friedmans' allusion to "the conditions now existing" in the context of this era of world antisemitism was striking, and other petitioners made similar allusions. In his 1942 petition to change his name to Saul Robert Gilford, for example, Solomon Goldfarb stated:

> I desire that any offspring of my marriage shall not labor under the handicap of going through life with the name such as Goldfarb. This is an unfortunate situation in the world we live in, but it is a situation not of my making, and I feel that we must face reality.[8]

Other petitioners both during and after the war spoke of their names as "handicaps" or "impediments," and spoke of their desire to spare their children the embarrassment the petitioners themselves had experienced.[9] Some of this language was legal boilerplate, and probably few of these petitioners changed their names because they feared violent antisemitism. Nonetheless, many of these petitioners were responding to the ways that Jewish names had been isolated and ridiculed during the era of the Holocaust and its immediate aftermath.

The handful of survivors of the Holocaust who submitted petitions for name changes after migrating to New York City similarly responded to the isolation and ridicule of Jewish names, while their petitions also reflected anger against German culture. Ignaz and Lina Rothstein, for example, believed their surname was "typically German and therefore objectionable to them," and sought to change their name to Rhodes, believing it in their "best interests ... that their names be more Americanized."[10] A few immigrants were open in their desire to escape all memories of their persecution as German Jews. Ronald Philip Steinberg, for example, sought to change his name to Stanton after facing persecution and being forced to flee Germany because he wanted "to remove as much as possible all associations with or thoughts of the German regime from his mind and also to give up the surname which is of German origin and association."[11] One contemporary observer in 1958 estimated that roughly four percent of Central European immigrants to the United States in the wake of the Holocaust changed their names. They frequently did so, he said either because they feared antisemitism in the United States or because they bore scarring memories of the antisemitism they had experienced in Europe and hoped to expunge those memories by effacing their German names.[12]

The large numbers of Jewish name-change petitions submitted to the New York City Court in the middle of, and in the aftermath of, the Holocaust suggest the ways that American as well as European Jews were racialized during these years— particularly through the linguistic marks of Jewish names. Ironically, those same petitions offer significant evidence of Jews' efforts to escape or negate those racial labels and to acquire a different status. Historians such as Gary Gerstle, Deborah Dash Moore, and Eric Goldstein have all suggested that the years of World War II were a watershed in American Jews' acceptance as white Americans, in part because Jews were integrated fully into white military troops.[13] Name-change petitions, however, offer a more complicated portrait. Because Jews were not readily welcomed as white Americans during the war—indeed, they faced antisemitism, even when serving in white troops—Jewish soldiers and their families felt they needed to abandon crucial markers of Jewishness in order to become members of the white American mainstream.[14]

Given the fact that large numbers of people changed their names during and after the war, it is not surprising that the larger American Jewish community was affected by name changing, since either they or someone they knew had probably changed their names. Not surprisingly, the widespread nature of name changing inspired intense public discussion and debate during and after the war.

A number of commentators, particularly during the war, perceived the growing numbers of name changes with equanimity and even with some support. Perhaps the most extensive exploration of name changing during the war was Louis Adamic's popular book, *What's Your Name?* (1942). Adamic's approach was pragmatic and sympathetic. As a Slovenian immigrant who had himself altered his name from Adamič, Adamic described the agonizing pressures immigrants and their children felt to change their names, as well as the alienation they frequently felt in the wake of having made those changes. While he wrote eloquently of ethnic Americans' turmoil as they changed their names and criticized native-born Americans who felt that their English names were the only ones that reflected American culture, Adamic ultimately supported name-changing that was "organic," that came about "with very little inner conflict," and that "[grew] or emerge[d] naturally out of an undistorted interrelation among all the pertinent circumstances."[15]

Other writers during the war offered similar pragmatic solutions. In a 1943 editorial in *Aufbau*, a journal for German Jews in exile, émigré Manfred George approved generally of the idea of name changing, and suggested that it might be particularly acceptable for Jews.

> Of course, there is no reason to change strictly Jewish names, for, like Italian names, these are generally known and respected. But there can be no objection if Jews starting a new life try to drop names which arrogant anti-Semitic officials in Europe at one time pinned on their forefathers.[16]

Nonetheless, George warned his readers to change their names sensibly, without attracting ridicule by selecting names like Lincoln: "A person who decides to change his name should be guided by three principles: moderation, tact and unobtrusiveness."[17]

During the war, then, writers like George and Adamic noted that name changing had become an ordinary part of American ethnic life, and although they might regret the chauvinist conditions that made individuals feel they needed to change their names, they embraced a pragmatic approach to name changing rather than decrying the phenomenon or attacking its practitioners. Indeed, George contrasted the freedom of the United States—a place where Jews could change their names—with the far harsher antisemitism that Jews had faced in Europe. All the same, these pragmatic perspectives did not openly address the persecution of Jews in Nazi-occupied Europe.

There *were*, however, some bitter and angry arguments against name changing before and during the war, and they sometimes did refer to the Nazi regime. Louis Adamic reported that after 1938, foreign-language and second-generation ethnic newspapers began publishing editorials describing name changing as being "tanta-mount to treason in the estimation of one's countrymen."[18] Jewish journals joined their ranks. In September 1939, the *Jewish Opinion* published an angry editorial about a Jewish family named Einstein who had petitioned to change their name to Easton in order to help their children advance in the military. Calling the family's "passion for advancement at the cost of self respect" a "disease," the editors contrasted American freedom with Nazi oppression: "Incidentally, it may be observed that Albert Einstein had to change his country but his name remains unchanged. Hitler's Reich rejected him. But our country will celebrate the day … which gives Albert Einstein (not Arthur Easton) to [sic] American citizenship."[19] The *Opinion*'s anger towards name changers in 1939, as well as its contrast between American freedom and Nazi tyranny, would be echoed and amplified in the years after World War II.

After World War II, the debate over name changing became far sharper and more vocal. More circumspect voices supporting name changing faded, and instead, angry attacks from name changers' critics dominated the pages of magazines, short stories, and novels. These attacks frequently featured both oblique and direct references to Nazism and to the Holocaust, suggesting that the impact of the war and the revelations of Nazi camps changed the ways that American Jews perceived name changing.

Literature after the war, for example, explicitly portrayed name changing as an act that revealed some American Jews' shame over Jewishness, and they contrasted this pathetic shame with the devastation faced by European Jews during World War II. Name changers were portrayed as striving fools who had allowed their vanity and their insecurity to cloud their attachments to the Jewish people—so much so that they even forgot the bonds that linked them to murdered European Jews. In the 1946 Laura Z. Hobson novel, *Gentleman's Agreement*, the Jewish secretary who has changed her name from Estelle Walovsky to Elaine Wales is portrayed as a self-hating Jew and an antisemite—one who uses the word "kike" openly to refer both to herself and to the "objectionable" Jews she worries will tar her own reputation.[20] A 1949 *New Yorker* short story by Joseph Wechsler centered on the pathetic figure of Walter Blum, an Austrian Jewish refugee who had changed his name to Walter Bradford. Austrian friends mocked him for betraying his family—"Dr. Redlich, a lifetime friend of Walter's dead parents, had said that Blum was an old Jewish name, nothing to be ashamed of. It was good enough for your grandfather in Poland, and for your father, when he moved to Vienna"—while Bradford's Americanized daughter was ashamed of her father and his friends' inability to assimilate.[21] In both of these pieces, the murder of European Jews is the subtext of American Jews' insecure social climbing.

In his 1958 short story, "The Lady of the Lake," Bernard Malamud was even more overt in his scorn for American Jewish name changing, and its consequences for Jewish identity and Holocaust memory. His central character, New Yorker Henry Levin, begins calling himself Henry R. Freeman on a trip to Europe.[22] Upon meeting a beautiful Italian woman, Isabella, who asks if he is a Jew, Freeman tells her he is not: "he did not look Jewish, could pass as not—had."[23] As he falls deeper in love with Isabella, he takes elaborate steps to insist upon his name as Freeman, so she does not uncover his identity as a Jew. By the end, she reveals herself to be a Jew, a survivor of Buchenwald: "I can't marry you," she tells him, exposing tattoos on her breast, "We are Jews. My past is meaningful to me. I treasure what I suffered for."[24] Malamud's piece quite explicitly linked Levin's name changing with his forgetting of the Jewish past, and his particular lack of connection to the memories of the Holocaust.

Non-fiction after the war similarly revealed simmering anger among Jews over the subject of name changing—including one equally angry defense from a Jew who had changed his name. The recent destruction of millions of Jews in Europe became an image in the debate as both sides laid claim to American freedom and the memory of Nazi violence. A 1948 article in the *Atlantic*, "I Changed My Name," by an author who ironically insisted on remaining anonymous, set off a spirited public conversation over name changing in America. "Anonymous" began by describing his name change: after the war, he and his brother had decided that a name change would afford them an easier, better life. The two paid $60 and became proud owners of a new name—and then were set upon by angry friends who called them cowards and deserters.

The author insisted to his friends that he had broken no ties by changing his name—he identified himself as a universalist, as someone who had just "joined the human race." In response to his friends' question—"But don't you bleed … for the Jews trying to get to Palestine?"—he responded, "I am appalled by all of man's inhumanity to man, everywhere." Perhaps most fascinating was Anonymous's response to his friends' charge that he was a liar:

> I think we should be only too pleased to misinform those gentlemen who like to know how to put their finger on Jews. Lies are too good for them, these lovers of an orderly world where each sect and breed comes plainly labeled and Jews good naturedly make their living at pawnbroking, clothes manufacturing, or junk dealing. Such gentlemen may not always be deceived, but if enough names are changed, they will certainly be confused. Therefore to hypocritical universities, polluted employment agencies, churchgoers ignorant of Christianity, canting business leaders, haters of people they haven't met, it seems a good idea to say, I won't make your dirty work easier, like a sheep considerately running up the plank into the slaughterhouse. Try and find me.[25]

Anonymous' essay illustrates the various ways in which memories of the Holocaust were put into the service of debates over name changing. On the one hand, Anonymous describes the ways that many American Jews, like the author's friends, perceived of the post-Holocaust plight of survivors as a problem for all Jews and a symbol that should rally Jewish loyalty and unity. On the other hand, however, the author's coded but meaningful reference to Jews as sheep "considerately running up the plank into the slaughterhouse" as they submitted to antisemitic discrimination is certainly a reference to the Holocaust.[26] Although he describes American antisemitism (employment agencies, university quotas), the anonymous author seems clearly to be drawing on his readers' knowledge of the Holocaust, and their beliefs about Jewish murder in Europe. Name changing, Anonymous seemed to suggest, was a rational response to antisemitism; indeed, it was even an ingenious strategy that might help American Jews avoid the violent persecution that had decimated the Jews of Europe.

"I Changed My Name" had wide readership and sparked substantial debate. Although it was initially published in the mainstream but upscale intellectual journal the *Atlantic*, it was also reprinted in the more middlebrow *Readers' Digest*, thereby engaging millions of ordinary Americans in the question of Jewish name changing. Two articles, moreover, appeared in print soon afterwards to refute Anonymous' enthusiastic defense of name changing and his use of Nazi genocide. In the April *Atlantic* Mississippi writer David L. Cohn produced a rebuttal, "I've Kept My Name," (also reprinted in *Reader's Digest*), which testified to the opportunities provided to American Jews, even those with distinctive Jewish names, while in the American Jewish Congress publication, *Congress Weekly*, editor Shlomo Katz railed against Anonymous in an editorial entitled "So You've Changed Your Name." Both pieces suggested that Anonymous—and by extension, other name changers—had abandoned Jewish pride and identity for the thin promises of acceptance into racist elite circles. While Cohn testified to the "kindliness" of the United States and insisted that only social climbers felt the need to deny their identity, Katz lashed out at Anonymous, suggesting that the writer had abandoned the Jews.[27] When his new bigoted friends confided in him their prejudices against Jews and Negroes, Katz pointed out, Anonymous had to keep up his disguise: "you have to grin and approve their fascist obscenities. You are not confusing the enemy, as you claim; you have joined him."[28] Both Katz and Cohn thus rewrote Anonymous' paeans to American freedom and his appropriation of Nazi genocide, suggesting that America could provide freedom for Jews with their names intact and arguing that name changers actually joined racists in their attacks upon the Jewish community.

In this context, J. Alvin Kugelmass's piece on name changing fit right in: like Katz and Cohn, like Hobson and Wechsler, Kugelmass portrayed name changing as the act of an insecure, pathetic coward who had separated himself from the Jewish people and betrayed his Jewish identity. And even though a few other authors offered less damning portraits—in 1958, Ernest Maass, for example, wrote a sympathetic scholarly article about name changing among Central European immigrants—the tenor of the public conversation on name changing remained harshly judgmental.[29]

Most literature of the post-World War II era, then, portrayed name changing as a flawed enterprise, one animated by insecurity, anxiety, and even bigotry or self-hatred. At their most extreme, writers after 1945 suggested that name changers betrayed the Jewish people in the wake of genocide. This dominant perspective on name changing demonstrates the impact of the Holocaust on postwar American Jewish thought. Far from repressing their knowledge of the Holocaust, American Jews in the late 1940s and 1950s used European genocide as a lens through which to interpret their most fundamental public identities in the United States.[30]

Yet, it is worth noting that some authors during the war perceived of name changing as a rational act that could be undertaken pragmatically. It is also worth noting, moreover, that large numbers of ordinary individuals chose to change their names in the years during and after World War II, even in the face of communal scorn. Although few of those individuals chose to defend their actions in print, as did Anonymous, their decisions to change their names may have reflected a different understanding of the lessons of the Nazi genocide: name changing was a freedom offered to Jews in the United States and denied to European Jews. Far from viewing their actions as a betrayal of the Jewish people, many may have viewed name changing as a means of maintaining the well-being of the Jewish people, a defensive response to the treatment of Jews as a despised race in the 1940s.

Notes

1 J. Alvin Kugelmass, "Name-Changing and What It Gets You," *Commentary* 14 (1952): 145; 150.
2 I am grateful to the Civil Court of New York City for allowing me to examine its name-changing records—a remarkable scholarly resource. I am particularly grateful to Ernesto Belzaguy and to Michael Boyle for facilitating my research. In my research, I examined the name-change petitions filed with the City Court from 1882 through 2002. I collected records for every fifth year (1892, 1897, 1902, etc.). I also examined a few outlying dates – 1918, 1940 and 1946. I chose 1918 because accounts of anti-German prejudice during World War I suggested that name changing might go up during those years. I chose 1940 and 1946 because simply an eyeball examination of the records demonstrated that name change petitions skyrocketed during those years. Between 1892 and 1927, I collected every single petition or judge's order in each year I examined; between 1932 and 2002, I collected 1 in 10 petitions because of the larger numbers of petitions during those years. I selected the 1 in 10 petitions randomly—I selected the first of every 10 I counted. When I saw particularly interesting petitions, I gathered them but marked them separately so they could be included for qualitative, not quantitative analysis. It is important to note that the records held at the Civil Court were actually submitted to the City Court before 1962 (in 1962, City Court and Municipal Court were merged to form Civil Court). Moreover, City Court was not the only place where New Yorkers could officially change their names during the twentieth century. Residents of the Bronx, Brooklyn, Queens and Staten Island could also change their names in separate borough courts, and residents of all five boroughs could also change their names at the Court of Common Pleas before 1895 and in Supreme Court after 1895. Furthermore, immigrants could officially change their names on naturalization petitions after 1906. Some information on the history of name changing in the New York City court system can be found in Arthur Scherr, "Change-of-Name Petitions of the New York Courts: An Untapped Source in Historical Onomastics," *Names* 34, no. 3 (September 1986): 284–302 and at the website for the New York City court system: http://nycourts.gov/courts/nyc/civil/civilhistory.shtml. Accessed August 12, 2010.
3 To determine Jewish identity, I either looked for the first or last name to be categorically Jewish: Israel, Yakov, or Chaim; Levine, Shapiro, or Kaplan. If either name was categorically Jewish, the person was Jewish, and so was his/her family. If not that simple, I generally looked for *both* the first and the last name to be a Jewish-identified name in

the United States. That is, I included first names like Rose, Ceil, Fanny, Harry, Max, and Sam as Jewish, and I also included last names like Lubinsky or Warshawsky as Jewish, but only if those Jewish-identified names matched one another. If the first name was a name rarely used by Jewish Americans – Thomas, James, Anthony, Frederick, Patricia, or Mabel, for example—I did not count the person Jewish, even if the last name seemed Jewish. If neither the first name nor the last name was a common or categorical Jewish name, but both names were used by Jews and together seemed to connote Jewish identity—for example, in a name like Victor Kavarsky—I used other markers in the petition, such as residential address, occupation, and birthplace, to help make judgments: if Victor Kavarsky was born in Russia, lived on the Lower East Side, and worked in the garment industry, I counted him as a Jew; if he lived in Queens and worked as a chauffeur, I did not count him as a Jew. When in doubt, I did not count individuals as Jews. This methodology is not perfect—given the wide-ranging origins of Jews and other immigrants in America and the varieties of names that they and their families adopted in various corners of the world, I am certain that I am making some mistakes when I guess at ethnic origins. But I believe that, in general, given my methodology, I am probably undercounting Jews, rather than overcounting Jews. Since my argument revolves around high numbers of Jews, I believe that underestimation should not negatively affect my conclusions.

4 For the Jewish population of New York, see C. Morris Horowitz, Lawrence J. Kaplan, Hon. James Felt, *The Estimated Jewish Population of the New York Area* (Federation of Jewish Philanthropies of New York, 1959), 22–23. Researchers for this study used the Yom Kippur method of calculating Jews—that is, they calculated the numbers of children absent from public schools on Yom Kippur, the holiest day of the year for Jews. The method, of course, has flaws: it links Jewish identity to Jewish religious practice, and it tends to understate Jewish population where the population is small.

5 See, for example, Gary Gerstle, *American Crucible: Race and Nation in the Twentieth Century* (Princeton, NJ: Princeton University Press, 2001), 164–66; Charles Silberman, *A Certain People: American Jews and Their Lives Today* (New York: Summit Books, 1985), 59–60; Leonard Dinnerstein, *Anti-Semitism in America* (New York: Oxford University Press, 1994), 124–25. One significant exception is historian Arthur Scherr, who wrote a valuable article introducing readers to the name-change petitions in the New York Courts, and encouraging researchers to do further study of their historical significance. See Scherr, "Change-of-Name Petitions of the New York Courts."

6 New York City Civil Court, Name-Change Petitions Collection, Box 1942, N207–1942.

7 New York City Civil Court, Name-Change Petitions Collection, Box 1942, N207–1942.

8 New York City Civil Court, Name-Change Petitions Collection, Box 1942, N155–1942.

9 See, for example, New York City Civil Court, Name-Change Petitions Collection, Box 1952, N72–1952; N375–1952; and N415–1952. See also Name-Change Petitions Collection, Box 1947, N191–1947.

10 New York City Civil Court, Name-Change Petitions Collection, Box 1952, N244–1952; see also N284–1952.

11 New York City Civil Court, Name-Change Petitions Collection, Box 1946, N129–1946.

12 Ernest Maass, "Integration and Name Changing among Jewish Refugees from Central Europe in the United States," *Names* 6 (1958): 141–42; 168–69. Far fewer than four percent of my name-change petition documents were submitted by Central European refugees. One reason for the discrepancy between my numbers and Maass's is that many immigrants may have changed their names on their naturalization petitions.

13 Gerstle, *American Crucible*, 187–237; Deborah Dash Moore, *GI Jews: How World War II Shaped a Generation* (Cambridge, MA: Belknap Press of Harvard University Press, 2004); Eric Goldstein, *The Price of Whiteness: Jews, Race, and American Identity* (Princeton, NJ: Princeton University Press, 2006), 192–93.

14 Although I disagree with his evaluation of the significance of white fighting troops, my conclusions here agree essentially with those of Goldstein, who argues that Jews in the 1940s were welcomed into the white mainstream, so long as they kept their group differences to a minimum. Goldstein interprets those group differences primarily as expressions of racial liberalism, but another (and more uniquely Jewish) measure of group difference was a Jewish-identified name.

15 Louis Adamic, *What's Your Name?* (New York: Harper and Brothers, 1942), 22–23.

16 Manfred George, "Müssen Sie Washington heißen?" *Aufbau* (August 6, 1943), cited in Maass, "Integration and Name Changing Among Jewish Refugees," 166.

17 Ibid.

18 *Armenian Mirror-Spectator* (October 9, 1940), cited in Adamic, *What's Your Name?*, 85.

19 *Jewish Opinion* (September 1939), cited in Adamic, *What's Your Name?*, 86.

20 Laura Z. Hobson, *Gentleman's Agreement* (New York: Avon Books, 1968; orig. pub. New York: Simon and Schuster, 1946), 127–29.

21 Joseph Wechsler, "The Rules of the Game," *New Yorker* (October 1, 1949): 29.

22 Bernard Malamud, "The Lady of the Lake," in *American Jewish Fiction: A Century of Stories*, ed. Gerald Shapiro (Lincoln: University of Nebraska Press, 1998), 94. Originally published in *The Magic Barrel* (New York: Random House, 1958).

23 Malamud, "Lady of the Lake," 100.

24 Malamud, "Lady of the Lake," 100.

25 Anonymous, "I Changed My Name," *Atlantic* 181 (February 1948): 72–74; reprinted in *Readers' Digest* 52 (June 1948): 13–15. Accessed at http://www.theatlantic.com/doc// 194802/changed-name (October 21, 2010).

26 According to Anita Shapira, the phrase "like sheep to slaughter" had been used as early as 1941, in a leaflet written by Abba Kovner describing the murder of Jews in the Vilna ghetto. By late 1942, the phrase began to appear in print in Palestine, and it became a dominant trope in Zionist self-understanding. At least by 1946, if not before, the phrase had begun to appear in print in the United States as well. Anita Shapira, *Land and Power: The Zionist Resort to Force, 1881–1948* (Palo Alto: Stanford University Press, 1992), 330–42; "Aid Pledged Here to Palestine Army," *New York Times* (July 3, 1946), 5.

27 David L. Cohn, "I've Kept My Name," *Atlantic* 181(April 1948): 42–44; reprinted in *Readers' Digest* 52 (June 1948): 16–18. Accessed at http://www.theatlantic.com/doc/ 194804/kept-name (October 21, 2010).

28 Shlomo Katz, "So You Changed Your Name," *Congress Weekly* (February 1948): 9.

29 Maass, "Integration and Name Changing."

30 For other arguments that suggest American Jews did not repress memories of the Holocaust in the years immediately after the event, see, for example, Jeffrey Shandler, *While America Watches: Televising the Holocaust* (New York: Oxford University Press, 1999), Michael Staub, *Torn at the Roots: The Crisis of Jewish Liberalism in Postwar America* (New York: Columbia University Press, 2002); Rona Sheramy, "'Resistance and War': The Holocaust in American Jewish Education, 1945–60," *American Jewish History* 91, no. 2 (June 2003): 287–313; Lawrence Baron, "The Holocaust and American Public Memory, 1945–60," *Holocaust and Genocide Studies* 17, no. 1 (Spring 2003): 62–88; Eric Sundquist, *Strangers in the Land: Blacks, Jews, Post-Holocaust America* (Cambridge, MA: Belknap Press, 2005); Kirsten Fermaglich, *American Dreams and Nazi Nightmares: Early Holocaust Consciousness and Liberal America, 1957–1965* (Hanover, NH: Brandeis University Press, 2006); Beth Cohen, *Case Closed: Holocaust Survivors in Postwar America* (New Brunswick: Rutgers University Press, 2007); and Hasia Diner, *We Remember With Reverence and Love* (New York: New York University Press, 2009).

12

THE MYTH OF SILENCE

Survivors tell a different story

Beth B. Cohen

From 1946 through 1954, 140,000 surviving souls of the remnant of European Jewry settled in the United States.[1] Unable to bear their recent traumatic experiences, the survivors repressed their painful Holocaust memories in its immediate aftermath and channeled their energy and emotions into rebuilding new lives. Decades later, in the quietude of retirement and impending old age, survivors began to find their voice. Finally, beginning in the 1980s, they were able to face their Holocaust years and raced against the clock to do so. From New York to Los Angeles, from Dallas to Providence, from San Francisco to Buffalo, America witnessed a proliferation of Holocaust oral history projects, memorials and museums driven, in large part, by survivors' urging and participation.[2] This awakening signaled a major shift in survivors' confrontation with their past. Or so popular as well as scholarly observers from historians to sociologists to psychoanalysts have traditionally described this narrative.[3]

Survivors, however, tell a very different story. Prompted by their remarks, which contradicted the accepted explanation of postwar silence, I probed this question.[4] Did survivors speak in the immediate aftermath? If so, to whom? How was this expressed? And, if they did, why would we think they did not? Scrutinizing oral histories taken after the war, analyzing contemporary case files of survivors in Jewish refugee agencies' archives, and studying postwar media helped illuminate and synthesize various strands of this thorny issue.

It is true that most, though by no means all, Displaced Persons (DPs) quickly began the process of acculturating to life in America. They looked for jobs, searched for and settled into apartments, and began raising families. The newcomers found that moving forward was possible but ignoring their memories less so. Forgetting was difficult. They could not forget, nor did they want to. Far from repressing their memories many were eager, willing, indeed compelled to speak. But few in the American Jewish world were inclined to listen.

Survivors' recollections of this are vivid. "We were very bitter," said one camp survivor. Because "in the beginning the people in America didn't want …" his voice failed. "We started to tell, nobody wanted to listen. And if somebody listened, they thought that we told them stories, that it is not true. From the first minute I spoke," he continued, "… When I came to America, when I told the people, they thought I'm crazy … they didn't want to listen," he repeated.[5] Hanne was ready to tell her new family about the war years but when her American cousin asked her if she had had orange juice for breakfast in Auschwitz, she knew she could not and would not share her story. "People had no—no understanding," she said, explaining her cousin's crushing ignorance. Even more, they "didn't really want to know." Hanne suggested that guilt rather than disinterest played a key role. But she remembered, too, that (American) Jews "were also complaining that they suffered … they didn't have enough meat and sugar."[6]

The attempt to equate their wartime experiences with survivors or to suggest that they empathized with their European relatives' suffering because of their own did not sit well with the newcomers. To the refugees, this signaled a deep, even unbridgeable chasm between the two groups and reinforced the belief that their American hosts did not care to hear about nor did they appreciate what survivors had endured. One woman recalled her frustration: "when I made an attempt to explain something sometimes, about the war, there was such lack of comprehension on the part of people I was talking to, that it shut me off … And I—I just couldn't—couldn't cope with that."[7] A young Auschwitz survivor recollected a time when a classmate asked about her tattooed arm, inquiring "Why did you put your telephone number there?" It was question to which she knew she could not possibly offer an explanation.[8] "[I] saw the lack of understanding in the first years, so I decided not to waste my time," remembered another woman. "It was too emotional to open my wounds," she explained.[9]

Not long after her arrival in 1949, one young woman, a refugee reporter for the Yiddish daily the *Forward*, was asked to assist at a fund-raising event for a women's organization in Baltimore and readily accepted the invitation. Thinking she would find empathetic ears, she recalled looking out at her audience and began, "your faces remind me of my mother, murdered by the Nazis."[10] The organization's president quickly interrupted and reminded the guest that her bad memories were in the past. As the hostess urged the band to resume playing, the survivor fled, resolving never to speak publicly about her experiences again.[11]

Some tried to broach the subject with their American kin, but in other instances the topic never came up. "How could the relatives not wonder about their murdered aunts and uncles?" puzzled one woman, whose father was the only child out of his large family who survived Auschwitz.[12] But they did not inquire about their relatives' fate. And the silence hung like a curtain separating the newcomers from their hosts. Commented another woman with finality, "No one ever asked."[13]

Similarly, at the New York Association for New Americans (NYANA), a Jewish agency created in 1949 to help those refugees who settled in New York, professional social workers showed little curiosity about their clients' past. In the hundreds of NYANA case files I scrutinized, few asked or encouraged conversation about wartime experiences. But it was not because of reluctance on the DPs' part. One woman told her caseworker that she "suffers severe dizziness, heart palpitation, high blood pressure and a variety of anxieties." She went further, describing how she "wakes in the middle of the night screaming and although she does not remember exactly what the dream was all about, she does know that she has very bad dreams and nightmare [sic]."[14] Her traumatic experiences plagued her days, as well. She feared the dark and subways, and "occasionally, she suddenly gets the idea that they are about to be deported and worries about that for days at a time," her social worker noted. While she was most eager to find employment, her nightmares kept her awake for hours and she had difficulty rousing herself in the morning. The social worker pressed the woman to continue her job search.

Mr. H. was a widower who arrived in New York City in August 1949.[15] His murdered wife's sister and brother-in-law sponsored him but quickly referred the newcomer to NYANA when they felt that they had more than met their obligation to him. Mr. H.'s wife had been killed in 1942, and he continued to struggle with the loss. The agency referred him to a psychiatrist when his condition interfered with his search for employment. The examining physician wrote:

> Mr. H, 43 years old, was examined by me on June 1, 1950. The patient told me that he had never been seriously ill before, and that he had developed no complaints during 4 years in concentration camps but that his complaints started after his liberation. He has been here for 9 months, and complains now that he perspires excessively, that sometimes he has a weakness in his hands and gets severe headaches.
>
> He attributes his complaints to the severe emotional upsets he has suffered during the last 10 years. ... On physical examination there was no evidence of an organic disease of the nervous system but he showed increased perspiration and some trembling of the hands, disappearing when distracted.
>
> This patient suffers from a psychoneurosis with depressive and hysterical symptoms. I told him that the best way to get over his complaints would be to start a new life here by getting a regular occupation, and that his chances for recovery would not be good if he would have to spend the whole day without useful work. To this he reacted rather violently, saying that this meant an accusation that he was not willing to work. Nothing of this kind has been expressed by the examiner. It is my opinion that this patient should be put to work as soon as feasible.[16]

The message that work was seen as a remedy for the client's ills echoed throughout the case files. Repeatedly, in their rush to get the refugees off relief, the agency workers ignored, minimized or even mocked the newcomers' references to the war, believing that the newcomers wanted special treatment because of their experiences. At times the case workers suggested that the refugees were weak and dependent, or that they were better off because of their experiences, and urged their clients to move ahead as quickly as possible and leave the past firmly behind.

What accounts for these responses? A former social work intern at the Montefiore Hospital offers one explanation for her own and her colleagues' seemingly unsympathetic stance. "We had no sense of the Holocaust as we know now, with a capital H. We really didn't understand what people were telling us," she remembered. "The stories were too horrible. We simply did not believe them," she admitted.[17] The social worker's response is illuminating. It highlights an attitude, which prevailed among the professionals. It also confirms that refugees were hardly repressing their experiences.

The comment by the young intern professing disbelief, however, is worthy of a closer look. Numerous accounts in the postwar media, including newspapers, memoirs, and professional journals (not to mention film and television), make it clear that there was considerable information about the Holocaust available to the public.[18] With a steady stream of information flowing from reliable sources, why would anyone who came face to face with the victims react to their stories with disbelief? How can we understand this? Or grasp why American Jews would ignore or trivialize survivors' attempts to speak—effectively silencing their efforts?

Clearly, some may have dismissed or showed little interest in survivors' stories because, when they finally confronted them, the Americans wished to avoid the pain—either their own or the survivors'—that they imagined discussion would evoke. Profound guilt on the part of American Jews that they were spared while Europe's Jews were slaughtered has also been suggested. In some instances, acculturated American Jews were likely embarrassed by the predominantly Eastern European refugees or the then-popular perception of European Jewry having gone as "sheep to the slaughter" and therefore distanced themselves from survivors. The records certainly reveal that many American Jews did not want the financial or emotional burden of newly arrived relatives. It was one thing to read about genocide but quite another to be confronted with the living proof. The idea of disbelief seems implausible, and yet there may be a nugget of truth in it. While Americans may have seen 1945 newsreels of camps and their emaciated victims, or read searing accounts of camp life and the effect on its victims, the newcomers arriving particularly after the DP Act of 1948 were outwardly healthy. Perhaps the American hosts simply could not or did not want to push their imaginations to bridge this dissonance. Finally, there is the possibility of saturation. Americans may have felt they had already heard enough and did not need to hear more directly from the source. I suspect that all of these reasons contributed to the silence that survivors consistently remember greeted them.

Can we hold the mental health professionals who worked with the refugees to a different standard? One might argue that we cannot expect otherwise in the immediate aftermath of the war, that in those years they simply did not have the tools to help Holocaust survivors. After all, it is only with the Vietnam War that the notion of post-traumatic stress disorder became a widely accepted diagnosis. Is it unfair, then, to think that those who worked with the survivors would treat these victims of genocide any differently than they did? I believe not. The response of the Jewish Family and Children's Services in Boston (JFCS) argues most tellingly and persuasively for the possibility that the professionals, at least, could have behaved differently. In

1946, the agency decided to experiment with placement strategies for refugee children who were beginning to arrive in the United States. One effort was a separate New American unit at an already existing Jewish summer camp, Camp Kingswood, in Bridgton, Maine. Beatrice Carter, JFCS director, delivered a paper to a national social work conference in which she stressed the therapeutic nature of this initiative. The New American unit was intended to offer a supportive setting in which the youths "are able to utilize many of the skills acquired in European experiences to master the rugged environment, which the new campsite offers."[19] This unique program began with seven children in 1946 and by 1949 had grown to include nineteen orphans.[20]

Leonard Serkess was a young social worker whose involvement with the New Americans began in 1947 at the summer camp. Speaking in 2002, he noted the staff's response to the refugees' attitude toward food. "One of the biggest problems we had was the kids would steal food and bring it back to the tents. And we tried to explain to them ... that there would be plenty of food," he remembers. Still, "they found it hard to believe. There was a perpetual hunger. ... [T]hey just never felt secure that there would be enough food for them."[21] The staff recognized the special significance of food for the young DPs and allowed for it.

That understanding pervaded the camp. The youngsters spent some of their time learning English, but there were also opportunities for creative expression. This included an original play by the teens about their lives during the Holocaust. In a literary magazine of the campers' work, one boy wrote "Why We Put the Play On," in which he describes the unusual production:

> One day Szmul came out with the idea of a play about concentration camp events, and, in talking, he had already acted out parts of the future play. At first we were stunned and resented to be overcome again by the flood of evil memories. Then we resolved to face once more the reality that had been. We only needed to pass out roles, never learned any parts and never twice said quite the same words during the life-like rehearsals. Within a week we were ready to perform in front of the entire camp. During that week we had little time for classes. We lived only partly in the present. Some of us sang the songs of the concentration camps; some, who were to act as Nazis, sang the songs which before we so often had heard and hated. Then the Friday night came. We were deeply steeped into the past and we played from our hearts ... In some way we are freer now to live for the future.[22]

In this environment the young people, encouraged, spoke often and freely about their past.

Responses such as the Jewish Family and Children's Services' were, however, rare among the Jewish communal organizations. Among newfound family members they were also glaringly absent. Even the expression of genuine sympathy was unusual and for that reason important to note. In an oral history, one survivor recalled her despair after arriving in the United States. She mourned her murdered family so intensely that she could not stop weeping. At night she screamed from her nightmares and woke her young cousins. "Why are you crying?" they wanted to know. The young woman told her relatives. The response was simple and direct. "Cry, if this will help you," her aunt encouraged her. Moreover, she told her, "I know it's not easy for you, but we love you and we want you to be happy." Her aunt's understanding meant a great deal. "I appreciate those words what [sic] she said to me," recalled the woman in an interview nearly forty years later. "Till now I remember them," she emphasized.[23] Although such examples are conspicuously absent from survivor testimonies and case files, those that do appear indicated that survivors could, would, and did speak under certain circumstances.

Certainly there were those who chose to keep silent. Bernie Sayonne of Denver believes some did not speak because they could not shake the internalized fear of persecution that shadowed their lives in America; better to keep a low profile, he reasoned, than to become a possible target of antisemitism.[24] Some simply could not articulate their experiences.

But many, many others' recollections belie the myth of silence. "We, the survivors, even me, I'm talking personally, I wanted to, I wanted to talk about it," emphasized Nessie Godin, who settled in Washington, DC, in 1949. "Why?" she asks herself. Because "in the most horrible times during the Holocaust, we used to sit and talk to each other, the women, hungry, cold, all the women used to say, please don't forget us. If you survive," she was instructed, "tell the world of what happened."[25] Nessie, as have others, takes this obligation seriously. "Those women asked me to talk about it," she affirmed.[26] And talk she did. But, if the outside world was largely indifferent, to whom did Nessie and others turn? At first it was largely amongst themselves that they found the persistent desire to recall, a common language of mutual grief, and sympathetic ears.

No matter where they settled, the newcomers created groups. Many who stayed in New York turned to *landsmanschaftn*, or hometown social clubs, which had been established by earlier Jewish immigrants after their arrival in America at the turn of the 20th century.[27] During the Great War, the majority of the Eastern European Jewry in the United States still had parents, siblings, and cousins overseas who kept them strongly and directly attached to the towns of their birth. But by the late 1940s these connections had attenuated. Their identities had shifted so that, as historian Daniel Soyer has noted, "the immigrants came to see themselves clearly as American Jews, a community distinct from those in the countries in Eastern Europe."[28] So much so that when DPs eagerly sought out their *landslayt* (descendants from their hometown) once in the United States, they were not necessarily received with open arms. These encounters were disappointing, noted survivor Hiller Bell, president of the United Belchatower Assistance Committee, when the old-timers did not welcome the refugees.[29] The existing groups mobilized to send money to Palestine or to DPs in Europe, but welcoming the newly arrived *landslayt* in the United States who were both part of the surviving remnant of European Jewry and also the last link to their own communities was not a priority. The lack of unconditional acceptance by his fellow Bellchatowers still rankled Mr. Bell more than fifty years later. Still, the growing number of refugees in New York like Mr. Bell jump-started existing societies, many of which were on the decline or defunct.[30] Some felt the need to form their own groups within established organizations. Such was the case with a core of surviving Bialystokers who formed the Club of Bialystoker Friends, promising "to preserve the cultural and spiritual heritage of Bialystok."[31] Yet others, such as the New Cracow Friendship Society, differentiated themselves from the original Cracow group, noted survivor Roman Weingarten and former *landsmanschaft* president, because the earlier immigrants had no interest in the newcomers.[32]

Whether newly formed or recently revamped, *landsmanschaftn* promised the new members a connection to their lost homes and murdered families. Within these circles, survivors discovered others who might have known their parents and who, in turn, were eager for information about their own relatives. Imagine the joy when a survivor found "someone who knew something about the family," remembered Hiller Bell.[33] Similarly, Roman Weingarten emphasized, "We came together as survivors and as friends; half of us … we knew each other from Crakow or we knew the family. You must understand [that] people came here after the war … they had no family. We were each other's families."[34]

The need to be with others was consuming. In the absence of *landsmanschaftn*, the immigrants created alternatives where identity as a survivor, not one's country of origin, defined one's membership. The postwar landscape was dotted with these groups wherever survivors settled. In 1950, Indianapolis refugees created a New Americans Club, as did those in Boston. In Kansas City, Missouri, newcomers quickly joined together. Twelve Polish refugees in Los Angeles banded together in 1952 to form the 1939 Club, so named to remember the year Hitler invaded Poland. Denver was home to two clubs: Club 1939 for German Jews who had survived in Shanghai and the New Americans Club for those from Eastern Europe. Some DPs in Dallas dubbed their association "New Texans." Refugees in Cleveland, Ohio, formed the Menorah group.[35]

In community after community, New American Clubs sprang up and took root. In smaller communities, survivors met informally without an official organizational framework. Some families in Providence, Rhode Island, congregated in one another's homes on a weekly basis, recalled Heinz Sandelowski, a German survivor who arrived in 1947.[36] Nearly fifty years later, he recounted, "We got together at our houses, every Saturday night at somebody else's house. We played cards and in the summertime, we went to the ocean or to the park."[37] Sidi Natansohn, an Auschwitz survivor, described how young adult refugees met regularly in the late 1940s on the boardwalk of New York's Brighton Beach. It was there she met another survivor, Sam, who became her husband.[38] Mr. Krell, a Polish refugee, began meeting with a small circle of other men in a local coffee shop. Soon it became a regular event.[39] So great was his need to be with other newcomers after his arrival in 1949 that Naftali Lis traveled by train from Hartford, Connecticut, to New York City every Sunday. He recalled going to the temporary refugee hotels in New York in order to spend time with other DPs even if they just "walked the streets together."[40]

And, once together, what did the refugees discuss? Nessie G. recalled "five, six couples, survivors coming to our house on the Sabbath, having a little lunch, what did we talk about? … comparing each other's suffering, telling how it was, talking about how by miracle we survived this selection and that selection and in a way, I think this was really beneficial to us … we didn't keep it inside."[41] Mr. Weingarten of the New Cracow Friendship Society unequivocally stated, "There was no conversation that did not end up on the subject."[42] "Even in social situations," remarked one woman, "the topic always came up."[43] When Denver's New American Club socialized, the discussion "always came back to the same thing," recalled Bernie Sayonne. Mr. Paul Krell continues to meet with a small cadre of other male survivors at a local coffee shop in the Bronx. "No matter what we start talking about; politics, the stock market … we always end up talking about the war," he asserted.[44]

The newcomers sought one another out. The structures varied but the intent was clear: they wanted the comfort of others like themselves. These groups provided sustenance on many levels, from mutual aid to casual socializing to profound and lasting bonds. For many, these groups became the family and the community that had been brutally and irrevocably destroyed. Those whose physical and existential past had been shattered longed to be with others who shared a common history; to reclaim their past and ensure that it existed outside of their imaginations. Whether by virtue of their refugee status and their Holocaust experiences, or because of a hometown association, these bonds formed the basis of new communities.

The desire to be together and create or re-create a community clearly motivated the formation of their first groups, but many quickly came to address the complex and pressing need to remember in a more formal way. Many of the groups became the springboards for some of the first Holocaust memorials in America. Some created *yizkor* (memorial) books, and commemorations, others erected monuments. There were those who did both.

By the late 1940s and early 1950s, monuments began to crop up in cities or towns with a survivor community. Providence survivors purchased a plot in the city's Jewish cemetery for their stone. The Hillel Academy, an Orthodox Jewish day school in Denver, donated space on their grounds to the New American Club.[45] Somewhat later, in 1961, the New Cracow Friendship Society erected three stones. "Our first monument that went up has our parents' names," explained Roman Weingarten.[46] The inclusion of names became a common practice and crucial component of the monuments. It not only guarded against oblivion but as scholar James Young notes, also acted as a symbolic grave for those who had none.[47]

Monuments were not the only acts of memorialization. Survivors from numerous *landsmanschaft* and New American groups recall that communal *yizkor* services also began as soon as, or very soon after, the groups were established and continue even as their numbers diminish. "We have a monument for the people who died by the Nazis and every year we go there for yizkor to remember our people" emphasized Mr. Bell of Belchatower.[48] While Jewish tradition mandates the recitation of *yizkor* on the deceased's *yahrzeit* (anniversary of date of death) many, of course, did not know the exact date of relatives' deaths. Therefore, groups adopted the custom of communal *yizkor* on a date that carried a particular significance. "Every year the organization [New Cracow Friendship Society] commemorates the liquidation of the ghetto in March 1943," Roman Weingarten explained.[49] "We chose August 11 when they sent out all the people from our little ghetto," commented Mr. Bell.[50] The Grodners in New York picked the date in March that marked the deportation of their hometown's twenty-nine thousand Jews.[51] The Denver New American Club chose the anniversary of the Warsaw Ghetto Uprising as the annual date for their service.[52] The 1939 Club in Los Angeles did likewise.[53] Still others chose a day during the week between Rosh Hashana, the Jewish New Year, and Yom Kippur, the Day of Atonement, when Jews traditionally visit a cemetery to pay their respects to the deceased.

A third profound and compelling example of survivors' early acts of memorialization is the recording and remembering embodied by yizkor books. Immediately after the war, survivors began the process of memorializing their devastated world in a tangible form. Culled from members' rich collections of photographs, anecdotes, and descriptions, these books paid homage to the vanished Jewish world in general and specific places, in particular. "For Lithuanian Jews, like Jews from all of the murdered communities in Europe," wrote Uriah Katzenelenbogen in his introduction to the Lithuanian memorial book, "are in mourning."[54] Written primarily in Yiddish or Hebrew, and largely the effort of *landmanschaft* groups, the memorial books focused on recording and restoring to memory, in as much detail as possible, the people, life and vibrancy of a place. The books followed a chronological narrative, however, which inevitably led to the survivors' accounts of the final days of their hometown during the *khurbn* (Holocaust). The close to eight hundred yizkor books that were written and published as early as 1947 testify to the fact that rather than repressing their memories, survivors acquired a purposeful and collective voice in the immediate postwar years.[55]

Survivors were by no means silent immediately after the Holocaust. While their American hosts typically encouraged the newcomers to move on and abandon their memories, the surviving remnant found this to be impossible. As they acculturated to American life, refugees joined forces and created a range of social networks. In these groups, they confronted their past and the need to remember. And remember they did—through speaking, building the first Holocaust monuments, creating memorial books and commemorations. Ample evidence contradicts the myth of silence. Survivors had much to say but not because relatives, social workers, or the outside world encouraged them. It would be some years before survivors' stories found the receptive audience that they wanted and deserved from their American brethren and, indeed, from the wider society.

Notes

1 Leonard Dinnerstein. *America and the Survivors of the Holocaust*. (New York: Columbia University Press, 1982), 288. The records of the United Service for New Americans and the National Refugees Service agree with this figure.
2 It was during this period that the United States Holocaust Memorial Museum was erected as well as regional Holocaust museums including the Rhode Island Holocaust Memorial Museum where I was Director of Education from 1988–98.

3 See Martin Bergman and Milton Jucovy, eds. *Generations of the Holocaust* (New York: Columbia University Press); T.L. Brink, ed., *Holocaust Survivors' Mental Health.* (Binghamton, NY: Hayworth Press, 1994); W. Helmreich, *Against All Odds: Holocaust Survivors and the Successful Lives They Made in America* (New Brunswick, NJ: Transaction, 1996); Dorothy Rabinowitz, *New Lives: Survivors of the Holocaust Living in America* to name a few that reinforce this notion that survivors repressed their past in order to move forward and build new lives.

4 See B. Cohen's *Case Closed: Holocaust Survivors in Postwar America* (New Brunswick: Rutgers, 2007), which draws on hundreds of oral histories and case files from Jewish Communal agencies to analyze survivors' early postwar years.

5 Bernie Sayonne, interview with the author, tape recording, Rockville, MD. 2 December 2004.

6 H. Liebman, RG-50.407★0086, Postwar Interviews, 5 July 1998, United States Holocaust Memorial Museum (USHMM) Archives.

7 S. Lipman, RG-50.02★0018, Postwar Interviews, 4 August 1998, USHMM Archives.

8 R. Gelb. RG-50.02★0013, Postwar Interviews, 18 March 1998, USHMM Archives.

9 A. Salsitz, RG-549.02★0054, Postwar Interviews, 5 July 1999, USHMM Archives.

10 S. Taube, interview with the author, tape recording, Rockville, MD, 14 December 2004.

11 Ibid.

12 Anat Bar-Cohen, interview with the author, Washington, DC, 6 January 2005.

13 Amalie Sandelowski, interview with the author, tape recording, Providence, RI, 3 March 2000.

14 NYANA Case file 322–49, New York Association for New Americans Archives (NYANA), New York, NY.

15 NYANA Case file 324–50,NYANA Archives.

16 Ibid.

17 As quoted in Barbara Burstin, "Holocaust Survivors: Rescue and Resettlement," *in Jewish Women in America: An Historical Encyclopedia,* ed. Paula Hyman and Deborah Dash Moore (New York: Routledge, 1997), 656.

18 See Cohen, Op.Cit.155–72, Hasia Diner, *We Remember with Reverence and Love: American Jews and the Myth of Silence after the Holocaust, 1945–1962* (New York: NYU Press, 2009) and Lawrence Baron "The Holocaust and American Public Memory, 1945–60," Holocaust and Genocide Studies, 17:1 (Spring 2003), 62–88 for discussion of the Holocaust in the public eye.

19 Beatrice Carter, "Social Case Work with the Adolescence in a Program of Social Case Work with Displaced Persons," paper read at the National Conference of Social Work, Atlantic City, 1950, cited in Glantz, "Factors in the Adjustment of New American Children in their First Year in the United States" (master's thesis, Simmons College, 1950), 27.

20 Ibid.

21 Leonard Serkess, interview with the author, tape recording, Newton, MA, 27 February 2002.

22 Harry Plow, "Why We Put the Play On," in *Twice Born,* ed. Joshua Rosenberg, writings from the New American Unit, Camp Kingswood, Bridgton, ME, Summer 1948, 21.

23 E. Beder, RG-50.091★0004, National Council of Jewish Women Oral History Project, Cleveland, 27 August 1984, USHMM Archives.

24 Sayonne, interview.

25 N. Godin, RG-50.549.01★0009, Postwar Interviews, 14 December 1995, USHMM Archives.

26 Godin, interview.

27 Studies of *landsmanschaftn* include Daniel Soyer's *Jewish Immigrant Associations and American Identity in New York, 1880–1939* (Cambridge, MA: Harvard University Press, 1997), which provides an excellent analysis; a work produced by the WPA Yiddish writers' project (Yiddish Writers' Group, *Di yidishe landmanschaftn fun nyu york*), which is the

most comprehensive contemporary description of the societies in the 1930s; Hannah Kliger's *Jewish Hometown Associations and Family Circles in New York: The WPA Yiddish Writers' Group Study* (Bloomington: Indiana University Press, 1992).

28 Soyer, Jewish Immigrant Associations, 162.

29 Hiller Bell, telephone conversation with the author, Sharon, MA, 12 January 2003.

30 Ibid.

31 I. Rybal, L. Kronick, and I. Shmulewitz, eds., The Bialystoker Memorial Book (Brooklyn, NY: Empire Press, 1982), 171.

32 Roman Weingarten, telephone interview with the author, Sharon, MA, 20 January 2003.

33 Bell, interview.

34 Weingarten, interview.

35 "Around the Nation," *New Neighbors* (United Service for New Americans newsletter) 3 (May 1950): 7.

36 Heinz Sandelowski, interview with the author, tape recording, Providence, RI, 9 March 2000.

37 Ibid.

38 Sidi Natansohn, interview with the author, tape recording, Sharon, MA, 4 February 2003.

39 Paul Krell, interview with the author, Bronx, New York, 7 March 2002.

40 Naftali Lis, interview with the author, Sharon, MA, 21 March 2002.

41 Godin, interview.

42 Roman Weingarten, telephone interview with the author, Sharon, MA, 20 January 2003.

43 T.R. telephone interview with author, Sharon, MA, 3 December 2002.

44 Krell, interview.

45 Sayonne, interview.

46 Weingarten, interview.

47 James Young, *The Texture of Memory: Holocaust Memorials and Meaning* (New Haven, CT: Yale University Press, 1993), 7.

48 Bell, interview.

49 Weingarten, interview.

50 Bell, Interview.

51 Yizkor Flyer, United Grodner Relief, Inc. of New York, N.Y., 1954, YIVO Institute for Jewish Research Archives, RG 996, Box 1, New York.

52 Sayonne, interview.

53 *To Remember Is to Know* (Los Angeles: Club 1939, 1982), 3.

54 M. Sodarsky and J. Katzenelenbogen, eds., *Lithuania*, vol. 1 (New York: Futuro Press, 1951), 33. Translated from Yiddish by the author.

55 Jack Kugelmass and Jonathan Boyarin, *From a Ruined Garden: The Memorial Books of Polish Jewry* (Bloomington: Indiana University Press in Association with the United States Holocaust Memorial Museum, 1998).

13

ORIGINS AND MEANINGS OF THE MYTH OF SILENCE

Hasia R. Diner

The title of this volume *After the Holocaust, Challenging the Myth of Silence* alludes to my 2009 book, *We Remember with Reverence and Love: American Jews and the Myth of Silence After the Holocaust, 1945–1962*. In that book I explored the multiplicity of ways, times, places, and genres in and by which American Jews in the period from the end of World War II and the defeat of Nazi Germany into the early part of the tempestuous decade of the 1960s made the Holocaust part of their communal culture. I examined how the Jews of the United States through their many institutions—including but not limited to synagogues and seminaries, philanthropic and defense organizations, schools, summer camps and youth groups, political and human relations bodies, their press and other organs of opinion and information in English, Yiddish, and Hebrew—wove the details of the catastrophe into their public works. I asked how, text by text, artifact by artifact, deed by deed, they attempted to accomplish several chores. How did they, so divided by political ideology, class, region, religious affiliation, and language, experiment with words and actions to hallow the memory of those who had been so brutally extirpated as well as that of their destroyed communities and cultures? How, through the thousands of organizations scattered in hundreds of communities which made up the inappropriately labeled "American Jewish community," did they employ the details and images of the horrendous disappearance of one-third of their people to affect political and cultural changes in their own Jewish world, in America, and indeed in the world writ large?

Having set that as my task, the phrase "myth of silence" should have had no place as part of my title. After all, that myth, a term I use to actually refer to a false history, first surfaced in the late 1960s, an era so different from the one I focused on. During the years I studied nearly no one complained that American Jews did not talk, write, and act in the name of the Holocaust. Writers and educators, rabbis and community leaders articulated a fear that forgetting would take place and directed much of their attention to imbuing in children and young people a sense of connection to the destroyed Jews and their culture. American Jews, representing the many interest groups which flourished, surely sparred with each other over the correct way to go about this memorialization, and each swathe derived different political and religious lessons as to how the Holocaust did and ought to reverberate in their present. One segment after another considered that it had devised the best and most effective way to remember the victims and the most appropriate way to act in the name of those who had been liquidated. But all converged around a shared perception that recognized how much American Jewish public life had become an arena which put the Holocaust in a prominent place.

In contrast, in the late 1960s and continuing into the present, a period of time I had not chosen to study, a narrative took hold which asserted emphatically that post-war American Jews either could not or would not make their communities venues for the memorialization of the Holocaust and that failed to use the Holocaust as they presented themselves to their American neighbors, and certainly not to those who wielded political power. In this rendition of the past, whether told as a matter of volition on the part of 1950s American Jews, or by compulsion, in those years, with its affluence, its increase in religious and ethnic tolerance, its rush to the suburbs, and under the threatening cloud of the Cold War, American Jews had nothing to gain and much indeed to lose if they kept alive the narrative of the six million Jews destroyed by the German Nazis and their allies. This understanding of what they believe happened in the post-war, or better, what did not happen, which arose at the end of the 1960s, continues to dominate the thinking of many American Jews, who in general dismiss evidence to the contrary. The myth prevails.

Since I had wanted to write about the years from 1945 until the early 1960s when Holocaust commemoration and the political action in its name took place on an experimental, grass roots, scattered, and nearly spontaneous basis, the subsequent decades did not enter into my scholarly calculus. The texts of the earlier years, not those of the later era, constituted the vast archival and published trove of material that provided me with the stuff of research. I was not concerned with the false history but rather the actual one.

Yet the "myth of silence" did end up on the cover and spine of the book, although in a circuitous way. When I spoke to my colleagues, historians of the United States and those who studied in particular the American Jewish past, when I presented at scholarly conferences, or shared my ideas with my doctoral students, they all asked me, in one way or another, where did the myth come from? Why had the material I retrieved gotten lost? Why did the ceremonies, liturgies, political and philanthropic writings and speeches, the ceremonies, journalism and pedagogical works get cast into oblivion? When I lectured to community groups, mostly in Jewish communal settings, I got not only the adamant response that I had to be wrong because they did not remember the post-war years as I presented them, but also if I am right, which they doubted, how come everyone else got it wrong? My editor at New York University Press and nearly everyone else pressed me to tackle the myth, not only to explore where it came from and how it developed, but why it has proven to be so resilient.

Initially I answered quite glibly, that answering those questions, important ones, did not fall into my purview. Let some other scholar tackle them. This subject would make an important book, or better, books. Perhaps I would put one of my doctoral students on to this. But ultimately my interlocutors convinced me that without the myth, *We Remember with Reverence and Love* would be incomplete and would leave my readers dangling. So I ended up tackling it, in what I realize is a tentative and hopefully suggestive manner, by devoting a chapter, entitled "The Corruption of History, The Betrayal of Memory," to the question hurled at me by so many.

That chapter, which in fact lay beyond the scope of my extensive primary material research, led me to see how the myth of silence sprouted in the latter part of the 1960s as an engaged and enraged generation of young Jewish activists, imbibing, and indeed playing a formative role in creating, the heady youth rebellion, began to challenge the elders of their communities, whom they defined as the "Jewish establishment," a subset of the hated establishment responsible for racism, the war in Vietnam, class inequalities, and the like. Like so many other young people, college students in particular, they castigated the dominant practices and prevailing rhetoric of the America they had grown up in. They took it to task for its emphasis on consensus and compromise with evil, its pressures towards conformity and willingness to shed ideology in order to get ahead. No institution lay outside the scope of the fury of the youthful rebels as they trained their attention on the corrupt workings of the government, the universities, the families and communities of the middle class.

For those insurgents who had been raised in a variety of ethnic communities, the late 1960s provided a time to lambast the leaders of the organizations and institutions that represented their group. According to these young people, the adults who ran the institutions that made up their ethnic enclave had too long faced the larger society with an accommodationist, conciliatory and assimilationist persona, ignoring the violence which American society had perpetrated upon them. Among the energized young people of the late 1960s, African Americans, Japanese Americans, and Native Americans, among others, stood out as examples of those who held up their establishments for harsh criticism for the sin of having neglected to condemn American society harshly enough for the sins of the past and present directed against their people, for having given America a too-easy pass for its crimes. They reserved some of their harshest rhetoric for group leaders who went out of their way to understate the evil perpetrated by America and to counsel soft rather than harsh rhetoric.

This barb, heard broadly in the heated discourse of the era, gave a prominent place to narratives of the past, as articulated by students and young adults in the various communities. Why, militant young Japanese Americans asked, did our parents, leaders of our communal institutions, our ethnic press, and the like fail to tell us and others about the horrors of the World War II internment camps? Why, militant young African Americans asked, did the community leaders, the creators of our texts and communal practices, downplay, almost to the point of suppression, the brutal history of slavery in favor of a narrative which emphasized achievement over adversity? They all made the tragic history of their group an element in a vast generation gap.

American Jewish college students and others who associated with a group we might roughly call the "new Jews," not only helped shape the general youth rebellion of the late 1960s, but some among them turned their attention to their own Jewish communities and its leaders. In a rhetorical flood which echoed in tone, tenor, and message that of their peers, they lobbed a critique at their own establishment, and in that condemnation of the status quo they had much to say about the Holocaust and what they believed to be the failure of the Jewish communal institutions and their leaders to confront it, either as it proceeded along its deadly pace in the 1930s and 1940s, or in its post-war aftermath.

These young "new Jews" took on a variety of issues, not just that of the Holocaust and its memory. They also critiqued the Jewish leadership for devoting too little attention to education, squandering resources on superficialities, and not instilling genuine group pride. They condemned rabbis, Jewish community center workers, federation activists, educators, and others for going along too willingly with the corruption of American society. Despite the programs at the summer camps that they had attended, despite the community events, pedagogic material, and sermons, they boldly claimed that the subject of the Holocaust had never surfaced. They charged with utter certainty that the adults who held tightly to the reins of power purposely blotted out the memory of the Holocaust because it jarred with the communal agenda of accommodation and assimilation.

Powerful and long lasting implications flowed from the words composed by this generation of young Jews, who like their peers put little stock in subtlety or nuance. For one, these young people grew up to become an establishment, as it were, in their own time, and they continued to assert the truth which had seemed so right when they first trumpeted it. That is, they continued, whether they became rabbis, historians, journalists, literary critics, directors of communal organizations, and active members of a range of Jewish institutions who shaped and participated in community projects, to believe in what they had said decades earlier. In the decades beyond their youth, as they matured and made up the leadership and membership of the Jewish communities, they consistently repeated this assertion as an incontestable fact. That fact, that the post-war generation had ignored the Holocaust, allowed them to claim that not only had they "discovered" it but also that they, unlike those who had directed the organizations, institutions, schools, summer camps, community centers, synagogues, and such in the post-war period, did so from an assertively particularistic and uncompromising perspective which in an unembarrassed manner asserted Jewish difference and distinctiveness. Unlike those who came before them, they said starting in the late 1960s and then into the end of the twentieth century and into the twenty-first, that they had exchanged the shallow obsequiousness which characterized the Jews of the much demonized 1950s for a willingness to boldly shriek, as the phrase went, "truth to power," even if they had to do so in uncomfortable ways. That is, the myth of silence served to confirm a generational narrative.

Because the young Jewish militants of the 1960s, so much in line with the style and substance of their era, produced so much in the way of written texts, they left behind a compendium of documents on which future historians, from the 1980s and beyond, could draw as they began to write the history of post-war America. Until then historians did not yet engage with the developments of the years after World War II, but by the 1980s, with just enough distance and enough archives, the subject emerged as a focus of scholarship. By the 1980s younger scholars entered the profession and for many of them the post-war existed as history as opposed to part of their own lived experiences. These scholars also could turn to the rhetorical output of the "new Jews" to learn what had happened in the post-war. Thus by the second to last decade of the twentieth century we began to see the first journal articles and then books, or chapters in books, which focused on the years following the conclusion of World War II and the 1950s.

For anyone wanting to write something about the history of post-war American Jews and their relationship to the Holocaust, the words of the late 1960s generation proved to be foundational. Here they had broadsides, articles, manifestos, and books that offered a very clear statement as to what had happened. These polemical works provided the evidence not only of the culture of criticism which rocked America in those years, but also proof of the now assumed truth that the post-war years had been resoundingly silent when it came to the Holocaust. As they were used, these works served as handy and accessible primary documents, less of the late 1960s than of the period which preceded it.

These words proved to be useful to historians who wanted to achieve a variety of ends, which could be seen as fundamentally political. For those who hoped to write a history of the period which took as its theme the post-war American Jewish generation's assimilationist goals, pursued in order to win acceptance into the white middle class during an era shaped by an emphasis on compromise and fitting in, then American Jewry's unwillingness to talk about the Holocaust, to remember it publicly to act upon it politically, served as a compelling piece of evidence. Insofar as it confirmed the historians' assumptions that winning acceptance into the post-war American mainstream, which emphasized sameness, abhorred ideology and suspected deviance, a world that opened up to American Jews in the years immediately following the war's end, then the "fact" that they eschewed talking, writing, thinking, or acting upon the Holocaust made ample sense.

Many of the historians who helped build and sustain the myth of silence put a great deal of stock in the momentous days of early June 1967. The myth of silence in fact pivots on the war between Israel and the Arab countries which commenced that month. According to the dominant paradigm of American Jewish history, that war transformed the Jews of the United States. It functions as a key watershed in the periodization of that history.

Some scholars have seen Israel's military victory as a critical moment that finally gave American Jews something to be proud of, and which shook them out of their post-war lethargy. The brilliance of Israel's military might pushed American Jews into a "sudden" willingness to be demonstratively Jewish. Once invigorated by Israel, American Jews could now confront, as articulated by these makers of the myth, that which they could not before, memorialize that which they previously shunted aside, and go public with a story that heretofore they had veiled in obscurity. Israel's

1967 military bravado, an event which, by coincidence, took place as the youth rebellion churned, provided American Jews with the backbone which they had lacked. That backbone made it possible for them to bring the Holocaust out of its hiding place.

Other historians, writers, and intellectuals have offered a different kind of take on the meaning of 1967, but for them that date resonates just as profoundly in terms of American Jews' willingness to go public with, and derive political capital from, the Holocaust. They have claimed that until 1967 Israel occupied a relatively low place on the American Jewish agenda, just as the Holocaust did. But after that *annus mirabilis* in modern Jewish history, Israel climbed to the top of their political and communal concerns, and in order to support, sustain, and advocate for Israel, American Jews, the leadership in particular, extricated the Holocaust from its marginality and pushed it into the center of the rhetorical arsenal. According to this particular iteration of the myth, as American Jews sought to make their case for Israel and also transformed Israel into a sacred religious symbol, they found use for the Holocaust, something which they had not done or needed to do before. The memorialization of the Holocaust as such had, according to one set of perpetrators of the myth, little or nothing to do with the tragedy of the six million and everything to do with contemporary politics.

Whatever their aims, scholars who have pinpointed the turning point in the prominence of the Holocaust in American Jewish life and culture at the moment of the 1967 war, have turned to rhetoric of the late 1960s radical youth as evidence that justified their conclusion. In doing so they have violated what I consider to be a bottom line necessity in the practice of history, namely, a thorough, deep, systematic, and broad immersion in the primary sources. Historians have an obligation to not make claims about silence without a careful analysis of the historic record. They can claim that silence reigned only after digging deeply and widely in the sources.

Likewise the myth of silence owed something of its tenacity with the Jewish public and its attractiveness to historians because it dovetailed with the words of the survivors living in America in the years beyond the post-war period, the 1970s into the present. By the 1970s and especially in the two subsequent decades, Holocaust survivors, now mature adults who had settled down firmly in their once new homes, finished struggling for a living, and completed the raising their American children, began to behave in relatively new ways. While they had always acted politically as a bloc and had always participated in building the memorial culture in America, as I demonstrate in *We Remember with Reverence and Love*, survivors now, like many Americans in this end of the twentieth-century mode, insisted on telling their stories and sharing their memories of what had happened to them both during the most dreadful days of their suffering and upon their liberation and resettlement in America. While this is not the place to interrogate how they recalled what had happened to them and what their agendas may have been, they shared their memories many decades after the events took place. In sharing those memories they have insisted on the superiority of oral history over archival and other paper sources, and historians have accepted their words as true statements of past events.

The survivor witness programs, like those undertaken with many other people, operated on the assumption that memory equaled fact. Notwithstanding the overwhelming conclusion of cognitive scientists and others who have studied the spurious and flawed nature of memory, historians already predisposed towards the myth, now had yet another form of corroboration which confirmed the truth that the public world of post-war American Jewry constituted one in which no one wanted to hear what had happened to those who had undergone the ordeal of the Nazi conquest of Jewish Europe. If no one in the American Jewish community cared to learn the details, then surely the places Jews occupied—schools, synagogues, organizational gatherings, and the community press—must surely have been devoid of discussion of the Holocaust. Because of the nearly sacred role adopted by the survivors and accorded to them by late twentieth century American Jewry, few historians have been comfortable with the idea of interrogating those memories and this further ground the myth of silence firmly into the soil of the communal culture.

The historians who have bought into the words of the late 1960s radicals and the retrospective statements of survivors, among others, frankly ought to have known better than to take what emerged as communal memory and inscribe it into their scholarship. Those memories and politically-charged declarations should have served not as the stopping points for scholars but rather as the starting point. If most or even all survivors, for example, have said in their oral histories that in the communities where they settled no one ever mentioned the Holocaust, then it behooves the historian to search the primary sources of that city, read the programs of public meetings, discover the documents of the organizations, immerse themselves in the local Jewish press. Do those documents confirm the memories of Holocaust avoidance or do they offer an alternative portrait?

I pose these here as rhetorical questions because they provided me with my research plan, and what I found amounted to the complete opposite of the survivor memory. Nearly all American Jewish communities into the early 1960s (and no doubt beyond) staged, for example, an annual Warsaw Ghetto Memorial program. Organizers invited survivors to stand on the platform and light memorial candles, and asked one or more of them to talk about what had happened to them. The same questions must be asked about the claims of survivors that when they came to America they met indifference and even hostility everywhere, including in the *landsmanshaftn*, the hometown societies of the Polish communities that had been founded in America a half century or more earlier. They may remember it that way, but the records, the minute books and program notes of these groups, tell a very different story. Besides documenting the clubs' efforts to find survivors from their town and offer them material assistance, the minutes of the meetings testify to the joy when survivors showed up, the excitement articulated in a nearly sacred tone, that one of their "*geblibbene*," those who had been left, physically appeared. Narratives of what had happened to them as individuals and to the destroyed community made up the stuff of the societies' documentary material. Further, as organizations made up of septuagenarians and beyond whose American-raised children had little or no connection to the home town, the *landsmanshaftn* recognized the need from a very practical stand point to have the dues of new, young working members. Rather than slamming the door on the survivors they eagerly tried to get them to join. While no systematic oral history project like the ones that would blossom decades later developed in these years, these community documents provide a very different picture of post-war American Jewish life.

How deeply in fact has the myth of silence been planted into organized American Jewish community life beyond the small community of historians? How tenacious a hold does it have in the American Jewish popular imagination? To what degree does it continue to dominate the memory culture down to this day? I might answer that in two ways by pointing out the reactions I received to both public presentations about this project and then to the published book. I do so, particularly the former, not to deprecate or mock the people who attended, and still attend, the lectures or to be ungrateful to the institutions around the country which have invited me to speak. But rather their incredulous reactions say much about the iron-strong hold of the myth.

Some set of audience members who may have been young children in the 1950s or teenagers decidedly declaim that where they lived, where they went to camp, the synagogues or Hebrew schools they attended, no mention of the Holocaust was ever heard. When I note, however, that *The World Over*, a publication of the Jewish Education Association given out free to every child enrolled in a Jewish school in the 1950s, contained articles in many issues that had something to say about the Holocaust, they will tell me that I am wrong. When I point out that the most widely circulating Jewish history textbook for children, Deborah Pessin's *The Jewish People*, contained in its third volume, which dealt with the modern period, a lengthy chapter on the catastrophe of the World War II era, they are certain it was not there. In reaction to my statement that the weekly radio broadcast "The Eternal Light," sponsored by the Jewish Theological Seminary, aired many dramas set during the catastrophic years of the Holocaust, they reply, that their family listened to the show regularly and do not remember any like that. While they express fond memories of the magazine, the book, and the radio dramas, they manifest a deep resistance to my statement, based on empirical evidence, that they contained Holocaust related material. With utter certainty those attending the lecture will similarly note that their hometown Jewish newspaper, the *Wisconsin Jewish Chronicle*, Boston's *Jewish Advocate*, or the *Chicago Jewish Sentinel*, made little of the Holocaust in the post-war years. Indeed, even when I come in armed with handouts, photocopies of articles from these publications, I tend to get from more than one individual a firm, "you cannot be right," articulated often in a tone between anger and dismay.

What I hear instead from those in attendance, some of whom serve as professional Holocaust educators, are a string of memories of that era, statements as to what they think they remember, what their parents may have told them about the post-war era, what they heard in a sermon, or read in a book which disseminated the myth of silence. They do not want to let go of the myth because its tentacles have grabbed the communal culture.

So too, some of the reviewers of *We Remember* cannot distinguish between fact and received wisdom, reflecting a communal will to not part with the comfortable truth of the myth. Reviews in such publications as *Commentary*, the *Forward*, and others have made what I consider to be a leap in logic which points to the importance of the myth in sustaining communal ideas about itself. Diner, they have said, on the one hand, has hit us over the head with too much evidence, too many examples, a surplus of details. She drowns her readers in a surfeit of sources, hoping to convince by the sheer volume and weight of her material. But having admitted that the gravitas of the evidence clearly lies on my side, the reviewers contend that what I have presented does not constitute evidence which would undermine the truth that post-war American Jews could find no place in the public realm to confront the Holocaust. The memorial texts, ceremonies, political and fundraising action, the sermons, textbooks, and letters to the editor and to public officials, just do not constitute remembering and acting upon those memories. Despite my deliberately assembled tsunami of material, the paradigm holds, and basically asserts that because they, the Jews of the post-war period, did not do what we–American Jews shaped by the upheavals of the late 1960s—do, then it just does not amount to their having constructed a memorial culture.

None of the reviewers have been able to offer an alternative interpretation of the appearance and dissemination of the books, articles, sermons, songs, pageants, memorial markers, calls to political action, fundraising propaganda, film strips, poems, editorials, radio broadcasts, and on and on that American Jewry, in its great diversity based on ideology, class, age, region, language, religious sentiments, produced in the post-war period which took as their theme and the reason for their creation the horrific experiences of the Jews of Europe under the German Nazi boot. If the Jews of the United States in the years after World War II through the end of the Eichmann trial in 1962 did not remember the Holocaust and did not care about it, how to explain these works?

American Jewry has since the end of the 1960s become so wrapped up in a narrative of the post-war period that takes the silence as a given that it cannot, at least not to date, depart from its myth. This myth frankly makes it feel good about itself, as a community, which it believes does remember, directed by a leadership group which in large part is made up of the veterans, figurative and literal, of the late 1960s who want to be able to claim that they themselves undid the evils of the pernicious post-war period when the Holocaust constituted taboo topic, an uninvited guest to the community table, a reflection of a widespread, self-imposed collective amnesia.

Inherent in the constant iteration and perpetration of the myth of silence is a valorization of what a later generation of American Jews did vis-à-vis the Holocaust and the kind of memorial practices which it constructed. As they have come to celebrate their own patterns of Holocaust remembrance, they have felt compelled to contrast themselves with the Jews of the post-war period, and to lay at their feet the claim that in those years American Jews had turned their backs on the harrowing images of the destroyed six million Jews. These late twentieth century and early twenty-first century Jews are firmly convinced that they would never have behaved in such a seemingly timid manner when it came to memorializing the Holocaust.

As long as community leaders and intellectuals have a stake in repeating the myth of silence, the more they will distort history and obscure the complicated history of the earlier era when American Jews had much to say about the European Jewish catastrophe, doing so in a multiplicity of ways. Whether in liturgy or journalism, in pedagogy or sermons, in staged ceremonies or in the deliberations of their organizations and the discussions of their youth groups, the tragic fate of European Jewry coursed prominently through their public culture. It moved them, frightened and angered them. It stirred them to action and they consistently designated times, places, and modes to say so.

They reflected widely and broadly on the horrific set of events, the Holocaust, so as to remember it for its own sake, and to teach and learn more about the fate of its victims with whom they identified, referring to them as "we," "us," and "ours." They incorporated into their communal cultures images, words, names, and references to the catastrophe.

Yet in perpetuating the myth of silence by claiming that the shallow, assimilating Jews of America in the two decades that followed the end of World War II had shunned the Holocaust and made it utterly marginal to their public lives, historians and others produced a flawed history and perpetrated an injustice to the past. By ignoring the full and variegated historic record, they essentially defamed a group of Jewish women and men who had in fact confronted, as they could, the enormity of the losses, had taken note of the gravity of the cultural destruction, tried to pick up the pieces of a shattered Jewish world, and experimented with language and modes of expression to create memorials and other projects that fit their time and place. The Jews of post-war America, rather than ignoring the Holocaust, instead should be seen as a group which constantly sought ways to fit it into their communal culture and political action. They searched for ways and times to weave it into the texture of their Jewish projects, and what they created they believed to be fitting memorials to the six million. They did what they could and took pride in having done so, believing that they simultaneously kept alive the memory of what had been lost and helped improve America and the world in the process.

SILENCE RECONSIDERED

An afterword

Eric J. Sundquist

We now know—beyond argument, it would seem—that there was no silence about the Holocaust in the first decade and a half of its aftermath. And yet there was. How else explain the counter-claims of silence so frequently stated and adamantly professed that no collection of essays will ever fully refute it?

"Silence," of course, implies a categorical condition, and any effort to refute "the myth of silence," no less categorical in its own way, may well compound the problem. By comparison with the "era of the witness," as Annette Wieviorka calls the post-Eichmann trial years,[1] during which testimony, along with scholarship and representations in many media, began to flow more rapidly toward the flood tide of the 1990s, the years 1945–60 might better be thought of as "quiet" or "reticent," an era of response to the Holocaust marked first by an explosion of testimony and inquiry, and then intermittently by shock, incredulity, evasion, and repression. If historians writing in Yiddish, along with ghetto scribes and camp prisoners, began to document the Nazi genocide even before the term "genocide" existed—coined by Raphael Lemkin in 1943, the term first appeared in print in his *Axis Rule in Occupied Europe* the following year—and survivors soon told their stories in many languages, the effective integration of the stories of the victims and the stories of the perpetrators lay far in the future. If impressive scholarly work emerged as quickly as documentary evidence could be assembled, some of the postwar era's most widely read English-language studies, such as Alan Bullock's *Hitler: A Study in Tyranny* (1952; rev. ed. 1962) and William Shirer's *Rise and Fall of the Third Reich* (1960), clearly subordinated the mass murder of Jews to the greater cataclysm of the war in Europe. If some survivors willingly told their stories in print or orally, and if some families and communities willingly heard those stories and commemorated the dead in the early years, later survivor testimony and the psychological and interpretive literature devoted to it abound in claims of silences both painfully chosen and painfully imposed.[2]

Writer-survivors have been particularly eloquent on this point. Although Aharon Appelfeld's assertion that the many collections of Holocaust testimony are actually "repressions" whose dexterous weaving of facts "veil the inner truth" is surely reductive, his contention that "the survivor did not know what to do with his experiences" and therefore oscillated between speech and silence is incisive. "If he had been able to keep silent," Appelfeld writes, the survivor would have done so willingly, yet neither his own "impulse to seek a moral" nor the requests of others for an explanation made the telling any easier. Indeed, "the reckoning was impossible," and "because it was beyond one's power, one took refuge in silence."[3] Second-generation writers have often felt the silence just as acutely. "Silence was the bitter syntax of survivors. The secret codes that could never be cracked," writes Thane Rosenbaum, a son of survivors, in his novel *Second Hand Smoke* (1999),[4] while David Grossman, though not himself the child of survivors—his mother was a native-born Palestinian Jew, his father a 1936 immigrant from Poland—has described his generation, the Israeli children of the early 1950s, as living "in a thick and densely populated silence" about the Holocaust, one broken only by the daily ten-minute reading of the names of missing relatives on the radio.[5]

Even if such testimonies, and not only among prominent writers, can easily be multiplied, the counter-evidence amassed by Hasia Diner and others demonstrates that such claims cannot simply be taken at face value. It is also the case, however, that commentary on the question of silence was from the very outset pervasive in reactions to the Nazi genocide, a fact that has surely contributed, paradoxically, to the idea that silence itself was pervasive in the postwar years. A thorough account of Holocaust "silence," as well as the mythology surrounding it, remains to be written. It would require that silence be understood from multiple angles and investigated in many settings, many languages, and many different historical moments.

By way of reflecting on the convincing arguments against silence by the contributors to this volume, we should also recall some of the many ways in which Holocaust silence has always been with us and always will be. A phenomenon that touches on the most sensitive and profound issues in theology, epistemology, and ethics; that has the power to convict or exonerate those swept up in a monstrous crime; and that plays some role, whether literal or figurative, in most every eyewitness testimony or artistic representation—such a phenomenon demands our continued scrutiny. In speaking of silence, in probing its deep recesses and measuring its dark implications, survivors and others, it might be said, broke silence and kept it at the same time. Silence, yes, but on whose part, of what kind, and for what purpose?

"For the first time in years, the tortured of Europe dare to cry out in their suffering," wrote Isidore Sobeloff, Executive Director of the Detroit Jewish Welfare Federation, in a fundraising note carried in the *Jewish Social Studies Quarterly* in late 1945. "Now, after all these years, we can hear their cries. We can reach them, we can help them—those who before military victory did not know whether their voices would ever be heard again by the outside world."[6]

In years to come the seeming silence of the victims would often be construed as a function less of their own muted cries than of the world's refusal to hear them, even its active suppression of them. Arguments about the "silence" of President Franklin Roosevelt's administration and those in the Jewish community with whom it consulted, notably Stephen S. Wise, became an indictment with the publication of Arthur Morse's *While Six Million Died* (1967) and later a field of scholarship whose foremost articulation is David Wyman's *Abandonment of the Jews* (1984).[7] Such arguments may never prove completely that the Roosevelt administration, by taking earlier action on the ambiguous evidence of genocide it was presented or by employing different wartime tactics once the evidence was more conclusive, could have made more than a marginal difference in the number of Jews or others rescued—arguably, any difference would have mattered—and rebuttals have assumed the form of charging Wyman and company with propagating another myth—namely, "the myth of rescue."[8]

What they have clearly demonstrated, however, is that war-time protests on the part of groups such as the Committee for a Jewish Army of Stateless and Palestinian Jews, led by Peter Bergson (Hillel Kook)—notably, its ongoing ad campaigns about the refugee crisis and the onset of genocide in the *New York Times* and other venues, as well as its 1943 staging of "We Will Never Die," a theatrical pageant written by Ben Hecht, in New York, Philadelphia, Boston, Chicago, and Los Angeles—broke through the official silence in a pointed way. Whether made as a public call to arms in Europe, the United States, and Mandate Palestine, or recorded in the clandestine words of those imprisoned in ghettos and camps, condemnation of silence on the part of Allied leaders and the world in general began during the war and has been reiterated through the present day. "How was it possible that men, women, and children were being burned and that the world kept silent?" asked Elie Wiesel in a famous passage in *Night* (1958; trans. 1960).[9] Although Wiesel became the foremost prosecutor of the world's silence—the original title of his book when it appeared in Yiddish in 1956 was *Un di velt hot geshvign* (*And the World Was Silent*), and a three-volume collection of his shorter writings is aptly titled *Against Silence* (1985)—his protests throughout many works of fiction and commentary against man's silence, as well as God's, passionately recapitulated ideas that were notable less for being new than for the fact that they have seemed to require stating time and again, often in conjunction.

In his opening address of the new school year at Hebrew University in November 1944, for example, Judah Magnes quoted from a document given him four months earlier concerning the arrival and processing of 1,600 French Jews at Birkenau. Of these, one thousand were immediately gassed, and the document described the operation in some detail: the structure of the gas chambers and crematoria; the deception of the "shower" room; the role of the Sonderkommando; and the use of Zyklon B, "a preparation of cyanide which becomes gaseous at a given temperature. In three minutes all were dead." Yet despite the accumulating evidence of Nazi atrocities, Magnes observed, "our minds prefer to reject the truth," and he wondered how it was possible "that this can happen under God's heaven."[10]

The rejection of evident truth, its cloaking in stunned silence, was a perennial concern in discussion of the Holocaust both while it was happening and in the aftermath, but the remainder of Magnes's address pursued a more vexing question.

After considering a variety of ways to comprehend God's reticence, he concluded that anyone seeking "the meaning of these massacrings, this wanton butchery," will not be answered: "from that man God hides His Face." One could only hope, therefore, to emulate Rabbi Isaac Levi of Berdichev, who asked not to comprehend God's ways "but only this: Do I suffer for *Thy sake?*" For us too, Magnes determined, "it would be enough to ask, not *what* is the meaning of this anguish, but that it *have* a meaning; and that our need of asking be so sincere that it becomes a prayer: Teach us only this: Does man suffer for Thy sake, O Lord?" And yet the title of Magnes's address, taken from Psalm 44:23, was not a question but an affirmation: "For Thy Sake Are We Killed All Day Long"—and one, in fact, whose subsequent line in the scripture, not quoted but surely taken for granted by Magnes, makes God's purpose more mysterious and demanding: "It is for Your sake that we are slain all day long, that we are regarded as sheep to be slaughtered."[11] By this account, not only was God silent but the voice of scripture, one that especially haunted postwar Israel's confrontations with the Holocaust and its immigrant survivors, appeared to enjoined the victims to passivity and silence in the face of their own destruction.

Condemnations of the world's silence also led at times to calls for judgment and punishment. Such was the case in Zvi Kolitz's short story "Yossel Rakover's Appeal to God" (1946), a work of fiction originally taken to be recovered eyewitness testimony written in the final hours of the Warsaw Ghetto uprising and later found in a bottle. Before his message concludes with the words of the *Shema*, Rakover proclaims his belief in God, despite God's having turned away from the Jews of Europe, and his pride, indeed, his honor, in being a Jew when it is hard to be one. Insofar as humanity has evidently been "abandoned to its evil instincts," however, Rakover issues a challenge to God: "I should like to ask You, O Lord—and this question burns in me like a consuming fire—*What more, O, what more must transpire before You unveil Your countenance again to the world?*" Those who have been "murdered by the millions" have a right to know: "What are the limits of your forbearance?" It is not with God's silence alone that Rakover is concerned, however, for he pleads that God's vengeance be visited not specifically on the perpetrators ("the murderers have already passed sentence upon themselves and will never escape it") but rather on "those who are silent in the face of murder ... those who express sympathy with the drowning man but refuse to rescue him."[12]

There were multiple reasons why victims might go silently to the slaughter—delusion, catatonic shock, exhausted resignation, religious faith, stoic defiance—but eyewitnesses who wrote from inside the inferno of the death camps both corroborated that silence and called it into question. After describing the increasingly adept forms of deception by which the SS reassured arriving transports about their future in Auschwitz, Filip Müller, a survivor of the Sonderkommando, reflected on his own and his comrades' mute paralysis while new prisoners seemed to file unknowingly past them on their way to the gas chamber. Their reticence grew from a tangle of motives—a sense of futility, an instinct for self-preservation, the slim hope that some might survive to bear witness—but Müller added one that is no less surprising for appearing to be a rationalization after the fact:

> We stood rooted against the wall, paralysed by a feeling of impotence and the certainty of their and our inexorable fate. … Hitler and his henchmen had never made a secret of their attitude to the Jews nor of their avowed intention to exterminate them like vermin. The whole world knew it, and knowing it remained silent; was not their silence equivalent to consent? It was considerations like these that led my companions and me to the conviction that the world consented to what was happening here before our eyes.[13]

Unlike Müller, who wrote retrospectively and may have composed his conscience accordingly, Zalmen Gradowski, a member of the Sonderkommando who left four testimonies buried at Auschwitz, gave a more complex and nuanced account. The uncommon lyricism that marks his portrait of a transport of Czech Jews on their way to the gas chamber is pierced by the voices of those who by no means went silently to their deaths. Gradowski witnessed songs of solidarity and protest among the victims, as well as accusations flung in the faces of the killers:

> Another woman, this time a lovely, blond girl, had addressed the officers: "Wretched murderers! You look at me with your thirsty, bestial eyes. You glut yourselves on my nakedness. Yes, this is what you have been waiting for. In your civilian lives you could never have dreamed about it. You hoodlums and criminals, you have finally found the right place to satisfy your sadistic eyes. But you won't enjoy this for long. Your game's almost over, you can't kill all the Jews. And you will pay for it all." And suddenly she leaped at them and struck Oberscharführer Voss, the director of the crematoria, three times. Clubs came down on her head and shoulders. She entered the bunker with her head covered with wounds, and the warm blood caressed her body lovingly; she laughed for joy, for her hand still tingled from the blow she had dealt the notorious killer's face. She had achieved her final goal, and proceeded calmly to her death.

Having done his terrible work of collecting and burning the bodies, Gradowski, against the backdrop of "ovens blaz[ing] furiously, like waves in a storm," reiterated the woman's promise of vengeance when he addressed an audience he could only hope would one day hear his voice:

> If you who are free should chance to notice this great fire; if some evening you should raise your eyes to the deep, blue sky and see that it is covered by flames, then you will know that this is the same hellfire that burns here endlessly. Perhaps your heart will feel its heat, and your hands, as cold as ice, will extinguish it. Or perhaps, your heart bolstered with courage, you will exchange the present victims of this never-ending inferno for those who first ignited it, that *they* may be consumed by its flames.[14]

Not only fear that their voices would never be heard but also fear that their words would fall on deaf ears, rendering witnesses silent even when they found words in which to convey their experiences, is a hallmark of many of the most evocative testimonies. After describing the black market that surrounded the extraction of gold teeth from corpses Miklos Nyiszli reaffirmed his doubt that his story, should he live to tell it, would be believed. Because "words, descriptions are quite incapable of furnishing anyone with an accurate picture of what goes on here," he wrote, "my efforts to photograph in my mind all I see and engrave it in my memory are, after all, completely useless."[15] "Useless knowledge," the French political prisoner Charlotte Delbo, who survived Auschwitz and Ravensbrück, called it. Like Delbo, who "learned / over there / that you cannot speak to others," Primo Levi recorded his recurring Auschwitz dream in which he was tormented by "the ever-repeated scene of the unlistened-to story."[16]

It was not victims alone who feared that those presented with incontrovertible evidence of the Holocaust would either not believe it or quickly forget it. In an essay published in the *New York Times Magazine* in January 1944, Arthur Koestler placed himself among the "screamers" whose reports of Nazi atrocities were greeted with disbelief. Facts, photographs, and eyewitness reports were of no avail, wrote Koestler, whose lectures on starvation, transports, and mass murder to Allied troops in England over a period of three years had made little impression. "You can convince them for an hour," he said, "then they shake themselves, their mental self-defence begins to work and in a week the shrug of incredulity has returned like a reflex temporarily weakened by a shock."[17] If soldiers going into battle suppressed such truths about the enemy, it may be no surprise that others, learning of the events at a greater distance, might "prefer to reject the truth," as Magnes said, or absorb the shock and then reflexively shrug it off.

By the end of 1944 and certainly by the time of liberation in 1945, and even more certainly within a few years following, it would have been difficult to speak of silence about the events that later came to be known as the Holocaust. Although the discovery and evaluation of archival materials from the ghettos of Warsaw, Lodz, Vilna, and elsewhere would take years, historians and survivors writing in Yiddish, Polish, German, and other languages produced a wealth of information during and soon after the war, much of it quickly translated into English. Consider just the dozens of articles in leading American newspapers and popular journals with titles such as "Nazi Mass Killing Laid Bare" (*New York Times*, 1944), "Merchants of Murder" (*Newsweek*, 1944), "Here the Nazi Butchers Wasted Nothing" (*Saturday Evening Post*, 1944), "Slaughter of 4,000,000 in Nazi Camp Disclosed" (*Los Angeles Times*, 1945), "Dachau: Experimental Murder" (*Colliers*, 1945), and "Eyes of Breathing Cadavers Reflect Grotesque Flicker of Hope in Nazi-Made Hell" (*Washington Post*, 1945), as well as works by survivors and observers written in English or quickly translated with titles such as *One Year in Treblinka* (Jankiel Wiernik, 1944), *This Was Oswiecim: The Story of a Murder Camp* (Philip Friedman, 1946), *Balance Sheet of Extermination* (Jacob Lestchinsky, 1946), *Smoke over Birkenau* (Seweryna Szmaglewska, 1947), *Escape from the Pit* (Renya Kulkielko, 1947), *Five Chimneys* (Olga Lengyel, 1947), *I Was a Doctor in Auschwitz* (Gisella Perl, 1948), *I Did Not Interview the Dead* (David Boder, 1949), *The Theory and Practice of Hell* (Eugene Kogon, 1950), *The Final*

Solution (Gerald Reitlinger, 1953), and *Harvest of Hate* (Léon Poliakov, 1954)[18]. Confronted with such evidence, the public, at least in the United States, would have been hard pressed to believe that silence was a problem to be overcome.

If there was no silence about the Holocaust, however, there was still significant apprehension about silence as wartime fears about the world's silence bled into post-war fears that the events would be ignored or forgotten. Writing in the same month as Koestler, Shlomo Katz was already wondering how to "transform the memory of this experience into a civilizing force that will tend to prevent the recurrence of such calamities." He worried, however, that once legal retribution had run its course the nations of the world would "erase the memory of what has happened from their minds even while they are rebuilding their ruined cities," and he asked what could be done about the "deep scar" that would be left in human consciousness: "Will it suffice merely to comb our hair back over the place where the skull was broken and where perhaps permanent damage was done to the brain?"[19] Repression prompted by horror, in other words, might give way to repression prompted by political expediency.

Soon after the war a further apprehension about forgetting was expressed. Instead of a lack of knowledge or its repression or erasure, knowledge itself, some feared, could lead to silence. Isaac Rosenfeld was tormented by the surfeit of information about the Jewish genocide—a surfeit that was, nevertheless, inadequate. "By now we know all there is to know. But it hasn't helped; we still don't understand," he observed in his 1948 essay "Terror beyond Evil." As an event "beyond all extremes—incomprehensible, unattainable to reason," what happened to the Jews of Europe constituted for Rosenfeld a "terror absolute" that yielded only "numbness" and could not be penetrated despite the fact that "it lies so close at hand."[20] Writing a year later, Solomon Bloom worried that the world was in danger not of forgetting the "extraordinary catastrophe [that] struck the Jewish people" but rather of "fearing to think about it." In discounting it as a consequence of fascism, sadism, or militarism gone mad, said Bloom, we risk "killing true knowledge by premature under-standing."[21] Whereas Rosenfeld recoiled from terrible knowledge that began where "our old evil left off," Bloom recoiled from terrible knowledge too blithely cate-gorized by an age that "abhors the unexplained event."

Nearly two decades after Katz feared that the world would forget the Holocaust, and Rosenfeld feared that no degree of knowledge could make it comprehensible, and Bloom feared that it would be chalked up to aberrant ideologies, the same questions surged forth once more during the trial of Adolf Eichmann in Jerusalem— as though the questions had never been asked and no answers ventured. For all of the ways in which the claim that the Eichmann trial "broke the silence" about the Holocaust is misleading, then, it cannot simply be set aside. "What had been silenced and suppressed gushed out and became common knowledge," Haim Gouri has written of the trial's effect in Israel.[22] There and elsewhere its extensive media coverage provoked public discussion of a kind not previously witnessed.[23]

Other kinds of broken silence were also evident. The dead themselves, it was said repeatedly, were to be given a voice. Gideon Hausner, the chief prosecutor, proposed in his opening speech to represent the "six-million accusers" who "cannot rise to their feet and point an accusing finger towards him who sits in the dock." Because "their blood cries out, but their voice is not heard," proclaimed Hausner, "I will be their spokesman and in their name I will unfold the awesome indictment."[24] The living, too, now had a voice. In contrast to the Nuremberg trials, the Eichmann trial was notable for the testimony of survivor witnesses, who one by one condemned the accused and the regime for which he stood—or spoke all the more dramatically by falling into convulsed grief or complete silence, the most famous instance being the testimony of the Israeli writer Ka-Tzetnik (Yehiel Dinur), who spoke haltingly about the other-worldly terrors of "planet Auschwitz" and then fainted dead away.[25] The Third Reich likewise had a voice in the testimony of Eichmann himself—on the radio in Israel, on television in the United States and elsewhere, and even in the glossy, middlebrow pages of *Life* magazine, where a version of his testimony, garishly entitled "I Transported Them ... To the Butcher," put his prevarications and moral myopia fully on display. "It would be as pointless to blame me for the whole Final Solution of the Jewish Problem as to blame the official in charge of the railroads over which the Jewish transports traveled," Eichmann averred. "Where would we have been if everyone had thought things out in those days?"[26]

Above all, however, the trial was about remembering—or rather, about never forgetting. For his part, Israeli Prime Minister David Ben-Gurion dismissed comparisons to Nuremberg and even treated Eichmann's guilt as a secondary consideration. He contended rather that the purpose of the trial, beyond its domestic and international implications for the state of Israel itself, was hortatory, a means to demonstrate the long reach of justice, to clarify the particularity of the Jewish genocide, and to prevent future generations from forgetting this essential point. As Ben-Gurion told the *New York Times* on December 19, 1960: "We want to establish before the nations of the world how millions of people, because they happened to be Jews, and one million babies, because they happened to be Jewish babies, were murdered by the Nazis. We ask the nations not to forget it."[27]

How, it might be wondered, could anyone have forgotten the systematic, often industrialized slaughter of some six million Jews? And yet, it seems, they had forgotten, and discussion of the fact circled continually around the question of silence. The highly inflamed controversy over Hannah Arendt's *Eichmann in Jerusalem* (1963), wrote Irving Howe, grew from "a guilt pervasive, unmanageable, yet seldom declared at the surface of speech or act." One useful result to be salvaged from the "debris" of the quarrel, Howe remarked, was that people were at last "acknowledging emotions that had long gone unused."[28] It was thus not only the young radicals of the late 1960s who later attacked the silence of their elders; the elders accused themselves of having been silent. While avoiding the misinterpretations that characterized some replies to Arendt, Harold Rosenberg maintained that the anguish of Arendt's critics represented a

> recovery of the Jews from the shock of the death camps, a recovery that took fifteen years and is by no means complete (though let no one believe that it could be hastened by silence). Only across a distance of time could the epic accounting begin.[29]

Although there was no shortage of published testimony and documentary images in photographs and film alike during the 1950s, it did take time for the awful magnitude of the event—in conception, in scale, in method—to come more clearly into view and for the Nazis' programmatic effort to eliminate the world's Jews to be comprehended as a distinctive kind of racial murder set apart from the catastrophic violence of total war. As Rosenberg emphasized, it was not that the Holocaust had gone unmentioned or that the facts were unavailable, but instead that their import remained elusive: "For most who lived through this period, the Nuremberg Laws, asphyxiation buses, rabbis scrubbing pavements, boycotts, death marches, the Crystal Night [Kristallnacht] atrocities, gas chambers, are all jumbled together in a vague hurt as of a bruise received in the dark. ... Perhaps no crime in history has been better documented and more vaguely understood." Whether or not Rosenberg was right to characterize the trial as a Greek tragedy with Eichmann the fated protagonist and survivors a chorus shouting their judgment from the gallery—Arendt had advanced a comparable argument—his focus on the proceedings as a media spectacle made a key point:

> It was possible for the first time to visualize the massacres that had taken place across the face of Eastern Europe not as disconnected atrocities, like outbursts of violence in an insane asylum, but as a planned and centralized undertaking aimed at the annihilation of all Jews. By his presence, Eichmann removed the crime from the madhouse and situated it in history.[30]

In the wake of the trial the idea that dormant emotions had been aroused and moral consciousness awakened was commonplace. Although good examples to the contrary make it hard to credit Saul Bellow's contention, expressed in a 1987 letter to Cynthia Ozick, that Jewish American writers had "missed what should have been for them the central event of their time, the destruction of European Jewry," his judgment, in which he included himself, is representative. "Growing slowly aware of this unspeakable evasion," he said, "I didn't even know how to begin to admit it into my inner life."[31]

One might argue that Bellow's early novel *The Victim* (1947), along with his later *Mr. Sammler's Planet* (1970), stands in partial qualification of his censure. So do other postwar American novels of the late 1940s through the 1960s such as Irwin Shaw's *The Young Lions* (1948), John Hersey's *The Wall* (1950), Michael Blankfort's *The Juggler* (1952), Leon Uris's *Exodus* (1958), Edward Wallant's *The Pawnbroker* (1961), Katherine Anne Porter's *Ship of Fools* (1962), Meyer Levin's *The Fanatic* (1963), Jerzy Kosinski's *The Painted Bird* (1965), Meyer Levin's *The Stronghold* (1965), and Richard Elman's trilogy *The 28th Day of Elul* (1967), *Lilo's Diary* (1968), and *The Reckoning* (1969), as well as works such as Isaac Bashevis Singer's *The Slave* (1962) and Bernard Malamud's *The Fixer* (1966), which dealt with entirely different historical eruptions of anti-Semitism as a means of approaching the Holocaust. It could be the case, however, that Bellow's judgment was affected by the many European, American, and Israeli writers who actively took Holocaust silence as one of their themes—a list that would include, just through the 1960s, Porter, Wallant, and Kosinski, as well as Tadeusz Borowski, Paul Celan, Nelly Sachs, Primo Levi, Elie Wiesel, Ka-Tzetnik, Charlotte Delbo, Piotr Rawicz, Jorge Semprun, Jurek Becker, and Jakov Lind.[32] Along with the upsurge in theological inquiry into God's silence that commenced in the early 1960s—"the *cri de coeur* of the memorialists of the *tremendum* is the silence of God,"[33] Arthur A. Cohen could write by 1981—the propensity of imaginative writers to make psychological, emotional, and mystical forms of silence constitutive of Holocaust memory no doubt played a significant role in promoting the myth of postwar silence.

Equally important, however, is the fact that no historians, no poets, no novelists, no psychologists, and no theologians, survivors included, up to this point had a shared terminology, let alone a single defining word, with which to frame their reactions. If Eichmann and his victims gave the genocide of the Jews faces and voices previously missing or forgotten, the word "Holocaust" itself, which came into more common use during the trial, gave events well documented but vaguely understood, as Rosenberg put it, a name.

Writing in the *Nation* in January 1943, Philip Bernstein had lamented the failure of the world to have recognized where Nazism could ultimately lead: "A clearer perception ten years ago of the meaning and intent of Hitlerism might have spared the world this holocaust."[34] Although there were a few other such early uses of the word "holocaust"—including the state of Israel's 1948 Declaration of Independence, which referred, in its English translation, to "survivors of the Nazi holocaust in Europe"—it is not irrelevant to the question of silence that the destruction of the European Jews, to borrow the title of Raul Hilberg's pioneering 1961 study, did not become "the Holocaust" until the 1960s, when the term was more frequently adopted as a singular way to conceptualize terrifying events whose significance was still inchoate.

The many terms employed previously—"disaster," "destruction," "catastrophe," "final solution," *khurbn* (in Yiddish), *shoah* (in Hebrew), "genocide," "Hitlerism," and "Auschwitz," among others—were serviceable each in its own way.[35] But the near impossibility of writing about the events nowadays without using "Holocaust," despite its burden of contested ancillary meanings, helps to explain why later generations could look back on the outpouring of wartime and postwar writing and hear silence. It may, however, be more accurate to say that coalescence of usage around "holocaust" and especially "the Holocaust," notwithstanding its problematic connotations of ritual sacrifice, served to distinguish a relatively quiet past from an increasingly garrulous future. Within a matter of decades historians could worry about the proliferation of "Holocaust kitsch," rabbis could bemoan "the Holocaust cult" that had supplanted traditional forms of Jewish identity and observance, and polemicists could decry "the Holocaust industry" as a mercenary shake-down operation.[36]

In worrying that the term obfuscated more than it clarified, moreover, others introduced the danger of new kinds of silence. Bruno Bettelheim contended that its adoption was a defense mechanism comparable to declaring the Holocaust "unimaginable, unspeakable." Seen as a technical term with its own euphemistic qualities, he remarked, "Holocaust" might permit us to "manage [the events] intellectually

where the raw facts, when given their ordinary names, would overwhelm us emotionally."[37] Coming of age with the era of the witness, "Holocaust" at times acquired
its own qualities of talismanic silence. Survivors might seem to have broken their
own silence in the post-Eichmann trial (or at least the post-Six-Day War) years, but
their very demand to be heard, according to Zev Garber and Bruce Ackerman,
threatened to add a "second silence" to that of the victims. When a survivor
"demands that we understand 'The Holocaust' as the most profound, cataclysmic
calamity in history," argued Garber and Ackerman, it forecloses the possibility of any
argument "with those who have suffered and witnessed so much." Like Job, "we
wish instead to lay our hands upon our mouths and speak no more."[38]

The perils of sacrilization were further exacerbated by the temptation on the part
of some survivors to enclose the event in enigmatic silence. The most captivating
instance is Primo Levi's argument that it is not the survivors whose testimony is
recorded who are "the complete witnesses" but instead the "drowned," those "who
saw the Gorgon, [but] have not returned to tell about it or have returned mute." For
Levi, in close quarters with the dead and barely separated from the *muselmänner* at the
very edge of death were the members of the Sonderkommando, whose immersion in
the grisly work of the gas chambers and the crematoria made them "the bearers of a
horrendous secret."[39] Levi's acute testimony has been the subject of much commentary, but to the extent that it endows witness in extremis with a nearly mystical
quality, unknowable in its horrid essence, it also presents the truth of the Holocaust as
a kind of black hole that swallows meaning into itself.

Levi's conception also, one may venture to say, stands in an uncomfortable
relationship with the Nazi claim that the destruction of the Jews was a kind of
sacramental undertaking to be shrouded in silence. The defining example of this
psychic strategy was Heinrich Himmler's notorious October 1943 speech to senior SS
officers, in which he addressed their moral duty to exterminate the Jews by enjoining
them to silence. "I ask of you that what I say in this circle you really only hear and
never speak of," Himmler requested, before discussing the necessity of killing Jewish
women and children, as well as men, lest avengers from this "festering plague" be
born to menace the children and grandchildren of Nazi Germany. Himmler's
incredible proposition "that we [must] take the secret with us to the grave"[40] put
silence to demonic use. Although Levi's veneration for "the drowned" is its precise
antithesis, both may be said to relegate the "Holocaust" to "an incomprehensible
cosmos," in the words of Eva Hoffman, one that risks making us "faithful" to "a
terribilitas that we simultaneously declare to be unimaginable."[41]

In simpler terms, crystallization of Nazi depredations into "the Holocaust" set in
motion an irresolvable debate about the scope of its reference. The planning of the
United States Holocaust Memorial Museum that commenced in 1978, to take a
prominent example, was beset by sharp disagreement about whether it would memorialize only the Jewish dead or all those killed by the Nazis. Although the latter
position ultimately prevailed, this did nothing to forestall continued arguments about
the "uniqueness" and "intentionality" of the mass slaughter of the Jews. It may,
indeed, have obscured the fact that the reciprocal slaughter of some fourteen million

Jews and other non-combatant state enemies, along with prisoners of war, instigated by Hitler and Stalin in the "bloodlands" of Europe between 1933 and 1945 might well be thought of as a set of unified actions whereby "Europe's most murderous regimes did their most murderous work."[42]

Debates about such intricacies in terminology, like debates about more abstract forms of silence, are largely a feature of the post-Eichmann trial era, but that does not mean they have no precedents in early commentary. Long before the precise scope of "the Holocaust" became the subject of ongoing and often acrimonious discussion, there were warnings against silence about the particularity of Jewish destruction as well as the particularity of *this* destruction of Jews within a history of Jewish destruction. Introducing a 1949 conference on "Problems of Research in the Study of the Jewish Catastrophe 1939–45" at the New School for Social Research, Salo Baron addressed the latter problem when he challenged his audience to reexamine its basic understanding of "the great Catastrophe." Too many of us, scholars and laymen alike, said Baron, have come to believe that the event was "but the climax of a long succession of massacres and persecutions which have repeated themselves throughout the history of Jewish dispersion," and he went on to emphasize the available evidence of the Nazis' plan "to eliminate all Jews" and the "immutability of the fate" of Jewish victims who could not have been saved, as might Jews of an earlier era, by conversion.[43]

Describing the new crime of "Hebrewcide"—the murder of a human being solely because of his Jewish birth or ancestry—Marie Syrkin had already insisted four years earlier on Jewish particularity in her critique of "atrocity" films about the liberation of the camps then appearing, though often in truncated or edited form, at movie theaters in many American cities. Despite the visceral emotions experienced by American audiences when confronted with "the carefully contrived equipment used to burn human beings ... [and] the methodically assorted piles of shoes, of eye-glasses, of children's toys, belonging to the murdered," Syrkin argued, movie-goers could too easily come away without any comprehension of the fact that "the faces they had seen were Jewish faces, that the dolls and babies' shoes lying in their appropriate heaps belonged to Jewish children." Because the audience will not know the identity of those "who came in sealed wagons to fill the gas chambers," memory of the Jews, *as Jews*, will be "annihilated in death, just as their bodies had been annihilated in life."[44] Lost among the mass of Nazi victims and forgotten as the unique target of an intentional act to destroy them as a race, Jews would thus be consigned to silence.

Syrkin's fears were unwarranted, but it could easily have proved otherwise—and in some respects has proved otherwise, in both the comparatively tranquil realm of scholarship and in the more vociferous realm of political rhetoric. At a time when indiscriminate use of the word "Holocaust" has nearly drained it of meaning, when Holocaust denial flourishes in new and more rancid forms, and when the state of Israel is accused of playing the trump card of the Holocaust in order to justify or conceal its own war crimes against Palestinians, silence has assumed forms unanticipated but no less disturbing than those with which Hitler's survivors had to contend. Once the last eyewitnesses—whether victims, perpetrators, or bystanders—pass into history, such problems are hardly likely to be diminished. Perhaps, however, we have now reached the point where we can dispense with the myth of silence without dispensing with the question of silence.[45]

Notes

1 Annette Wieviorka, *The Era of the Witness* (1998), trans. Jared Stark (Ithaca, N. Y.: Cornell University Press 2006).

2 See, for example, Shoshana Felman and Dori Laub, *Testimony: Crises of Witnessing in Literature, Psychoanalysis, and History* (New York: Routledge, 1992); Aaron Hass, *The Aftermath: Living with the Holocaust* (New York: Cambridge University Press, 1995); and Henry Greenspan, *On Listening to Holocaust Survivors: Recounting and Life History* (Westport, Conn.: Praeger, 1998).

3 Aharon Appelfeld, *Beyond Despair: Three Lectures and a Conversation with Philip Roth*, trans. Jeffrey M. Green (New York: Fromm International Publishing, 1994), pp. 13–14.

4 Thane Rosenbaum, *Second Hand Smoke* (New York: St. Martin's Press, 1999), p. 18.

5 David Grossman, "Individual Language and Mass Language" (2007), *Writing in the Dark: Essays on Literature and Politics*, trans. Jessica Cohen (New York: Farrar, Straus and Giroux, 2008), p. 71, 73.

6 Isidore Sobeloff quoted in "Notes on Fundraising," *The Jewish Social Service Quarterly* 22 (December 1945), 177.

7 Arthur D. Morse, *While Six Million Died: A Chronicle of American Apathy* (New York: Random House, 1967) and David S. Wyman, *The Abandonment of the Jews: America and the Holocaust, 1941–1945* (New York: Random House, 1984). See also Monty Noam Penkower, *The Jews Were Expendable* (1983; rpt. Detroit: Wayne State University Press, 1988) and David S. Wyman and Rafael Medoff, *A Race against Deth: Peter Bergson, America, and the Holocaust* (New York: New Press, 2002).

8 See William D. Rubinstein, *The Myth of Rescue: Why the Democracies Could Not Have Saved More Jews from the Nazies* (New York: Routledge, 1997). See also Henry L. Feingold, *Bearing Witness: How America and Its Jews Responded to the Holocaust* (Syracuse, N. Y.: Syracuse University Press 1995) and Frank W. Brecher, "The Western Allies and the Holocaust: David Wyman and the Historiography of America's Response to the Holocaust: Counter-Considerations," *Holocaust and Genocide Studies* 5 (1990), 423–46.

9 Elie Wiesel, *Night*, trans. Marion Wiesel (New York: Hill and Wang, 2006), p. 32.

10 Judah Magnes, "For Thy Sake Are We Killed All Day Long," J. L. Magnes, *In the Perplexity of the Times* (Jerusalem: Hebrew University, 1946), pp. 65–67.

11 Magnes, "For Thy Sake Are We Killed All Day Long," pp. 77–78. The scripture continues: "Why do You hide Your face, ignoring our afflictions and distress?" (Psalm 44: 25). For God's promise to hide His face from those who break the covenant, see Deuteronomy 31: 16–18.

12 Zvi Kolitz, "Yossel Rakover's Appeal to God," in Kolitz, *The Tiger beneath the Skin: Stories and Parables of the Years of Death* (New York: Creative Age Press, 1947), pp. 91–94. The story was first published in Yiddish in Buenos Aires in 1946, reprinted in Israel in 1954, translated into German and French in 1955, and into Hebrew in 1965, all the while being taken as an authentic eyewitness document, with the misunderstanding finally corrected in an English edition published in New York in 1968. A 1996 edition, with a text established by Paul Badde, appears in English as *Yosl Rakover Talks to God*, trans. Carol Brown Janeway (London: Jonathan Cape, 1999). In Badde's biographical sketch of Kolitz and his story's strange fate, however, he does not mention that the story appeared in *The Tiger Beneath the Skin*.

13 Filip Müller, *Eyewitness Auschwitz: Three Years in the Gas Chambers*, trans. Susanne Flatauer (Chicago: Ivan R. Dee, 1979), pp. 36–37.

14 Zalmen Gradowski, "The Czech Transport: A Chronicle of the Auschwitz Sonderkommando," in David G. Roskies, ed., *The Literature of Destruction: Jewish Responses to Catastrophe* (New York: The Jewish Publication Society, 1988), pp. 559, 564.

15 Miklos Nyiszli, *Auschwitz: A Doctor's Eyewitness Account* (1946), trans. Tibere Kremer and Richard Seaver (New York: Fawcett, 1960), p. 64.

16 Charlotte Delbo, *Useless Knowledge* (1970), in *Auschwitz and After*, trans. Rosettte C. Lamont (New Haven, Conn.: Yale University Press, 1995), p. 225; Primo Levi, *Survival in Auschwitz: The Nazi Assault on Humanity* (1958), trans. Stuart Woolf (New York: Touchstone, 1996), p. 60.

17 Arthur Koestler "On Disbelieving Atrocities" (1944), in *The Yogi and the Commissar and Other Essays* (London: Hutchinson, 1945), p. 90.

18 For more on books and other publications during these years see the essays by David Cesarani and David Roskies in this volume, as well as Hasia Diner, *We Remember with Reverence and Love: American Jews and the Myth of Silence after the Holocaust, 1945–1962* (New York: New York University Press, 2009), pp. 86–149, and David G. Roskies and Naomi Diamant, *Holocaust Literature: A History and Guide* (Hanover, N. H.: University Press of New England, forthcoming 2012).

19 Shlomo Katz, "Shall We Forget?" *Jewish Frontier* 11 (January 1944), 19.

20 Isaac, Rosenfeld. "Terror beyond Evil" (1948), in *An Age of Enormity: Life and Writing in the Forties and Fifties* (New York: World Publishing Co., 1962), pp. 197–99.

21 Solomon Bloom, "Dictator of the Lodz Ghetto: The Strange History of Mordechai Chaim Rumkowski," *Commentary* 7 (February 1949), 111.

22 Haim Gouri, "Facing the Glass Booth," in Geoffrey H. Hartman, ed., *Holocaust Remembrance: The Shapes of Memory* (Cambridge, Mass.: Blackwell Publishers, 1994), p. 155.

23 On media coverage, especially in the United States, see Jeffrey Shandler, *While America Watches: Televising the Holocaust* (New York: Oxford University Press, 1999), pp. 83–132.

24 Gideon Hausner, *6,000,000 Accusers: Israel's Case against Eichmann*, trans. Shabtai Rosenne (Jerusalem: The Jerusalem Post Press, 1961), p. 29.

25 See, for example, Tom Segev, *The Seventh Million: The Israelis and the Holocaust*, trans. Haim Watzman (New York: Hill and Wang, 1993), pp. 3–4, and Wievioka, *The Era of the Witness*, pp. 80–81.

26 Adolf Eichmann, "I Transported Them … To the Butcher," *Life* 49 (November 28, 1960), 21.

27 David Ben-Gurion, "The Eichmann Case as Seen by Ben-Gurion," *New York Times* December 19, 1960. SM7.

28 Irving Howe, *Decline of the New* (1963; rpt. New York: Harcourt, Brace & World, Inc., 1970), p. 245.

29 Harold Rosenberg, "The Trial and Eichmann," *Commentary* 32 (November 1961), 374.

30 Rosenberg, "The Trial and Eichmann," 374–75.

31 Saul Bellow, July 19, 1987, letter to Cynthia Ozick, in Saul Bellow, *Letters*, ed. Benjamin Taylor (New York: Viking, 2010), pp. 438–39.

32 For relevant studies that take up a number of these writers see Alvin H. Rosenfeld, *A Double Dying: Reflections on Holocaust Literature* (Bloomington: Indiana University Press, 1980) and Sara R. Horowitz, *Voicing the Void: Muteness and Memory in Holocaust Fiction* (New York: State University of New York Press, 1997).

33 Arthur A. Cohen, *The Tremendum: A Theological Interpretation of the Holocaust* (1981; rpt. New York: Continuum, 1993), p. 95.

34 Philip Bernstein, "The Jews of Europe: The Remnants of a People," *Nation* 154 (January 2, 1943), 11.

35 See, among others, Anna-Vera Sullam Calimani, "A Name for Extermination," *Modern Language Review* 94 (October 1999), 978–99.

36 Saul Friedlander, *Reflections of Nazism: An Essay on Kitsch and Death* (1982), trans. Thomas Weyr (Bloomington: Indiana University Press, 1984); Michael Goldberg, *Why Should Jews Survive? Looking Past the Holocaust toward a Jewish Future* (New York: Oxford University Press, 1995), pp. 41–66; Norman G. Finkelstein, *The Holocaust Industry: Reflections on the Exploitation of Jewish Suffering* (New York: Verso, 2000).

37 Bruno Bettelheim, "The Holocaust—One Generation Later," in *Surviving and Other Essays* (New York: Alfred A. Knopf, 1989), pp. 90–91.

38 Zev Garber and Bruce Ackerman, "Why Call the Holocaust 'the Holocaust?': An Inquiry into the Psychology of Labels, *Modern Judaism* 9 (May 1989), 209.

39 Primo Levi, *The Drowned and the Saved*, trans. Raymond Rosenthal (New York: Vintage, 1989), pp. 83–84, 52.

40 Heinrich Himmler quoted in Peter Padfield, *Himmler: Reichsführer SS* (London: Macmillan, 1990), pp. 468–70.

41 Eva Hoffman, *After Such Knowledge: Memory, History, and the Legacy of the Holocaust* (New York: Public Affairs, 2004), pp. 175, 177.

42 Timothy Snyder, *Bloodlands: Europe Between Hitler and Stalin* (New York: Basic Books, 2010), p. xviii.

43 Salo W. Baron, "Opening Remarks," *Jewish Social Studies* 22 (January 1950), 14–16.

44 Marie Syrkin, "On Hebrewcide," *Jewish Frontier* 12 (July 1945), 10–11.

45 I am grateful to David Cesarani, David Roskies, and Michael Bayzler for their helpful comments on a draft of this Afterword.

Index